Memoirs

of

the Great War

Complete and Unabridged

Volume I

Marshall Joffre

Memoirs

of

the Great War

Complete and Unabridged

Volume I

By Joseph Joffre

Translated by Robert B. Marks

Legacy Books Press
Military Classics

Published by Legacy Books Press
RPO Princess, Box 21031
445 Princess Street
Kingston, Ontario, K7L 5P5
Canada

www.legacybookspress.com

The scanning, uploading, and/or distribution of this book via the Internet or any other means without the permission of the publisher is illegal and punishable by law.

This translation first published in 2022 by Legacy Books Press
1

This translation © 2022 Robert B. Marks, all rights reserved.

ISBN: 978-1-927537-65-7

First published as *Mémoires du maréchal Joffre (1910-1917)*, by Librairie Plon, Paris in 1932.

Printed and bound in the United States of America and the United Kingdom.

This book is typeset in a Times New Roman 11-point font.

Table of Contents

Translator's Note 3

Preface 5

Part I – Before the War 7
    Chapter I 9
        I entered the Superior Council of War (February 1910). – I was appointed Chief of the General Staff (July 1911). – Plan XVI. – The XVI bis plan. – Mr. Millerand and the reorganization of the high command: decrees of January 20, 1912 and May 14, 1912.
    Chapter II 34
        The transformations of the army from 1911 to 1914. – The evolution of doctrines.
    Chapter III 47
        The preparation of the war budgets.
    Chapter IV 64
        Light and heavy artillery.
    Chapter V 77
        Ammunition supplies.
    Chapter VI 81
        The training camps.
    Chapter VII 87
        The three-year law.
    Chapter VIII 102
        Plan XVII. – The external situation of France in 1912 and 1913. – Overview of the different powers of Europe. – The neutrality of Belgium and the Grand Duchy of Luxembourg. –– Russia. – What we knew about Germany and its intentions.
    Chapter IX 138
        Plan XVII. – Ideas that served as a basis for the concentration plan.
    Chapter X 156
        Plan XVII. – The setting up of the plan.

Part II – 1914: The War of Movement 199
    Chapter I 201
        The last days before the war. July 24 – August 2, 1914.
    Chapter II 222
        Mobilization. – The concentration. – Belgium and England enter the war on our side. – The first meetings in Alsace. – August 2-16, 1914.
    Chapter III. 259
        The Battle of the Frontiers. – August 17-24, 1914.
    Chapter IV 291
        The preparation of the battle of the Marne. – August 25-September 5, 1914.
    Chapter V 370
        The battle of the Marne.
    Chapter VI 401
        The autumn campaign. – The stabilization of the Western Front.

Index 455

About the Author 472

Translator's Note

Although an English translation of Joffre's memoirs has existed since 1932, it is incomplete. The translator, Colonel T. Bentley Mott, abridged Joffre's manuscript in multiple places. In this first volume, Mott removed approximately 15,000 words, excising half of the chapters of the first part, including detailed discussions of pre-war artillery development, training camps, and more (a summary of this content was translated and attached to the end of volume II as an appendix by Lt.-Colonel S.J. Lowe). As such, a new and complete translation is warranted, particularly for those interested in the modernization of the French army prior to the First World War and Joffre's perspective on it.

This translation was created with the assistance of DeepL Pro translation software. While efforts have been taken to avoid translation errors, some errors may still be present in the text. I am also grateful for the assistance of Franklin Delehelle on the War Studies subreddit.

Where Joffre has quoted an English-language document or correspondence, I have attempted to locate and use the original English version.

Translator's Note

To improve general readability, some modifications have been made to the formatting of paragraphs throughout the text. All efforts have been made to preserve the author's voice and meaning while making these changes.

– Robert B. Marks

Preface

It was in 1921, after his official trip to the Far East, that the Marshal was asked by one of his oldest and most faithful friends to write his Memoirs. After some hesitation, he decided to undertake this task. The reason that motivated him was, as he proved sufficiently by his attitude up to his death, neither the desire to attract attention, nor the thought of provoking polemics or answering criticisms and attacks. He recognized that in the high office he had held before and during the war, he owed it to himself to leave behind an account of his actions and a record of his thoughts, and that he owed to the country he had passionately served for sixty years of his life the vast sum of lessons that can be drawn from the gigantic events in which he had taken such an important part.

Begun in 1922, these Memoirs were completed in 1928. They form a typewritten manuscript of 1218 pages of which each sheet bears the signature of the marshal at the top right:

They include four parts:

The first is of the pre-war period since the moment when General Joffre was called to the High Council of the War, until August 2, 1914.

The other three are of the war from the beginning of the hostilities until the moment when, elevated to the dignity of Marshal of France (December 1916), he left the command of the French armies.

These Memoirs also contain, in a brief epilogue, the story of his trip to America in the dark days of the spring of 1917.

– N. D. E.

Part I – Before the War

Chapter I

I entered the Superior Council of War (February 1910). – I was appointed Chief of the General Staff (July 1911). – Plan XVI. – The XVI bis plan. – Mr. Millerand and the reorganization of the high command: decrees of January 20, 1912 and May 14, 1912.

In September 1909, while I had been commanding the 29th Army corps in Amiens since the previous year, General Trémeau announced to me, during the cavalry maneuvers that he was directing at Sissonne, his intention to have me appointed as Director of the Rear, to replace General Lefort who was going to move to the reserve section of the general staff. I expressed to General Trémeau my desire not to be confined to these rather special functions, but to be able to initiate myself into questions of operations. General Trémeau answered me that these functions would only be temporary and that he understood my desire so well that he intended to entrust me with an army inspection at the same time.

On January 23, 1910, General Brun, Minister of War, appointed me as a member of the Superior Council of War and Director of the Rear. At the same time, I was appointed inspector of the 7th, 13th and 14th Army corps.

The following May 2, I took part in the first session of the Council. Mr. Fallières was president; General Trémeau was still vice-president. It was about the defensive organization of the northern and eastern borders. It was a question which was familiar to me, having already had to deal with it as director of the engineers, and my opinion had been made for a long time. I considered that there was reason to classify only those works that were in a state to present a serious defense. Now, on our northeastern frontier, we had a series of *bicoques*, absolutely incapable of resisting modern machines; by persisting in considering them as places, we put the officer in charge of defending them in an unacceptable situation.

Also when it came to discussing the forts of Montbard, Montmédy, Lormont, and Longwy, I expressed the opinion that they should, like all those of the same nature, be put, such as they were, at the disposal of the general-in-chief who would use them, if necessary, as points of support for the campaign, if it was not possible to make modern fortifications of them. I was not followed by the other members of the Council, who considered that the capacity of resistance of these places was only limited by the supplies of any nature which would be constituted there.

However, I found the opportunity to expose another idea that had been worrying me for a long time; I indicated that in order to reinforce its places, it would be necessary to have a very flexible heavy artillery equipment. However, on this point, we were clearly behind the Germans. And in my mind, this equipment that I was asking for had to serve two purposes: to reinforce the defense of the attacked places and to cooperate in the operations of the light siege batteries.

The president seemed moved by the question: he turned to the Minister and asked for his opinion. The latter acknowledged that our siege equipment was the same as our field equipment and added that, for lack of funds, we could not maintain these two types of equipment on the same basis. This was a dilatory answer that reflected General Brun's mentality; it did not satisfy Mr. Fallières, who asked that this inferiority be addressed in order to remedy it. "It is necessary," he added, "to reach a practical conclusion to this discussion; studies must be undertaken without delay and actively pursued with a view to the constitution of easily transportable local equipment."

The minister therefore entrusted me with a basic study to

determine our heavy artillery needs in the fortress war.

It seemed to me necessary to place this study in the framework of the general hypothesis of war against Germany, such as it could be envisaged at that time; it was necessary, in particular, to take into account the advantage that the Germans had then on us in the concentration.

I based the general idea of my maneuver on a combination of offense and defense. A defensive zone encompassed a bridgehead created at Nancy, Toul, the Hauts-de-Meuse upstream of Verdun, and extended by the temporary fortification to Buzancy and Rethel. To the right of this well-held economic position, a first mass counter-attacked in the direction of Sarrebourg-Sarreguemines, covered in front of Strasbourg by a secondary attack. To the left of the defensive front, a second mass was held in reserve; in the face of a partial failure of the counter-offensive on the right, it was enlarged by men taken from the right and transported by rail. Thus reinforced, it took the offensive through the Belgian Ardennes.

Generals Pau and Léon Durand were willing to join me in these studies, and, with them, a certain number of young officers among whom were commanders Payot, de la Boisse, Pouydraguin and Carence. The result was two studies: one, carried out by my office, aimed at the strategic conditions of the maneuver and its tactical execution; the other, with the help of some officers of the 4th Bureau, studied the new problem of transport during operations that I was considering. I must say that Colonel Favereau, then head of this office, was not very supportive of what he called "innovations" and declared himself skeptical about the practical possibilities of these improvised transports, so rigid and timid was the old conception of the use of railways in wartime.

The first study, which dealt with the tactical part of the problem, allowed me to develop many questions, especially in modern warfare, and also, which was the initial goal of my study, the question of artillery.

However, the defense of the Hauts-de-Meuse posed a problem that could not be solved by the tense trajectory of the 75: there were considerable blind spots all along these steep hills that could not be bombarded.

This general study was pushed in October-November 1910 in

all its details; we considered both the holding of the initial defensive front and the siege of the German positions, and I came to the conclusion that it was necessary for us to possess a light 105 or 120 mm howitzer capable of firing from wide angles and therefore fulfilling the same tasks as the field gun, but against defiladed targets.

The detailed report that I sent to the Minister on this subject was transmitted to General Michel, who had succeeded General Trémeau as vice-president of the Superior Council of War, and was at the same time president of the high commission of fortified towns. General Michel replied that the adoption of a light howitzer was not necessary; he considered that the 155 mm Rimailho was sufficient as a siege and field gun; he asked that each army corps receive only one group. I did not share his opinion concerning the Rimailho, which was unsuitable for the best tasks expected of it.

Thus this question was buried with the complicity, it should be said, of the Directorate of the Artillery which, under the pretext of not breaking the unit of gauge, directed its research towards the organization of a projectile of 75 mm likely to work under great angles.

But if this study that I had undertaken had not given any results from the practical point of view, it had been very useful for the preparation of my war functions as Director of the Rear. In particular, it had drawn my attention to the importance of transportation during operations; I had come to the conviction that in modern mass warfare the real strategic instrument of the general-in-chief should be the railroad.

In order to clarify this fundamental question, I took advantage of every opportunity. In particular, as an army inspector, I had to direct two staff maneuvers, one in February 1911, the other in June of the same year. In retrospect, these maneuvers are of some interest because they seem to me to contain the characteristic elements of the Marne maneuver, i.e. the formation on an outer wing of the enemy of a mass of attack constituted by forces taken from the other end of the front, transported by rail, and using for their exit a place of the moment.

In the first exercise, the theme of the maneuver was inspired by the Situation of Bourbaki's army during the winter of 1870-71:

Chapter I

An army transported by rail was concentrated between Dijon and Besançon; in the presence of an enemy offensive similar to that of General Manteuffel, it took cover in the direction of Vesoul against enemy forces reported in this region, and made a front in the region of Mircheau, its left near Dijon considered as the place of the moment. At the same time, the 13th Corps was massing in the Dijon area to break through the enemy's flank, which was continuing its offensive towards the Saône.

The second exercise was intended to serve as a framework for a trip to the rear. This time, I wanted to study the transportation by rail of an entire army for strategic purposes. I assumed that two armies were forced to retreat in front of a superior enemy, towards the southwest on both sides of the place of Langres. A third Army, formed in the interior, was placed at the disposal of the commander in chief. The latter transported it by rail to the Saône valley to concentrate it on the enemy's left flank.

From all these studies I drew fruitful lessons: I concluded, in particular, that our regulation on transport during operations was too timid and that it was necessary to recast it, by posing, in spite of the resistance of what I will call the old 4th Bureau, the principle that these transports, instead of being exceptional, would become the rule in the next war. In addition, I had a great number of variants studied for Plan XVI, in all sorts of hypotheses; this work had the effect of making the staffs and the technical organs more flexible, which were thus better prepared for their role in war. In passing I point out that it is one of these variants studied when I was Director of the Rear which became the variant of Plan XVI, carried out in September 1911.

But the external situation had suddenly worsened. The months of April, May and June 1911 had been filled with the march of our troops on Meknes and Fez. The Germans had, so to speak, demanded their retreat. The police operations that we were pursuing in Morocco had required the dispatch of large forces drawn either from Algeria-Tunisia, or from the colonial troops, or even from the garrisons in France. The result was a profound disturbance in the organization of our mobilization precisely at a time when fate seemed to be pursuing the Ministers of war: in fact, since the death of General Brun on February 11, in six months, three ministers had succeeded each other at rue Saint-Dominique. The last one, Mr. Messimy, arrived at power in a tragic hour. The very next day after his installation at the ministry, on July 1, the *Panther* anchored in Agadir; the German ambassador, Mr. de Schoen, spoke with the new Minister of Foreign Affairs, Mr. de Selves, in such a tone that at the end of this interview a conference was held at the home of Mr. Caillaux, President of the Council, where the question of sending troops to Agadir was discussed. In London, a bellicose speech by Lloyd George; a tremendous drop in the stock market that turned into a panic. For a long time the possibility of war had not seemed so close. At the Ministry of War, there was a battle cry; all mobilization measures were prepared. Finally, to complete the picture, it should be added that the internal situation of France was far from being satisfactory.

The new minister found before him a hard and difficult task. A former staff officer, he was surrounded by several of his old comrades; they were for the most part officers of value in whom he had all confidence; well oriented on the needs of the army, they had a large share in the work carried out by the Minister. Among them, we must particularly mention Captain Duval, Commanders Brissaud-Desmaillet, Mesple, Guillemin, and the Controller Boone, who had a happy influence on Mr. Messimy.

No sooner had the Minister taken office than a serious crisis occurred in the high command.

The designated generalissimo at that time was General Michel. A few days before General Brun's death, he had submitted a memorandum to the latter which had caused a sensation. Studying the French military situation in regards to Germany, he proclaimed the quasi-equivalence of the active and reserve formations. General Michel planned a new use of the reserve regiments. He proposed to form under the command of the colonel commanding the active infantry regiment a half-brigade constituted by joining to each active regiment the corresponding reserve regiment. The war division and the mobilized army corps would thus have double the number of infantrymen as in peacetime; the project foresaw for each army corps the assignment of a group of 155 mm Rimailhos to two batteries.

In order to understand the excitement that such a preposition was capable of arousing, it is necessary to refer to the political mentality of that time; for, strange as it may seem, this question of reserves had become a political question.

On the one hand, the parties of the right maintained that the only true force on which the fatherland could rest for its defense was the active army; they declared themselves hostile to the principle of the armed Nation in which they saw the beginning of a militia army; they consented to consider the use of the reservists only as a supplement, necessary moreover to the army of the time of peace to bring this one to its war strength; convinced that the war would be of short duration, they consented to mention only this active army of which they made the pillar of all the national edifice. From then on, no sacrifice seemed too great to them that would be destined to reinforce the latter. As for the reserve formations, because of their mediocre training, and the necessity to use all the reservists and therefore relatively old men, they denied them any solidity and any capability to take part in operations of war properly speaking; they envied the use of them, after they would have been subjected to a preliminary training, only for secondary tasks.

The parties of the left, on the contrary, conceived only the Nation in arms, did not admit any long-term service, but only a few months of instruction, intended to create the citizen soldier recalled under arms at the time of the war. And one remembers the discussions raised by Jaurès when he published his famous book *The New Army*.

In the light of the history of the long war we have endured, it is clear that both were exaggerating and that the truth was, as is often the case, somewhere between these two extremes. But there was no need for the great ordeal we had just undergone to realize that the reserve formations were mostly lacking in leadership, and that after a period of recovery they would be ready to fight alongside the front line units. If, however, opinion was inclined to judge this question with passion, it is fair to say that the Superior Council of War knew how to free itself from these contingencies, and judge it impartially. I believe that the same preposition submitted today to the Superior Council of War would be judged as it was at that time.

In the discussions that General Michel had with the Minister during the first two weeks of July, he insisted that the organization that he proposed be submitted to the deliberations of the Council. Mr. Messimy accepted without enthusiasm to put the question on the agenda of the next Council meeting. I say without enthusiasm because, a few months earlier, on the occasion of two conferences given at the Centre des Hautes Études by the head of the 3rd Bureau of the army staff, Lieutenant-Colonel de Grandmaison, General Michel had rather awkwardly tried to justify his strategic ideas, and his credibility had come out of it much discussed.

The Superior Council met on July 19, under the presidency of Mr. Messimy. On the agenda were three questions: the decommissioning of the citadel and the fortress of Laon and La Fère, the creation of a field howitzer and a heavy mobile artillery, and finally, the proposals of General Michel on the constitution of the mobilized units and the use of the reserve troops.

The Minister opened the meeting by expressing the desire that, given the gravity of the hour, the discussions should be inspired only by the desire to increase the efficiency of all the organs of National Defence.

On the first question, the Council expressed the opinion that it was necessary to present a project for the decommissioning of the fortresses of Laon and La Fère.

I took the floor as soon as the discussion of the second question began. I explained that, in many exercises, I had been able to note that to bombard areas escaping the 75, one was often obliged to have recourse to the 155 mm and to use thus projectiles of 40 kilos, whereas shells of 15 kilos would have been enough. It seemed to me therefore essential to adopt a light howitzer allowing both to bombard the dead angles that the 75 could not reach and to accompany in certain cases the infantry attacks. General Michel immediately rose against my opinion, by showing the disadvantages of the multiplicity of calibers. A vote was taken, and, for the first time, the Council proved him wrong by declaring that it was necessary to adopt a light howitzer.

Then the proposal of General Michel came up for discussion. The minister said that it was on the express request of the general that it was submitted to the Council.

Chapter I

It was a real outcry. The Council members, in turn, presented their objections: lack of homogeneity and cohesion in the face of German units that we knew to be so well organized, complete upheaval of our organization, unwieldiness of the army corps with their sixteen infantry regiments, delay of five days in our concentration which obliged us to postpone our deployments as far as the Marne, too low a proportion of artillery for the number of infantrymen, the creation with the half-brigades of a new level of command, which would entail an increase in the number of headquarters, etc...

General Michel showed some bad mood during the discussion. When the question was put to the vote: "Should the principle of half-brigades be adopted?" the answer was unanimously "no."

Immediately a campaign began in the press in which reference was made to the unfortunate position in which the vice-president of the Council had found himself; without precedent, the newspapers published an account of the session. I have always thought that the Minister was not a stranger to this campaign. The public opinion was so charged that soon the situation of general Michel became impossible.

On July 21, the German crisis marked a particularly serious upheaval. The government hesitated and decided to withdraw the general's letter of command. A successor had to be chosen without delay. On the other hand, Mr. Messimy intended to take advantage of the crisis thus opened to bring to a successful conclusion the reform of the high command to which he was attached; he considered, in fact, that a regrettable duality existed between the Superior Council of War and its vice-president, and the administration of the war placed under the orders of the chief of staff of the army. The vice-president of the Council was indeed without action on this important organ in charge of the preparation for war.

Mr. Messimy first thought of General Pau to succeed General Michel as eventual generalissimo. No one seemed more worthy of these high functions. But in an interview he had with the Minister on this subject, he put an absolute condition to his acceptance which the latter did not want to accept: the control of the nominations of generals.

It was then that Mr. Messimy called me. "Would you accept the supreme command in time of war?" he asked me.

I said that my colonial career had for a long time kept me away from questions relating to European warfare, that I had only recently become involved in the conduct of operations, and that others in the Council were better prepared than I was for such a role. And I suggested General Pau.

"But if it were not possible for the government to appoint General Pau," the Minister replied, "would you accept?"

"If the government believes it must override my objections, I will bow to its decision."

After this interview, I met General Pau at the ministry; I told him about the conversation I had just had, he insisted very kindly that I accept the heavy responsibilities that were offered to me.

Following a new discussion that he had with Pau, the Minister informed me that the government had decided to entrust me with the command of the armies in case of mobilization. At the same time he informed me of the reorganization of the high command that he planned: the title of vice-president of the High Council of the War was suppressed and replaced by that of Chief of the General Staff, which would be given to me to better mark my authority with respect to the staff of the army. Moreover, if the title of vice-president of the Council were abolished, the functions with respect to this Council would remain the same: in the absence of the Minister, it would meet under my presidency. At the head of the army staff, General Dubail remained, taking the title of Chief of Staff of the Army. He would continue to go daily to the Minister's office, but for all matters he would report to me and would retain autonomy only with regard to personnel appointments. The chief of staff of the army would be assisted by deputy chiefs. In the event of mobilization, the Chief of Staff of the Army would remain under the authority of the Minister with all the powers that the latter would then believe he should delegate to him.

As for the Chief of the General Staff, he would receive the command of the main group of armies, having the first Deputy Chief of Staff as his Major General; because of the possible functions that the latter would have to fulfill with me, I was invited to choose him.

This solution seemed to me likely to eliminate the frequent duality of thought that had existed for so long between the vice-president of the Supreme Council of War, the designated generalissimo, and the army staff in charge of preparing the mobilization, the concentration and the operational plan.

So I nodded, and immediately thought of fixing my choice for the first Deputy Chief of Staff, who would be my wartime Major General.

On reflection, three names caught my attention: Foch, Lanrezac and Castelnau. All three of them seemed to me very suitable for these delicate functions because of their high intellectual value and the proofs of military knowledge that they had given.

All my preferences were clearly for Foch, who appeared to me as the best brain and the best prepared for the studies of tactics and strategy. But, if I recognized these eminent qualities, a particular consideration prevented me from fixing my choice on him: Mr. Messimy had prejudices against him, the origin of which I do not know. I had proof of this shortly afterwards: having learned that the Minister hesitated to give him his third star, I had to make an urgent request for Foch to be named major general.

Thus remained Lanrezac and Castelnau. After long hesitations, I fixed my choice on the latter, for the reason that having been major general of General Trémeau, he had already worked on Plan XVI and already knew admirably the various workings of the staff.

So I asked the Minister. His nomination appeared at the same time as mine in the *Official Gazette* of July 28, 1911. I have always thought that the government was quite satisfied with this coincidence, which made it possible to disprove the rumors that gave a political color to the choice of which I had just been the object.

At the same time two decrees appeared, one bearing on the reorganization of the Council of National Defense, the other specifying my attributions as Chief of the General Staff, those of the chief of staff of the army and those of the first deputy chief. As far as the Superior Council of War was concerned, it was specified that the letters of command of the armies would only be valid for one year. In addition (and this was a most fortunate innovation, which soon bore fruit), each designated army commander would have, as of peacetime, a cabinet including the chief of staff and the chief of the operations office, who would be assigned to his wartime staff.

The state of the army was divided into three groups: the first, placed under the authority of General de Castelnau, included the services that had to prepare directly for the war (the office of military operations and the general instruction of the army, the office for the study of foreign armies, the office of railroads and stages); the second group was made up of the offices and sections dealing with the organization of the active army and the mobilized army; the third group had in its portfolio the current service, the personnel, the material, and the troop movements in time of peace

The Staff Committee was also profoundly modified. Henceforth composed of the chiefs of staff of the armies of the general commanding the Superior School of War and placed under my chairmanship, it would have to study all the questions raised by the members of the Committee during their annual inspections, to find a solution to them, and to ensure the application of the appropriate measures.

Finally, the Center for Advanced Military Studies,* intended to prepare future army chiefs of staff, as well as the Superior School of War were placed under my immediate direction: the Staff Committee was to assist me in this task.

Thus was settled this question of the high command, which for so long had preoccupied public opinion and had raised violent controversies in the Chamber.

This reorganization constituted a great advance: it ensured in my hands a concentration of powers capable of creating an effective convergence of military efforts; the unity of doctrine so long desired was going to be able to be achieved because of the links created between the Superior School of War, the Centre des Hautes Études, the Comité Technique d'État-major, the General Staff and the Chief of the General Staff.

---

* Created by ministerial decision dated October 21, 1910.

Chapter I

In carrying out this work, Mr. Messimy rendered the country an immense service; he allowed the intense work of organization and transformation of the army which characterized the years 1912, 1913 and 1914. And it is a great honor for me to have been appointed the first to direct the work of these great military organs in the years that prepared the great war.

I will, however, make a reservation with respect to the reorganization of the army staff. Mr. Messimy had not thought it necessary to subordinate the Ministry's directorates of arms to the Chief of the General Staff; the decree of July 28 made them directly dependent on the Minister. This was, in my opinion, regrettable, and I frequently had to deplore their independence from me, especially that of the artillery directorate. I will have to come back to this subject.

As soon as I was appointed, I asked for an audience with the President of the Republic, who, in response, invited me to lunch at Rambouillet.

I have always had for Mr. Fallières the greatest respect and the highest esteem; I have always found him deeply attached to the interest of France. His good sense, his finesse, his uprightness did not exclude in him either firmness or authority.

It is thus with pleasure that I found myself at the end of July in front of the Head of State. He greeted me with these words: "I am happy to see an engineer officer at the head of the army. War, in my opinion, has indeed become an engineer's art."

I have often thought of these words; they are profoundly true: military genius alone would be insufficient today if it were not helped by a spirit of organization able to combine the multiple means that science and industrial progress put at the service of the army. How these words take on even more weight in the aftermath of a mass war which has brought to light the immense complication of all the organs which participated in it.

However, the crisis opened by the arrival of the *Panther* in the waters of Agadir was far from over. I remember on this subject an interview that I had at the beginning of August with Mr. Caillaux in the presence of Mr. Fallières. The President of the Council asked me this question: "General, it is said that Napoleon did not fight until he thought he had at least a 70 percent chance of success. Do we have a 70 percent chance of victory if the situation forces us to war?"

I was embarrassed to answer. I finally said, "No, I don't think that we do."

"That's fine," replied Caillaux, "then we'll negotiate."

This answer undoubtedly helped to decide the government to continue the negotiations. In any case, a few days later, Mr. Cambon, who had come from Berlin, returned to his post bearing for Mr. de Kiderlen-Waechter a note that he gave him on September 4, and which served as the basis for the November 4 agreement on Morocco.

This crisis, so serious, had at least one happy result as far as France was concerned; the Entente Cordiale came out of it stronger. It is, in fact, from the beginning of this period that the first conversations between the French and British staffs date. General Wilson came to France to work with us and to prepare the eventual landing of a British expeditionary force. He was the first and a good contributor to this cooperation.

I made, in addition, the choice of my first appointments to form my staff. The head was the commander Gamelin, and I took, in addition, – the captains Renouard and Bel and the commander Alexandre.

I do not have to praise these officers, whom I kept with me for a long time and who only left me for the time necessary to complete their command training during the peace, or to go, during the war, to rejoin the troops. During these forced absences, I replaced them with captains de Galbert and Fétizon. They all did their duty magnificently; two of them were killed: Bel at the head of a group of battalions of *chasseurs* in Italy, de Galbert at the head of the 13th battalion of *chasseurs* on the Somme; as for Renouard, he died during the summer of 1918 at the head of an infantry division.

As soon as I was installed in my new position, I began to study the concentration plan then in force, known as Plan XVI; I had already been aware of it as Director of the Rear; it was now necessary to examine it from a strategic point of view.

It is important to recall here the essential provisions:

From an organizational perspective, the two main features of this plan were:

The addition to each mobilized corps of an additional brigade of two reserve regiments with three battalions (except in the five frontier corps: 6th, 7th, 20th, 14th and 15th Corps);

The constitution in each region – except the 19th – of one or two reserve divisions. One thus obtained twenty-two new divisions of which twelve were assigned to the armies of the northeast, two to Paris, four to the Alps, and four to the fortresses of the east.

This organization made it possible to assign to the northeast front, in a firm manner, sixteen two-division army corps, two three-division army corps, twelve reserve divisions, eight cavalry divisions, and twenty-one heavy artillery groups.

Eventually, four army corps with two divisions: 14th, 15th, 21st, army corps of Algeria.

If circumstances permitted, it was possible to assign the two reserve divisions from Paris and the two available territorial divisions to this main theater.

As a whole, the established concentration scheme presented:

In the front line, between Épinal and Verdun, a front of ten army corps divided into three armies; behind the wings of this mass, two armies, one in the Vosges, the other in the region of Vouziers; a group of three cavalry divisions covered the left of this formation in the region of Rethel.

In the rear of his armies of first line the remainder of our available forces was gathered in view of maneuvers in a formation articulated near railway lines: four army corps and twelve reserve divisions which would come eventually to join the 14th, 15th, 19th and 21st corps.

All this concentration was done under the shelter of our fortifications in the east; in front of these, the cover was ensured in first emergency by three frontier army corps, the 6th, 7th and 20th Corps and by three cavalry divisions; from the fifth day at noon, the cover was reinforced by elements of the 1st, 5th and 8th Corps.

Our fighting forces were able to go into action from the seventeenth day of mobilization.

The most striking characteristic of this concentration was the proportion of forces maintained south of the Paris-Metz line; indeed, out of eighteen corps planned for the northeast front, fifteen of them were grouped south of this line with their center of gravity in the Neufchâteau region. This concentration obviously took little account of the violation of Belgium by the Germans, which however appeared to be a very likely hypothesis. A German maneuver enveloping the left side of our system, which was rather weakly garrisoned, would put our entire system in danger. This scenario had obviously not been considered. Plan XVI was based on the conviction that the Germans would direct a "straight blow" against us in the Metz-Toul-Verdun region.

On the other hand, the maintenance of the reserve army, the 6th, far behind the front line, corresponded to the strategic conception of the time; considering that our numbers were appreciably lower than those of the Germans, and that we had a delay in our concentration compared to our adversaries, Plan XVI had assumed, as had a part of the plans that had preceded it, that we should first receive the first shock in a defensive situation, and then counter-attack with reserve forces transported to the wing or to the point that would seem most favorable.

I found in the safe of the former vice-president of the Superior Council of War a draft of a concentration plan which showed that my predecessor had rightly been concerned about the possibility of a German invasion through Belgium. This project, which was the consequence of the general reorganization that he had ordered, constituted the second part of the note that he had given to the Minister in January 1911: it had not been communicated to the Superior Council of War in the session of July 19.

General Michel, in this note, assumed *a priori* the violation of Belgium. He established an extremely stretched line, a sort of cordon extending all along our border from Switzerland to Dunkirk. The center of gravity of our forces was this time moved to the extreme left; on the Lorraine front it left only the two covering army corps; the general reserves were reduced to five divisions in the region of Paris, three colonial divisions at Troyes, the 19th Army corps towards Dijon, the English in the region of Soissons.

Obviously, by placing the greatest density of his forces on his left, General Michel sought to compensate by the concentration of his troops for the inferiority of the natural lines and artificial defenses of the Franco-Belgian border.

But such a plan exposed us, on the other hand, to a rupture either of our center, or of our right, risking to expose to the enemy the heart of the country, and allowing our adversaries, in case of success, to leave behind our armies in an eccentric direction and to cut our lines of operations. It was possible, in connection with this plan, to repeat the famous terms of the note that Napoleon addressed in 1808 to Major General Berthier: "Do we want to prevent smuggling? Should we return to this nonsense?" Who could assure us that having figured out our intentions, the Germans would not change their plan of operations to march on Paris by Lorraine, by abandoning the bulk of our forces in the region of the north? In such a situation, the planned reserves would have been insufficient to restore the situation.

I found myself in front of, on the one hand, a plan in force which, obviously, did not correspond to the most probable scenario of German maneuver, and on the other hand, of a project which exaggerated the importance of this scenario, and included the most dangerous hazards.

First of all, it was necessary to determine exactly how likely it was that the Germans would violate Belgium. In a more general way, what did we know about their preparation for war and what could we conclude from it?

Our intelligence service, although disorganized for some years for political reasons, had been aware of the mobilization plan established in 1907 by the German general staff, and which was still in force with our adversaries. On this basis, which seemed solid, it was determined that Germany would initially mobilize against Russia the value of about twenty divisions, of which about half were reserves, and three cavalry divisions, and against France, about sixty-five divisions, of which one third were reserves, and eight cavalry divisions. From the thirteenth day, all the units destined to participate in active operations could be assembled at the concentration point.

We thought we knew that the plan of the old Moltke had been abandoned. Schliefien, his successor, head of the great German military staff until 1906, had kept it until about 1894, the date of the Franco-Russian alliance treaty. From that moment on, it seemed clear that Schlieffen had reversed the plan, counting on taking the offensive against France first, while maintaining a defensive attitude against Russia. It appeared from many indications that Schlieffen's successor, Moltke the Younger, had adopted this idea.

Thus, in all probability, the Germans would take the offensive immediately on our front.

On the plan of offensive operations against France we did not know anything precise.

However, the study of the debarkation stations and the German railroad network, on the one hand, and of their defensive organizations, on the other hand, provided us with useful indications. In Upper Alsace first of all, the stations and the railroads seemed to allow to concentrate there only five army corps at the most, which, with the two garrison divisions, seemed insufficient to attempt an eccentric maneuver through Switzerland. Moreover, the reinforcements brought to the Strasburg-Mutzig fortified barrier, the organization of the Rhine, from Strasbourg to the border, seemed destined to make this part of the battlefield a purely defensive zone, where only a small number of troops would be engaged. On the other hand, the distribution of platforms and debarkation sites led us to believe that the bulk of the German forces would deploy north of the Metz-Strasbourg line, and that a significant part of them could be north of the Sierck-Merzig line; out of a total of one hundred and ten stations or platforms existing north of this line, ninety or so had been built after 1896, and since 1904, constant improvements had been made to the railway network in the Eifel region.

It was however difficult to prejudge if it was necessary to expect to see disembarking in the area in the north of Trier a strong proportion of active corps intended to gain by Belgium the left wing of our armies, or, if this zone was intended to receive only reserve corps, flank-guards of an attack in force carried out against the front of the French armies without violating the neutrality of Belgium.

To the first scenario, the work carried out on the railroads for the last ten years and the German strategic tendencies gave the greatest likelihood.

But one was bound to greet with some reserve the statements published by German authors on the necessity of violating Belgium. This could be a concerted maneuver to draw us northward, and to divert us from the east where the decision could be more quickly obtained by our enemies.

Plan XVI took little account of the probability of the violation of Belgium. As I have already said, our left hardly exceeded the region of Vouziers; it was weak and the reserves only allowed it to be reinforced and extended under insufficient conditions.

But this was not the only criticism that could be made of Plan XVI.

Indeed, in the face of the sixty-five German divisions that we expected to appear on the northeastern front, Plan XVI provided only for the concentration of thirty-eight active French divisions and four reserve divisions in the area; the twelve reserve divisions maintained far away towards Dijon, Troyes, Soissons and Laon were intended, as we have seen, for secondary missions only.

This resulted in a significant numerical inferiority to our detriment, which, combined with the feeling that we had of a more rapid mobilization and concentration of German troops than ours, explained the strategic intentions to which this concentration responded. This was the theory of the "defensive-offensive" that had been in vogue in France for the last twenty years. It was based on the Russian operations in Poland and the British operations on the sea, in the sense that it was intended to weary the German offensive by a defensive battle supported by our fortified barrier, long enough to allow the Russians, whose mobilization was very slow, to make their offensive action felt and to force the Germans to clear our front before having obtained a decision. At that moment, it was thought, the Russians on one side, the French reinforced by the English on the other, would simultaneously begin a general and decisive offensive. In this scenario, the French army had to play first of all the role of cover for the Triple Entente.

This conception seemed to me to be based on a sophism; namely that during the first month of the war no decision would be obtained against us, in spite of our obvious numerical inferiority and the initiative of the operations that we left deliberately to the adversary. It had moreover the disadvantage of transporting, from the beginning, the war into French territory; it corresponded neither to our warlike traditions nor to our national temperament so quick to be alarmed at the first reverses; it still carried the imprint of defeat, in spite of the efforts that the Republic had made for forty years to ensure its safety.

Finally, it did not take into account the probable eventuality that the Germans would take up the plan of old Moltke: an immediate offensive against the Russians in order to overcome them before the latter had finished their mobilization, combined with a temporary aggressive defense against France.

All these considerations led me to look for possible changes in our concentration.

First of all, was it possible to reduce the inequality of manpower that condemned us to the initial defensive position? It seemed to me that this could be achieved by making better use of our reserve units and by modifying the general distribution of the French front. Facing Italy, the plan initially maintained the two army corps of the Alps (14th and 15th), the elements that were to constitute the 21st corps, and four reserve divisions. Now, Italy had a large part of its land and sea forces occupied in the conquest of Tripolitania or engaged in the war against Turkey. It was therefore possible, without serious risk, to reduce the forces assigned to the army of the Alps and to provide for the transport of the 14th and 15th Corps to the northeast, under the same conditions as the other army corps.

As for the reserve divisions, it appeared that the ostracism of which they were the object was exaggerated and that it would be possible to make use of them in the maneuver combinations of the front line army, and consequently to bring them immediately closer to the battle front. In this way, one could bring to fifty-eight divisions (including the four divisions of the east) the total of the forces immediately concentrated at the border. If, in addition, one prepared in a more complete way the possible transport of the 21st and 19th Corps, it was possible to expect a total of sixty-three divisions to be employed in the operations.

Of this number, only sixteen divisions were in reserve: we thus arrived at an almost complete equality with the Germans.

So how do we organize our system?

Chapter I

First of all, it was necessary to move the left wing of our deployment further north; in view of the resources at our disposal, it did not seem possible to extend it beyond Mézières. It was then necessary to reinforce this wing: for this purpose, the fourth group of reserve divisions could be added to it, and the 19th Corps could eventually be assigned to it. But this extension towards the north created a dangerous gap between the 3rd and 5th armies, opposite the Metz-Thionville position.

This led me in August 1911 to establish a modification to Plan XVI in the form of a variant to the initial plan according to the following guidelines:

> To move up northward the left of our line formed by the army wing and the cavalry contingent, from the Vouziers-Rethel to that of Mézières;
>
> To bring the four reserve division groups together to our deployment line;
>
> To bring the maneuver army to the read of the Verdun fortifications;
>
> To firmly plan the transport of the 14th and 15th Corps to the right wing towards Lure and Belfort;
>
> To extend the possible transport lines of the 19th Corps to Laon in view of its assignment to the left wing army and that of the 21st corps to Meaux in view of its assignment to the maneuver army, 6th Army.

In truth, these directives were still only an expedient. They were in my mind only provisional and only valid until the day when we could seriously undertake a resolutely offensive attitude that would protect us from any German maneuver.

The complete redesign of a plan is always a delicate period. I decided, on these general directives, to bring to the plan a simple variant. The preparatory studies were finished when I left for the great autumn maneuvers. These studies gave birth to Variant No. 1 of Plan XVI which became effective in September 1911.

> In this variant, the first emergency cover was assured by the 7th, 20th and 6th Corps, and by the 8th, 2nd, and 4 th Cavalry divisions, on a line marked out by Delle, Giromagny, Corcieux, Bayon, Saint-

Nicolas-du-Port, Domèvre-en-Haye, Vigneules-les-Hattonchâtel, Fresnes-en-Woëvre. Damvillers, Montmédy.

Behind this cover, our six armies were gathered from south to north in the following order:

4th Army (3 army corps and a cavalry division) in the region of Belfort, Lure, Remiremont;

1st Army (4 army corps and 2 cavalry divisions) in the area of Épinal, Toul, Chaumont, Langres;

2nd Army (2 corps) in the Saint-Dizier, Joinville, Gondrecourt, Ligny-en-Barrois region;

3rd Army (2 army corps and 2 cavalry divisions) in the Pierrefitte, Heiltz-le-Maurupt, Bar-le-Duc perimeter;

6th Army (4 army corps, plus possibly the 21st) in the triangle Sainte-Menehould, Reims, Châlons;

5th Army (2 corps, plus possibly the 19th) between Amagne and Mézières.

In addition:

A group of three cavalry divisions in Renwez;

A group of reserve divisions in Vesoul;

A group of reserve divisions in Toul;

A group of reserve divisions in Bar-le-Duc, Sainte-Menehould;

A group of reserve divisions towards Mézières.

In my mind, this concentration could, at the moment of need, be modified according to the information that I would obtain: it served, if I may say so, only as an average adjustment of the deployment. The studies of transport by railroad that I had pursued while I was Director of the Rear had convinced me that it was possible to utilize our railroads with enough flexibility and to easily vary, when the time came, our deployments; if, for example, for reasons of policy that I was obliged to foresee, the decision to mobilize was taken with some delay, I could find myself in the necessity of postponing my deployments; I considered the thing easy thanks to the flexibility to which our railroad service had arrived. If, on the contrary, I decided to take the offensive before the completion of the deployments, I considered that it would be possible for me to follow our vanguards by extending my lines of transport, and thus to catch up one or two days of march. If finally some information reached me before the end of the strategic transports, I assumed that I could vary the last transports to prepare

Chapter I

another maneuver.

Thanks to these various measures, we had managed to reduce the numerical disproportion that existed to our disadvantage, and we had acquired greater flexibility in our initial maneuvers. But it appeared that we would have to bear the main weight of the German armies, no matter what, as long as the Russian armies did not take the offensive themselves. In order to frustrate the German intentions, to restore the balance of forces in favor of the Triple Entente, to enable us to free ourselves from a purely defensive attitude, the surest way was to obtain from our Russian allies an intensive effort.

General Dubail left in August for Russia; his trip was fruitful in terms of results; after interviews with the Tsar and the Russian general staff, he received the assurance that mobilization and concentration would be carried out as soon as possible, and that in any case they would not wait for this concentration to be completed before acting. The offensive would be taken as soon as the front line forces were in position, and from the sixteenth day the border would be crossed. By common agreement, it was determined that a decided offensive alone could give success: "It is in the very heart that Germany must be struck," the Tsar had said, "the common objective must be Berlin." A commitment was signed in this regard by the Russian Chief of Staff on August 18-31.

The importance of this agreement cannot be overlooked; this jointly affirmed offensive will was likely to cause the German plan as we suspected it to fail, by causing our adversaries to modify the initial distribution of their forces, perhaps even to abandon the fundamental idea of an offensive against us from the outset, and to reverse their plan once more. In any case, it removed the root cause which, for so long, had condemned us to a circumspect conduct of operations.

At the beginning of January 1912, a new ministerial crisis arose as a result of the Selves incident before the Senate Commission on the Franco-German agreement. A Poincaré cabinet replaced the Caillaux cabinet; at the Ministry of War, Mr. Millerand replaced Mr. Messimy.

I did not know my new minister. I will often have the occasion in the course of these memoirs to say the immense services which he rendered to the country. For the moment it is enough for me to give this testimony that his first passage at the ministry was beneficial for the army, which had immediately given him its confidence.

The same day, when Mr. Millerand settled in his office in the rue Saint-Dominique, he had an interview with me of about half an hour. He asked me my opinion on the decree of July 28, 1911, and let me know that in his opinion, the maintenance at my side of a chief of staff of the army charged to deal directly with the Minister with the questions of personnel and current service was a mistake. I answered him that indeed, with use, it had revealed itself an inconvenient combination. Undoubtedly, between General Duhail and me, no difficulty had arisen, but it had not been the same between General Dubail and General de Castelnau, because of the role that the latter had to fill with me in case of mobilization.

Mr. Millerand told me, as he has said publicly since, that this organization seemed to him to be the result of political rather than military considerations. Determined to do everything possible to strengthen the bodies responsible for national defense, he informed me of his decision to abolish the position of Chief of Staff of the Army and to give General de Castelnau the title of Deputy Chief of Staff.

Indeed, five days later, the decree of January 20, 1912, which was later completed by the decree of May 14, 1912, abolished the function of chief of staff of the army. General Dubail was given an army corps.

Thus was concentrated into my hands almost all of the military functions; it was the first time that such powers were entrusted to only one man: I had action on the instruction of the army, its doctrine, its regulations, its mobilization, its concentration. For questions of promotion, the new minister made known to me his intention to consult me. For the first time, we arrived at this logical conception of the chief responsible in time of war centralizing in time of peace: all the functions to prepare for war. After a thousand discussions of all kinds, considerations of persons as well as of politics, it had taken the crisis of Agadir to make people admit a solution which would have seemed too audacious some time before; it had taken, moreover, two ministers animated one as the other by only patriotic feeling to give this reform all its scope.

It was now up to me to use these powers in the best interests of France, and to prove myself worthy of the trust placed in me.

Chapter II

The transformations of the army from 1911 to 1914. – The evolution of doctrines.

The first question I had to answer was what general direction to give to the whole of our military organization for which I was now responsible. Above all, it was necessary to provide our army with a firm doctrine of war, known by all, and unanimously accepted.

In order to fully grasp the mental state in which the army found itself at the beginning of 1912, it is necessary to take a quick look back.

After 1870, our strategy had been dominated by the fact that we intended to wage only a war of defense; impressed by the German victories, convinced of our military inferiority vis-à-vis our eastern neighbors, we had first sought our safeguard in permanent fortification. We had built, according to the program outlined by General Séré de Rivière, a barrier of forts along our border. Because of the mediocre efficiency of our railroad network, the concentration of our active forces was slower than that of the Germans; so we only envisaged it happening in the shelter of this fortified zone, and intended to deliver a series of defensive battles on the concentric ridges of the Parisian basin. One hoped thus to

Chapter II

exhaust the German armies, and to tear off with their weariness a difficult victory. Mediocre conception, to the truth, entirely dominated by the haunting of the German power, but forgetful of the lessons of 1870, which had shown that the passive defensive is the mother of the defeat.

From 1890, our strategy became less timid. A major event had just revolutionized the fortification, it was the appearance in 1885 of the mortar shell; experiments undertaken at the fort of Malmaison in the following year showed that our fortifications of the east were no longer in a state to resist the new machine. From then on, the barrier built at great expense between our four major cities, Belfort, Épinal, Toul and Verdun, was no longer sufficient to protect the country. We were therefore led, our railroads having improved considerably, to ask the field armies for a less passive attitude. Massed for the most part behind the holes reserved in our defensive curtain, in particular in the Charmes-Neufchâteau region between the places of Toul and Épinal, they were ready to defend these artificial defiles and to counter-attack the adversary if he came to force these defenses.

But, following the Anglo-Boer war, that is to say around 1900, a whole series of false doctrines, some of them supported by the most brilliant military personalities such as General de Négrier, came to take away from our officers the weak offensive feeling which had just appeared in our war doctrines, and to ruin in the mind of the army its confidence in its leaders and in its regulations. Basing himself on the system used successfully in the Transvaal by Lord Roberts in front of the Boers, excellent shooters but ignorant of any maneuver, frozen in an inert defense, General de Négrier proclaimed the impotence of any strong action, declared himself the enemy of so-called decisive attacks and launched the famous theory of the inviolability of fronts. For him and for General Kessler, one of the most eminent personalities of the time, the height of the art consisted in avoiding battle and seeking success in an envelopment obtained by an extension of the front. When defending this theory, one did not take into account that it required, above all, an absolute superiority of manpower.

Others, admitting the same dogma of the inviolability of the front, claimed to seek the decision in the cut-off points where the enemy's fire lost its power. They thus neglected the necessary action of the artillery in a decisive operation.

Finally, others became the protagonists of the doctrine summarized in the formula: tactical defense, strategic offense. Starting from the dogma that any frontal attack is impossible even with superior forces, and that advanced weaponry favors the one of the two adversaries who is on the defensive, they systematically considered it advantageous to be attacked. The supporters of this doctrine accepted the risks of a decisive battle to wear down the enemy, without wearing down themselves. Then the "event" would occur with the help of the strategic reserve: but it was not a question any more of enveloping a flank, nor of counter-attacking with this reserve, because "movements of this kind would have required troops of combat formation, ready to use their weapons." On the contrary, it was a question of bringing this reserve to a point such that the enemy could not give up possession of it and which was free of troops. By striking a blow "in the wings which will be empty of troops," one thought to see "the morale of the leaders and especially that of the high command collapse in the adversary."

Thus the incomplete study of the events of war led the military intellectual elite of that time to think that the improvements of the armament and the power of fire had so much increased the power of the defense that in front of it the offensive had lost all virtue. One fled the battle, and one sought the decision in a maneuver.

These theories had an immense repercussion in the army. They favored the secret instincts of self-preservation, seriously undermined the very foundations of our regulations, and shook the confidence of officers in their leaders. The harm was serious and deep.

Without doubt, General Langlois pointed out the speciousness of such theories; he showed that the events of the South African war had been studied in a false light and that, from a particular case, one had concluded to general rules; no, the fronts were not inviolable, provided that at a given point one had a superiority of fire capable of dominating the adversary. Finally, he proclaimed the eternity of the Napoleonic principle: "War is an act of force. In strategy, one must seek battle and want it with all one's energy."

Chapter II

The Russian-Japanese war brought a striking confirmation to the words of General Langlois. At the Superior School of War, under the direction of the Fochs, the Lanrezacs, and the Bourderiat, the young intellectual elite of the time got rid of all the phraseology that had upset the military world and returned to a sound conception of the general conditions of war.

At the same time, around the year 1905, a movement against the importance that we gave to permanent fortifications took shape: the advances in armament seemed to decrease its power of resistance, while increasing the value of the field fortification, of which Russians and Japanese had just made such a large use. On the other hand, our fortresses were reproached for absorbing too much of our troops. And a great number of places and forts were downgraded to second and third category.

This disfavor in which the permanent fortification fell, joined to the reaction brought by the theories resulting from the Boer War produced in what I will call the "Young Army," following its brilliant leaders of thought, a current of ideas which sought, in the action even of the troops of field, the defense of the country which the fortification did not seem any more capable of ensuring.

But, as it happens every time it is a question of going back up a current of established ideas, one came in these circles to an exaggeration of the offensive doctrine. One spoke of a "mystique of the offensive." The word is undoubtedly excessive; however, it marks quite well the somewhat unreasonable character that the cult of the offensive took on, in the years following 1905. It was up to Lieutenant-Colonel de Grandmaison, the head of the operations office of the army staff, to support in 1911, in two famous conferences that I have already mentioned, this outrageous theory with a brilliance that made it dangerous in its turn!

Only a small military nucleus, hard-working, educated, daring, having the cult of energy and mastery of character, not having known the misfortunes of 1870, not obsessed by the idea of German superiority, was touched by the new ideas. In 1911, the new doctrine had not yet penetrated very far into the mass of the army, but the latter was beginning to be moved. For many years it had been tossed back and forth between the most extreme theories, framed by officers who rebelled against all innovations, and yet it remained absolutely apathetic and indolent. No doubt they knew that the offensive was in fashion in high places, and they tried to do "the offensive," but under what conditions!

The maneuvers of 1911 made this clear. The infantry, which was not very maneuverable, revealed the shortcomings of its training; the fronts of attack were disproportionate to the means used; the terrain was poorly used; the artillery and the infantry did not try to link their efforts; the most elementary notions of cover were ignored; the various arms were profoundly ignorant of the needs and possibilities of each other; the high command lacked unity of vision: at every moment one saw the emergence of particular "instructions" which commented, according to the temperament of the chief who wrote them, on the maneuver regulations.

In the end, the mass of the army, long maintained in a defensive mold, had neither doctrine nor instruction. Uncertain of the path to follow, it did not form a tool capable of applying the harsh doctrine of the offensive; the high command, aged in outdated ideas, made suspicious by a period of agitated politics, showed itself skeptical and impotent; it is within this framework that a young and ardent generation, believing itself to have built up a body of doctrine in conformity with the traditions of war, allowed itself to be carried away by its enthusiasm and its faith to the point of dangerous exaggerations. Such was the character of the army when I took office.

There was an obvious truth in the assertion that only the offensive allows one to free oneself from the will of the adversary. Military history proves this abundantly. It also shows that wars of waiting have never led to anything but defeat. It was also my feeling that our fortresses were no longer strong enough to serve as a basis for a system of war.

But if I was persuaded of the superiority of the offensive, I considered that we should not carry it out insensitively, without precautions, without intellectual and moral preparation of the army, without putting our material at the level of this higher form of the war.

This will to give to the operations an offensive form and to prepare our army to carry them out, corresponded moreover so deeply to the enlightened opinion of the country tired of carrying eternally the weight of the German threats, that the peaceful Mr. Fallières himself at the Elysée, on January 9, 1912, in the course of a superior council of national defense, was pleased to state that defensive projects, which constituted an admission of inferiority, were being renounced. "We are," he added, "resolved to march straight to the enemy without any ulterior motive; the offensive suits the temperament of our soldiers and should assure us of victory, on the condition that we devote all our active forces to the struggle without exception."

To create a firm body of doctrine, to impose it on the command and the troops, to form an instrument capable of applying what seemed to me to be the sound doctrine – such appeared to me the urgent task to which I had to devote myself.

First of all, it was necessary to establish the reasonable bases of an offensive doctrine, and to make this doctrine penetrate from the Superior Council of War, the Army Staff and the Superior School of War to the last echelons of the troops.

For the development of theories of the offensive, I resorted to the only practical method available to us: exercises on the map and in the field.

I have said that, since the reorganization of the Superior Council of War, each of its members had a small number of officers with him who represented the core of the general staff which would be assigned to him in the event of mobilization, and in particular the chief of this general staff. The meeting of these chiefs of staff constituted the staff committee. It was appropriate to use the members of the Superior Council of War and their staffs for these concrete case studies; in this way I achieved the double result of fixing the doctrine and training the staffs in their war functions. I therefore organized a series of exercises on the map of army group against Army group, with the members of the Council and their staffs as participants. Following these strategic exercises, these generals in turn had a new exercise carried out within the same framework, in which the army corps under their inspection took part. In the spring, the maneuver studied on the map was repeated in the field, with each level of command in its actual place and with all the means of communication for the transmission of its orders. In turn, the army commanders repeated the theme studied during the winter in cadre maneuvers. The result was an intense general work in which the trainees of the Center for Advanced Military Studies and the professors of the School of War participated. All the ideas, all the conceptions, all the audacity, all the timidity were aired; little by little a doctrine was elaborated; the conditions of an offensive energetically but prudently conducted were specified.

It was the first time that such exercises were organized on this scale. For my part, I attached the greatest importance to them. They served to bring the realities of war as close as possible in peacetime, despite all the distortions that a long period of peace always imposes on the military mind. In my eyes their importance was increased by the fact that the continuous relations between the members of the Superior Council of War and their staffs were constantly developing. The daily contacts between the officers belonging to the Technical Staff Committee, the Army Staff, the Center for Advanced Military Studies , and the School of War were eminently fruitful. They contributed to creating the indispensable unity of views between these various bodies. And above all, this work prepared the proper functioning of the army staffs at the beginning of the war. It should not be forgotten, in fact, that if the command of large units sometimes proved, at the beginning, to be inferior to its task, if moral failures. It is to their work, their professional knowledge, their exact preparation, their role that we owe the fact that the failures of the first days did not turn into disasters.

To give an idea of the intensity of the work thus done, I will say that in the first six months of 1914 alone, the army exercises on the map directed by the members of the Council, Generals de Castelnau, de Langle, Lanrezac, Ruffey, Dubail, Sordet had, over seventy study sessions, brought together, in addition to the direct staffs, ten professors from the School of War and thirty officers from the army staff. The preparation of the maneuvers with Army group cadres carried out under my direction had brought about constant relations between the members of the Council, party leaders, army commanders or directors of the rear, their staffs and quite a large number of officers from the army staff and the War

College. The preparation of the maneuvers with Army cadres brought together, apart from the permanent staffs of the members of the Council, about ten officers from the War College and the army staff. On the other hand, some members of the Staff Committee, army chiefs of staff such as Generals Anthoine, Demange and Lindet, themselves directed a large number of army corps, army or divisional studies at the Center for Advanced Military Studies during the winter of 1913-1914.

I have just said that, little by little, a logical and wise doctrine of the offensive was established in a working atmosphere. Let it not be imagined that it was an innovation or that it was made of novelties. Our studies only brought back the eternal principles of the necessity of the offensive, of the obligation to fight only with all forces united, of the economy of forces, of the necessity of an

The Grand Duchess Asastasia and the Grand Duke Nicholas received by M. Millerand and General Joffre at Nancy

Chapter II

Generals Joffre and de Castelnau at the 1912 Grand Maneuvers

implacable will, of the subordination of all secondary missions to the main goal. Nothing in all this was revolutionary or simply debatable: these are the very principles of all military history; those to which we owe both the victory of the Marne and the victorious campaign of the second half of 1918.

It will be the eternal honor of this generation of officers to have contributed to getting the French army out of the vague theories that troubled it for so long.

The great western maneuvers in the fall of 1912 were an opportunity to test the high command with the troops.

Two army staffs, four army corps, two cavalry divisions, a reserve division, and a large number of services took part. It was the first time that maneuvers were carried out between armies. They were interesting. General Gallieni was opposing General Marion. These two team leaders showed a very accurate strategic sense; they knew how to assemble and engage their forces in the battle in due time. The troops showed a lot of endurance and spirit. The various executors seemed to be animated by an offensive and commendable spirit. But, from the tactical point of view, there was a lot to criticize, although it was not strictly speaking the goal of these maneuvers: actions not linked to each other, poorly covered, imprudent maneuvers leading to surprises, serious errors in the use of artillery. These maneuvers also made it possible to study the use of the reserve divisions.

On the other hand, these maneuvers demonstrated how insufficient our equipment was. In the zone of action of both armies, there were deep and wide valleys whose bottoms could not be bombarded with our guns; the necessity of curved fire guns and long range guns, able to reach from one side the objectives located on the other, was once again clearly demonstrated.

At the great maneuvers in the southwest in September 1913. From left to right: General de Castelnau (from behind), General Joffre, President Poincaré.

The following year, the great maneuvers in the southwest revealed the same shortcomings, and in addition, highlighted serious deficiencies in command. If the two army commanders, Generals Pau and Chomer, were up to their task, some corps commanders appeared totally incapable. These maneuvers showed me that from the corps level up, minds were not prepared for the conditions of modern warfare. It was to be the task of 1914 to accomlish this preparation. To achieve this, I planned to have all the large units stay in training camps; they would be trained there

From left to right: President Poincaré, Mr. Etienne, Minister of War, General Joffre, General de Castelnau

under the direction of members of the Council, and, during these periods, it would be possible to proceed to a purification of the command which appeared to me as a task of primary necessity. Many of our generals revealed themselves, in fact, incapable of adapting to the conditions of modern warfare; for the good of the army, they had to be replaced as soon as possible by younger, more open-minded men. The war came before this important work of regeneration of our senior staff had been accomplished. We left for the campaign with insufficient cadres, and it was in the middle of battle, under the pressure of events, that we had to make the drastic cuts that I proposed to make in peacetime.

Now that the doctrine had been developed, it was important to codify it into a basic document intended to serve as a guide for the high command and the staffs. This new regulation, which was called the *Regulations for the Conduct of Large Units*, was to serve as a body of doctrine for the teaching given at the Superior School of War and at the Center for Advanced Military Studies; it was also to serve as the starting point for a new *Regulations for the Service of Armies in the Field*, a fundamental document for the troops: the practical instructions and maneuver regulations of the various armies would be linked to it.

It seemed to me that, in this way, all the prescriptions concerning the tactical use of the troops would form a unified whole, and that would thus be established all along the hierarchy this common understanding of principles so desirable and so necessary to the convergence of efforts.

Commissions, in which an important place was reserved for members of the Technical Staff Committee, were formed to draft its various regulations. At the end of October 1913, the Minister of War submitted for the signature of the President of the Republic the decree bearing the *Regulations for the Conduct of Large Units*: it was written in an ardent prose, a bit like a profession of faith, some sentences even reminding one of the style of the Convention decreeing the victory. It affirms as a kind of dogma that success in war goes only to the one who seeks the battle and knows how to deliver it offensively with all his means. He based the idea of safety on the necessity for the command to get away from the enemy's hold. This regulation was a novelty in that, for the first time, the principles relating to the conduct of the army corps and superior units were set out in an official text.

The decree concerning the *Regulations for the Service of the Army in the Field*, concerning the rules and procedures for the use of the division and lower units, was signed on December 2, 1913 by the President of the Republic: it countered the idea of the 1895 decree, which indirectly encouraged the command to prefer defense to attack, because the value of a position allowed it to hope to engage in combat under good conditions. Another novelty of this decree was that field work took an important place in it.

The new *Infantry Maneuver Regulations* of April 20, 1914, brought profound changes to the previous regulations dating from December 3, 1904.

Unfortunately, its rules were still being studied by the troops when the war broke out. It takes a long time for a doctrine to penetrate to the lowest echelons, especially after a period of doctrinal anarchy similar to the one the army had gone through. Thus in August 1914, the situation was as follows: in the high command, the minds were still too often paralyzed by routine habits, and strategic education especially was almost entirely lacking. The staffs, in their generality, were well trained, well oriented, rid of the exaggerations that had arisen at the time of the offensive revival. From a tactical point of view, the staffs had not yet understood the offensive necessities. If they saw in the offensive a sort of dogma in which they only wanted to believe by tradition and temperament, they had not yet grasped all its requirements; in particular, they had a too general tendency not to take sufficient account of the conditions of modern warfare, which no longer allowed for an attack as it was done in the days when the rifle and the cannon were loaded from the muzzle. As for the troops, they were ardent, trained, and ready for any challenge and any sacrifice. This was very dangerous, given the shortcomings I have just mentioned in its cadres.

Chapter III

The preparation of the war budgets.

Without a doubt, numbers are of primary importance in warfare; but, apart from the conditions of direction and execution, the organization of materiel is a factor that grows with the progress of science.

It was a question of giving the army the materiel corresponding to the possibilities of our finances. When I accepted the position of Chief of the General Staff, I sensed what kind of difficulties I was going to encounter in this last area. Indeed, during the two years that I had been director of engineering at the Ministry, I had been able to measure how difficult it was to achieve results and to obtain the necessary funding. Without doubt, it is true that the House did not refuse the appropriations requested for national defense, but we must know what was going on behind the scenes and how the requests for appropriations were made.

It does not seem to me to be without interest to note here my memories of this period: they can serve to clarify this question on which one often discussed and to show that it would be unfair to put the responsibility for our mediocre preparation on the Ministry of War; they will make it easier to understand, in addition, the insufficient state of materiel in which the army was in 1911.

In January 1904, when I arrived at the direction of the engineering, I found, as far as the fortification was concerned, a detailed program in progress, which had been decided in 1900 by the high commission of the fortified places for the restoration of the four great fortresses of the east. This program, approved on June 1, 1900 by the Minister of War, provided for the execution of the work at a cost of 90 million francs. Until my arrival at the ministry, the annual budget had remained so insufficient that a delay of twenty years would have been necessary for the complete execution of the program. This was an unacceptable delay, since it was not likely to allow the completion of the program before it was overdue. In 1903 and 1904, for example, a sum of 3,800,000 francs had been allocated only to the eastern frontier; these credits had been almost entirely devoted to Verdun and Toul, Épinal and Belfort having been allocated only insignificant sums (100,000 francs on average per year for each of these two places).

As a result, when I had to present my proposals for the 1905 budget in February 1904, I insisted on pointing out the serious disadvantages of this situation in my budget proposal:

> It would be essential that this work be continued with great speed. However, due to a lack of sufficient funds, it has so far only been possible to undertake the work in Verdun and Toul, despite the essential interest of also carrying it out in Épinal and Belfort, since these places are no less threatened than the first. Under these conditions, one should not conceal from oneself that it will be necessary, in a short time, to devote to this work much higher budgetary funding, if one does not want to risk leaving these places in a state of obvious inferiority over an almost indefinite time. One cannot think of devoting more than ten to twelve years to the complete execution of the program, which would lead to a budget of approximately 10 million from 1906. This allocation is not excessive if one considers that Germany has devoted the following sums to fortification work in recent years: 45 million in 1899 and 1900; 22,800,000 francs in 1901 and 20,900,000 francs in 1902.

In any case, taking into account the budgetary situation, I requested for 1905 only an appropriation of 4,700,000 francs, approximately equal to that which had been allocated for this purpose in the 1902 budget. This sum seemed to be the minimum necessary to continue the work, most of which was carried out by contracts in progress; any slowing down of the work would have constituted a false economy prejudicial to the interests of the Treasury. In spite of its modesty, this request for an increase was not accepted: a note from the Directorate of Control dated March 23, 1904, informed me that the Minister had decided to reduce the requests to the figures of the budget voted for 1904, that is to say, to 3,800,000 francs for the four large projects in the east. Thus my requests were nipped in the bud without even being referred to Parliament.

The situation however appeared to me so critical that when Mr. Berteaux replaced General André, who had resigned, at the ministry I thought I had to bring the matter to the attention of the new minister in October 1904, in a note which, moreover, had received the full approval of the army staff: I took up again the arguments developed during the preparation of the budget of 1905, and I insisted in the most pressing way that the funding intended for the realization of the program of 1900 be very notably increased, so as to ensure, within an acceptable time, the full execution of the program in the four large fortresses of the east. This request still had no result.

At the beginning of 1905, I presented my new proposals for the 1906 budget, asking for an increase of 8 million on the 3,800,000 francs allocated in 1905. I pointed out that the work already carried out made it possible to specify the expenditures remaining to be made on January 1, 1906 and to fix them as follows:

Verdun	11,500,000 francs.
Toul.....................	19,900,000 –
Épinal	19,600,000 –
Belfort...................	23,000,000 –
That is to say in total.........	74 000 000 francs.

I considered it essential to reduce the duration of the work to six years, starting in 1906, which implied an annual allocation of about 12 million francs; I therefore asked that the credit be increased to 11,800,000 francs, thus distributed:

Verdun	3,500,000 francs.
Toul	4,000,000 –
Épinal	2,150,000 –
Belfort	2,150,000 –

These proposals were once again rejected. A note from the Direcorate of Control, dated July 5, 1905, informed me "that in the presence of the conditions imposed by the Minister of Finance to balance the general budget for the year 1906, the Minister has had to give up introducing in the draft budget all the increases requested by the different services under the third section, that is to say, the extraordinary expenses. The allocation of the chapters had therefore been maintained at the following figures: Chapter 90. Fortifications: Eastern frontier: 3,800,000 francs."

Now, this refusal takes on a particular flavour if we compare it to the situation created, at that time, by the tension resulting from the question of Morocco in our relations with Germany. It was, in fact, in March 1905 that the sensational visit of Kaiser Wilhelm II to Tangiers had taken place, a visit whose direct consequence had been the forced resignation in June 1905 of Mr. Delcassé, Minister of Foreign Affairs of the Bouvier cabinet. The tension was so great at that time that the Minister had summoned to the ministry, on June 23 and 24, the chiefs of engineering of the four major eastern cities to examine with me the measures to be taken as a matter of urgency, in order to remedy, as far as possible, the defects of these cities resulting from the delay in the execution of the 1900 program.

However, at the end of that same month of July, that is to say, a few days after receiving the note from Control, the government recognized the need to adopt the exceptional measures required by the seriousness of the situation, and to open important credits "outside the budget" in order to immediately undertake the most indispensable fortification work in the four eastern cities, and on

July 25, a sum of 3,200,000 francs was allocated to us, in addition to the normal budgetary credits. In spite of the difficulties and delays that the opening of new sites inevitably requires, this additional sum could be usefully employed before the end of the 1905 fiscal year.

In the meantime, in response to a question from Mr. Klotz, reporter for the 1906 budget, I had the opportunity to insist again, in a note dated September 13, 1905, on the imperative need for a rapid execution of the 1900 program.

However the international situation remained as tense as ever: there was, on November 25, 1905, a bellicose speech by the emperor, soon followed in January 1906 by the opening of the conference of Algeciras which was announced at first under unfortunate auspices.

Mr. Berteaux resigned on November 10, 1905. Mr. Étienne succeeded him. I represented to my new minister the necessity to complete the works in the east with the most extreme haste. A new "off-budget" allocation of 13,500,000 francs was provided on January 24, 1906, to the 4th directorate to be applied to the acceleration of this work: it was added to the normal funds of the 1906 budget reduced, as we have seen, to 3,800,000 francs. It was at this time that I left the 4th directorate to take command of the 6th infantry division.

If I have insisted on quoting these facts, prior to the period of which I have undertaken in this narrative, it is in order to show the secret combinations which presided over the preparation of the budgets. It is true that the Parliament never refused the credits which were requested by the various minsitries; but these were forced to ask only for what the Ministry of Finance, in agreement with the parliamentary committees, considered possible to allocate to each department. One cannot, therefore, in all fairness, blame the Ministry of War for the shortcomings that the world conflict revealed later regarding our materiel. To give definitive proof of what I have just said, I will cite the cuts made from 1901 to 1910 in the credits requested by the Services:

Year	Budget requested by the Services	Budget received through the Finance Act
1901	95,926,350 francs.	60,708,150 francs.
1902	98,541,600 –	49,136,475 –
1903	59,457,800 –	31,063,000 –
1904	61,638,000 –	28,723,000 –
1905	44,997,100 –	26,917,150 –
1906	59,853,710 –	26,917,150 –
1907	133,053,700 –	76,308,516 –
1908	89,884,971 –	60,260,079 –
1909	98,582,221 –	66,049,443 –

As can be seen from this table, the requests were never satisfied except in a small proportion. Thus the army staff obtained for the railroad service, from 1901 to 1911, only such reduced allocations that it was not possible for it to seriously improve our railway network on which our concentration depended. However the protests had been numerous, as testified by a whole series of notes addressed to the Directorate of Control on March 13, 1902, June 20, 1903, February 5, 1904, July 7, 1905, and January 19, 1907. On January 13, 1909, the Directorate of Control warned the staff of the army that, following an agreement with Finances, the annual endowment not to be exceeded by the service of the railroads would be 850,000 francs. As a result of this imperative note, the requests of the army staff were reduced to this figure for the fiscal years 1910 and 1911. It was the same for the Directate of Intendance: in 1908 it was notified of a global reduction of 5,500,000 francs. In January 1909, it was notified that its total forecast for the period 1911-1913 should not exceed 15,355,050 francs. On June 2, 1910, this share was further reduced to 4,770,350 francs.

In June 1909, the 4th directorate had requested 36,062,395 francs for the 1910 fiscal year; it was ordered to reduce its requests and presented new expenditure accounts reduced to 26,214,375 francs.

In reality, France had believed, at the beginning of the

Chapter III

twentieth century, in the chimera of universal peace. She woke up halfway in 1906 after the crisis of Tangier; she only came out of her dream definitively after Agadir.

During this period of French somnolence, our eternal enemies were preparing themselves, and nothing is more instructive than to compare with ours the average expenditure which they made during this same period for their various services. From 1901 to 1905, while we spent an average of 47 million, as shown in the table on the previous page, the Germans spent 115 million; from 1906 to 1910, while our average was 95 million a year, the Germans spent 190 million. Is it surprising, under such conditions, that in 1911 we had a formidable backlog to make up in the field of materiel?

I knew therefore very well, in August 1911, through the experience I had acquired, all the difficulties there would be to overcome to obtain the necessary funding to equip the army and the country for the war.

What was the situation of the army from the materiel point of view when I was appointed Chief of General Staff?

Let's take first the question of the armament of the infantry. It was rumored that our rifle was no longer up to the task, and that a certain number of shared weapons were in poor condition, which had led to their being classified as supplies for the territorial army. Articles by Generals Bonnal and Langlois had echoed these concerns. The truth was less critical. In reality, a general classification of all the rifles had revealed 42,000 weapons that were a little tired, and only 40,000 out of use. This was a small number out of a total inventory of about 3 million guns. The weapons in perfect condition, 2.5 million, were only assigned to the front line formations. It was therefore an exaggeration to conclude that our armament was in urgent need of replacement. Without doubt, it did not have the latest improvements as a portable weapon, but it was still safe and its inferiority to the German rifle did not justify the 465 million that it would have cost to put a new rifle into service.

If we now consider the armament of the artillery, we see that our field artillery was complete and in good condition. But the supply of ammunition was insufficient: since 1906, it had been progressively increased up to 1,280 shells per piece. It was necessary to reach at least 1,500; it was necessary, moreover, to take measures to prepare the mobilization of the industrial establishments likely to feed in wartime this supply by an intensive production. The majority of our establishments were in no state to carry out this condition, and important funding were necessary for that.

Others would be needed for the constitution of our heavy artillery. The Germans had, in fact, large-caliber pieces in each of their army corps; they also had light siege equipment. In France, we had made little effort to keep up with them, and our situation in this regard was worrisome. The Rimailho (155 T.R..) existed only in small numbers: the number of batteries planned was only forty-two, each battery having only two pieces. It seemed to me that the progress to be made to improve this state of affairs should be carried out in two stages. During the first, it would be necessary to resort to makeshift means, using the 120 and 220 pieces included in the siege crews or the armament of the forts. During the second stage, it would be necessary to progressively replace this provisional equipment with heavy artillery, composed solely of rapid-fire pieces and meeting the needs of the future war. It would take time and considerable expenses to succeed. I will return to this important question in a future chapter.

In the armament of the forts, there was still a great number of pieces to be transformed, and cast iron projectiles to be replaced by steel shells.

As far as the fortifications are concerned, great efforts had been made during the last years. Perhaps we had even pushed too far the concern to maximize the power of our defense system. It was necessary to maintain the existing works at the level of modern warfare, but to abstain from building new forts. There were more urgent needs, in particular those which concerned the training of our troops by the extension of the existing camps and the creation of new camps which was imperatively necessary. In fact, because of the reduction of the time of service, the instruction had to be intensive; combat firing, the combined operations of troops for all weapons in varied grounds had the most extreme importance. Because of the difficulties of the execution of musketry in open field and the impossibility, during maneuvers, to go into private properties, the troops needed vast grounds especially arranged. Consequently, the program that I had adopted provided for a camp for two army corps; the funding necessary for this reform were requested in the 246 million program, and reconnaissance was carried out by that year's corps with a view to choosing the most practical and least costly sites. I will also come back to this question in a later chapter.

There was another problem which for being less important did not deserve less the attention, that of the mobile kitchens. The first tests went back to 1905, without the interested directorates having succeeded in choosing a type; at each period of great maneuvers, these tests were continued, without ever reaching a conclusion. However, all foreign armies were already equipped with mobile kitchens.

The accommodation of the infantryman was also a pending issue; the need for cars designed to carry part of the soldier's load, the need to replace in the camp the sheet metal with aluminum were still discussed; the clothing of the troop with less conspicuous colors, the transformation of metal bridges to make them suitable to support the heavy vehicles used by the army, the bridge crews – all these issues unresolved.

It is fair to say that one of the causes of this inability to carry out reforms was the fact that the army staff had not yet exercised the role of leadership and coordination over all the directorates of the ministry, which is the pre-requisite of command.

There were several reasons for this:

First of all, the chief of the army staff had had neither the hierarchical situation nor the authority that the decree of July 28, 1911 conferred on me as Chief of the General Staff: a brigadier general, my friend General Delanne, had exercised the same functions in 1900. As a result, the army staff appeared only as a directorate equal to the others, and did not enjoy the preeminence necessary to ensure the coordination of the multiple workings of the ministry.

Secondly, the Vice President of the Superior Council of War lived completely apart from the administrative organs of the Ministry, which ignored the needs recognized as necessary by the

Council.

Finally, it was a long-standing practice to deal with all questions of appropriations, under the chairmanship of the Minister, between the Directorate of Control and the directorates of the arms and services, with the army staff being involved only for its own appropriations.

The creation of a Chief of General Staff was a happy opportunity to change these mistakes. As early as August 26, 1911, during a visit I made to the Minister, I pointed out to him the urgency of the work, the considerable improvement to be made in our war equipment, and the role I thought it would be useful to play in the coordination of the organs of the ministry and in particular in the establishment of requests for appropriations. I must say that I found Mr. Messimy quite willing to follow me on this ground and to support me with his authority. We agreed on the fact that in the presence of the defects of equipment which appeared on all sides, and by taking account of the offensive will which animated us, it was necessary first to equip the armies of field before thinking of the fortresses. Already the requests for the budget of 1912 had been established; the services had asked for the materiel approximately 113 million; at the ministry, this request had been reduced to 95 million, finally one had agreed with the Finance Commissions on the figure of 84,867,174 francs. In studying this request with Mr. Messimy, we agreed that this sum was insufficient; it was necessary either to ask for extraordinary funding, or to increase the budget of the 3rd section. After an informal agreement with the Finance Commissions, we decided on the first solution, and 21,300,000 francs of expenses could be incurred in 1912 outside the budgetary appropriations. Adding to this the 12,950,000 francs provided by the law for the implementation of the aeronautical program, the War Department thus had a total appropriation of 119,167,174 francs to spend in 1912.

But this was only the first step: a general equipment program had to be drawn up. The order was given to the various services to study completely the totality of their needs, and from the 20th to the 31st of October several conferences took place in the Minister's office between the Directorate of Control, the interested directorates and myself. They resulted, in November, in the establishment of a statement of particularly urgent expenditures, to be carried out in five years, the amount of which amounted to 246,600,000 francs. Of this total, 33,200,000 francs were to be provided for the year 1912.

On January 6, 1912, the Minister of War communicated to his colleague in Finance his draft budget requesting that authorizations for expenditures be granted in the form of off-budget funding; he wanted in this way to avoid the introduction of these appropriations under the heading of extraordinary expenditures, which would have delayed the possibility of beginning the work and drawn attention to the effort we were about to make. It should not be forgotten, in fact, that on that date the treaty of November 4, 1911, concerning Morocco had not yet been ratified either in France or in Germany.

Laborious discussions had just begun between the War and Finance departments when, on January 12, 1912, the Caillaux ministry fell. Once again, we were able to measure the disadvantages of ministerial instability.

Indeed, on January 17, Messrs. Poincaré, Millerand and Klotz, the new holders of the portfolios of the Presidency of the Council, War and Finance, met to examine the request for off-budget appropriations presented for 1912. During this discussion, some of the planned appropriations were greatly reduced, the appropriation for the training camps, which I will discuss later, was eliminated, and the appropriation intended for the transformation of cast iron shells into steel shells in the supplies of the fortresses was increased by one million. The principle of extraordinary funding established by the letter of January 6 being maintained, however, the amount of the appropriations was reduced from 246 million to 50,700,000 francs, and the appropriation for the year 1912 from 33,200,000 francs to 21,300,000 francs, which added to the 119 million of which I spoke earlier, opened up to the Minister of War a total budget of 135 million. (The Germans at the same time spent 216 million). The program no longer mentioned the funds planned for the field howitzers, nor for the heavy artillery, with regard to the substitution of metallic platform mounts for the current mounts in the forts; it no longer mentioned the project of substituting B powder for black powder in the fortifications, which had been planned for the fiscal years 1912 to 1917; nor did it speak of the funding requested for the auxiliary bedding and the camp, planned for the fiscal years 1912 to 1917.

On November 21, 1912, I learned indirectly that Mr. Chéron, general reporter of the Budget Commission, had written to the Minister of War to ask him if the credits requested by his department corresponded to the total needs of the services. Following this intervention, on December 1, 14, 18 and 19, 1912, conferences were held on the orders of the Minister between the directors concerned and the Directorate of Control in order to draw up a list of particularly urgent expenditures: the total was set at 469 million francs, including 109,400,000 francs for the year 1913. But a new change of ministry on January 13, 1913, brought a new delay to the execution of the program of works to be carried out.

However, events precipitated themselves; in spite of the arrangement concluded with Germany in November 1911 after long and painful negotiations, a strong emotion spread in France in February 1913, at the news of the enormous increases in armaments projected by Germany. The Superior Council of War met at the Elysée Palace and unanimously adopted the principle of returning to the three-year service; the Parliament voted shortly afterwards the necessary funds for the maintenance of the releasable class, and the country, faced with the imminence of the danger, seemed resolved to make the most severe sacrifices to ensure its defense.

On February 14, 1913, a conference was held at the home of Mr. Briand, the new President of the Council, with the Ministers of Finance and War, and the representatives of the Army and Finance Commissions of both Houses. The program decided in December 1912 was discussed, and it was decided that the question of authorizing the immediate commitment, by anticipation, of part of the expenses, would be examined in a secret committee by the Senate Finance Committee. But, in the meantime, the newspaper *the Times* divulged these talks by publishing the broad outline of the project. The consequence of this indiscretion, which violated the secrecy with which they had sought to surround themselves, was that the Finance Committee asked that the commitment of the planned expenditure remain subject to legislative authorization. A bill was introduced on February 27, 1913, which called for the commitment of 500 million in addition to budgetary appropriations. But at the time when the Budget Committee was examining this project, the experiments of Major Malandrin relating to a plate allowing the 75 to fire curved rounds appeared to be a sufficient reason for abandoning the request for a credit of 80 million planned for the constitution of batteries of field howitzers. The total program was thus reduced to 420 million.[*]

The bill was introduced on March 18, 1913 by Mr. Clémentel; it was never discussed. In fact, a few days before the bill was tabled, the Finance Committee unanimously authorized the Ministers of War and Finance to commit in advance the sum of 72,040,000 francs, after which the Minister of War notified the departments concerned of the sums that each of them was authorized to commit immediately. One had never seen such zeal or such promptness in meeting national needs. Fear is the beginning of wisdom.

Here are the main bases of the adopted program:

21,170,000 francs for the supply of 75 mm ammunition (to be carried out in two years);

54,400,000 francs for the substitution of steel shells for cast iron shells (to be finished in eleven years);

98,450,000 francs for the east and northeast forts (to be completed in five years);

6,000,000 francs for the fortifications of the southeast (to be completed in two years);

500,000 francs for the adaptation of 75 mm shells for curved fire;

20,000,000 francs for the heavy mobile artillery: 155 Rimailho and 105 T.R. (to be realized in two years);

15,000,000 francs for the transformation of the 120 L into 120 T. R. Rimailho carriage (to be realized in two years);

10,000,000 francs for the transformation of the 155 L. into 155 T. R. (to be completed in four years);

---

[*] This program is known as the "420 Million Program."

14,200,000 francs for the light artillery of place: 105 T. R (to be completed in three years);

6,000,000 francs for car-cannons against aircraft (to be realized in two years);

20,000,000 francs for the creation of a very long range artillery equipment (to be realized in five years);

27,350,000 francs for the training camps.

This program was a considerable effort, albeit late. Moreover, since I had had no part in its elaboration, it seemed to me that a number of urgent things had been omitted.

In particular, a series of experiments on breastworks had been pursued in parallel at Otchakof, in Crimea, by the Russian government, to which we had been invited, as well as at the Mailly camp. These experiments had proved that our breastworks were satisfactory, on the other hand our heavy artillery was not able to fight against the modern fortifications. The great maneuvers had, on their side, revealed a certain number of gaps to be filled urgently, such as the mobile kitchens which all the modern armies were now equipped with.

Consequently, in April 1913, I drew the attention of the Minister to the need to establish a new program, focusing in particular on the supply of 75 mm ammunition, which still seemed to me to be very insufficient, on the creation of heavy artillery equipment with a very long range, on the creation of automobile radio and telegraphic stations, on the increase of the telephone and telegraphic equipment, on the creation of mobile kitchens, on an increase of 100 pieces of 105 long in addition to the 120 pieces already planned, on the construction of 200 pieces of mobile heavy artillery with great power, on the creation of materiel with great power for the armament of the coasts, and on the modernization of the armament of the places. These were the main points that I felt were essential to understand in the revision of the 420 million program.

Following my interventions, the Minister decided that a conference would be held on April 23 between the directorates concerned to examine the measures to be taken. This time, the meeting of the directorates took place at the army headquarters, under the chairmanship of General de Castelnau, first deputy chief of staff, my delegate.

This conference produced a project amounting to 504,500,000 francs, which was added to the February 1913 program of 420 million, thus bringing the needs of the War Department to 924 million. The very next day, the Minister of War referred this new request to his colleague, the Minister of Finance. The latter replied, after examination by the Council of Ministers, on the following May 13, that he could not unreservedly support the proposal to present to Parliament an increase in expenses of nearly one billion. He indicated that only a simple increase in the 420 million program could be considered, if "the necessity were recognized," and suggested raising the February 27 figure to 450 million. In other words, to an additional request of 504 million, the Minister of Finance would offer only 30 million.

Mr. Étienne, Minister of War, then sought to resolve the difficulty: he invited the directorates concerned to inform the Directorate of Control of those expenditures included in the supplementary program which seemed indispensable and needed to be committed immediately. The total of these urgent expenses was then reduced to 235,720,000 francs. It must be recognized, moreover, that the administration of Finance was then faced with terrible needs; it was, in fact, around this time that, for the application of the three-year law, enormous expenses were going to be incurred: just for the barracks made necessary by the increase in personnel, 162,700,000 francs were planned for the year 1913 and 124,200,000 francs for the following year.

However, the Minister, energetically assuming his responsibility, and realizing that it was necessary to revise the order of urgency established for the work to be done, decided on October 8 to merge the two programs, that of 420 million and that of 504 million. Conferences were held on October 20, 21, 22 and 24 under my chairmanship. They led to the elaboration of an overall program amounting to the total sum of 1 billion 403 million of which:

803 million to be requested immediately off-budget to replace the 420 million in the February 27 bill;

305 million to be requested under extraordinary expenses (3rd section).

And 295 million requested as a second emergency.

This program was a misfortune. Indeed, having been the subject of a bill, it was transmitted to the Finance Department on 12 November. But it was not tabled, the government having declared to the Budget Committee on November 18 that it was sticking strictly to the draft of February 27. Immediately, new conferences were held at the War Ministry to establish new estimates which, while remaining within the limit of the 420 million imposed by the government, included certain urgent works which had been omitted from the February 27 program.

We were thus able to draw up a new project which, by ministerial decision of November 25, 1913, was set at the total sum of 1,147,000,000 francs, of which 420 million francs were not included in the budget and 727,820,121 francs in annual instalments of the third section.

But in early December 1913 there was another change of ministry, which caused a further delay. The question was, however, taken up by the new Minister of War, Mr. Noulens, who at the end of December obtained from his colleague in Finance the acceptance of an acceleration program of 1,408,741,571 francs. This program was included in the bill submitted on January 16, 1914; it included: 754,500,000 francs to be committed outside the budget and 416,450,571 francs to be included in the annual budgetary instalments under the third section.

The elections of April 26, 1914 delayed the discussion of this project, which was voted by the Senate only on the eve of the war in the famous sessions where Mr. Charles Humbert, reporter of the Commission of the Army, made revelations on our military situation which deeply moved the opinion. It is probable that these revelations had their echo across the Rhine and contributed to hasten the German decision to declare war on us. Following these revelations, Mr. Clemenceau went up to the rostrum and exclaimed: "Since 1870, I have not attended a session of Parliament as moving or as painful."

This time the whole country awoke. It suddenly realized the degree of impoverishment into which a long period of pacifist utopias had plunged it. But, even if it could measure the effort to be made, it was, alas, too late to accomplish it.

Such was the long and painful history of pre-war budgets. I have shown in the course of this account that one of the essential causes of disorder in the establishment of our military budgets came from the independence of the different directorates. Mr. Messimy had sensed this when, as early as December 1911, he invited me to attend the meetings of the directors to establish our needs. Mr. Étienne also understood this when, in October 1913, he asked me to preside over the conferences that led to the merging of the two programs of 420 million and 504,500,000 francs.

Another cause of our inability to succeed lay, in my opinion, in the instability of the Ministers. Eight ministers succeeded one another from January 1, 1911 until the declaration of war. They fell without having had time to get acquainted with the complicated functioning of their departments. Too many bodies led directly to the ephemeral minister. The result was an omnipotence of the directorates, who were no longer subject to any higher authority. As for the Directorate of Control, which worked directly with the reporters of the parliamentary committees, it had come to play a role for which it was not suited. It modified, reworked and coordinated the requests of the departments. It was it that, in reality, prepared the budget. Its position was all the stronger because it remained, while the Ministers passed.

Finally, public opinion was too little and too poorly informed about military necessities. If it had been better informed and more aware of the risks involved, it would have demanded earlier the realization of the financial effort before which Parliament had recoiled for too long, and which was agreed upon only on the eve of the war.

Chapter IV

Light and heavy artillery.

Until 1905, the superiority of our field artillery was unquestionable. The 75 had an unequalled rapidity of fire, and the percussive fire of the explosive shell with slightly delayed priming allowed us to hope to reach the sheltered troops. On the other hand, for the attack of the semi-permanent fortification works of the field of battle, captain Rimailho had, in 1904, very ingeniously modernized the 155 short of Bange, making it more mobile than the materiels of the light crews of siege. 140 of these pieces had just been ordered from Saint-Chamond. Unfortunately, the data that had governed the scope of this equipment did not allow the current use of ranges greater than 5,000 meters. I will only quote for memory the 120 and 155 short of the general Baquet already out of fashion.

On their side, the Germans had, at that time, only the 77 old model with direct fire, without brake, requiring a return to its initial position after each shot. Since 1901, they had introduced in their field artillery a howitzer of 10 cm. 5 intended to reach by firing rockets our batteries defiled behind the ridges, as well as the personnel placed in trenches or sheltered behind shields. But, because of the numerous defects of this equipment, we were entitled to admit that our artillery superiority was not compromised.

From 1905, the Germans began to make up some of their lost ground. They transformed their 77, making it suitable for rapid fire. At the same time, wishing to give the war a brutally offensive pace, they introduced in their field armament a heavy howitzer of 15 centimeters intended to undertake without delay the attack of our fortifications. In 1909, by ingenious modifications brought to the 105 howitzer, they made of it an excellent piece, with rapid fire. Around the same time, a series of experiments made them see the possibility of using their heavy guns more widely, by making them participate from the beginning of the battle in the artillery fight. From then on, their progress in this way was extraordinarily fast: in October 1910, at the Juterborg camp, with delay fuses similar to those we have been using ourselves for a few years, they proved that they could obtain in the artillery fight a fast result with a minimal expenditure of ammunition, even against a shielded artillery hidden behind ridges.

These results had very important consequences in Germany. It was considered necessary to start the battle with a systematic fight against the enemy artillery, by bringing the heavy artillery on line very early. Our firing methods were adopted for the 77 model 96 N/A; the 15 centimeter batteries were transformed into mounted batteries; the number of howitzer batteries of 10.5 cm. was doubled; the increase in the number of howitzers was achieved at the expense of an equal number of 77 guns which were suppressed.

In France, a period of semi-somnolence had followed the intense activity that had brought the artillery to the state it was in 1905. The disappearance of the Technical Committee, decreed on August 22, 1910, and especially the loss of the president of the Committee, who was at the same time the inspector general of the army, had resulted in a very noticeable decrease in the maneuvering ability of the troops and the technical value of the officers.

Mistaken ideas had come to increase the disorder and the confusion of the minds. A certain number of artillerymen estimated that the obstacles of the field fortification could be easily destroyed by the explosive shells of the 75, judged superior to the shells of similar caliber of our adversaries; at most, in certain exceptional cases, one would have recourse to the 155 C.T.R.; therefore one would avoid, by being satisfied with the 75, encumbering the columns, which appeared essential to the advocates of the offensive to excess, who wanted to see in the battle only a maneuver and a fight of infantry, simply supported by the artillery.

On the other hand, in the competent circles of the artillery, in particular at the Mailly firing range, it was well known that the German artillery had pieces that fired infinitely farther than our field gun; but it was considered that the German artillery could not take advantage of this benefit: in fact, it was considered essential that the captain remained close to his pieces; it was considered impractical, due to the difficulty of telephone transmissions on the battlefield, to place the observer far from the battery.

As, at that time, the use of the observation plane was unknown, it was concluded that it was useless to try to shoot beyond the normal radius of observation that the captain maintained near his pieces. Five to six kilometers seemed to be a maximum not to exceed. The war took care, within a few weeks, to show the poor value of these speculations.

In spite of this hostile spirit towards heavy artillery, it had to be noted that we had lost our advantage. As far as I am concerned, I had been so struck by our inferiority that I had been led, as soon as I entered the Superior Council of War, in 1910, as I have already reported, to draw the attention of the Minister, General Brun, and of my colleagues, to this question. In my opinion, it was necessary to have a long gun capable of prolonging the fire of the 75, a mobile howitzer, to attack the defiled objectives and to take part in the fight against the German pieces recently equipped with shields, and a mortar with large crushing effects against the fortifications. One remembers that the Superior Council of the War in its session of July 19. 1911 had approved my conclusions.

When I was appointed Chief of the General Staff, I was concerned with bringing these matters, which seemed to me to be fundamental, to a conclusion. I inquired about what had been done by the artillery directorate, which had officially announced that it intended to propose the adoption of certain equipment under construction in the artillery workshops of Puteaux in the near future.

Unfortunately the director of the artillery soon had to admit that he was not in a position to submit new gun models; none of the materials under study in the workshops of Puteaux had yet left the period of the first tests; and I was given to understand that a delay of two or three years would be necessary to succeed.

In the presence of these disappointing results, I realized that it was necessary above all to bring order to the technical studies, and to establish a firm program, giving an overall conception of the system of artillery sought and required to direct the minds of the inventors. I was convinced that the disappearance of the Technical Committee of the Artillery was, for a good part, in the impotence that I noticed; I obtained from the Minister a decision creating a commission of new materiel, at the head of which was placed General de Lamothe, a man of a remarkable clairvoyance and a high competence. This commission was ordered to establish the study programs for the field howitzer and the long gun.

One month later, General de Lamothe, after agreement with the army staff, presented to the Minister a test program concerning the field howitzer and the long-range gun.

The light howitzer had to be fast-firing, mobile enough to follow the 75 in all circumstances, powerful enough to produce destruction effects superior to those of the 75, with an extended field of fire, and with a range as large as possible.

The long gun had to be capable of firing at 12 or 13 kilometers on weakly protected targets; it had to be able to move at a walking pace harnessed to six or eight horses.

The goal to be reached being thus defined, it was advisable to address this program to the various manufacturers, and I represented to the Minister that it would be very useful to resort not only to the establishments of the artillery, but also to the private industry, of which certain firms built for foreign powers pieces giving all satisfaction. Mr. Messimy, a born enemy of any routine, welcomed this suggestion. The competition was thus opened between our industrialists and the technical section of the artillery; the date for the presentation of the various models was fixed for February 1912.

Chapter IV

This appeal to private industry seemed, at the time, almost revolutionary; the artillery establishments saw it as an attack on their prestige. The minister held firm and did not let himself be influenced.

But that was not all. It was not enough to organize the future. It was necessary at once, using the resources immediately available, to establish a makeshift heavy artillery, which would be gradually replaced by a modern artillery.

On January 9, 1912, at the High Council of National Defense, Mr. Messimy summarized our artillery situation:

> Our field artillery is complete and in good condition. For a long time, the supply of ammunition remained insufficient. Since 1906, on the initiative of Messrs Berteaux and Klotz, it has been gradually increased. Today it amounts to 1,280 cartridges per piece. A new effort is necessary to reach 1,500 rounds. On the other hand, measures must be taken in order to prepare the mobilization of the industrial establishments and to put them in a position, in case of war, to provide an intensive production. At present, most of our establishments are unable to meet this condition; new funds will be needed for this purpose. It will be necessary to obtain more new funding for the constitution of the army's heavy artillery. The Germans have large-caliber pieces in each army corps; they also have light siege equipment. In France, not enough effort was made to follow them. The Rimailho, although it is satisfactory, exists only in small proportion. The number of batteries planned for mobilization is 42, each battery has two pieces. The progress to be made to improve the present state of affairs will have to be carried out in two stages:
>
> During the first it will be necessary to have recourse to makeshift means. One will use pieces of 120 and 220 currently included in the crews of siege or in the armament of the places. During the second stage, a heavy artillery composed of rapid-fire pieces and answering the needs of the future war will be substituted for this provisional material; this substitution will require time and considerable expenses.
>
> The delay brought to the creation of a heavy artillery equivalent to that of our probable adversaries is due to the extreme slowness of our technical services, which, always pursuing new advances instead of seeking achievements, multiply the experiments and never succeed. Noting the impotence of the competent bodies, I have already thought of appealing to the private industry which for a long time has

manufactured artillery for foreign powers; perhaps, by means, it will be possible to arrive more quickly at the sought-after result.

The problem defined by the Ministry was well defined and the solutions clearly indicated.

But the question of the transformation of the artillery entailed as a corollary a question of personnel: to constitute and serve a new heavy artillery, it was necessary to have men; however, with the two-year service, and the new creations which it had been necessary to make, it was impossible to find available men. I then envisaged the use of some coastal batteries, some of which, assigned to points with little threat, seemed to me to be able to be more usefully employed by serving the embryo of our heavy artillery. When this project became known, it raised vehement protests in the parliamentary world and in certain military circles, who believed that removing a battery from Royan or Port-Vendres was equivalent to opening France to foreign invasion.

The Minister decided to ignore these protests. A decree dated February 6, 1912, transferred a certain number of coastal batteries to the foot regiments. And, to show my intentions, I had a regiment organized immediately. This regiment, constituted in Rueil under the command of colonel Bayel, was provisionally equipped with equipment from Bange, transported by makeshift horse-drawn vehicles, and served by the personnel of some disused coastal batteries. Later, part of this regiment was placed at the disposal of General Foch, then commander of the 20th Army corps, for the organization, begun at that time, of the Grand-Couronné of Nancy.

At the beginning of January 1912, Mr. Messimy was replaced at the Ministry of War by Mr. Millerand. It was the latter who was to continue the execution of his predecessor's plan.

In February, the workshops of Puteaux presented a 120, and a material with double calibre of 75/120. Neither one nor the other proved satisfactory.

In the first days of the following month, the Schneider establishments presented a 105 mm howitzer built for Bulgaria. The technical experiments took place in Calais in the presence of the Minister; I was also present; they gave complete satisfaction. This equipment met exactly the requirements of the program. The

Commission proposed that a battery, which was ordered immediately, be tested at Mailly and at the autumn maneuvers.

Because of the short time left to the competitors, Creusot did not have time to develop, for the long gun requested by the program, an original prototype; it was satisfied to present us with a 106.7 mm gun recently adopted by Russia. The test firings of this piece were satisfactory, but this material deviated significantly from the conditions of the program, particularly with regard to power and range. It was therefore refused by the unanimous vote of the Commission, minus two votes, including that of the president, General de Lamothe.

I agreed with General de Lamothe: in my opinion, it was urgent to achieve practical results. I insisted to the Minister that this equipment should not be eliminated *a priori*; by giving Creusot some time to improve the materiel that it had just presented to us, I was persuaded that it would manage to give us satisfaction in a short time. Indeed the tests were resumed, and the dispatch to the autumn maneuvers of two test pieces of this equipment was decided.

The test of the maneuvers of 1912 was clearly favorable to the two materials of Creusot, from the double point of view of mobilization and the ease of traction. The acquired results confirmed my conviction that we had to have a heavy field artillery: many tactical problems which occurred during these maneuvers could only be solved with the help of these materials.

In January 1913, I attended a new series of firings of the long gun from Creusot in Calais, which were so satisfactory that the Commission concluded to adopt it, provided that the caliber would be reduced to 105 mm. In reporting these results to the Minister, I insisted that the order for this equipment be placed without delay.

But, the technical services, in defiance against this materiel which had been neither conceived nor executed by them, exploited with the Minister the disadvantages recognized in the long gun of Creusot, and obtained the principle of the adaptation of a caliber close to 135 millimeters, launching at 18 kilometers a projectile of approximately 40 kilos. In addition, a series of studies were carried out in order to modernize our old 120 and 155 long Bange guns. This intervention risked delaying the outcome of this issue which

Chapter IV

had so far been too late.

At the same time, the first information on the Balkan war began to arrive. General Herr, commander of the artillery of the 6th Army corps, having spent the months of November and December 1912 in the theater of war, published his impressions in February 1913: he reported the absolute conviction that a long-range heavy artillery was indispensable in modern warfare: "It does not seem doubtful," he said, "that a long-range artillery will return, even in field warfare, frequent opportunities to take the lead against a medium-range artillery, like a duellist with a large rapier over an opponent armed with a court sword."

The publication of this report provoked a lively stir in military and parliamentary circles; once again, a lively polemic started between the exclusive supporters of the 75 and those who advocated the necessity of a heavy artillery. The experience of General Herr decided the doubters, and, on my insistence, in April 1913, 220 pieces of the 105 long model of the Creusot were ordered, with the simple authorization of the Budget Commission. Half of this order was to be built in the Schneider factories, the other half in the artillery establishments; the delivery of these pieces was to be staggered from August 1914 to July 1915.

It is this very well studied model which appeared at the front in the first weeks of the hostilities. It had a range of 12.3 km. and launched a 17 kg shell containing 1.87 kg. of explosive. Its role was, all in all, rather modest: it was only an enlarged 75, extending the range of the field gun. It had nothing of a piece with great destructive impact. Moreover, at the beginning of the hostilities, we had only a small number of these guns. Indeed, on the request of the technical services, the order of 110 pieces made in Creusot, was reduced to 36, and the order placed in Bourges was cancelled.

Following the experiments carried out at Mailly in 1912, and the favorable test of the maneuvers, the field howitzer of Creusot had been adopted; a credit of 80 million had been registered in the 500 million project deposited in February 1913 to contribute to the national defense. The high cost of the construction of this howitzer made a strong impression on the Parliament. Also, during the discussion, the government, relying on the opinion of the technical services, decided that it was still necessary to proceed to new experiments for the shells, and it declared that it gave up this credit of 80 million intended for the light howitzer. At the same time, a fact occurred which had singular consequences.

The technical services, which wished, as I said, not to encumber our army with heavy pieces for fear of damaging its maneuvering qualities, had sought a solution making it possible to avoid the disadvantages which the tension of the trajectory of the 75 presented to beat the dead angles and the strongly defiled objectives. Three ideas had been proposed:

The use of reduced loads. This process was criticized for complicating the supplies;

The fusing firing of the explosive shell to which the executants were hostile for technical reasons;

Finally the plate of the commander Malandrin, which made it possible to increase the curvature of the trajectory; this solution seemed to solve the problem in a simple and economic way.

This process was recommended on a provisional basis by the Commission of New Materiel, while waiting for the construction of light howitzers. In March 1913, a solemn session was organized for the conclusion of the tests of the Malandrin plate in front of the Minister, the members of the Superior Council of War, and the Commissions of the army. The experiments were followed with enthusiasm; a clever advertisement argued that the plate had the advantage of making the 75 a gun with two purposes, namely a gun with tense firing and a gun with curved firing. In vain it was pointed out that, in any case, the weight of the projectile remained much lower than that of the projectile of the German howitzer, and especially that the trajectory was reduced by the adoption of the plate. Nothing did it. The field howitzer was definitively discarded, and replaced by this rather crude makeshift means.

For my part, I did not share the general enthusiasm, and I persisted in thinking that the question of the howitzer was not solved. Undoubtedly, the Malandrin plate was a very ingenious solution; but its principal disadvantage was, as I have just said, to decrease the range of the pieces. This is what General Ruffey, then commander of the 13th Army corps, wrote in a note of October 1913: "The French artillery admires itself in its 75. The Germans will attack us with howitzers of 10.5 and 15; they have scales going

Chapter IV

up to 16 meters: we only oppose them with inferior shells; we count, it is true, on the aeroplanes which considerably lengthen the duration of the adjustment and on the telephone; we only have bad glasses, nightingales. Conclusion: the enemy superiority will be overwhelming."

Determined not to give up the game, I returned once again to the fray, and I obtained in February 1914, from Mr. Noulens, the new minister, that the directorate of the artillery would be urged to complete as soon as possible the studies relating to the improvement of the 75 mm projectiles, allowing in particular to shoot beyond 6,000 meters; and I called once again the attention of the Minister on the recognized need for a short field gun. On the 26th of the same month, a new note invited the directorate of the artillery to push the study of a 120 mm howitzer with a range at least equal to that of the German 15 howitzer. Our efforts were not absolutely vain, since experiments could take place on its design at the end of July 1914. These results came unfortunately too late, and the war broke out without us having a field howitzer.

The fight that I had undertaken in favor of the materiel had not made me lose sight of the general organization of our heavy artillery. We have seen that a first heavy regiment could be constituted in Rueil. It had not been possible to make more at that time because of the lack of available personnel. But, when the law of three years was put under study in 1913, I introduced proposals for the use of the additional manpower given by the law, the creation of fifteen new batteries; the Superior Council of War consulted on the question gave a favorable opinion, and the proposed organization was adopted on October 15, 1913; it took account of the materiel which we could then have and those which were adopted.

The law of April 14, 1914 organized five heavy artillery regiments; but these were still in the training period at the time of mobilization. This organization was only a beginning limited to what we could expect in terms of materiel in a short time: it was to continue during the implementation of Plan XVII. It was only provisional in character. In particular, it was impossible to permanently equip the army corps with heavy artillery as the Germans had done: indeed, our heavy field artillery was to include at the beginning only sixteen groups (not including the 5th regiment, provisionally armed with the 120 long equipment). As it was beyond discussion that the dividing of the heavy artillery could not go beyond the group level, it became impossible, with sixteen groups, to equip twenty-one army corps with heavy artillery. It was therefore necessary to make the heavy artillery an army organ.

At the beginning of August 1914, the French army corps had 120 guns of 75 firing a shell of 7.3 kg., and that was all; the German army corps had 108 guns of 77 mm, 36 howitzers of 10.5 cm firing a projectile of 15 kilos, and 16 heavy howitzers of 15 cm firing a projectile of 42 kilos. As heavy army artillery, we had only 104 Rimailho of 155mm short distributed in 26 batteries, 96 guns of 120 Baquet distributed in 15 batteries, and 20 batteries of 120 long with tractors or groups of hitches. On the other side, Germany had 360 long guns of 10 centimeters, 360 long guns of 13 centimeters and 128 mortars of 21 centimeters, that is to say in total 848 pieces.

As far as the siege crews were concerned, on 20 February 1913, the commission for new equipment submitted to the Minister a new program that partly took up that of the high commission for fortified places established in 1909.

On this question, the opinions were less divergent, and public opinion was less passionate about it, so it was easier to reach a solution. On October 31, 1913, in Calais, the Schneider establishments presented a long-recoil barrel for the 155 long guns, allowing for rapid firing with ranges of 12 to 13 kilometers, and a 280 mm mortar that gave excellent results with a range of 9 kilometers. On November 8, 1913, 18 of these mortars were ordered; the delivery was to be staggered from November 1915 to November 1916. In June 1914, 120 barrels for the 155 long model 1877, intended for the rapid-fire gun of Creusot, were also ordered, to be delivered from December 1915 to December 1917.

On his side, Captain Filloux had developed a powerful mortar of 370 mm which was ready, at the end of 1913, to undertake its first firings. In 1912, Captain Filloux had also happily transformed the 155 short 1881 into an accelerated firing mortar. The transformation of the 155 short rapid fire 1904 into a less cumbersome equipment was also explored.

Chapter IV

However, when mobilization occurred, the light siege crews were composed solely of 120 long guns, old models modernized by the use of hitches and tractors; 155 short guns on transportable platforms. The heavy siege crew divisions were supplied with 155 long hitched, 155 short, and 220 mortars with metal platforms.

In January 1914, I submitted to the members of the Superior Council of War a general note in which I had condensed the conditions of use of heavy field artillery. This note presented our situation *vis-à-vis* the Germans in a rather favorable light. It was for moral reasons, in particular to avoid discouragement, that I had given this note an optimistic form: our inferiority could not escape anyone, but, since for the moment, and for a rather long time, only a part of the forces in the field could use heavy artillery, it seemed necessary to me to represent the assistance of short artillery as sometimes necessary, and not as always indispensable. As long as our resources in heavy pieces were not developed, it was useless to insist more on the powerful help that this material had to bring to the men.

It is also for psychological reasons that I did not think I should insist too much in this document on the provisional character of the projected organization. I did not want to let the officers in whose hands they would be placed assume that everything would soon be changed, and that their exercises, their work, their reflections on the procedures of instruction and the mode of use were doomed to future changes.

Such were the motives which inspired this note. The members of the Superior Council of War did not rally without reservation to the proposed solutions. The opinions of the Council were quite divided. General Dubail wrote: "The note is marked by an optimism that I do not share." And General Chomer made the following observation at the same time: "It (the Note) gives the impression that the Germans are much better equipped and armed than we are."

I do not want to end this chapter on artillery without mentioning a point that is generally not well known.

Our intelligence services had made known to us in the course of 1913 that the Germans had recently put in service various types of "Minenwerfer." Very concerned about this information, I asked the 3rd directorate in October of the same year to pursue with the greatest activity the study of similar machines which were entirely lacking. In spite of three successive reminders, the directorate of the artillery made known in the first months of 1914 that it expected to be able to succeed in this inquiry only in a still undetermined time. I then considered, in agreement with General Chevalier, director of the Engineers, to request authorization to place an order for "trench mortars" with private industry, which could be quickly put into service in the engineer units. But this request – for what reasons? I do not know – was not accepted, and nothing was done to provide our army with "mine launchers," which it was completely lacking at the beginning of the operations.

General Chevalier was not discouraged. He had the problem studied by an engineer officer, Major Duchêne, which led to the development of a type of trench mortar. In November 1914, when the events proved the necessity to have "Minenwerfer," and when General Duménil was charged to solve this problem urgently, he could not do better than to join in the first place the battalion commander Duchêne.

Chapter V

Ammunition supplies.

The general program of works to be carried out for the urgent needs of the national defense established at the end of 1906 on the initiative of Mr. Messimy, then reporter of the budget of the War, had envisaged that the supplies of ammunition of 75 mm would be increased from 700 shots per gun to 1,200 at the end of 1912. It was also foreseen that this figure would be subsequently increased to 1,500 rounds within five and a half years. At the time of Agadir, that is to say when I took the responsibilities of Chief of General Staff, our supplies had arrived in the batteries and inside at the rate of 940 cartridges loaded and assembled, for a total of 3,900 parts; moreover, 200 shells per gun were stored to be assembled as of the first days of the mobilization. From 1906 to 1911, 62 million francs were spent to obtain this result.

This situation had seemed insufficient to some minds. General Langlois, in particular, had published that we were inferior to the Germans on this point. The artillery services did not share this opinion. We had, they said, sufficiently precise data on the supplies of our adversaries to allow us to make an exact comparison between the supplies of the French army corps and the

German army corps: assuming that the reorganization of the supply units had been carried out, which the Germans were not to complete until 1912, the Germans had at their immediate disposal only 375 rounds per piece, representing a tonnage of 400 tons of projectiles, whereas we had 500 tons, representing 615 rounds for each of our army corps pieces. The distribution of ammunition between the various echelons of the French corps allowed for 37,000 rounds to be available on the battlefield, while the German corps had only 18,000 rounds available in the front line. The solution adopted in France thus seemed to better meet the requirements of rapid-fire gun consumption.

I did not share this optimism; indeed, our information was very incomplete concerning the supplies built up in Germany in the army, stage and interior depots. On the other hand, rapid-fire artillery is a great consumer of ammunition, and since we were determined to give an offensive character to our eventual operations, we had to fear the fate of an army whose ammunition would be exhausted in front of an adversary still provided with shells. Moreover, if we had fewer guns than the Germans, we had to compensate for this inferiority by ensuring the ability of firing a greater number of rounds per gun. The infantry could only carry out their attacks supported by a hurricane of projectiles, and it seemed useless to possess rapid-fire weapons if we did not place at their disposal abundant quantity of ammunition to feed them. Moreover, the inferiority of our heavy artillery made it our duty to achieve an overwhelming superiority for our 75 mm artillery.

Also, when, at the end of 1911, I was called to preside over the conferences which fixed the program of the needs of the national defense, I posed in principle that the supplies of 75, which were to be increased from 1,200 to 1,500 rounds, were to be acquired not in five and a half years as it had been planned, but in four years.

In 1912, 10 million were spent on this objective, and 14 million and a half in 1913. Unfortunately, manufacturing was slowed down by the impossibility in which the Service of the Powders found itself to increase its production. However the experience of the last Balkan wars had come to confirm us in the impression that it was necessary to estimate very broadly the supplies of ammunition. At the beginning of 1914, a series of judiciously conducted experiments showed the need to increase the supplies of manufactured ammunition to 3,000 rounds per piece. It was curious to note that the conclusions of these experiments carried out in Mailly agreed with the figures that General Langlois had proclaimed indispensable. However, we were far from meeting these figures, since at the time of mobilization we had only 4,866,167 shells, that is to say 1,390 rounds per 75 mm gun, of which 1,190 rounds were assembled and 200 represented by their parts.

The manufacture of ammunition had been ensured until 1911 by the artillery manufacturing establishments, with a supplement provided by the private industry which delivered 3,000 shells per day.

The production of 75 mm ammunition after the mobilization was regulated by the manufacturing plan of the artillery establishments of December 28, 1909, which included first of all the assembly and loading, before the fiftieth day, of 800,000 75 mm cartridges, including 554,000 bullet shells and 246,000 explosive shells at a rate of 25,000 cartridges per day, using the manufactured components stored in the assembly workshop reserve distributed between Bourges, Tarbes, Lyon and Rennes.

From the fifty-first day, it was planned to manufacture 13,600 cartridges per day from scratch, including 7,900 rounds and 5,700 explosives. A manufacturing reserve including as first supply a stock of raw materials was created for 600,000 cartridges of 75 and 10,000 of 155 C.T. The private industry contributed to this production with 3,500 75 mm shells per day.

On May 7, 1913, wartime manufacturing was reorganized and distributed among the general reserve depots of Bourges, Angers, Rennes, Clermont and Nîmes.

As far as industrial mobilization was concerned, the idea of collaboration with private industry had not yet penetrated people's minds to such an extent that, on February 20, 1914, the management of the Artillery Forges informed the few French industrialists who had worked for it up to that point that the agreements made for the manufacture of munitions in wartime were about to expire and would not be renewed. It was only planning contracts and the requisition of raw materials. The industrial competition was only planned for the manufacture of casings. On hearing this news, I went to Mr. Messimy to secure from him the continuation of the industrial competition. The minister was all for this idea, but he could not succeed in making it succeed before the declaration of war. On August 1, 1914, he decided that manufacturing would be intensified to the greatest extent possible, by calling on private industry, but this decision, which took the industrialists by surprise, could not have an immediate effect. It was not until the arrival of Mr. Millerand at the Ministry of War that this problem finally received a solution.

Chapter VI

The training camps.

The question of training camps was, along with that of the artillery which I have just mentioned, the object of my preoccupations and my efforts from the moment I took office as Chief of the General Staff.

This question was not new. Two successive programs had been adopted, the first in 1897, the second in 1907, towards which an average of 3 million per year had been devoted. At this rate, the 1908 program would not be completed until 1930, since it was estimated that 75 million dollars would be needed to complete it. At that time, about half of the workforce would be spending time in training camps each year. But in 1911, we still had only eight unfinished camps; barely a third of our active troops could spend a fortnight in the camps each year, and because of the distribution of the camps over the territory, the units of certain army corps were unable to go there. At the same time, on the other side of the Rhine, an effort was made for the same purpose, so that within a few years Germany would have a divisional camp for each army corps.

If we wanted to give our troops the practical training required for the formation of an army composed of active elements serving only two years and of reserves called up only for short periods, it appeared urgent to make a vigorous effort in the same direction as the Germans. In addition, the maneuver grounds, the stands, the cramped firing ranges of the garrisons were far from being sufficient for the proper execution of the technical exercises of the infantry: the introduction of the D bullet required firing ranges of at least 4,000 meters in depth for the musketry. The artillery, on its side, claimed each year, rightly, a greater number of days of fire training; the recent increase of this army fully justified this request. All the cavalry generals insisted that the regiments and brigades should spend time each year in the camps, especially for development. Finally, it was important that the elementary unit of troops of all arms, the infantry division, had camps large enough to execute its combined training.

To all these reasons was added another: the law of 1908 prescribed the sending to the camps of the reserve units of the second call-up in the spring; until now, for lack of fields, we had only been able to satisfy this legitimate requirement in the proportion of a quarter of the regiments called up.

Therefore, as early as November 1911, I had a program put forward for study based on the following principles:

First of all, a training camp had to be suitable for a complete division, and therefore had to have an area of 5,500 to 6,000 hectares.

Secondly, in order to minimize the financial burden on the country, the camps were to be distributed in such a way that one camp could be used for the training of two army corps.

The studies resulted in the following forecasts:

Two corps camps: Châlons (enlarged) and Mailly;

Ten divisional camps: La Courtine (existing), Coëtquidan (in transformation), Sissonne and Valdahon (enlarging), and 6 camps to be created;

The Larzac and Souge camps, defective, to be used in their current dimensions.

This program would require an expenditure of about 135 million to be spread over seven years: 12 million for 1912, and 20 million for six years from 1913.

Chapter VI

General Joffre inspects the school of Saumur. Behind him, on the left, General Wegand, then a lieutenant-colonel.

As soon as I had this preliminary study, I sent the Minister a report exploring the issue and the conclusions we had reached; on December 14, 1911, Mr. Messimy approved it. A few days later, the army corps were invited to carry out the necessary ground surveys and to draw up projects, which were to reach the Minister before April 1, 1912.

The greatest discretion was recommended on the real object of the recognitions, in order not to attract the public attention, and thus to avoid increasing of the price of the grounds.

While this preparatory work was being carried out, the matter came to a halt because of budgetary difficulties. I have already said, in fact, that on January 17, the new holders of the War and Finance portfolios, gathered around the President of the Council to examine the request for credits outside the budget presented by the previous cabinet, agreed to eliminate a certain number of our requests; among them, the allocation for the camps disappeared.

This amputation seemed to me to be serious, because it was useless to make an important materiel effort if one did not give at the same time to the army the means to educate itself. Also, when it came to establishing the proposals for the 1913 budget in 1912, I insisted strongly that the forecasts of the program of December 14, 1911 be completely taken up. Information that reached us at that time from the other side of the Vosges gave me the opportunity to confirm my conviction: the modalities of the German military law were beginning to be known to us; on May 23, when the Minister asked the army staff what measures he was considering to respond to the German military effort, I had the necessity of setting up training camps listed in the first place, by improving those that already existed and by creating those that were planned. In addition, on June 6, I asked the Minister to carry out the program of December 14, 1911 in its entirety. To this end, I requested the allocation of an additional credit of 2 million for 1912 to make Coëtquidan a camp usable for a division as early as 1913, and the opening of an annual payment of 17 million for 1913, to be followed by annual payments of 20 million for five years beginning in 1914.

On June 10, Mr. Millerand approved "in principle" the conclusions of this report, which was immediately transmitted to the Directorate of Control. On June 22, the latter replied that since the figures for the 1913 war budget had been decided by the Budget Committee, it was too late to request an increase in appropriations. "We would endeavor," it added, "when the time came, to come to an agreement with the Finance Commissions to determine the amount of expenditure commitments likely to be authorized outside the budget for the year 1913, and to obtain that the training camps appear in the authorizations concerning 1913."

As for the requested increase in appropriations for 1912, the Directorate of Control felt that it could only be presented in the omnibus bill to be introduced in October.

As a result, the entire development of the program was forced to slow down. However, the preliminary arrangements for the acquisition of land at the Coëtquidan camp were made in such a way that, when Parliament voted on the project, only the final administrative formalities had to be completed.

But we were not at the end of our troubles. In the middle of October, I learned indirectly that, according to information provided by the Comptroller, the 2 million franc appropriation would probably not be voted before the end of the year, and that there was reason to have reservations about the possibility of obtaining an additional appropriation for 1913 for training camps.

Chapter VI

I then drew the attention of the Minister in a note dated October 15 "to the capital interest for the training of the army which was attached to the fact that the necessary funding for the camps be granted in due time, with a view to the immediate implementation of the decided program."

Mr. Millerand willingly complied with my requests, and a few days later he informed the Ministry of Finance that, for the fiscal year 1913, it was necessary to add to the sum already provided for off-budget expenditures the 13 million requested for the training camps. Moreover, at the insistence of Mr. Millerand, the 2 million for Coëtquidan could be acquired before the end of the 1912 fiscal year.

In spite of the energetic help that I found with the Minister of War, the allocation for 1913 could only be raised to 7,350,000 francs: As for the 20 million requested for 1913, the amount was incorporated in the requests that led to the program of 420 million that I have already mentioned. We know what happened to this program and that, on the unanimous authorization of the Senate Finance Committee, the Ministers of War and Finance were authorized, on February 24, to commit in advance a sum of 72 million. On February 26, the Minister of War notified the departments concerned of the amounts that each of them was authorized to commit immediately. In this way it was possible to spend 7,350,000 francs on training camps in 1913.

However, all these delays had had deplorable consequences for the Treasury. In spite of the precautions taken, in all the regions where land purchases had been considered, word had spread; speculation had fallen on these regions. For the camp of Coëtquidan, for example, the land had been evaluated at 500 to 800 francs per hectare; when the 2 million necessary were granted at the end of 1912 to buy this land, the War Administration had to pay much higher prices out of proportion with the initial evaluation. As a result, the funds we had obtained were not sufficient to acquire all the land we had in mind, and it became necessary to spread our program over a greater number of years.

In short, it was only on the eve of the war that the question of training camps, which was fundamental to the training of the army, finally received its status. The necessary appropriations to ensure a sufficiently rapid execution of the 1911 program were finally granted, and it was hoped that this program would be entirely completed in 1918. The first studies on this question dated, as I have already said, from 1897!

When in 1913 the law of three years was adopted and the reinforcement of reserve units was planned, it seemed necessary to provide for the means of assembling, at the time of their convocation, these regiments in camps where it would be easier for them to work than in the garrison towns where they had been convoked until then. It was, moreover, in my intentions to form reserve brigades for mobilization; I was therefore led to consider the possibility of assembling these units during the reserve periods.

The delay brought to the establishment of the large camps led me to seek for the training of the reserve units an immediate solution. There was no need for large camps to ensure that regiments and brigades could be reorganized and held together. We had a whole series of artillery ranges and infantry firing ranges that had become too small for the training of these weapons as a result of the use of the D bullet, but which could very well, without being enlarged, provide housing and training for the reserve regiments. On July 17, 1913, I had a program established that dealt solely with the additional facilities to be provided for the purpose I have just indicated. The camps selected were eleven in number and distributed throughout the country. The planned expenditure was 15 million; a budget of 250,000 francs could be used for this purpose in 1913.

Chapter VII

The three-year law.

The law of March 21, 1905, on the recruitment of the army had, undoubtedly, achieved the equality of the military obligations between all the citizens likely to bear arms; but it seemed to have decreased appreciably the robustness of the mounted services, and quite particularly that of the cavalry.

The latter complained about the lack of manpower, the inadequacy of the instruction given to two-year-old soldiers with the methods then in use, the critical situation of the regiments after the departure of the class, the impossibility of carrying out the training of the horses and, above all, the shortage if not the absence of trained and well-saddled riders.

These complications were compounded by difficulties in mobilizing during the winter period, when only one class of riders could be mobilized.

The situation had seemed critical since the implementation of the two-year law. It was expected that there would be an abundance of voluntary enlistments and commitments, which, in the mind of the 1905 legislator, were to constitute the important core of experienced soldiers, indispensable in the mounted troops;

but this expectation had been disappointed.

In their inspection reports, the generals insistently drew the Minister's attention to this situation. He was convinced. Mr. Messimy, as early as 1911, had asked the study section which he had organized in his office to look for possible improvements to the law of 1905. For its part, the Army General Staff had not remained inactive, and it had undertaken a whole series of studies on the question; it had even tried, by separating some items from a proposal modifying the recruitment law, to have Parliament vote without delay on certain provisions which would have had the aim of reinforcing our peacetime manpower and increasing the number of our enlisted men, re-enlisted men and commissioned men destined for the cavalry and the mounted batteries. It sought, on the other hand, to multiply the number of the three-years-old recruits, by increasing the advantages allotted to these.

In the meantime, the Parliament was moved by the rumors that were circulating about the state of our cavalry and, on the occasion of the discussion of the law of the frameworks of this weapon, some speakers clearly asked the Minister questions relating to its numbers.

Mr. Millerand, concerned with a situation whose gravity did not escape him, then prescribed to the staff of the army to seek a solution which allows to give to the cavalry the experienced soldiers who were lacking, without worrying about the political side of the question of which it was the examination. It was then January 1913. The return to the three-year service was thus proposed; but this problem no longer concerned only the cavalry.

The whole army was, in fact, tested and weakened by the consequences of short-term service and by the shortage of career soldiers; everywhere, the numbers were insufficient; the liberation of the class left in the ranks only one contingent of trained conscripts, so that, during the winter period, our cover was in a precarious situation.

On the other hand, the reduced quota did not allow us to bring our units into line with the requirements set by the military laws, which were already very appreciably lower than the corresponding German figures.

The training of the troops was naturally affected by the scarcity of manpower; it could only be given with great difficulty in units with a small number of soldiers; it was hardly possible in units with a normal number of soldiers to have a few men without ranks available for exercise every day during their second year of service; and the cadres never handled the number of soldiers they would have to command in the field.

Moreover, it became impossible, for lack of resources in men, to respond, as the need was felt, to the creation of technical troops and to the new needs revealed each day by the progress of science and the experience of recent wars.

Finally, Morocco absorbed a significant fraction of our manpower; it was as much lost for the defense of the metropolis.

Such was the state of affairs when, in February 1913, the first information reached us about the new military arrangements that were to be made by the Reichstag. Already on March 27, 1911, the Reichstag had passed a military law increasing the established strength of the German army by 13,000 men. The essential feature of this law had been a significant development of the technical means placed at the disposal of the army; financial considerations explained the restraint of the demands of the war administration; this relative restraint moreover aroused, at this very time, violent attacks from certain political circles and the military press.

Fifteen months later, a new military law, known as the law of June 14, 1912, was passed by a considerable majority and implemented as a matter of urgency, increasing the Empire's military forces by a tenth.

Less than eight months later, the German government proposed a new increase in the number of soldiers, which raised the army's strength by a fifth.

What was the state of mind that could motivate such measures at such short intervals of time?

This is how our diplomatic agents explained it: on pain of dying of overpopulation, Germany had an absolute need not only to maintain, but also to create outlets for its industry and trade. It was therefore in competition with other nations. Until 1912, the German people, believing firmly in the superiority of their military organization, had thought that the mere act of throwing their sword into the international balance of power would always be enough to tip it in their favor. German merchants and industrialists were convinced that a few threats of dry powder and a sharpened sword would be enough to break down all resistance and conquer the world in the economic order.

Now, the attitude of France in the Moroccan conflict had been for Germany a subject of surprise and the solution of the conflict produced on it an effect of stupor. It regarded the concessions made by France as a humiliation that the latter had inflicted on it.

Convinced that the authority of peoples in peace is measured by the capacity they have to wage war, our eastern neighbors felt from that moment on that their military power was no longer great enough to impose it. A German consul in one of Europe's largest trading ports summed it up this way: "It is possible that war, especially an unfortunate war, will lead to the commercial decline of Germany, but it will not lead to it any more than would diplomatic retreats, because of the moral and economic consequences of the latter. Trade and industry are at present suffering very severely from the difficulties arising in Germany on all sides. These must be broken by force, if necessary, and armed accordingly."

It was from this state of mind that the military law of June 14, 1912, resulted; it was also this state of mind that had given birth in January 1911 to the League of National Defense "the Wehrverein," which had as its goal "to re-establish the feeling of confidence that the Germans possessed a few years ago, and which must be the point of support of the foreign policy." This same mentality made the generals Keim, Falkenhausen and Bernhardi demand, in numerous conferences, the full application of compulsory service.

Then came the Balkan War, the defeat of Turkey, which was subservient to Germany, and the blossoming of Slavism in the Balkans. "We can no longer count, in the event of a European conflict," wrote General von Bernhardi at the end of 1912, "either on Turkey, or on Romania, or on the entire Austrian forces. We will have against us not only the French and the British, but the main mass of the Russian forces. The reverses of the Turks have damaged our military prestige; there is not even Belgium that does not recognize a French heart and deride the poor results of German training in Turkey."

Chapter VII

Thus, for the past two years, Germany had seen France stand up to her with the support not only of Russia, but also of England. Knowing that she could not make much of Austria, and that she could not count on Italy, she strengthened her military power. Perhaps she desired peace, but a peace resulting from the satisfaction given to all her external ambitions, and from the subordination of the neighboring powers to her desires, a peace, to say the least, resulting from the fear that she would inspire.

It is now important to define the results of these military laws.

By the law of 1912, the German command had not sought to increase the number of its large active mobilized units. We knew, in fact, for a long time, that two army corps bearing the numbers 20 and 21 were to be formed at the time of mobilization by the addition to the 3rd Division of each of the 1st and 14th Corps, of surplus elements in neighboring army corps. The organic creation of these two army corps (20th and 21st) did not therefore constitute an increase in the number of large units. But the new law proposed to make these 25 active army corps immediately usable, considering that the formation of large units, at mobilization, is incompatible with the speed that the German general staff proposed to give, from the beginning, to the operations.

The new law in the pipeline at the beginning of 1913 had, according to the information we had at the time, a completely different character. It was to increase the budgetary target by 4,000 officers, 15,000 non-commissioned officers, 117,000 men and 27,000 horses. The new or increased numbers envisaged were exclusively related to the increase of the active nuclei, to the reinforcement of the management and to the development of the material organization in the already existing large units. The quality of each of the army's units was considerably increased; in particular, the leadership would be assured only by career officers with more than two years of service in the foot armies and three years in the mounted troops. No combat unit would have more than one-third reservists, almost all of whom would be from the last released class. In addition, and above all, in the covering corps, the peacetime strength was to be brought to figures very close to the wartime strength. The German command now had in its hands a very powerful army, whose mobilization was improved and accelerated, which gave it the means, if the desire arose, to begin the war against us by a sudden attack.

Such was the military situation of our neighbors at the beginning of 1913. It seemed to us that the maintenance of the balance of French and German forces was the only guarantee of peace in freedom and dignity.

As soon as the new effort decided by Germany began to be committed in France, it was understood that the brutal suddenness that it was trying to give to its mobilization constituted a threat for our borders weakly defended by insufficient coverage. It was necessary to increase our manpower, and to make better use of those we had. To this end, a whole series of proposals were launched, at the same time as the studies of the three-year law prescribed by Mr. Millerand were being carried out. All these proposals aimed at improving our military state without touching the 1905 law. Some of them asked for an addition of forces to our indigenous people in North Africa as well as to our contingents in the colonies: this was certainly feasible, but progressively, at the risk of raising great difficulties. Others sought salvation in a system of long-term commitments and reenlistments improved by the granting of very serious moral and material advantages: this solution presented too many uncertainties for it to be possible to make it the basis of our organization.

These different systems were, in short, only palliatives that could not remedy the situation. It was soon realized that it was not possible to achieve anything serious without touching the law of 1905. Solutions were then sought in this sense, some of which were ingenious.

First of all, a proposal was studied in which the length of military service varied according to the different arms. The time of service would have been extended by six weeks in the infantry, ten weeks in the artillery, twenty weeks in the cavalry. To compensate for this, long leaves of absence would be granted to soldiers of the mounted arms during their active service. The only advantage of this project would have been to keep two mobilizable classes under the flag during the first weeks of the winter period; on the other hand, it undermined the principle of equality of military duties for all citizens, and it was detrimental to the proper functioning of

Chapter VII

training by the frequency and duration of the leaves.

The system of staggered calls for reservists was also considered. This procedure would have made it possible to maintain our forces at a higher level and to ensure better training for our reservists by calling up each of the two complementary classes annually for one month; on the other hand, it would have had the disadvantage of preventing the reserve formations from being brought together for training; it would also have caused a profound disturbance in the social life of the country and in our military organization.

The twenty-seven month service, with incorporation on July 1, would have made it possible to have recruits available for mobilization as early as October 1. But this system would have taken away part of their cadres from the units trained during the summer period, which was favourable to general exercises and manoeuvres. Moreover, this system did not solve the problem of manpower.

Thirty months of service would have resulted in overcrowded units in all arms in winter, when individual training is given and work must be moderated for reasons of hygiene. In the summer, on the other hand, the units would have fallen back to their current size, precisely at the time when training is most active.

As for the biennial call-up system in October and April, it seemed likely to bring about a profound disturbance in our organization, and to put us in a state of constant inferiority *vis-à-vis* Germany.

Thus, all the studies undertaken tended to convince us that the only acceptable solution was the integral and compulsory three-year service for all.

It was under these conditions that, on March 4, 1913, at the Élysée Palace, the question of the principle of the three-year law was submitted to the Superior Council of War. For the first time, Mr. Poincaré presided as Head of State. Mr. Briand, President of the Council, and Mr. Étienne, Minister of War, were present.

I explained that the German measures taken in 1911 and 1912 brought the active army to 800,000 men on the footing of peace; under these conditions, it would only have to be mobilized by receiving a complement of horses; this accelerated mobilization of the twenty-five German army corps gave our adversaries the possibility of rushing our coverage without difficulty.

It therefore seemed necessary that our covering units be brought to a strength close enough to the war footing, so that, from the first night of mobilization, by simple recall of the reservists domiciled on the spot, they would be in a position to conduct the campaign with war strength.

In addition, the number of large covering units was to be increased by the participation in this role of the 2nd Corps and a division of the 8th. We would thus arrive at eleven divisions in cover, with which we could hope to resist a sudden attack. Supported by the fortified places, these eleven divisions were to be sufficient to guarantee our mobilization and our concentration.

If, now, we consider the army corps of the interior, we find there, as a result of the deductions made from the infantry for the new branches (aeronautics, artillery, technical troops), numbers so low that the training given there was fruitless: 150 men per company were needed to form a solid nucleus around which the reservists would come to agglomerate in the proportion of 2 to 3; 150 men per company were also needed to allow training.

Thus, the proposed three-year service would not increase the number of units mobilized, but would first strengthen coverage, then facilitate mobilization, and finally significantly improve the quality of the troops.

After this presentation, Mr. Briand affirmed that the government was determined to do everything possible to put the army in a position to fulfill its role. He asked that, because of the difficulties he foresaw in getting the Chambers to accept the return to the three-year law, the most striking arguments be provided to him.

The question was then put to the Council, "In the presence of the German effort, should we strengthen our military forces, and especially our coverage?"

The Council unanimously answered yes to this question.

The different systems studied were then discussed: the system of reenlistments, the twenty-seven month system proposed by General Pédoya, the thirty month system.

The problem was essentially as follows:

Chapter VII

If the reinforcements I had indicated were accepted, the minimum strength to be achieved was 674,300 men. To take into account the waste which occurs at the time of conscription and which experience allowed to fix at 8 percent for the combat arms, it was necessary to conscript 727,000 men.

However, the resources with the full three-year service broke down as follows:

210,000	men for the last class called up.
200,000	men for the class that had already served one year and lost 5 percent of its strength.
194,000	men for the class that had served two years and lost, during that second year, 3 percent of its strength.
90,000	men of the permanent metropolitan contingent (enlisted and re-enlisted).
20,000	men of the permanent colonial contingent.
9,000	men from the three contingents donated by the old colonies.
15,000	men from sources supplied by the third medical examination following two adjournments, and from the passage of men from the auxiliary service into the armed service.

Total: 738,000 men.

This total figure was only a relative value; it was subject to variations in plus or minus which probably amounted to about fifteen thousand men.

We can see that our needs corresponded approximately to the

resources provided by the simultaneous presence of three classes under the flag.

The Council therefore unanimously declared that the three-year service was the only one likely to allow the necessary reinforcements; it expressed the wish that no attenuation of the principle of equality of service be made.

It was in this sense that the bill was drafted to be tabled before the Chambers. However, at the formal request of Mr. Chéron, taking note of the slight excess of expected resources over needs, the Minister decided at the last hour to introduce a reduction in favor of the sons of large families. It was to be feared that this concession, legitimate as it was, would constitute a crack that would gradually widen.

In the meantime, Messrs Reinach and de Montebello had introduced a counter-proposal whose essential provisions were to fix a minimum number of soldiers for each unit and to make a large appeal to voluntary recruits. The authors of this proposal assumed that the duration of service was increased to three years for the entire contingent, with the proviso that when the minimum number of soldiers was reached, conscripts belonging to certain categories (sons of families with more than four children, married men with families) could be sent on leave.

The Minister of War, in agreement with the authors of the counter-proposal and the reporter appointed by the Army Commission, agreed to a compromise solution which borrowed some of their essential provisions from the original proposal and from the one that Messrs Reinach and de Montebello had submitted.

It was this draft that served as the basis for the discussion in Parliament, and which was tabled on March 6 by the government on the desk of the Chamber. As it stood, the draft was to provide us with an active army of 700,000 men and officers against 870,000 men in Germany; as it was logical to assume that one fifth of the German forces, or about 175,000 men, would be immobilized by Russia, only 695,000 would remain against us. Thus the balance was restored, taking into account what we would eventually be obliged to maintain on the border of the Alps.

It will undoubtedly be objected that, in these calculations, there is no mention of reserves. The reason is that their importance depends on the number of active units, because it depends on the number of available active cadres who are destined to command them; a proportional relationship exists between the numbers of peacetime and wartime personnel: these depend on those.

As soon as the decision was made by the government to request the three-year service, that is, as early as the end of February, a vigorous campaign was launched in the press to orient public opinion towards this solution. In addition, the various members of the government, and especially Mr. Étienne, devoted themselves throughout the country to demonstrate the necessity of this heavy sacrifice.

It must be said here that a new argument, which could not be publicly mentioned, had come to reinforce the conviction of the French government by showing it clearly the goal towards which Germany was moving. Indeed, at the end of March, the Minister of War received from a reliable source an open and secret report on the reinforcement of the German army; this document emanated from a high German military authority and its authenticity could not be doubted. As it has since been published in the French *Yellow Book*, it is important to quote a few passages to recall its spirit:[*]

> It is necessary, said the author, to accustom the German people to think that an offensive war on our part is a necessity to fight the provocations of the adversary. It is necessary to conduct business in such a way that, under the heavy impression of powerful armaments, considerable sacrifices, and a tense political situation, an outbreak is seen as a deliverance. The war must be prepared from the financial point of view; we must not, however, arouse the distrust of our financiers. It will be necessary to create unrest in North Africa and in Russia; this is a way to absorb the forces of the adversary. In the next European war, it will also be necessary that the small states be forced to follow us or be tamed.
>
> On the side of our northwestern frontier, the goal towards which we must tend is to take the offensive with a great superiority from the

---

[*] Report by Colonel Ludendorff, March 19, 1913. *Yellow Book* No. 2, Appendix 2.

first days. For this, it will be necessary to concentrate a large army followed by strong formations of landwehr that will force the armies of the small states to follow us, or at least to remain active in the theater of war, and that would crush them in the event of armed resistance. If we could convince these states to organize their fortifications in such a way that it would constitute an effective protection of our flank, we could renounce the projected invasion. But for that it would be necessary, particularly in Belgium, to reorganize the army so that it offers serious guarantees of effective resistance. If, on the contrary, its defensive organization was established against us, which would give advantages to our adversary of the west, we could not, in any way, offer to Belgium a guarantee of the safety of its neutrality. A vast field is thus open to our diplomacy to work in this country in the pursuit of our interests.

The arrangements in this sense giving hope that the offensive can be taken immediately after the complete concentration of the army of the Lower Rhine, an ultimatum at short notice, which must immediately follow the invasion, will allow us to sufficiently justify our action from the point of view of the law of nations.

These are the duties of our army, which require a high level of manpower. If the enemy attacks us, or if we want to tame him, we will do as our brothers did a hundred years ago: the provoked eagle will take flight, seize the enemy in its tight talons, and render him harmless. We will then remember that the provinces of the old German Empire: the county of Burgundy and a good part of Lorraine are still in the hands of the Franks, that thousands of German brothers in the Baltic provinces are groaning under the Slavic yoke. It is a national matter to give back to Germany what she once possessed.

At this time, after the events of 1914-1918, the reading of this document takes on a particular importance, because it shows the German premeditation, the German dreams and the German preparations. One can judge the effect that it produced in 1913 within the government, and how much it served to strengthen it in its will to make the return to the three-year law succeed.

The question seemed so urgent that the government took the decision to keep the releasable class under the flag in October, in order to have, without delay, the three classes considered necessary for our security. It had already stated this intention before the Army Commission. A few days later, on May 4, in Caen, in a political speech, Mr. Barthou again announced this resolution; and on May 15, in the Chamber, the President of the Council read a declaration asking Parliament to approve this decision. And, by 322 votes to 155, the Chamber of Deputies gave its assent.

On the same date, Mr. Henri Paté, reporter of the Army Commission, submitted his report on the three-year law; on June 2, the discussion of the law began in the Chamber. I attended all the sessions with General Pau, as Government Commissioner.

The discussion was extremely long. It was clear that most of the deputies understood the need to vote for the law, but that electoral issues were holding them back: therefore, interventions, counter-projects, and amendments multiplied, dragging out the debate in vain.

We must also pay tribute to the patriotism of those who, like Mr. Joseph Reinach and Mr. André Lefèvre, gave their all to make the proposal triumph. Mr. Reinach, in particular, is one of those to whom belongs a great part of the honor of having had this law of national salvation voted. It caused him not to be reelected in the following elections.

The discussion continued for eight sessions. At the end, on Monday, June 16, the Minister of War, Mr. Étienne, had to speak. He had truly been the soul of this law; he had worked on the opinion of the parliamentary circles by an incessant and skilful personal action; moreover, he had spent himself in the provinces in numerous speeches, to demonstrate the necessity of the law. On June 15, he had gone to pronounce in Rennes one of these speeches; he had returned on the 16th in the morning and he was visibly tired; he did not have all his strength to enter the decisive struggle before the Chamber. His speech was affected by this, and it made little impression on the assembly. I was seated next to Mr. Barthou, President of the Council, who, sensing the bad effect produced on the assembly, leaned towards me and said: "But, didn't you prepare the speech of the Minister? – Excuse me, here is the text that I gave him. – It is well, give it to me." He took it, and a few days later, on June 26, on the occasion of an amendment proposed by Mr. Augagneur, taking the floor in his turn, he presented the issue with such force and clearness that from that moment the success of the government was assured.

However, one incident almost put everything in question. Among the innumerable counter-proposals presented, one was by Messrs. Paul-Boncour and Messimy. Paul-Boncour was the first to speak: he asked for the maintenance of the two-year service with different incorporation dates, so as not to leave the army during the winter with only one educated class, the second one being trained. The system in itself did not solve the question, but the speaker was so astonishing in his persuasiveness and skill that at the end of the session I had the distinct impression that if we had voted after this speech, our proposal would have been compromised. Fortunately we did not vote until a few days later; the effect produced by Paul-Boncour's speech had had time to evaporate, and when the vote was taken, his proposal was rejected.

For my part, I had to take the floor on July 8, on the occasion of the discussion of Article II. This article modified the number of men in the active army of the different units fixed by the previous laws. General Pau was supposed to speak, but suffering for some time, he had to leave me, at the last moment, to speak in his place. It was his speech that I presented more or less unchanged and I only made a few modifications of detail. I tried to demonstrate that the quality of the troops is a function of two main elements: training and cohesion, both of which require an increase in the number of peacetime troops. It was important, in fact, that the active elements, in whom the force of cohesion resides, be able to assimilate the reserve elements, and not be drowned by the influx of the latter.

These considerations had led us to fix at 140 men the minimum strength for the infantry companies of the interior; this figure corresponded in the mobilized company to a proportion of reservists at most equal to those of the men of the active army: in this way, we could hope not to be in too appreciable inferiority compared to the similar German units, where the peacetime strength was going to be raised to 160 men per company.

As far as covering units were concerned, the need to be able to bring our covering units up to their mobilization strength in a few hours led us to ask for 200 men per company.

The House was willing to listen to my argument and to listen to the improvised orator that I was with an attention that marked all the importance that it attached to the issue.

Finally, the final vote of the law was passed on July 19 by 358 votes against 204.

Three days later, Mr. Étienne deposited the text voted by the Chamber on the desk of the Senate, thus marking the urgency that there was to succeed. A favorable report from the Senate's Army Commission was tabled by Mr. Doumer, president of that Commission, on July 25, and on July 31 the debates began in the High Assembly. The discussion was rather brief, in spite of the fact that inevitable counter-proposals had been tabled. I did not attend the meetings. But. already, it seemed that the atmosphere of the Senate was favorable, and August 3, when I embarked for Russia, in order to attend there, on the invitation of the Tsar, the grand maneuvers, I carried the conviction that this essential work of national defense was going to be carried out.

Indeed, on August 7, by 244 votes to 36, the Senate approved the text of the law voted by the House.

Chapter VIII

Plan XVII. – The external situation of France in 1912 and 1913. – Overview of the different powers of Europe. – The neutrality of Belgium and the Grand Duchy of Luxembourg. –- Russia. – What we knew about Germany and its intentions.

I have already explained the conditions under which modifications were made to Plan XVI, in order to constitute variant no. 1 of this plan, which was put into effect in September 1911.

I will briefly recall that Plan XVI was based on the sole hypothesis of a German right blow coming from the Metz-Toul-Verdun region. It stated that Germany would respect Belgian neutrality, and that military action would be limited to the Franco-German border. As the most serious doubts on this respect had come to us, it appeared that we risked, if the enemy did not play fair, to see our left enveloped. To counter this danger, the variant no 1 had carried towards the left our reserve army, the 6th. In addition, Plan XVI, based on a counter-offensive on our part, abandoned a large strip of national territory to the enemy; the concentration took place behind the barrier of our fortresses; the Meuse and the Moselle were defended, leaving Nancy to its fate; the number of troops in cover was weak, the sectors allocated to the: border army corps were very large.

As we can see, this variant appeared only as a temporary expedient, while waiting for a total overhaul of our mobilization plan.

I was therefore determined to study the problem methodically and in all its breadth.

There was, in the first place, to have the government determine the situation of France in regards to the powers of Europe, taking into account our alliances and the probable grouping of the European forces.

The grouping of the powers in Europe was such that a war between two of them could no longer be envisaged without examining what might be the political situation in the face of this conflict which would be dictated to the others by the more or less strict observance of agreements and treaties of alliance or neutrality. This political position of each of the powers not directly interested in the conflict would probably manifest itself either at the beginning or during the hostilities by a military action such that the struggle would extend over a greater or lesser number of theaters of simultaneous operations. If we were to consider, for example, the possibility of a war between France and Germany, we had to foresee which would be our possible allies, which would be our enemy's, and which states would remain neutral. It was necessary to try to determine the form and the value of the military intervention of each of them. Only then would policy, giving operations their purpose, distribute our forces among the particular theaters before leaving the field open to strategy in the main theater of operations where the decision would be sought.

It was thus necessary for us to be enlightened as precisely as possible on the most probable attitude of Russia, England, Austria, Italy, Belgium, Switzerland, and the Balkan powers.

Already the Minister of War, at the beginning of July 1911, that is to say at the beginning of the Agadir crisis, had asked the President of the Council to submit to the Superior Council of National Defense a series of questions intended to enlighten him on certain precise points of foreign policy, with a view to making changes to the concentration of our armies. The minister had asked, in addition, by virtue of article 9 of the decree of April 3, 1906, that the Chief of the General Staff (it was then General Dubail) attend this meeting of the Council.

The Minister's request was not met with a satisfactory

response.

On July 28, 1911, the Council had been reorganized, and its first meeting in this new form was to be held in October. I took advantage of the circumstance to ask Mr. Messimy that these basic questions be examined at this session. I explained to the Minister that, until now, the external situation and the consequences that it should entail in the general distribution of forces had never been studied in a precise and complete manner. I argued that the Franco-Italian agreement signed on November 1, 1902 between Mr. Prinetti and our ambassador, Mr. Barrère, had only been known to the Chief of the General Staff on June 10, 1909, and that, as a consequence of the ignorance in which the general staff of the army had remained throughout this period, we had continued to maintain in the Alps an important and useless army.

The minister willingly agreed with me, and on September 28, he insisted in writing to Mr. Caillaux, President of the Council, that the questions I had just mentioned be studied at the next Council of National Defense. But he was not successful, and Mr. Caillaux replied with a refusal to accept.

However, at the beginning of the following month, a new note was sent to the President of the Council:

> Our war plan is a function of the situation of France in relation to other nations. It is up to the government to define the goal to be reached, to lay the foundations of the war plan, leaving all initiative to the competent ministers to prepare the means of execution, and to the generals commanding the armies to decide on their operational projects.
>
> The preliminary work must be done in collaboration by all the Ministerial departments. Thus, before any elaboration of the war plan, the external situation must be clearly indicated by the Ministry of Foreign Affairs. By reciprocity, the latter must be exactly informed on the military and maritime resources of the European powers, because of the repercussion on the foreign policy; in addition, it must be fixed on the importance of our armed forces, our finances, and directed on our military projects.
>
> However, until 1906, the Ministry of War was guided only by the reports of its military attachés and the personal conversations of the Chief of the General Staff and the Minister of Foreign Affairs. As a result, it lacked an overall view: this is how we maintained a large and

excellent army on the southeastern frontier for a long time, because we did not know about the Prinetti Convention.

However, if one reads the minutes of the meetings of the Superior Council of National Defense, which was charged with examining all questions requiring the cooperation of several ministerial departments, one finds only incidentally some indications on the possible attitude of England and Italy. We believe that it is time to do better, to ensure the convergence of the efforts necessary for the preparation of the war plan,

As a conclusion, and as a consequence of the recent reorganization of the Superior Council of National Defense, it seems necessary to have a memorandum drawn up by the competent ministers giving a complete overview of the political situation, a summary of the military forces and financial means of the various States and a financial and military situation of France.

With this information, the Council will be able to identify the most likely hypotheses of conflict, provide advice and prepare guidelines to address these hypotheses.

The Superior Council of National Defense was to meet at the Elysée Palace, on October 11, under the presidency of Mr. Fallières. I was summoned. The questions raised by the Ministerial note were discussed.

The Minister of Foreign Affairs, Mr. de Selves, declared that, in his opinion, it was for the Minister of War to indicate his intentions for war and his plans; the Foreign Affairs would then respond by making known the diplomatic possibilities. "In diplomacy," he added, "one counts on probabilities, never on certainties."

I retorted by showing that, for example, from the only military point of view, our interest would be to carry the war in Belgium, and that however this question belonged above all to the diplomatic field. Mr. de Selves answered me that at the time when the war had recently almost erupted, the Belgian question had been discussed between the Chief of the General Staff and himself, and it had been agreed that we would be ready to penetrate Belgium if the Germans violated the neutrality of Belgium first; in this case, we could extend our operations in Belgian Luxembourg. In conclusion, he declared himself to be opposed to any memorandum, and preferred the system of conferences between representatives of the Foreign

Affairs and the War. The Council was interrupted by the entry of the President of the Council, Mr. Caillaux, who immediately took the floor and strongly supported the position of Mr. de Selves. Mr. Fallières tried to intervene, but Mr. Caillaux was able to cut him off. The game was lost. The Council refused to take on the responsibilities that I felt were within its purview. Finally, it was decided that a conference would be held shortly between representatives of the War Department and the Foreign Office "with a view to establishing an understanding on diplomatic matters which might influence operations." Another conference was decided upon between representatives of the War and Finance Departments "to ascertain whether the armies would have the financial resources necessary for their maintenance during the first months following mobilization."

Five days later, on October 16, I met the director of Political Affairs of the Ministry of Foreign Affairs. I gave him a note based on the information we had from our military attachés; this note was intended to clarify the points that were most important for us to know. Here is a summary:

> We regard Germany as our principal adversary; all the incidents which have taken place since our setbacks in 1870, the threats of war in 1875, the Schnoebelé affair in 1887, the imperial trip to Tangiers in 1905, the incidents in Casablanca and Agadir were provoked by the government in Berlin. War with Germany is therefore by far the most likely, and the one we must foresee above all.
>
> Austria is linked to Germany by a treaty signed in 1879 and published in 1888. The alliance had been renewed. Under the terms of the 1879 treaty, the *casus foederis* was to come into play if there was aggression by a third power against one of the two empires or if the aggression was supported by Russia. It would seem, therefore, that the treaty is intended only for defensive purposes. However, more and more, Austria is increasingly linked with Germany as the incidents in Bosnia and Herzegovina have shown, and we believe, therefore, that in all probability Austria would be ready to support Germany in any eventuality of conflict with France supported by Russia, without investigating where the aggressor comes from and whether it is a defensive war.
>
> We would like to know if Foreign Affairs has any information that would confirm or deny this view.

Chapter VIII

On the other hand, there are many indications that Romania would unite with Austria in case of war with Russia. Do we have any information on this subject?

As far as Russia is concerned, the Franco-Russian convention states that "in the event that the forces of the Triple Alliance or of one of the powers which are part of it should come to be mobilized, France and Russia, at the first announcement of the event, and without the need for a prior consultation, will immediately and simultaneously mobilize the totality of their forces, and will bring them as close as possible to their frontiers. Should we consider that this convention has the same force as a treaty?

England is frightened by the development of the German navy and trade; this is the reason which has brought her closer to France. Our staffs have just entered into contact through our military attaché; they have examined together the course of action to be taken in case of war with Germany. It appears from the most recent conferences held that we can hope to see 150,000 British soldiers come to our left around the fifteenth day of mobilization; on the other hand, the combined action of the two fleets has also been considered, the English seeking superiority in the North Sea and the French in the Mediterranean.

We would like to know if the relations established between staffs are the consequence of a treaty or a written or verbal agreement between the two governments, or if they result from a tacit consent between them.

Moreover, can we assume that, *in all probability*, England would be on our side in a conflict against Germany?

As far as Switzerland is concerned, it seems more and more that she is under Austrian influence and nourishes unkind feelings against France. It seems to us, however, that it is unlikely that it will leave its neutrality, because of the great advantages that this gives it. Germany, on the other hand, would have little interest in violating this neutrality; Austria, in all probability, would make her main effort against Russia. Under these conditions, we believe that there is no reason to be concerned about a Swiss intervention.

Because of the small extent of the common border between France and Germany, which was bristling with fortifications on both sides, and because of the difficulty of moving considerable armed masses across it, the Germans, like the French, would have an advantage in carrying out their maneuvers through Belgium. The Belgian army would be unable to oppose a violation of its territory. The French General Staff never believed that it could be the first to violate the neutrality of Belgium; besides the fact that it would be a denial of our agreement, it would be a provocation capable of alienating us from Russia and England. But according to all the information in our possession, we are justified in believing that the Germans do not respect this neutrality as we do.

In view of the seriousness of the question, it would be useful to know the opinion of the Superior Council of National Defense on the authorization to be given to the Commander-in-Chief to extend his zone of operations into Belgium on the sole news of the violation of this country by the Germans; on the other hand, is there complete agreement on the prohibition for our troops to violate Belgian territory first?

Moreover, in a recent conference, General Wilson made it known that his government had made representations to the Belgian government and had obtained the reinforcement of the garrison of Liége. By analogy, would it not be possible for the French government to obtain a reinforcement of the area of Liége which would make it safe from a *coup de main*?

As far as Holland is concerned, the French general staff assumes that the Germans could violate the Maëstricht area, but this violation is only of indirect interest to us.

The London Conference of 1867 guaranteed the neutrality of Luxembourg. But the Grand Duchy seems so subservient to Berlin that it is almost certain that the Germans will not hesitate to violate it. The question is whether we can take the same initiative and plan a maneuver through the Grand Duchy? Would there be diplomatic complications to fear?

We assume that the treaty of the Triple Alliance is clearly defensive. For the last ten years or so, we thought we had noted an improvement in Franco-Italian relations; the Prinetti convention, in particular, was signed in 1902. It seems, on the other hand, that at present Italy is entirely oriented against Austria: thus, even recently, at the time of the war against Turkey, the Italians cleared the French front to take troops from it, and on the other side they maintained their garrisons facing east.

In these circumstances, we at the General Staff believe that Italian neutrality is very likely: we would like to know if this is also the opinion of the Foreign Affairs.

The affairs of Morocco have singularly cooled Franco-Spanish relations. Last month, we even had to take some precautionary measures.

Is there a secret agreement between Spain and France regarding

Chapter VIII

Morocco?

In short, the General Staff considered Germany to be its most probable and most important adversary; it considered it certain that Russia would be on our side in an armed conflict; it assumed that Austria and perhaps Romania would join Germany; it considered it probable that England would join us, that Italy, at least at the beginning, would maintain a strict neutrality; it considered it a possible scenario that Spain would declare itself against us; it posed in principle that we did not have to take into account the neutrality of Luxembourg, but on the contrary that we had to rigorously respect Belgium, with the proviso that as soon as the Belgian border was violated by the Germans, our armies could penetrate into Belgian Luxembourg.

We wanted to know if we agreed on its various points with Foreign Affairs.

My interlocutor, Mr. Bapst, discussed a certain number of the conclusions of my questionnaire, but our conference did not lead to any clarity on his part. However, on October 19, he wrote to the Minister of War that the Department of Foreign Affairs was in general agreement with the Ministry of War on the future role of the powers mentioned in the note I had given him concerning the hypothesis of a great conflict.

In addition, on the following day, October 20, we received a series of notes from the Foreign Office clarifying certain points that concerned Romania, Austria, Switzerland, Luxembourg, Belgium and Spain in particular.

As far as Austrian-Romanian relations were concerned, the great intimacy between the sovereigns was pointed out. "Between Austria and Romania, there is no need for written conventions," said the King of Romania in 1910. A former president of the Romanian Council, Mr. Carp, had announced that a verbal agreement existed between Romania, Austria and Germany against Russia. The price of this agreement was to be Bessarabia.

All the information suggested that the Germans might violate Switzerland to turn Belfort and that, presumably, given the Germanophile and Austrophile influence that dominated the Swiss general staff, it was to be expected that Switzerland would defend itself rather feebly.

With regard to Luxembourg, which was subservient to Germany, France could take without hesitation all the measures that circumstances would make necessary; moreover, there would be no complication to fear, since England did not have the same interest in seeing this neutrality respected as that of Belgium.

As far as the latter was concerned, the note said: "We have the duty not to take any initiative which could be considered as a violation of neutrality. But it seems certain that Germany will have its troops cross Belgian territory, and we would then have to take all the measures necessary for the care of our defense."

Finally, the state of mind in Spain was represented as very hostile to France, but it was considered that the internal situation of the country would not allow it to take part in a war action against us; we therefore had to consider as negligible the Spanish intentions.

This last point of view was moreover soon enlightened by a report of our military attaché which reached us on October 26. In a conversation that King Alfonso had had with him, the sovereign had affirmed that there was no agreement between Spain and Germany, and that, on the contrary, he, the king, wished to pursue a policy of friendship with France; the court and the queen mother were undoubtedly in favour of the German alliance, but this influence had no effect on the king, who had stopped all attempts at negotiation with Germany from the start. The king had added, however, that if the Spanish policy in Morocco failed, it would also ruin his policy of friendship with France.

A few days later I also met in conference with the director of the public accountancy to study if the armies would have at their disposal during the first months which would follow the mobilization the financial resources which would be necessary for their maintenance. According to our calculations, we foresaw in the army staff as necessary, for the first twenty days of the mobilization, a sum of 700 million francs, then, from the 21st to the 60th day a new sum of 1,800 million, that is to say in total 2,500 million francs. This conference showed us that the financial resources had been well foreseen.

As we can see, if from the financial point of view the situation was clear, in the field of general policy the questions I had raised had only partially clarified the very complex problem that represented for us the prospect of a war against a country that would respect Belgian neutrality only insofar as it found its interest there.

Without wasting any time, I sent a note to the Chief of Staff of the Army on October 27, inviting him to put the following questions under immediate consideration:

1. Possibility of hastening the mobilization operations of a certain number of army corps, in order to gain a notable advance (twenty-four hours at least) on the date of the beginning of their transport by rail;

2. Possibility of increasing the efficiency of transport lines, so as to significantly reduce the duration of concentration transport;

3. Conditions of using on the northeast frontier of troops from Algeria, Tunisia and later from Morocco; instead of grouping these troops into army corps, it would perhaps be advantageous to group them into divisions, each of which could be assigned to a different army. This way of doing things would make it possible to leave in Algeria the commander of the 19th Corps, whose presence might become necessary in North Africa; this solution would also be more flexible, and would lend itself to staggered transports according to the political circumstances of the moment; it would place at the disposal of the army commanders a reserved division, made up of excellent troops, whose prestige was considerable on the other side of the Rhine;

4. Conditions of using of the troops of the Alps which constituted the 21st corps. For the same reasons that I have just mentioned for the troops of Africa, it was convenient to form three divisions with the troops of the Alps: the first two formed of battalions of Alpine hunters, the third of active troops of place;

5. Transporting of the 14th and 15th Army corps, as well as the first elements of Alpine troops on the right of the concentration of the armies of the northeast in the Vosges region, where they were well suited;

6. Possibility of pushing forward the deployment zone of the 6th Army (reserve army, called the army of Paris), in order to push the head of the concentration areas to the Meuse. Replacement of the early division of the 2nd Army corps sent to the Stenay region by a division of one of the army corps that made up the army of Paris;

7. Possibility of bringing closer to the Belgian border the deployments of the 5th Army, called the army of Amiens, and to foresee the transport in the Givet-Fumay region of an early division provided by an army corps of this army; modifications that this displacement of the army of Amiens would entail for the deployment of the three cavalry divisions which were to operate on this side

8. Possibility of organizing a variant which, decided before the beginning of the period of concentration transports, would allow the deployment north of the Paris-Avricourt line of two or three army corps whose deployment was normally planned south of this line (for example, the two army corps constituting the 2nd Army (Fontainebleau army) and one of the army corps of the Dijon army).

These guidelines were based on the following considerations:

First of all, one could assume as certain that the two belligerents would gather face to face, at a distance of a few marches: great clashes would thus immediately follow the concentration, and would probably occur in the vicinity of the common border. Now, the theories that we knew in favor among the Germans could not leave us any doubt: we knew that they would seek by a merciless offensive to reach their war goal, that is to say the destruction of our forces. We knew that their concentration would be followed by an immediate general attack.

On the other hand, because of the power of the materiel implemented and the moral effects that one could expect, it seemed that these first shocks would be brief and that a decision would be quickly obtained. It was thus a question of hastening as much as possible the meeting of our forces so that we could go to the decisive battle with all our means united. Indeed, because of the short duration of the first battles, our reserves would only have time to participate if they were on the ground. Now, in Plan XVI, and in its first variant, the reserve army or army of Paris was kept several marches behind; because of the burdens incumbent on the railroads, it would have to move by land to the side where its intervention would be decided: its movement having to last several days, it was almost certain that it would arrive in the zone of operations only after the first major battle had been lost or won. In these conditions, it seemed to me essential to bring it closer to the front and to put it within range of intervention.

Chapter VIII

On the other hand, in order to avoid seeing the first clashes on our soil, we had to avoid being overtaken in our concentration by the Germans; we had to gather on the northeastern front the maximum of our resources, including our 14th and 15th Corps of the Alps and our troops from Algeria and Tunisia, since the political situation allowed it.

Above all, it was necessary to be in a position to prevent a German violation of Belgium.

On this last point, in fact, the information we received was in agreement with the deductions we could make about the probable intentions of the German general staff. In particular, when we tried to figure out the reasons for the extraordinary development given for a certain number of years to the fortified system of Alsace-Lorraine, we arrived at suggestive conclusions.

In fact, this fortified system took the following form: in Alsace, an organization of the Rhine between Strasbourg and the Swiss border combined with a complete blockade of the Alsace plain; in Lorraine, a vast fortified region encompassing Metz and Thionville, ensuring the inviolability of the Moselle between the French border and that of Luxembourg, at the same time as a bridgehead on the plateaus of the left bank. Between Metz and the Vosges remained about 80 kilometers of open border. But this field of action was itself divided into two corridors by the Etangs region – one, the Delme gap, 40 kilometers wide, the other, the Sarrebourg corridor, which was barely 20 kilometers wide.

We had been led to investigate what the general types of German concentration could be, and what role the German fortified system could have to play in it. Our studies had led us to consider three types of concentration: the first one corresponding to the case where the neutral territories would be entirely respected; the second one, in the case where Belgium would be violated *a priori*, with maintenance of a defensive attitude in Alsace and Lorraine; the third one, in the case of an offensive starting from Lorraine with limited and perhaps delayed violation of Belgian Luxembourg.

The first scenario corresponded to the plan that had animated the old Moltke in 1870: to reject the French armies towards the north by an attack on the Épinal-Toul front combined with a secondary attack in Woëvre. In this case, the Metz-Thionville fortified system would only have a secondary role to play, that of an offensive bridgehead for the benefit of the secondary attack; this role did not seem to justify the enormity of the fortifications built in this region since 1870.

The second scenario transported the maneuver to Belgium. It recalled the plan studied in a great *kriegspiel* made in 1906 by the German general staff, and which had come to our knowledge. In this scenario, the role of the Moselstellung became considerable: on the one hand, it would reinforce the defensive front of Lorraine by threatening the flank of any French offensive which would come between the Vosges and the place of Metz; on the other hand, it would be used as a pivot for the marching wing while masking the displacement of forces towards the region of Trier.

The third scenario could answer the following concerns: not to allow the French to violate the land of the Empire, to deceive them on the true intentions of the German command, and to delay if possible until a first success the violation of Belgium. One could assume that, in this case, the maneuver would take place in two stages: the first aimed at crushing the French forces engaged between the Vosges and Nancy, the second stage leading to the crossing of the Belgian border by armies gathered north of Trier which would attack on the Meuse downstream from Verdun. In this last scenario, the Moselstellung would seem to be called upon to play a fundamental role: it would make it possible to concentrate, sheltered from any investigation, a mass of maneuver which could engage towards the south, the southeast, the north or the northwest, and to be able thus, at will, to move the center of gravity of the forces.

Of these three hypotheses, the first was the least likely because it took little account of the possible intervention of the English, and that it engaged the German main mass through the rather difficult massifs of the high Moselle; in addition, it failed to explain the material effort concentrated for several years in the area of the north of Trier, and, as I said, the extraordinary development of the Moselstellung.

The last two, on the other hand, which envisaged the deployment of large forces towards the Eifel, destined to fall back

Chapter VIII

through Belgium on the French left wing, amply justified the enormous expenses incurred over the last ten years in developing the Thionville-Metz group.

Thus, the study of the presumed role of the Metz-Thionville fortified region led us to consider the violation of Belgium as likely. It explained the judgment formulated in the criticism of the exercise made in 1906 by the German staff:

"One gave to the place of Metz," read this document, "the great extension that it possesses today so that it can cooperate in the operations. Forts pushed far away give an army composed of a large number of corps the possibility of gathering completely under cover from the enemy and outside his sight, and of producing an effect of surprise by a sudden eruption. The square of Metz was not created to be defended by an army, but to facilitate the movements of an army in its area."

Thus, it seemed essential to clarify our position towards the Belgians in this scenario, and to obtain from the French government that it accept its responsibilities, and that it establishes the necessary position.

It was under these conditions that the following question was asked at the High Council of National Defense on January 9, 1912, chaired by Mr. Fallières:

"Will our armies be able to enter Belgian territory at the first news of the violation of this territory by the Germans? Do they have the right not to acknowledge Luxembourg's neutrality?"

The answer of the unanimity of the Council, after Mr. de Selves had declared that such was our right, was that which I desired. I pointed out that it was indispensable for us to have information on the English intentions before the fourth day of mobilization, because on that date the strategic transports were to begin, and it would be possible to vary the center of gravity of our concentration.

In this same session, I had proposed to have the general directives approved, of which I had prescribed the study, on October 27, to the staff of the army. I therefore asked the Council to decide:

1. If the defense of the Alps, the Pyrenees and the coasts could be entrusted to reserve units and the territorial army;

2. If, in addition, he was of the opinion that our active corps should all be transported as quickly as possible to the northeast front;

3. If, finally, the transport of the 19th Corps should be assured as soon as this corps is mobilized.

To its three questions, the Council answered: yes, unanimously. It was at the beginning of this discussion that President Fallières took the floor to note with pleasure that the defensive projects, which constituted an admission of inferiority, were finally abandoned. "We are resolved to march straight to the enemy without ulterior motive," he added; "the offensive suits the temperament of our soldiers, and must secure us victory, but on condition that we devote to the struggle all our active forces without exception against the enemy in the northeast."

On the strength of this approval, I then submitted to the Council the general distribution that I had prepared for our land forces, taking into account the Russian and English possibilities and the information provided by Foreign Affairs in October 1911:

Against Germany: 22 active army corps, 8 cavalry divisions and 12 reserve divisions;

On the Alpine front: 4 reserve divisions (not including the garrisons of the strongholds);

To the mobile defense of the coast: 4 territorial divisions;

To the defense of the Pyrenees: possibly the 68th reserve division currently assigned to Paris, where it would be replaced by a territorial division, a detachment of the reserve division of Perpignan and 2 territorial divisions.

On the British side, I estimated that we could count on the support of 6 active infantry divisions, 1 cavalry division and 2 mounted brigades.

On the Russian side, we could assume that our allies would field 28 army corps, 30 reserve divisions, and 27 cavalry divisions into the line.

Finally, eventually, 4 army divisions, 2 cavalry divisions, that is to say 100,000 men concentrated in the region of Brussels, the front in Antwerp at two stages north of the Meuse, could be brought into play on the Belgian side.

Thus were fixed the general conditions in which it was now

Chapter VIII

necessary to establish our new plan of concentration, and to prepare our maneuver.

I have highlighted above the very important role that the fortified group Metz-Thionville was to play in the first operations; it is essential to insist on this point, and to note that the existence of this fortified massif placed the French armies in a dilemma. Either we were obliged to renounce the initiative of the strategic offensive, with all the risks that such an approach entailed with regard to an adversary as determined as the German, or else, if we wanted to take the initiative of the offensive, it was necessary to commit ourselves in the closed field engineered between Metz and Strasbourg.

We could only escape this dilemma by directing our operations towards Belgium, but this solution was only allowed to us if this country had been previously violated by the German armies. It should be noted here that the intensive period of the concentration transports starting only on the seventh day of the German mobilization; we could not count, at this time, to receive before the tenth or the eleventh day at the earliest information likely to provide us indications on the orientation of the enemy maneuver.

The problem was therefore extremely delicate for us. I wanted to enlighten the government on the possible consequences of its decision concerning the attitude to be observed towards Belgium. I found the opportunity, on the following February 21, in a secret meeting held from 9 o'clock in the evening to midnight at the Ministry of Foreign Affairs. Only Mr. Poincaré, President of the Council and Minister of Foreign Affairs, Mr. Millerand, Minister of War, Mr. Delcassé, Minister of the Navy, Mr. Paléologue, Director of Political and Commercial Affairs at the Foreign Office, Admiral Aubert, Chief of the General Staff of the Navy, and myself were present at this conference. The purpose of this meeting was to discuss the latest state of concerted measures between the Russian and French staffs for the possible application of the alliance, as well as the state of the secret talks between the British and French staffs.

The Minister of the Navy outlined the naval measures agreed upon between the British Admiralty and the French Naval Staff: the British fleet would reserve operations in the North Sea, the

English Channel and the Atlantic, while the French fleet would conduct operations in the Mediterranean.

In my turn, I made known that our talks with the British staff about the ground forces, had concerned 6 infantry divisions, 1 cavalry division and 2 mounted brigades, that is to say, in total, 125,000 combatants.

After examination, it had been assumed that this army, embarked in the ports of England and Scotland, would come to land in Boulogne, Le Havre and Rouen. After landing, a stay of twenty-four hours in camps had been planned; then, the British units would be transported in the Hirson-Maubeuge area. Under these conditions, our potential allies would be in a position to enter into operations as early as the fifteenth day of mobilization.

Speaking solely from the military point of view, which my duty obliged me to present to the government, I then observed that if we could carry out our offensive through Belgium – assuming that no other consideration opposed it and that we could come to an agreement with the Belgian government in advance – that would simplify the problem which was posed to us, and would singularly increase our chances of victory. Invited to develop this idea, I expressed myself thus:

> The most fruitful plan in terms of decisive results in the event of a war with Germany consists in taking, from the beginning of the operations, a vigorous offensive, to finish off at once the organized forces of the enemy.
>
> The existence of natural obstacles and fortified barriers near the Franco-German border confined our offensive to narrowly limited regions: Alsace was closed off to the north by the Strasbourg-Molsheim system; it was horned in the east by the Rhine, where our adversaries had installed organized bridgeheads. An offensive on Strasbourg stopped from the front, and threatened from the flank, could only lead to limited results. In Lorraine, the border was blocked north of Metz by the fortified Metz-Thionville complex; it was cut off towards Dieuze by a region of ponds and east of Sarrebourg by the Vosges mountains.
>
> Between the entrenched camp of Metz and Dieuze on the one hand, and the Vosges on the other hand, there are two wide corridors, the first one of 30, the second one of 20 kilometers only.
>
> It is obvious that we can only develop relatively limited means in

Chapter VIII

these corridors. Assuming that our attacks manage to progress there, they will not be long in coming up against organized positions head-on, while at the same time they will be threatened from the flank by counter-offensives from Metz and Strasbourg.

In short: neither in Alsace nor in Lorraine will we find favorable grounds for an offensive aiming at immediate decisive results.

The situation would be infinitely more advantageous, if it were possible for us to extend our left beyond our borders in the Grand Duchy and on the Belgian territory: on this side, we could develop all our means of action, and we would pass to the north of all the fortified systems built at great expense by our adversaries. In case of success, our armies would push back the German masses towards south Germany, and would directly threaten their main direction of retreat and their communications to Berlin; moreover, the passage through Belgium would give us the means to make the British army participate in a more effective way in our operations, the addition of which provides us with a marked numerical superiority over our adversaries.

From this presentation, I concluded that we had a major interest in being able to get our armies into Belgian territory and not only when the Germans, as was likely, would have violated it themselves. I added that, through diplomatic channels, it might be possible to suggest to the British and Belgian governments the solution that seemed most advantageous to us. The Minister of War, Mr. Millerand, agreed with my way of seeing things, on the results to be expected from a plan of operations leading to an offensive action through Belgian territory; Mr. Delcassé, Minister of the Navy, pronounced himself with the same firmness in favor of my opinion.

But the President of the Council then pointed out that the passage of the French army through Belgium would risk upsetting not only Europe, but the Belgians themselves because of the difficulty of reaching an agreement with them in advance; under these conditions it seemed necessary that our entry into Belgian territory was at least justified by a positive threat of German invasion. It was, moreover, the fear of invasion of Belgium by Germany which had been the primary cause of the military agreements with England. We would therefore have to make sure that a plan based on our entry into Belgium would not cause

England to withdraw her support.

Then, placing himself in the purely diplomatic point of view, Mr. Poincaré declared that the British ambassador, in a recent conversation, had expressed to him the thought that our military agreements might have reached the ears of the Germans and provided them with pretexts for the reinforcement of their army. Sir Francis Bertie had also made it very clear that in his opinion the Franco-English agreement was as useful to his own country as to France. In Berlin, Lord Haldane had reserved England's freedom of action for the eventuality of Germany attacking France. The President of the Council added that it would be in his interest that the military agreements receive diplomatic consecration.

Finally, the President of the Council asked me about the arrangements made on the Italian front as a result of the secret agreement of 1902.

In answer to this question, I explained that Italy, even if it took sides against us from the beginning of the war, could only put 6 army corps in line at first, which would not arrive on our border before the 18th day of mobilization, too late therefore to exert an influence on the first operations against Germany. It would therefore be a serious mistake to leave active army camps on the southeastern front; it was enough to foresee the case where, the first clashes having remained undecided, the French and German armies would have to reorganize themselves before resuming the fight. Our goal on the Alps was therefore to prevent the Italians from emerging from the mountainous zone into the plain, before the moment when the Russian troops would begin to make their action felt in an effective way, that is to say before the end of the sixth week. To obtain this result, 4 reserve divisions reinforced by 13 reserve alpine groups, relying on the strong points, seemed to me to be sufficient in this terrain eminently favorable to the defense.

For his part, the Minister of the Navy made it known that the naval army of the Mediterranean was to move quickly to meet the Italian fleet, as soon as mobilization began. This fact should not be ignored by Italy and would in all likelihood contribute to making it respect the pact of 1902, and at least to making it carry out its mobilization with a wise slowness that would not compromise it.

Chapter VIII

He concluded by saying that in his opinion it was well with respect to Germany that it was necessary to concentrate all our ground forces. And the President of the Council declared that he shared this opinion.*

From this important conference, of which I have retained a very precise memory, we can draw the following conclusions:

First of all, the threat of a German invasion through Belgium had not only not escaped us, as has been repeated too often, but it appeared so probable that we had agreed with the government on the right we should have to enter Belgium as soon as it was violated by our enemies. During the discussion, as we have just seen, the President of the Council, Mr. Poincaré, in spite of his natural prudence, had even gone further in this direction than I had expected, by assuming that an intervention of our years beyond the neutral frontier could be justified by a "positive threat of German invasion" in Belgium. But what was meant by a "positive threat"?

---

* Mr. Paléologue, who took the minutes during this deliberation, is willing to communicate to us, according to his unpublished notes, a remarkable prediction by General Joffre on the duration of the future war.

The Director of Political Affairs had just told the Conference that he was studying ways to provide the Treasury with the resources it would need to meet the enormous expenses of a war. He had concluded in these terms:

"If the war is to be short, say, four or five months, as many people think, our present cash resources would be sufficient. But, if the war is to be long, very long, as other people affirm, we must establish as of now the project of a vast loan which would be negotiated in New York as soon as hostilities begin, in order not to be outdone by our enemies on the American market. I therefore beg Mr. General Joffre to tell us what might be, in the present state of Europe, the duration of a great war."

The general answered:

"I make, in this regard, two predictions. *First prediction: we are victorious at the beginning.* I estimate that it will take us at least six months to reach the Rhine. Then, but only then, will the real national resistance of Germany begin, the entry into the scene of all the powers, an indefinite duration... *Second prediction: we are defeated at the beginning.* I estimate that I will be able to support our retreat to the Morvan for four months. Then, but only then, will begin the true national resistance of France, the entrance on the scene of all the powers, an indefinite duration."

"So, in both hypothetical cases, you're anticipating an indefinite duration?"

"Yes, in both hypotheses, an indefinite duration." (Original editor's note.)

Chapter VIII

It did not seem that a German concentration in Prussia on the Rhine could denote an obvious intention to invade Belgian Luxembourg; gatherings between Trier and Malmédy could be presented as a precautionary measure against a threat of invasion of Belgium by France. Thus, if the conference of 21 February 1912 had the essential result of posing the problem, it did not solve it.

The phrase so characteristic of M. Poincaré's speech during this conference deserves to be considered. The president of the Council had, undoubtedly, in mind all the warnings which the English had given us concerning Belgian neutrality: in 1906, at the time of the first conversations on the subject of the Franco-British military agreement, we had formally promised to respect Belgian neutrality; about the same time, an official voice[*] had warned us: "Do not let yourselves be tempted to enter Belgium on the basis of mere threats from Germany; it could be in Germany's to push you down this path." In 1911, Lord Esher had also insisted on this same warning.

However, I have every reason to believe that following my declarations in this session of February 1912, and on the initiative of Mr. Poincaré, the English diplomat studied the question I had just raised. Indeed, I learned that the British military attaché in Brussels, Colonel Bridges, tried, in the course of 1912, to enter into conversation with General Jungbluth of the Belgian general staff; but the exchanges of views could not go beyond the prejudicial question of knowing what arrangements could be made in common in the event of a German violation of Belgian territory. Even on this limited basis, the conversation did not lead to any result.

Nevertheless, on November 27, 1912, General Wilson, with the consent of Lord Grey, came to the French headquarters and told us that the Foreign Office considered "that Belgium was hesitant as to which side to take in the case of a Franco-German conflict, and that she seemed to be leaning towards Germany. But," he added, "if France violates Belgian neutrality first, the Belgian army will surely march with the Germans, and the British government could

---

[*] Lieutenant Colonel A. Court Repington.

then be summoned to enforce neutrality: it would thus find itself in a very embarrassing situation. There is, therefore," he concluded, "not in the interests of the French army to violate the neutrality of Belgium first."

This communication was of the utmost importance, because it obliged us to definitively renounce any idea of *a priori* maneuver by Belgium.

We had, moreover, to worry about the state of mind of the Belgian people, in case their neutrality was violated.

In this order of ideas, a small book had appeared in 1911 which had held our attention. It was entitled *The situation in Belgium in Anticipation of a Franco-German Conflict*. It was authored by the pseudonym O. Dax, under which was hidden, it seems, a high military personality. The conclusion of this book was as follows:

"Let us not hesitate, if need be, to direct events in such a way that our alliance with the strongest of the belligerents can be justified by the facts."

This opportunistic recommendation was no surprise to us. Many good minds thought that Belgium would limit itself at the beginning to gathering its forces in the shelter of Liége and Namur in order to allow itself the possibility of joining the winner.

We had also tried to find out the measures taken by the Belgians to ensure the security of their Liége-Namur front, and particularly of these two places. In December 1911, the 2nd Bureau of the army staff informed us that Liège was exposed to being taken by a *coup de main* until the third day of the Belgian mobilization. From the fourth day, the measures taken for the defense of the area seemed sufficient to force the enemy to attempt a surprise attack. Experience had shown us that in case of political tension, as in 1911, for example, the Belgians took precautionary measures and reinforced the garrison of the fort. As far as Namur was concerned, the information was even less favorable, so I considered the possibility, in case the Belgians would allow us to enter their territory in arms, of having the place occupied by an infantry division: the 1st. The survey that I made revealed that this division could be concentrated from the fourth to the fifth day, either between Jeumont and Maubeuge, or, if one could use the Belgian railroads, between Jemmapes and Charleroi. In the first case, it could be in Namur on the seventh day in the morning; in the second case, on the fifth day in the evening, Jemmapes being 12 kilometers from the place.

A last element of the Belgian problem consisted in the reorganization of the army, to which Mr. de Brocqueville, President of the Council, had devoted himself. As a result of patient efforts, he succeeded in getting the Belgian Parliament to pass the law reorganizing the army on August 30, 1913. But the provisions of this law were to have their full effect only after ten years. On the other hand, during the discussion, Mr. de Brocqueville had declared that the Belgian army thus reconstituted was destined "to tip the balance in favor of the power that would not have violated the neutrality of Belgian territory first."

Let's now look at our situation with respect to Russia.

It is necessary, for that, to go back to the secret military convention which bound us to our eastern allies. This convention had been signed in Saint Petersburg, on August 17, 1892, by general Obroutcheff, chief of the general staff of the Russian army, and general de Baisdeffre, then Deputy Chief of Staff of the French army, sent to this end on a mission in Russia. The emperor and the French government had approved this convention in December 1893; born of the Triple Alliance, it was to have the same duration as it. In August 1899, following new talks, the scope of this agreement was singularly extended, since the two governments, "always concerned with the maintenance of general peace and the balance of power between the European forces," decided together that the convention would remain "in force for as long as the diplomatic agreement concluded for the safeguarding of the common and permanent interests of the two countries."

It does not seem useless to give here the text of this convention:

> France and Russia being animated by an equal desire to preserve peace, and having no other aim than to ward off the necessities of a defensive war provoked by an attack of the forces of the Triple Alliance against one or the other of them, have agreed upon the following provisions:

Chapter VIII

1. If France is attacked by Germany, or by Italy supported by Germany, Russia will use all its available forces to attack Germany.

If Russia is attacked by Germany or by Austria supported by Germany, France will use all its available forces to fight Germany;

2. In the event that the forces of the Triple Alliance or of one of the powers that are part of it should be mobilized, France and Russia, at the first announcement of the event, and without the need for a prior consultation, will immediately and simultaneously mobilize the entirety of their forces and will bring them as close as possible to their borders

3. The available forces, on the French side, to be employed against Germany, will be 1,300,000 men, on the Russian side 700,000 to 800,000 men.

These forces will be fully engaged, with all diligence, so that Germany will have to fight both in the east and in the west;

4. The staffs of the armies of the two countries shall consult each other at all times in order to prepare and facilitate the execution of the above measures.

They will communicate to each other, from peacetime, all information relating to the armies of the Triple Alliance which is or will come to their knowledge.

The ways and means of correspondence in wartime will be studied and planned in advance;

5. France and Russia will not conclude a separate peace;

6. This agreement shall have the same duration as the Triple Alliance;

7. All the clauses listed above will be kept strictly secret.

At the time I took over as Chief of the General Staff in July 1911, we knew that Russian mobilization and concentration were very slow because of the low density of Russian railroads, their low efficiency and the shortage of rolling stock. Therefore, when General Dubail, then Chief of Staff of the Army, left in the middle of the summer of 1911 for Russia to exchange views with the Russian General Staff in accordance with paragraph 4 of the military convention, his main mission was to represent to our allies the serious inconveniences that could result from the delays due to the inadequacies of their railroad network. He was fortunate enough to obtain, on August 18/31, the formal commitment of Russia to make every effort to activate the mobilization and concentration. Our allies undertook not to wait until the concentration of their armies was complete before acting. The offensive would be taken as soon as the front line forces were in position, and it was calculated that the Russian-German border could be crossed, thanks to this measure, as early as the sixteenth day. Finally, it was agreed that only a determined offensive could give success.*

This was a significant first step. The following year, it was the turn of the chief of staff of the Russian army, General Gilinsky, to come to France. He arrived on July 6, the day after the famous meeting of the Tsar and Emperor William I at Port-Baltique. General Gilinsky was accompanied by Admiral Prince Lieven, Chief of Staff of the Russian Navy, who was to sign a naval convention similar to the military convention with Vice-Admiral Aubert, Chief of the General Staff of the French Navy, on July 16.

After an exchange of views on the plans to be followed by the two allied armies, General Gilinsky took, on July 13, the commitment that the Russian armies would begin the offensive on the fifteenth day by flanking actions which would have the objective of clearing the center of the Russian zone. It is necessary, indeed, to notice that the layout of the Russian border was not very favorable to a defense against an Austrian attack coming from Galicia: this one, coming from the south to the north, would take the lines of the Niemen, the Narew, the Pilica, the Vistula upstream from Warsaw, and the Bug. If therefore the first Russian operation was to be, as we requested, directed offensively towards the Koenigsberg-Thorn front, it was necessary that at the same time a part of the Russian forces penetrated simultaneously into Galicia, in order to straighten the front, and neutralize the offensive that the Austrians would probably begin starting from this convenient base.

It should be noted that the military convention, from its inception, obliged the two allies *"to engage their mobilized forces with all diligence."*† In addition to the reasons which logically led

---

* Deposition of Mr. Messimy before the commission of Briey, p. 149.

†Paragraph 3 of the military convention of August 17, 1892, quoted above.

Chapter VIII

us to seek the initiative of operations on our front by an offensive as prompt as possible, the will to be faithful to the very terms of the convention forced us to this same attitude. And we can affirm that the certainty of our offensive spirit and the attachment to the clauses of the convention noted by the Russian General Staff in each contact with our General Staff strongly contributed to directing the Russian General Staff towards an intensification of its own effort. If they had sensed less decision on our part, there is no doubt that our allies would have been more reserved at the beginning of the war.

The agreements were at this point, when in September 1912, the Grand Duke Nicolas came to attend the great maneuvers in Poitou. I did not yet know the man who was to be the commander-in-chief of the Russian armies in 1914.

Born in 1856, Grand Duke Nicholas Nicolayevich, commander of the Imperial Guard and the military district of St. Petersburg, was the son of Grand Duke Nicholas Nicolayevich, the third son of Emperor Nicholas I, who had been the commander-in-chief of the Russian armies in 1877-1878 in the war against the Turks. Physically, Grand Duke Nicholas was very tall, slender and vigorous; he had a reputation in the Russian army as an intelligent and energetic leader, very knowledgeable in all military matters, knowing and loving his job, and constantly training for the heavy duties he would have to perform in wartime. Many good spirits regretted that, during the unfortunate Manchurian campaign, the emperor had not called upon his services to restore a situation which had never been so desperate. But it was said that the Grand Duke Nicolas had a very upright, whole, independent character, and that for these qualifications the emperor liked and appreciated him, but also feared him a little. I did not delay to rejoice, from my first encounters with him, to know the fate of the Russian armies henceforth in his hands. Events showed that he deserved the eminent place to which the emperor had called him. And I am honored to have remained his friend since that already distant time.

At the time of his departure, at the end of the maneuvers, the Grand Duke asked me very kindly to visit him the following year and to attend the next Russian grand maneuvers.

Arrival of General Joffre at the station of Krasnoie-Selo

General Joffre and the French military mission. To the right, the Grand-Duke Nicholas.

On August 3, 1913, I left for St. Petersburg, accompanied by Generals d'Amade, Dor de Lastours, Desaleux, Hély d'Oissel, Delarue, Colonels Dumasnil and Berthelot, and Major Renouard.

Chapter VIII

The French mission attending the parade of Simionovsky's regiment

After the review. The tsar goes to his tent for lunch.

We were received in the most cordial and warmest manner by the emperor and the Grand Duke. The conversations that I had with the latter during our three weeks stay were numerous. I took the opportunity to insist to him several times on the necessity that I saw to hasten the Russian mobilization and to start as soon as possible an offensive with the fraction of the Russian armies immediately mobilized; my request took all its value from the more than probable scenario where the concentration of the major part of the German armies would be made against us.

The Grand Duke gave me the assurance that we would have satisfaction; he understood admirably the necessity for the Russian army to launch an offensive quickly, whatever the risks that such an approach could make it risk; it was necessary at all costs to relieve our front, if the Germans tried, from the beginning of the hostilities, to come to terms with our forces. We have seen, since then, in what generous and loyal way this great leader kept his word. I consider it a duty to say it. I will say it again later. And France has a duty not to forget the service that our allies have rendered us.

Apart from these conversations, our stay in Russia was very useful because of the exchange of views that took place between the officers of our mission and their Russian comrades. Some of them were full of zeal and sought to learn from us. In particular, Grand Duke Sergei, Grand Master of the Russian artillery, had taken a liking to Lieutenant Colonel Dumensil, and never left him, asking him a thousand questions to find out how the French artillerymen were solving the various problems on the battlefield.

Unfortunately, in spite of the sympathetic reception which was given to us, we felt in the entourage, even of the Tsar, a whole faction which gave us, undoubtedly, external testimonies of friendship, but which regretted to see the leaders of Russia so clearly directed towards France. The Minister of War Sukomlinoff, in particular, promised everything we wanted, but never kept anything. I will say no more about this man who died in Berlin after the war.

During our stay in the camp, we attended many maneuvers. They seemed to us to be mainly directed towards parade effects, without taking sufficient account of the realities of war. The troop looked good, the men seemed vigorous and well trained.

From these various contacts with the Russian army, it was possible for us to have a rather precise knowledge of the capabilities of our allies.

Chapter VIII

We knew that in addition to its 27 active army corps, Russia would be able to mobilize 28 reserve divisions. Thanks to the materiel progress of all kinds, we could count that on the fifteenth day of mobilization, the border army corps could be at work: 8 to 9 corps facing East Prussia on the Kowno-Grodno-Warsaw front and 7 corps facing Galicia on the Lublin-Cholm-Rowno front. By the twentieth day, the army group in the northwest facing Germany could be increased to 11 corps, and that in the southeast to 9 corps. In addition, a reserve army of 4 corps could be assembled in the region of Brest-Litowsk. It is thus towards the twentieth or the twenty-third day only that 24 out of 27 active corps could give all its weight to the offensive. Finally, around the twenty-sixth day, most of the reserve divisions could be landed in the concentration area.

The main offensive was to have, in principle, as its objective the German army. This mission fell to the Northwest Army Group, which would advance by its main body on Allenstein and Thorn, while its right would advance from the Niemen on Koenigsberg. South Army Group would have as its objective the Austrian army in Galicia.

It will not escape anyone how delicate the situation was for the Russian army, and how, by agreeing to a major offensive before having concentrated all its means, it showed abnegation. Indeed, from Warsaw to Kowno, there are 350 kilometers. An offensive of 8 to 9 army corps on such a front was full of risks. It was difficult to lead such a large army over such a large area, and the armies could not support each other, as they were separated not only by great distances, but also by a region full of rivers and lakes. A German army, even if inferior in number, but concentrated, could easily break through the cordon of Russian armies unrolled in front of it, especially in the direction of Thorn-Warsaw, by combining its action with an Austrian offensive directed from Przemysl on Brest-Litewsk.

It seemed therefore that the mass of Russians assembled in Poland on the Narew, with its bulk in the Warsaw area would better stop the German attacks directed from Thorn on Warsaw. Moreover, from this central region of Warsaw, the bulk of the Russian forces could better either take the offensive towards

Allenstein, or maneuver by the left bank of the Vistula to march on Berlin.

In summary, the Russian concentration presented a formation too extended in width, with a center of gravity too much thrown back towards the north; and the forces of the center seemed to me to have to be disembarked too far behind compared to the wings.

In my opinion, it would have been necessary to accelerate the concentration, because, until the twenty-third day, the 9 army corps of the northwestern group and the 7 corps of the southern group were going to be alone in front of the enemy; it would be only at this date that the offensive effort could have some intensity. This delay was very long, if we wanted to ensure the simultaneity of the Russian and French attacks. But in order to shorten this delay, profound improvements to the Russian railroads would have been necessary.

Unfortunately, such transformations could only be made at the cost of important works and studies which would have deeply upset the mobilization and the Russian campaign plan. In fact, the war would find Russia in the same military state as in 1913.

It is now appropriate to say what we knew about the German force and the intentions of our adversaries.

In 1912, it was generally accepted that the mobilized German army would consist of: 23 active army corps and 3 newly formed army corps; in addition, a number of reserve units, 6 fortress divisions, and 11 cavalry divisions.

In reality, the number, formation, and mode of use of the German reserve units remained a mystery until about 25 August 1914.

The German mobilization plan, which came into effect on April 1, 1914, stipulated that reserve troops would in principle be employed from the beginning of hostilities in the same tasks as active troops; it therefore provided for the formation of reserve army corps generated by active army corps.

Until then, we had been convinced that the Germans would only ask their reserve troops to do secondary tasks, under the same conditions that we intended to use ours. "No fathers in the front line," William II had said. And these words had been repeated, in

Chapter VIII

June 1913, in the Reichstag.

These imperial words seemed to agree with the theories in honor at that time in the German army which based success on the brutal violence of the first shock. We were therefore justified in assuming that our adversaries would not entrust the fate of the first encounters to obviously inferior troops.

The new German mobilization plan aroused a doubt in us when it came to our attention. But, considering that the reserve army corps were equipped with a reduced artillery, we were still inclined, on the eve of the war, to believe that these army corps, following in the second line, would only be used for the siege of strongholds, the guarding of communications, the holding of passive fronts, or the occupation of conquered territories.

It is important to say that this mistake we made had a heavy impact on the way we organized our concentration, as we will see later, and consequently on the beginning of the operations.

In the years leading up to the war, the German army had become much stronger.

The law passed in June 1912 had promptly borne fruit. While we had 519,000 men under arms, the Germans had 657,000; moreover, Germany had called up 551,000 reservists in 1912, compared to 456,000 in 1909; finally, the German army, which until the 1912 law had only 23 army corps in peacetime, had 25 since October 1, including the 21st corps in Saarbrucken. We have been aware for a long time of the German plan to form two army corps upon mobilization. But, as the Minister of War had declared before the Reichstag, this creation obtained at mobilization by the addition of surplus elements in neighboring corps to the third Divisions of the Ist and XIVth Corps represented a delicate operation. The formation, as of peacetime, of 2 covering army corps with reinforced manpower was likely to protect our adversaries from any miscalculation.

In particular, the creation of the XXIst Corps at Saarbrücken represented a barely disguised threat to us. This corps, inserted into the German covering system barely two marches from the Nancy area, with a strength such that it was likely to enter the field immediately, tilted the balance of covering forces, which had hitherto been more or less equal, in favor of the Germans in a disturbing manner.

On the other hand, from the beginning of 1913, we learned that a new military law was being considered in Germany, intended to complete and improve the existing units, to maximize their war value by the increase of their staff and by the reinforcement of their active nuclei: thus the 6 corps which bordered our border would be reinforced in number; we had, consequently, to envisage the possibility of a sudden attack in the very first days of the mobilization, and even on the first day, if our adversaries managed to conceal the first operations of their mobilization. As for the rest of the German army, it seemed certain that its concentration would take place in a shorter period of time than previously anticipated. However, our 3 army corps that were guarding the border were too numerically inferior to the 5 German army corps that were facing them. In the previous chapter, I mentioned how the three-year law voted in France on July 6, 1913, allowed us to ward off the danger that threatened our coverage.

Having defined what we knew about the German army, it is now important to indicate the assumptions we made about the operational plans of our future adversaries.

First of all, it was possible that the German general staff took up the plan of old Moltke – the post-war documents proved to us that our adversaries thought of it – by engaging the principal offensive against Russia, and by being satisfied, at the beginning, on the Western Front to observe a defensive attitude. It was obvious that in this scenario the Germans had no interest in violating the neutral territories of Belgium and Luxembourg, and that the right of their strategic deployment would be limited to the region of Trier. In this case, given our commitments, Belgium would have been similarly forbidden to us.

This plan offered undeniable advantages for Germany; in particular, it made the intervention of the English on our side very unlikely. This solution condemned us to deploy all our forces between Luxembourg and the Vosges, in front of the formidable position of Metz. Another scenario was that the Germans would first take the offensive against us, maintaining a defensive attitude towards the Russians, as long as a decision had not been obtained on the Western Front.

Chapter VIII

In this scenario, it was almost certain that the Germans would violate Belgian neutrality. But, from then on, they would open the doors of the only field of maneuver where we could deploy our armies.

But then the question arose as to how far the Germans could go with their maneuver.

A map exercise performed at the German General Staff in 1905, in which the maneuver of the German right through Belgium was precisely studied, had come down to us. In this study, the German right wing did not rise north of the Meuse from Namur to Liège. This document had, obviously, only the relative value of a theoretical study, but it was nevertheless an indication.

This serious question was discussed at length by us and particularly with General de Castelnau, the head of the 3rd Bureau, Colonel Hallouin and the officers of the 2nd Bureau.[*] It appeared to us that the necessity for the Germans to first of all reduce the fortifications of Liége and Namur would incline them to limit the scale of their movement to the south of the Meuse.

We estimated, on the other hand, that the more complete violation of Belgium would be likely to make the English enter the fight, because of the threat against Antwerp, whereas limited to the southern bank of the river, it was possible that the English remained indifferent.

In addition, the use by the Germans of the Grand Duchy of Luxembourg and Belgian Luxembourg allowed them to have at their disposal fifteen rivers and three railroads, which seemed sufficient to move the forces that they were devoting to their right wing.

Indeed we assumed – and this was mainly the opinion of General de Castelnau – that the Germans would not use their reserve units in the front line. "From then on," he said, "unless they extended their front dangerously and gave it insufficient density for vigorous action, they would be unable to get beyond the Liége-Namur line."

I must admit that, after much reflection, I agreed with this

---

[*] 3rd Bureau: operations office; 2nd Bureau: information service.

opinion.

However, I did not reject *a priori* the hypothesis of a more extensive German maneuver north of the Meuse. But, in this case, I was entitled to consider the cooperation of the Belgians and the English.

This was our understanding of the possible German actions.

Also, in a conference which took place at Foreign Affairs on October 12, 1912, when I had to make known what would be, in the event of conflict, according to our evidence and our intelligence, the respective situation of the French and German forces on the northeastern front, it seemed possible to me to conclude that "in the case where we could not count on the English assistance, but where it would be possible for us, as a result of Italian neutrality, to constitute an army corps with the Alpine forces and to bring the 19th Army corps from Algeria-Tunisia to France, our active forces would be equal, within a few units, to the corresponding German forces; and that, should the British join us, our forces would be clearly superior to the German forces."

With regard to the German reserve formations, the number and composition of which were very inaccurately known to us because of the transformation of which the German army was then the object, I declared that it was not possible for me to give any particulars that could be compared with similar details concerning the French army.

It may be interesting to note here the figures that I believe I can give in support of the assessment one has just read. Here they are:

We estimated that in terms of active forces, the Germans would lead 550 to 600 battalions, 350 squadrons, 500 to 550 mounted batteries of 6 pieces, 24 batteries on horseback of 4 pieces and 100 batteries on foot of 4 pieces against France.

We would have to oppose to these forces, including the troops of the 19th Army corps and the army corps constituted with alpine units: 580 active battalions, 332 squadrons, 653 batteries of 4 pieces and 42 heavy batteries. It should be noted here that the sending of reinforcements to the expeditionary corps of Morocco had resulted in a reduction of 12 battalions and 5 mounted batteries in the forces to be directed against Germany; moreover, the colonial army corps, as a result of numerous withdrawals made in favor of the marching units sent to North Africa, only had a weak active core.

I estimated, at that time, the possible reinforcement provided by the English at 73 battalions (including 3 mounted infantry), 45 squadrons, 60 batteries of 6 pieces and 24 heavy batteries.

But, soon after, the reinforcements of the German army transformed the possible conditions of the struggle. As we have seen in the previous chapter, it was this new situation that brought us back to the three-year law.

Chapter IX

Plan XVII. – Ideas that served as a basis for the concentration plan.

Having recalled the atmosphere of the pre-war years, I will now trace the genesis of Plan XVII.

Before beginning studies to fix our ideas on our possibilities of maneuver, I insisted on having the ground studied on which the operations could possibly lead us.

In the spring of 1912, I had two officers of that army's staff, Lieutenant-Colonel Duport and Major Barthélemy, conduct reconnaissance in the Grand Duchy of Luxembourg and in southern Belgium. Both had the mission to study the terrain in relation to specific offensive scenarios. At that time, as I mentioned above, we still hoped to use Belgium for our offensive operations. Although this intention was not realized, these reconnaissances were not useless. They proved to me that the characteristic of these regions was a kind of partitioning presenting serious difficulties for the conduct of an overall action. But, all in all, neither the Grand Duchy, nor the Belgian Luxemburg were less favorable than the north of France and the region of Charleroi, which were dotted with important settlements and divided by fences, making the movement of the armies difficult. The Grand

Chapter IX

Duchy and Belgian Luxembourg even seemed to me, with their covered areas, rather favorable to a combatant having, like us, a significant inferiority in heavy artillery, but a clear superiority in field artillery.

I will now tell you the ideas that served to set my decisions from the point of view of concentration and operations. I will do so sincerely, saying without reticence all my thoughts at the time, even when later events came to invalidate them.

First of all, we all believed that the war would be short. In this respect, everyone was wrong: civilians and soldiers, strategists, diplomats, economists and financiers. Didn't Foch write in his admirable *Principles of War*: "The armies that we will set in motion will be armies of civilians torn from their families. War will bring discomfort with it; life will cease; hence the consequence that war cannot last long." In the *Conduct of Large Units*, written by a commission chaired by General Pau, one could read: "In the present form of warfare, the importance of the masses involved, the difficulties of their resupply, the interruption of the social and economic life of the country, everything encourages to seek a decision in the shortest possible time, in order to end the struggle promptly."

The Germans have the same belief.

General von Schliefien, chief of the General Staff until 1906, in a series of resounding articles published in 1909, limited the duration of the war to that of the first battle. In addition to economic arguments, he pointed to the pacifist tendencies of most European peoples as an element that would quickly circumscribe the war in time: "From the beginning of an unfortunate war," he said, "the government of a country will have to reckon with a current of opinion that will lead it to peace."

I leave to others more qualified the easy task of finding in the writings of politicians, financiers and economists, opinions similar to those I have just quoted.

Starting from this idea that the war would be short, it was necessary to do everything to deliver the decisive battle which, in the eyes of Schlieflen, was to begin and close the war, with all its forces. If one could discuss the fact that the first great battle would end the war, it was incontestable that general encounters would follow very closely the completion of the deployments, and that no artifice of maneuver would be able to defer the first shocks: in particular, the sacrifice of coverage would be powerless to delay them.

From then on, all the mobilized forces of the first line had to be put into action in due time to participate all together in these operations; it could no longer be a question of distant reserves transported during the first engagements, according to the turn that they would take.

So the essential principle that guided me was this: "Go into battle with all my strength."

The second simple idea that guided me was the following: I wanted to take the initiative in operations. This attitude was, in the first place, to avoid French territory becoming the theater of the first battles and undergoing the invasion; it would allow us to safeguard our freedom of action and to avoid that our maneuvers are from the beginning dominated by the will of the enemy; moreover, it was in conformity, as I said in the preceding chapter, with the military conventions between the French and Russian staffs.

I was also convinced that it was impossible to set a definitive maneuver to be carried out a long time in advance; it is necessary in fact to take into account all the unknowns which complicated the problem. As Lord Kitchener said, our strategic policy should be opportunistic. I stated this before the Briey Commission: "The plan of operations can only be made by taking into account the events and information that arrive in the course of operations. It is not an immutable plan that will be applied no matter what happens; it can only be drawn up a few days after mobilization, when things take shape, because it can only take shape little by little, according to the intelligence, both diplomatic and military, that arrives after mobilization."

Now, there were too many unknowns in our political situation, as well as in the German plans. The essential thing was to have one's troops ready at that moment, gathered in a formation that allowed for all solutions. The concentration was thus, in my opinion, to be considered as an initial arrangement of our forces in view of the realization of any plan of operations; it could not

Chapter IX   141

therefore be an arrangement arrested *ne varietur*. It was necessary to have a sufficiently flexible concentration to allow all possible maneuvers and combinations. These, of course, had to be considered and prepared by the general in chief, because, because of the proximity and the size of the masses in presence, it was necessary that the command had prepared at least in its broad outlines its maneuver so as not to be caught unprepared, the goal being not to reach geographical objectives, but to join the enemy under predetermined conditions. Moreover, since the intensive period of German transport did not begin until the seventh day of mobilization, one could not expect to receive information likely to provide guidance until the tenth or eleventh day at the earliest. Therefore, unless we wanted to remain in a strategic defensive posture and incur all the dangers of it, we were forced, without waiting for this information, to decide on an approximate plan with sufficiently flexible variants to respond to this information. A preconceived plan of operations was also made impossible by the unknown that Belgium represented for us.

For all these reasons, there was never a written plan of operations. In fact, no one asked me about it.

The operations plan is, in fact, essentially the personal work of the general-in-chief. No plan of operations was ever drafted by the army staff, whose work was limited to the preparation of the concentration. It is drafted under the sole authority of the general-in-chief, without any possibility of asking him for official communication with a view to discussion or approval: any attempt of this kind would constitute potent ammunition in the hands of those who denounce the dangers of government interference in military operations. The various generalissimos had understood this responsibility quite differently: some, like General de Lacroix, had informally communicated their intentions to the assembled Superior Council of War; others, like General Trémeau, had spoken directly to the army commanders alone; others, like General Brugère, had refused to explain themselves on this subject.

For my part, I considered the latter method to be preferable.

I therefore decided to postpone the decision on the maneuver to be carried out until the first days of the conflict: no preconceived idea, other than a stated desire to take the offensive with all forces gathered, the obligation to wait until the European alliances had been formed, until the territorial capabilities had been established, before deciding on the strategic maneuver.

In short, I was limited to an opportunistic afterthought, to use Kitchener's words, based on the developments of the early days of the war.

This is why I am justified in asserting that the *complete* plan of operations was never written. Moreover, when I signed Directive No. 1, of which I will speak later, my colleagues insisted strongly that in one word, in one sentence, it was indicated that the scenario envisaged in the Directive was not the only one possible. I refused to do so, believing that in such a document that would come to the knowledge of the English, there could not be, in any form whatsoever, any reference to maneuvers on neutral territory.

I therefore decided to limit our efforts to the determination of a concentration likely to respond to all possible maneuvers.

Moreover, when it was a question of determining the general zone of concentration, it is necessary to notice that the difficulty of positioning the considerable masses transported to the border, due to lack of sufficient space, the constraints imposed by the layout of the railroads, the disposition of the debarkation sites, had as a consequence restricting between rather narrow limits the scope of the modifications that one could make subject to this general zone. Moreover, the various proposals of operations that could be envisaged hardly differed as regards the assembly of the armies except by the conditions of the formation and the density of the forces inside this zone.

Since the number of troops in line was out of proportion to the size of the Franco-German border, the French armies were to be concentrated on a width corresponding to this size. Obviously, the line of the Meuse downstream from Pagny and that of the Moselle upstream from Toul, marked out by our large strongholds and protected by our covering troops, was to constitute the natural front of our concentration. This line seemed to me to be close enough to the border so that our armies would not waste the time saved in the gathering of forces, and so that too vast an area of territory would not be abandoned to the enemy in case we were forced to adapt a defensive attitude momentarily.

Chapter IX

In the shelter of this barrier, our armies could make their deployments in complete safety, assemble at the behest of the plan of operations that I had chosen, and then form up either to receive the enemy or to begin offensive operations.

This solution seemed favorable to me, because it placed us in a central strategic position, allowing the offensive or a defense facing east, if the enemy emerged directly from Alsace-Lorraine; it also allowed us to act facing north in the left flank of the enemy, if he marched on Paris by crossing Belgium, and facing south, in his right flank, if he passed by Switzerland. These flanking positions, which prevent the enemy from advancing straight ahead toward a geographic or political objective, always force him to make a difficult change of front.

A staggering of about two stages applied to the combat elements of the active corps was to make it possible to satisfy the condition of concentration of the forces, while guaranteeing to the armies the play necessary to their maneuver. The number of platforms and drop-off sites was great enough on our transport lines to allow this staggering. It was thus assumed that, in the central part of the zone of concentration, the fighting elements of the corps were to be maintained in front of the general line marked by Luxeuil, Neufchâteau, Saint-Dizier and the course of the Aisne up to Attigny.

On the flanks of the concentration zone, the depth had to be more considerable, to allow us to face the violation of the neutral Swiss or Belgian territories. If a German diversion were to occur through the Swiss plain in order to turn Belfort, this diversion would necessarily be late; we could therefore attempt to assemble on the right flank of the concentration zone, between the Saône and the Doubs, an army composed of reserve divisions capable of containing the enemy by using the escarpments of the Jura, by defending the middle course of the Doubs if necessary and by relying on the fortifications of Belfort and Besançon. The region of Vesoul seemed suitable for the concentration of this army, because, placed at equal distance from Épinal, Belfort, and Morteau, it allowed this army to follow our active forces either in Lorraine, or in Alsace, in case the Germans respected Swiss neutrality.

On the left flank of the zone of concentration, it seemed that an initial echelon extending to the region between Mézières and Hirson, would answer all requirements, without it being necessary to go beyond this last locality, by assuming, of course, that the mission of forming the extreme echelon of our left would fall to the British army. Indeed, in the case of offensive operations in Belgium, developing northward to Dinant, this left echelon could reach the Meuse in the vicinity of this city in three stages as quickly as if it started from Avesnes or Maubeuge. It would also be well placed to follow the bulk of the armies if, the enemy turning away his right, our offensive had to be maintained south of the difficult region limited by the Paliseul, Saint-Hubert, Houffalize line. In the case where we would be temporarily reduced to a strategic defense, this region still seemed to me to be suitable because, from there, our left could effectively confront the enemy obliged, in order to avoid the abstraction of the Ardennes forest, to push back either on Sedan or Dinant. Finally, in the case where the Belgian neutrality would be respected by the Germans, this echelon would have to be employed towards Luxembourg. It is true that in this case the last combatants would be in Hirson, about four stages away from the column heads. But this inconvenience was not very important if one takes into account the high number of troops involved and the need to always be able to ward off an enemy maneuver through Belgian Luxembourg.

As far as the English army was concerned, given the impossibility of extending the two transport routes assigned to it, only two divisions could be concentrated between Hirson and Mézières, the other divisions landing between Hirson, Avesnes and le Nouvion, the cavalry and artillery between Landrecies and Maubeuge. As a result, Hirson would be the center of gravity of the English concentration zone. This situation increased by approximately two stages the staggering in depth of the general lines; it still aggravated the disadvantages resulting from the late landing of the English divisions, ready to march only on the fifteenth or sixteenth day or perhaps even later still, if the date of the beginning of the English and French mobilizations did not coincide. Thus, until conditions for British transport could be improved, the involvement of British forces in the initial operations could hardly be counted upon.

These were the considerations that determined the general layout of the concentration area, should we be able to carry out the mobilization and strategic transport operations according to our forecasts.

It was certain that a significant delay in mobilization, or a series of accidents occurring during the period of transportation on the lines of concentration, would profoundly affect the situation; in this case, the zone of concentration of the armies would have to be changed, and we would be obliged to return to the project of strategic defense to which the fortified system that General Séré de Rivière had built responded. The cover, reinforced as much as possible by the cavalry and by hasty divisions, would then defend the line of the fortresses and delay the enemy in his crossing of the Meuse and the Moselle; our armies would wait for the enemy at the outlet of the truncations provided in our fortified system, ready for the attack at the same time of front and on the flanks. In this case, the concentration of the French forces would take place behind the general Aisne-Ornain-Faucilles front; the concentration of the British army, as well as that of the reserve army, could remain unchanged, which would eventually provide us with a base for a counter-attack at right angles.

The general zone of concentration being thus largely determined, it was a question of controlling within this zone the general disposition of the forces, so as to allow the army staff to prepare the concentration. I insist on the fact that, in my mind, it could not be a question of a plan established *ne varietur*, automatically triggering itself. In 1866, Moltke had repeatedly modified his plan of operations and his plan of concentration; in 1870, he had twice varied his deployments. Napoleon himself, carrying out his concentration by land, had had time to gradually give the "assembly of the army" the precise form corresponding to the maneuver envisaged. Now, our railroad networks had, in 1912, acquired enough flexibility to make it possible to modify the grouping and distribution of forces during the course of the concentration.

It was a question, to give a point of support to the preparatory studies of the staff of the army, of providing a plan of *average distribution* of our forces inside the zone of concentration defined as I have just said. I had to intervene for that purpose in a first study the various plans of operations which seemed to me compatible with the situation.

The feasible projects fell naturally into two categories: strategic offensive projects, or strategic defensive projects. In each category, a distinction had to be made between the case where the belligerent armies would respect the neutrality of Belgium, and the case where they would develop their means of action through Belgian Luxembourg.

To solve the problem of adapting the plan to the circumstances, I used the following ideas:

As the strategic maneuver of a group of armies always includes a principal operation and subordinate operations, it was the nature and the range of the principal operation to be carried out in each case which was to allow me to differentiate the projects between them; it seemed to me possible to determine the zones of grouping of the armies in a form sufficiently general to be used as a basis for all the scenarios of maneuver, allowing me by the use of the reserves to reinforce or widen the action envisaged destined in my thought to become the principal operation. Thus I considered that by a single choice of the point of application of the forces reserved for one or the other of the possible actions, it would be possible for me to give to the maneuver, when the time came, the scale and the form which would seem suitable to me. Because of the uncertainty of the situation, I could only see this way to solve the problem.

However, due to the division of the border zone into compartments separated from each other by major obstacles, our offensive, as soon as it penetrated the enemy's soil, would be confined to narrowly limited regions, where our armies could only develop a part of their means of action. Assuming that Belgium's neutrality would be respected, we would have to attack through the Sarrebourg, Château-Salins and Luxembourg corridors, which were respectively 15, 30 and 25 kilometers wide. An offensive in Alsace, leading to a dead end, could only be conducted with relatively weak forces. We had to *attack from all the available parts of our Lorraine frontier*, both to make full use of the limited space we would have, and to fix the enemy on his entire front and keep him uncertain about the direction of our decisive effort.

It was then a question of choosing, among the five corridors through which our attacks would be channeled, those in which we should push our efforts until the enemy battle system was broken. It was in the rear of the most important of these corridors that the forces in charge of supporting the front line troops, shoring up their flanks and completing their success should be spread out.

The main attack could be aimed at achieving the final separation of the enemy forces operating in Alsace from those operating in Lorraine. In this case, we would have to push our offensive on both directions toward Sarrebourg and Château-Salins with, as general objective, Sarreguemines.

The main operation could also have the aim of taking the enemy forces gathered in the Metz area, driving them back into the entrenched camp and to try to entrap them there. In this case, we would have to conduct a double offensive through Luxembourg in the north, through the Château-Salins corridor in the south, with these two actions being linked together by an operation that would initiate the blockade of the Metz-Thionville fortified group.

In the first plan, our two offensives, although originally separated by the region of the ponds, were intimately linked to each other. Both directed at the meeting point of the German armies of Alsace and Lorraine, they would act in concordance on a weak point of the enemy's formation and could produce a rupture in the center of this formation. If the attempt succeeded, the Germans could only regroup in the Rhine valley. But, on the other hand, during this operation our forces would be threatened to be taken in the flank by attacks emerging at the same time, in all probability from Metz and from the Molsheim-Strasbourg area; penetrating like a wedge inside the enemy's formation, we would in a way move towards envelopment. It was thus essential, as our progression was developing in German territory, to cover our flanks threatened by more and more important forces. In sum, the risks of this maneuver were high, while the results appeared to be hardly decisive, since, in case of success, we could hope at most to drive the main mass of the German armies of Lorraine towards the Rhine and north Germany, i.e. on its natural lines of retreat.

In the plan of a combined offensive through Château-Salins and Luxembourg, the main effort would be directed at both the center and a wing of the enemy. The latter could only act against the flank of our northern offensive by violating Belgian neutrality; but, if he decided to do so, we would be entitled, in turn, to develop our means of action in Belgian Luxembourg by simply extending our position, whose left would be, at the beginning, as we have just seen, strongly reinforced and widely spread out in depth. If our flank attack through the Grand Duchy were to succeed, part of the German armies of Lorraine could be locked up in Metz, and the exploitation of our victory by the north would lead us to the lines of retreat of these armies and would allow us to defeat them in the south of Germany.

However, I did not conceal the fact that this plan was not without serious disadvantages. First of all, the impossibility of deploying important forces towards the north without violating the Belgian territory obliged us to seek a decision by the combination of two attacks which were going to be separated by the fortified zone Metz-Thionville; in fact, they were two distinct actions between which a concordance would be difficult to establish. Secondly, the exit into Luxembourg could be very difficult, and in any case it could be prolonged, if the enemy took up an enveloping barrage position. Delaying our offensive in the north, the Germans could act with the bulk of their forces against the army emerging on Château-Salins and Faulquemont by offering its right flank to enemy attacks from the Sarrebourg area. Finally, a success of the German forces emerging from the Vosges and Sarrebourg on our right, in the direction of the Moselle gap, would place us in a difficult situation, since the main mass of our armies would be exposed to being cut off by the enemy from the rest of France.

As can be seen, the advantages and disadvantages of these two maneuvering plans seemed to balance each other out.

It was still necessary to briefly determine the subordinate Operations, common to both projects. These operations could be defined as follows:

1. Blockade of the western front of the fortified region of Metz-Thionville and of the southern front of Metz between the Moselle and the Seille;

Chapter IX

2. Protection of the left wing of the whole of our formation against an attack coming from Belgium;

3. Protection of the right wing against the German forces of Alsace and, possibly, against the corps which, violating the Swiss territory, would try to make a diversion in the region south of Belfort.

In the scenario of the offensive via Sarrebourg and Château-Salins, in the general direction of Sarreguemines, our attack by Luxembourg would be a subordinate operation aiming to attract towards the north the central mass of Metz and to maintain the enemy forces of the Prussian Rhine to prevent them from going down into Lorraine. Conversely, in the scenario that the main operation would be based on the offensive through Château-Salins and Luxembourg, the attack on the Sarrebourg corridor would be aimed at fixing the enemy and preventing the forces of Alsace from passing into Lorraine.

Thus, these two plans would result in an offensive on each of the three corridors, and, consequently, the constitution of three armies, those of the sides containing, in addition, important elements – army detachments – in charge of the protection of the flanks; the blockade of the western front of the fortified region Metz-Thionville was to be entrusted, because of its importance, to an army having a group of reserve divisions. The blockade of the southern front of Metz between the Moselle and the Seille rivers, which was of special interest to the army in charge of the offensive through Château-Salins, was to be assigned to an army with a group of reserve divisions for this purpose. Finally, an army would be reserved to reinforce either the offensive on Château-Salins, or that on Luxembourg, depending on the decision that would be taken. Finally, the troops of Africa, the Alpine garrisons, the divisions provisionally kept in the interior, would constitute a last reserve to be used according to the particular circumstances at the moment when they could enter the line.

Under these conditions, the distribution of our forces could be envisaged in the following way:

> An army of 4 corps in charge of the offensive on Sarrebourg and the coverage of the right wing;

An army of 4 corps reinforced by a group of reserve divisions, in charge of the offensive through Château-Salins and the blockade of Metz between the Moselle and the Seille rivers;

An army of 6 corps in charge of the offensive through Luxembourg and the coverage of the left wing;

An army of 2 corps and a group of reserve divisions in charge of the blockade of the western front of Metz.

In reserve:

An army of 3 corps in the Metz-Verdun area ready to support the main operation according to the adopted project;

An army of 3 divisions behind the right wing ready, either to reinforce the protection of the right wing by moving to the Vosges or Alsace, or to face a German diversion in the Jura;

An army of 4 or 5 divisions behind the left wing ready, either to reinforce the main action through Luxembourg, or to counter an overflowing movement of the enemy through Belgium, or to reinforce the 3rd Army for example for the blockade of Thionville.

Finally, the English army, spread out in the rear of our left, would cover our flank, or would be ready to extend our action towards the north, possibly passing through Belgium.

The concentration areas of the various armies were demarcated as follows:

The Army of the North should extend south to the Spincourt-Varennes line;

The army intended to invest from Metz-Thionville to the Toul-Dieulouard line;

The army from Nancy to Manonviller-Bayon;

The army from Épinal to the south of this line, to Belfort;

The support army of the right would be organized in the region of Vesoul; the support army of the left wing, in the rear of the Army of the North; finally, the reserve army in the region of Bar-le-Duc.

The second scenario to consider was that it would be possible for us to develop our maneuver through Belgium. Without recalling here all the advantages that this maneuver would give us, but it should not be forgotten that the President of the Council had assumed that an intervention of our armies beyond the neutral border could be justified by a *positive threat* of German invasion in Belgium, and in a case where we would have acquired the certainty of the consent of the English. It was therefore legitimate for me to envisage the case where an agreement with England was established on this subject from the very first days of the war, and we could implement a project of operations based on the violation of Belgian neutrality.

I realized, moreover, that the approval of England being problematic and subject to political considerations, it was impossible to base a strategic offensive plan *a priori* on eventualities that might well never occur.

However attractive at first glance, from a military point of view, a plan based on an offensive in Belgium might have been, this project entailed considerable risks. First of all, the intervention of Belgian forces against the left wing of our armies would be particularly dangerous if the Belgians were to link their operations to those of a German mass advancing to meet us through Belgian Luxembourg. It is true that we could expect, in this eventuality, the timely arrival of British contingents to counter this threat.

The situation would be more unfortunate for us if the Germans, completely ignoring their right wing, forced us to cover long spaces before giving battle. Our adversaries would thus place themselves beyond the reach of the British forces, who would not be able to enter the Trier region before the twenty-sixth day of the British mobilization; this situation would cause us to lose precious time, which the Germans could use to vigorously attack our armies in Lorraine. If they succeeded in beating our right in the region of Nancy and to the south, while our armies in Belgium, acting at first in a vacuum, would not yet have obtained any results, they would place us in a critical situation which would present some analogy with that of September 1870. In any offensive plan based on an immediate invasion of Belgium, this essential consideration should not be lost sight of; it is obvious that a French army on the left wing, moving from the region of Mézières in the general direction of Marche-Malmédy to attack German forces deploying south of Aix-la-Chapelle, might have to change its orientation along the way if the enemy were to evade towards the Eifel north of Trier. Assuming that this army moved on the twelfth day of the mobilization and did not meet any obstacle on its road, it would reach the Kill towards Gerolstein and Killbourg only on the twenty-second or the twenty-third day, i.e. at a date one week later than the beginning of the operations in Lorraine and Woëvre; and this date should be appreciably delayed if enemy rearguards put up continuous resistance to our columns in the region of the Ardennes, which is particularly favorable to a war of obstruction.

This example shows how important it was, in such a scenario of maneuver, not to lose time, and to extend only to good effect our concentration towards the north, at the beginning of the operations. It was the measures taken by the Germans during the concentration that would indicate to us the limits that should be given to this extension. If the German concentration was carried out solely in Lorraine, it would be in our interest to take at the beginning on Belgian territory only the space necessary to facilitate our movement in the general direction of Trier, while preserving the possibility of gaining ground towards the north if the circumstances required it.

Thus, our studies revealed the difficulties that would be encountered in the implementation of an offensive plan via Belgium. It was necessary to retain that an extreme precision would be necessary in the conduct of the strategic maneuver, to ensure that the displacement of our armies of the left does not take place either too early or too late.

Taking into account the particularities of the region to be covered, it seemed to me that the essential goal of an offensive through Belgium was to reach, in order to destroy more easily, the mass of the enemy armies whose deployment would take place in the Metz-Thionville-Trier triangle, by passing to the north of the fortified Metz-Thionville system.

According to the information of the moment and according to the extension towards the north of the German forces, for the army group of Belgium the principal operation was thus to consist of a march either on Luxembourg or on Saint-With, the left being supported at the Belgian Ardennes. In case of success, the enemy would be defeated in the Eifel, while a part of our forces, crossing the Moselle upstream of Thionville, could catch the German armies of Lorraine in the flank and the rear.

If, on the contrary, our adversaries ignored their right wing and directed their masses on Lorraine, our northern armies would cut as short as possible in the direction of Trier, would force the Moselle downstream from Thionville and as soon as possible would take the bulk of the German forces in the flank. Subordinate operations should facilitate the main operation: some would cover the flanks of the French armies in Belgium, others would keep the enemy in Lorraine and in the Vosges. These operations would include: north of the Nancy-Toul line, the investment of the western front of the entrenched camp of Metz to prevent the enemy from bursting into Woëvre, the narrow blockade of the works of Thionville on the left bank of the Moselle, the coverage of the left wing of the French armies by the occupation of the Belgian Ardennes and later by the arrival of the British Expeditionary Force which, according to the circumstances, could march either by Dinant on Verviers, or by Neufchâteau and Bastogne in echelon behind our left. South of the Nancy-Toul line, the number of troops should be sufficiently large to prevent the enemy from breaking through between Épinal and Toul. I envisaged a defensive attitude for this part of our forces. However, if the Germans did not attack into Lorraine themselves, they would move forward to fix the enemy and attract his reserves.

To fulfill these various missions, I envisioned the following distribution of our armies:

> A *main group*, "Belgium group," for the offensive north of Thionville;
> A *secondary group*, "Lorraine group," to keep the enemy south of the Nancy-Toul line;
> A *central army* linking the two groups and charged with investing the western front of the entrenched camp of Metz.

In my mind, the main group had to include two armies strongly enough constituted to be able to provide the detachments necessary for the protection of the wings:

One of these armies, formed of 6 corps and a group of reserve divisions, intended to march offensively on Saint-With or on Trier;

A second Army of 5 corps (and possibly 2 reserve divisions) intended to operate either on Thionville, or further north between Luxembourg and Thionville, its right side blocking Thionville.

Because of the extent of the front between Nancy and Belfort, I was led to divide the Lorraine group equally into two armies: one of 3 corps and 3 reserve divisions holding the enemy between Nancy and the Châtel-Manonviller line; the other of 4 corps operating south of this line as far as the Vosges; I envisaged, moreover, a group of 3 reserve divisions gathered initially in the region of Vesoul to cover the right flank of our armies. As for the central army, it could include 2 army corps and a group of 3 reserve divisions, and would be intended for the blockade of the western front of Metz. The British army would, in any case, have to operate in concert and in close liaison with the group of French armies in Belgium. Finally, the African troops and the division of the Alpine troops would form a general reserve that I could use, according to the circumstances, to reinforce the group of Belgium or that of Lorraine.

After having determined the general role of our forces in this scenario and their grouping, I still had to determine the zones of concentration of these various groupings to allow the staff of the army to prepare the work of the concentration.

To the group of the armies of Belgium, I assigned as a front of concentration the course of the Meuse from Mézières to the south of Verdun; to the group of Lorraine, the line of the Basse-Meurthe and the heights between the Moselle and the Mortagne, the right to the Hautes-Vosges; finally, the central army should advance as far forward as possible to begin without delay the investment of Metz.

These were the general guidelines on which I asked the army staff to work.

These studies had made me see the importance of the fortified Metz-Thionville massif. In the scenario that we would be obliged not to violate Belgium, it would be the principal danger for our offensive in Lorraine; in the case where we could pass through Belgium, this fortified region would allow the Germans to slide support forces from Lorraine to the Eifel; In any case, sitting on both banks of the Moselle and penetrating like a wedge into French territory would favor the German offensive, whether it was a partial and sudden offensive at the beginning of hostilities or a general offensive once concentration was assured.

Chapter IX 155

Therefore, it seemed to me to be essential to look for ways to limit the offensive power of this fortified massif. The solution seemed to me to be to create, from the very first days of mobilization, in front of our military frontier marked by the Hauts-de-Meuse, a sort of temporary position that the enemy, coming out of the Messina region, could not in any way neglect.

Similarly, I felt that, in the event that we respected Belgian neutrality, and where, as we have seen, an offensive in Lorraine would be necessary, our fortified system, despite its defensive value, no longer met these offensive requirements. If we had had no other claim than to wait for the Germans at the exit of the holes voluntarily made in this system in order to channel the invasion, the dams of the Hauts-de-Meuse and the chaîne des Ballons would still have been able to render the same services as at the time General Séré de Rivière had conceived them. But our positions in the northeast were now to facilitate the offensive departure of our armies destined to attack in Lorraine, by opening up all the useful channels for them. However, except perhaps in the vicinity of Verdun and in the region of Épinal, our fortified system was not likely to play a role similar to the one the Germans attributed to the Metz-Thionville group. From this point of view, the substitution of Toul for Nancy as the southern base of the Hauts-de-Meuse line was, in my opinion, particularly regrettable: sunken between the Haye and Queen's forests, Toul did not ensure us the possession of any important channel, and if the Germans succeeded in establishing themselves on the Couronne's of Nancy, we would probably be obliged to open up the campaign with difficult and costly operations to retake the Meuse line.

Now, for obvious budgetary reasons, it would have been too much to expect profound modifications to our defense: I therefore began to study the defensive arrangements available at the time, in particular around Nancy and in the region of Hattonchâtel, combined with those that I envisaged to counter the offensive power of Metz.

It was obvious that all these arrangements could only be carried out in time if they had been the subject of detailed reconnaissance and meticulous preparation during peacetime.

Chapter X

Plan XVII. – The setting up of the plan.

After having said how I envisaged the problem which was posed to me and in which way it seemed logical to me to solve it, it is appropriate now to explain how, from the domain of the study, these plans came to be realized.

In the autumn of 1912, when the complete revision of the plan seemed more and more imperative, I was obliged to postpone it: in fact, the plan which was under consideration mentioned the organizational laws submitted to the Parliament, and as long as we were not sure that they would be accepted, it was impossible to build something definitive.

It was under these conditions that, on October 24, I submitted to Mr. Millerand, Minister of War, a note highlighting the urgent need to rework the concentration plan, and as a consequence, the urgent need to expedite the vote of the cadre laws submitted to the Chambers. In this note, I explained that Plan XVI put into effect on March 1, 1909, corresponded to an external situation and to plans of operations that no longer reflected the present conditions. The complexity of the movements by rail of the 14th and 15th Army corps planned both towards the northeast and towards the Alps, the excessive rigidity of the transport routes, the organization of a maneuver army intended to move by land towards one of the wings of the operation, thus running the risk of not being able to intervene in good time on the decisive side of the conflict. In addition, Plan XVI had only made insufficient projections concerning the possibility of a German offensive through Belgium.

Undoubtedly, the variant of September 1911, adopted under the pressure of the world events, had appreciably improved the situation, but it offered all the defects of makeshift solutions. I said, "The transformation of the Russian army following the war in Manchuria had begun only in 1908, but it will be completed: the heavy field artillery will be complete, the equipment of the reserve formations is constituted; England seems more than ever resolved to support us: in July 1911, the War Office took the decision to send to the continent not part but all of its field army, and to hasten the mobilization and transportation of this army; the collaboration of the two navies is assured. As far as Italy was concerned, it was increasingly to be hoped that she would not seriously intervene in a conflict with France; in any case, her intervention would not be immediate."

As a consequence of this situation, it became possible to leave only reserve formations on the Alps, to transport from the beginning the 14th and 15th Army corps towards the northeast, and later the units left as coverage on the Italian border, and finally to count on the certain transport of the 19th Army corps to France. Germany, on the other hand, was obliged to take more precautions on its eastern border, which had just led it to create a XXth Army corps in Allenstein.

On the other hand, the efficiency of our railroads had improved considerably: the number of usable stops on the transport lines had been increased from forty-eight to fifty-six; all the work undertaken was going to be completed at the end of 1912; thanks to this greater emphasis on transport, it was going to be possible to shorten the period of concentration of the fighting elements by one day. Other works which were to be completed, one in 1913, the others in 1914, would give even more flexibility and would allow the grouping of the army corps in the zone of concentration at the discretion of command.

The latest intelligence reports, however, indicate German activity in the construction of the strategic network in the Eifel region, and the importance of the new military bases in the region east of Malmédy, "which proves," I said, "in the German general staff a growing tendency to bring the right wing of its concentration system northward, and to include Luxembourg and Belgium in the theater of its operations."

I ended my report by saying that the present concentration was no longer in keeping with the external situation, the state of our forces and the efficiency of our railroads. It did not seem to me to lend itself completely to the movements that an offensive in Belgium would require in the event of a German violation of Belgian territory. For all these reasons, a new plan seemed to me necessary; but it was essential that it rested on a perfectly defined organization of the army. "Now," I concluded, "Plan XVI, put under study on August 2, 1907, could not come into force until March 1, 1909, that is to say seventeen months later; at present we estimate at fourteen months the time necessary for the establishment of the new plan: if one wants that it is applied in the spring of 1914, it is necessary to hasten to pass the laws of the cadres of the infantry, the cavalry, the engineers, and to set to work on the preparation as of the beginning of 1913."

However, I could not be under any illusions. Taking into account the slowness of the legislation and the time necessary for the material work of the development of a new plan, I understood very well that this one could only be implemented in a still very distant time. Therefore, it seemed necessary to me to have recourse once again to a provisional solution which, by improving the conditions of the concentration, would allow me to carry out, when the time came, the maneuver that I would have decided. Obviously the variant No. 1 that I had approved in September 1911 proved to be insufficient for this goal. I recall that, faced with the possibility of the Germans violating Belgium, taking advantage of the flexibility of our transports to reinforce the northeast theater by withdrawals from the southeast theater, I had, at that time, decided to carry the left of the front line towards the north, to push also in the same direction the "maneuver army," and to tighten on the front line armies the reserves constituted by the groups of the reserve divisions.

This solution still left the 6th Army (army of maneuver) strung out between Châlons-sur-Marne, Reims and Sainte-Menehould, with its head at the Argonne. However, I have pointed out in the previous chapters that the strategic conduct of a maneuver through Belgium was only feasible on the condition that no time was lost. The distance of the 6th Army, in this scenario, was incompatible with these necessities. Also, I gave the order to prepare a variant which would take into account the projected organizational changes, while remaining based on the two-year service. The purpose of this variant was to move the head of the cantonments of the most advanced army corps of the 6th Army eastward, in order to hasten and facilitate the movements of this army beyond the Meuse, north of Verdun. The conditions that I imposed were to allow this army to break through either in the direction of the east by crossing the Meuse between Verdun and Stenay, which corresponded to the scenario of the non-violation of Belgium, or in the direction of the northeast, by approaching the Meuse between Dun and Sedan, in the case where Belgium, for one reason or another, would be opened to us.

These studies led to the concentration of the 6th Army up to the Grand-Pré front, Varennes, Clermont-en-Argonne, the 3rd and 4th Army corps already having numerous elements beyond the Argonne forest, the 10th and 11th Corps in the Champagne plain.

I also said that a strategic maneuver led either by the Grand Duchy, or by Belgian Luxembourg, required the absolute inviolability of the front of the Meuse, in addition to the need to limit in Woëvre the offensive power of the Metz-Thionville position. To the north, Verdun formed the core of our positions, and it was necessary to reinforce the occupation of the Hauts-de-Meuse around this place. It was therefore decided that the third group of reserve divisions, concentrated in the September 1911 variant between Sainte-Menehould and Bar-le-Duc, would henceforth concentrate on either side of Verdun with a view to the eventual occupation of the Hauts-de-Meuse between Damvillers and Hattonchâtel. To achieve this goal, it was necessary to modify the composition of the 3rd and 4th reserve divisions: the 4th Reserve Division Group, whose concentration was not modified, now included the 51st, 60th and 62nd reserve divisions, the 3rd Reserve Division Group, the 52nd, 53rd and 54th reserve divisions; the 52nd concentrated on the Meuse from Stenay to Dun, the 53rd in the Varennes-Montfaucon region, the 54th on the Meuse from Diane to Troyon.

These two principal modifications concerning the zones of concentration of the 6th Army and the 3rd Reserve Division Group constituted what took the name of variant No. 2 to Plan XVI. It took about five months for the preparation and setting up of all the documents intended for its possible execution; it was only in April 1913 that the new variant could come into force. It allowed us to wait in better conditions for the total revision of the plan.

If one considers the successive transformations that the initial Plan XVI underwent as a result of variants 1 and 2, one can see that they were motivated above all by the ever-increasing importance in our eyes of the possibility of the violation of Belgian territory by German forces. To counter this possible threat, the center of gravity of all the forces in the northeast theater moved more and more to the north. It should be noted, however, that if variant No. 2 did not include an extension north of the Mézières region, this was due solely to our capabilities at the time; indeed, it should not be forgotten that we were still under the two-year law.

On the other hand, the abandonment of defensive ideas and a more accurate appreciation of our possibilities in the face of an adversary who was concentrated on the frontier itself, led us to avoid as much as possible abandoning at the beginning a too large strip of national territory. This explains why the concentration of the bulk of our forces in these successive plans was planned on a line closer and closer to the border. Plan XVII was to mark a further step in this new direction.

In addition, the work of reorganizing our reserve formations with the dual purpose of making them more flexible and improving their training, allowed us to plan for their earlier use alongside the active troops. Finally, the development of these different variants allowed us to discover a series of improvements and simplifications to be brought in the execution of transport and concentration. Thus, in particular, the rules governing the movement of trains were simplified: until then, the route of each

Chapter X

train was regulated from beginning to end, and this route required a form for each train for each station crossed; the station of disembarkation was fixed in an absolute way; this rule was too strict and required a very long and very meticulous process. It was decided to regulate the route of each train only up to the controlling station. This was charged to determine, according to its availabilities on the network which was assigned to it, the final route and the station of debarkation.

The five months of work that the preparation of the variant no. 2 required were thus very useful, and enabled the improvement of the subsequent conditions for executing Plan XVII.

However, the cadre laws submitted to Parliament were to serve as a basis for a profound reorganization of the army; in particular, the one concerning the infantry had the essential aim of more solidly organizing the command and management of the reserve troops, and of allowing us to consider the use of certain reserve divisions in the front line armies. The law relating to the constitution of artillery cadres and manpower was promulgated on December 13, 1912. Mr. Millerand, Minister of War, in agreement with Mr. Étienne, President of the Army Commission of the Chamber of Deputies, worked to bring the laws in question to fruition as soon as possible; on December 12, the Chamber voted on the draft concerning the infantry cadres that had been submitted to it, and the Senate voted in favor of it on December 21, without discussion. As for the cavalry cadre bill, it was accepted by the House on December 20, but it was not finally adopted by the Senate until March 27, 1913. This law led to the division of most of the cavalry regiments.

Therefore, by the end of 1912, we were confident that we could build our new concentration plan according to the forecasts we had made on the general reorganization of active forces and reserve units. But at that time, new concerns came to challenge some of the elements of the plan I had just had reviewed. The law passed in June by the Reichstag had already borne fruit: our coverage, as we had envisaged it, was no longer able to stop the momentum of the five enemy corps that were opposed to it; it was therefore necessary that it be increased and brought up to the value of five army corps, so that the possibility of a sudden attack would become improbable, or, at least, if it were to occur, that we would be in a position to face it. These considerations, as I have already said, helped to convince us that the 1905 recruitment law was no longer sufficient, and that only a three-year service would be likely to bring the covering troops up to full strength, and the interior troops to normal strength.

It was under these conditions that, shortly after the meeting of March 4 where the principle of the three-year law was unanimously accepted by the Superior Council of War, on April 18, I submitted to the deliberations of the same Council the finalized bases of the new plan which was to be called Plan XVII. It was submitted to the Council in accordance with article 3 of the Decree of July 28, 1911, on the reorganization of the high command.

It seems necessary to summarize here the document given to the members of the Council for this meeting of April 18:

> First, the reasons for the new plan, the external situation and the internal military situation, were presented. Then the document studied the proposed organization of the mobilized army.
>
> Because of the division of the cavalry, the corps would have only one regiment with six squadrons.
>
> As for the reserve infantry brigade assigned to the corps until then, it was proposed to abolish it; indeed, its combat value was low, and yet, it had been observed, both in maneuvers and in exercises on the map, that corps commanders frequently tended to assimilate it into active units, and to use it for missions requiring strong cohesion; now, the law on infantry cadres was going to improve the management of these regiments, which had been reduced from three to two battalions. Under these conditions, the new plan provided for the assignment to each division of a reserve regiment with two battalions.
>
> As far as the artillery is concerned, we are obliged to note that, since the session of July 19, 1911, when the Superior Council of War had pronounced itself in favor of the creation of a heavy artillery, the projects undertaken had not been successful. The only important modification to the situation had been, as I have already said above, the presentation by commander Malandrin of a plate allowing, against the sheltered personnel and materiel, shots with an angle of descent of up to 12 degrees. Therefore, from the point of view of the organization of the artillery in the army corps, the new plan did not

Chapter X

bring any modifications to the old one.

Plan XVII anticipated twenty-one army corps, including the colonial corps and the 21st Army corps whose creation was planned in Épinal.

The mobilization of the 19th Corps, because of the levies for Morocco, could not be envisaged; consequently, Plan XVII provided that Algeria would supply two autonomous divisions, the 37th and 38th Divisions.

The normal army corps was to include: 28 battalions, including 4 reserves, 30 batteries, and 6 squadrons, including 2 reserves.

The 14th District could provide a division with 16 battalions.[*]

In total, the active army was mobilized with 46 infantry divisions, that is, with the same number as in Plan XVI.

As for the cavalry divisions, the plan called for the creation of 10 divisions comprising 6 cavalry regiments, a group of 3 batteries of 4 pieces, and a group of infantry cyclists.

The planned composition of the reserve infantry division was as follows: 2 infantry brigades with 3 regiments of 2 battalions, 3 groups of 3 batteries, 2 squadrons. The new plan called for the creation of 25 reserve divisions instead of the 22 divisions of Plan XVI. Each reserve division would have only 12 battalions instead of 18, but it would be heavier and more capable of maneuver. In Plan XVI, the reserve divisions were all kept away from the front at first, so that they would have time to develop cohesion; they were not intended for the first encounters. But, now that they were better organized, stronger in artillery than in infantry, they seemed likely to perform certain tasks alongside the active units. It is for this reason that, already in the September 1912[†] variant of Plan XVI, provision was made for the extension of the transport of certain reserve divisions.

For the heavy artillery, Plan XVII anticipated army artillery

---

[*] This division, which had been numbered 43, was numbered 44 after the creation of the 21st Corps.

[†] Translator's note: In the original text, this is printed as September 1921, an obvious typographical error.

groups of 3 to 4 batteries of 4 pieces of 155 C.T.R., or 25 batteries. The mobile heavy artillery, that is to say 15 batteries of 120 long and 6 batteries of 220 mortars, was assigned to the Northwest Group. It was envisaged that these allocations would be increased in line with the deliveries of equipment that would be made.

As far as aeronautics was concerned, elements of this new service were to be represented, from spring 1914, by 13 airships, 20 squadrons of 6 planes distributed among the armies. Studies were underway for the organization of light aircraft sections for the cavalry divisions and the artillery of the army corps. It was also planned to have sections of aircraft equipped to attack enemy airfields and to carry explosives and grapeshot.

The territorial divisions were intended for the defense of Paris, the coasts, the southwest front, etc.; they were to include 12 battalions, 3 to 6 batteries, and 2 to 4 squadrons.

The garrisons of the strongholds had until then been formed by active regiments. The new plan provided for the equipping of the 24 battalions forming the regiments 164 to 173 selected for the four major positions with means of transport, so that they could, as soon as possible, take part in campaign operations as soon as they had been replaced by reserve or territorial units.

The plan to protect North Africa included:

1. The forming of security garrisons on the coast in Bizerte, Algiers and Oran;

2. Mobile columns to reinforce the threatened points of the coast and to suppress insurgencies in the interior;

3. Territorial garrisons in peacetime garrisons;

4. The protection of the colonial centers was to be ensured by the territorials who were domiciled there.

With these security measures in place, the 37th and 38th Divisions with 16 battalions could be drawn from our entire African force for the Northeast Theater.

In Morocco, it seemed necessary to leave all the Expeditionary Corps troops in place until they were relieved by black troops.

To maintain the lines of communication, it was essential that the general-in-chief could, with complete freedom, modify the grouping of his forces for the benefit of the maneuver. As I have already had occasion to say, the railroad is the primary strategic

Chapter X

instrument. However, the organization provided for by Plan XVI lacked flexibility. Plan XVII therefore proposed to keep all the lines of transport at the end of the concentration, keeping only a certain number of regulating stations. In addition, a system of transverse lines was planned to allow for bypass movements.

Except for some detailed measures, nothing was changed in Plan XVII to the provisions of Plan XVI, as far as mobilization was concerned.

The corps must be ready to be transported:

> The cavalry, on the 3rd day at 6pm,
> The combatants, from the 4th to the 9th day,
> The convoys on the 10th day.

For the covering corps:

> The first echelons, from the first day, from the 3rd to the 8th hour,
> The complement of the first echelons at the 27th hour,
> The second echelons, the 2nd, 3rd and 4th day.

The cavalry divisions had to be ready to be embarked on day 3 at 6 pm.

For the reserve divisions, the two Paris divisions were to be ready to be transported from the 5th to the 10th day, all the other divisions from the 9th to the 12th day; the territorial divisions from the 5th to the 15th day.

The mobilization of the northeast areas was to be completed on the 7th day; that of the southeast areas from the 6th to the 10th day.

The project submitted to the Superior Council of War then examined the general distribution of our forces.

The Northeast Theater being the main one, it had to absorb almost all of our active forces, the second line formations being, as already mentioned, used for missions not requiring the same degree of cohesion as the active formations.

For the southeastern frontier, it was sufficient, in any case, to prevent the enemy from rapidly emerging from the mountains and prematurely exerting an impact on operations. By relying on the places that blocked the roads, it was possible to assume that French forces that were inferior in number would obtain this result quite easily. Indeed, because of the slowness of the Italian mobilization, if it even occurred, it would be a month before the Italian troops could make a serious effort. Under these conditions, it did not seem rash to entrust the first defense of this region to reserve divisions; they would certainly have time to gain cohesion before having had serious contact with their possible adversaries.

The southwestern region and the coasts were not very exposed. However, measures were taken on the coast to protect it from possible attacks.

The two reserve divisions provisionally assigned to Paris, the 61st and 62nd, were on the campaign trail; they could be called upon to operate in any theater, along with the 67th reserve division, a central reserve grouped at Mailly and left to the discretion of the Minister of War to deal with the unexpected. These three units made it possible to reduce the defense of the Alps and to put only territorial divisions on the coast.

Under these conditions, the general distribution of our forces was envisaged in accordance with the decisions of the Superior Council of National Defense of January 9, 1912, which had unanimously taken the following resolution:

> Our active corps must all be transported as quickly as possible to the northeast frontier. The protection of our secondary frontiers and coasts may be entrusted to reserve and territorial army units.

This resulted in the following distribution:

Northeast Theater of Operations:

21 army corps,
2 African divisions, 37th and 38th,
Division of the Alps, 44th,
10 cavalry divisions,
14 reserve divisions,
The mobile garrison of the northeast areas,

Chapter X

All the heavy army artillery and heavy mobile artillery.

Southeast Theater of Operations:

4 reserve divisions,
1 territorial division,
The mobile garrison of the southeast areas intended to eventually form the 44th Division.

Southwestern front and coasts:

6 territorial divisions.

General reserve of the territory:

3 reserve divisions (61st and 62nd in Paris, 67th in Mailly),
1 territorial division.

The concentration was to be ensured by *ten independent lines of transport* comprising:
A cluster of 3 lines ending between Belfort and Toul,
A cluster of 3 lines ending between Toul and Verdun,
A cluster of 4 lines ending between Verdun and Hirson.

These 10 lines were linked together by crossings allowing the execution of variants planned or to be improvised during the concentration; in particular the African divisions, and the 44th Division could be conducted by the great crossroads of Dôle, Dijon, Paris, Creil, Tergnier, to the point deemed necessary according to the circumstances.

On the other hand, the operation of the system of regulating stations made it possible to move the concentration as demanded by events backward or forward in the area between the general line Laon, Soissons, Reims, Troyes, Dijon, Besançon, and the front formed by the Moselle upstream from Toul and the Meuse downstream from Pagny.

Consequently, the transportation documents should only give the indication of a group of debarkation stations and the normal zone of the cantonments of each army corps; this resulted in a double advantage: first, a very great simplification in the creation of these documents, which would allow the new plan to be put into effect in significantly less time than that required for the preparation of similar documents in the previous plans; secondly, the army commanders would have enough latitude to order any necessary changes in their respective zones in good time.

With this new approach, it was possible to extend the lines of transport of the tail elements of the large units to the most advanced debarkation stations; one could thus hasten the moment when the armies could move forward by making them follow by consecutive stations.

These various measures were to give us a flexibility in concentration that the uncertainty of the situation made all the more valuable.

Strategic transports were to begin intensively on day 5, at a rate of 56 moves per line per day, and under these conditions we could have ready to go into action in the area of operations:

The cavalry, the evening of the 4th day,

The fighting elements of the corps from the 9th to the night of the 10th day,

Reserve divisions, half on the 11th day at noon, the other half on the night of the 13th day,

The Algerian-Tunisian divisions would be transported to Marseille for the 7th or 9th day; they could be on the morning of the 16th day between Toul and Épinal, or on the 17th day north of Toul. The Alpine division would be transported under similar conditions.

As far as the *coverage* was concerned, the document submitted to the members of the Superior Council of War highlighted the weakness of our numbers in the face of the German opposition and the excessive width of the sectors of our three border army corps. This situation motivated the recruitment law submitted to the vote of the Parliament, the bill requesting the creation of a 21st corps in Épinal, and the draft decree modifying the territorial zones of the 2nd, 6th, 7th and 20th Corps, so as to make the 2nd corps participate in the initial mission of coverage.

The preparatory studies had highlighted the importance of

Chapter X

holding the Meurthe line. The 20th Corps was in a position to ensure the defense, provided that its sector was limited to the Moselle on the left and the Parroy forest on the right. The remaining part of the sector of the 21st Corps, i.e. the Saint-Dié-Baccarat region, could be the object of a sudden attack by the German army corps recently created at Sarrebourg. Under these conditions, the creation of the 21st Corps, made up of the 7th, 20th and 14th Corps and the 19th Artillery Brigade, with garrisons placed between the Meurthe and Moselle rivers, seemed an essential safeguard. The sector of coverage of the 21st corps would extend from the Hautes-Vosges region towards Fraize to Manonvillers, including the access roads coming from Schlestadt, Strasbourg and Sarrebourg.

The main characteristic of the sector extending from the Schlucht Pass to the Swiss border was the connection between operations in the Hautes-Vosges and in the Belfort region. This led to the 7th Corps being given the task of guarding the border from the Schlucht to Switzerland, with the 14th Division spreading out from Belfort to Lons-le-Saunier, the 13th Division having to hold the Vosges, from the Schlucht inclusive to the Ballon d'Alsace, the other brigade towards Giromagny ready either to support the 14th Division, or to support the Vosges brigade. In addition, the 8th Cavalry division, which had deployed towards Montbéliard, would participate in the cover in front of Belfort.

From the first news of the violation of Belgium by the Germans, it was necessary to have towards Givet sufficient forces to occupy the Meuse from this city to Namur. The usefulness of having in this region an infantry division and a cavalry division led me to call upon the 2nd corps whose 4th Division was installed in Mézières with a regiment in Givet.

The defense of the southern Woëvoe was entrusted to the 6th Corps between the Verdun-Conflans line and the Saizerais plateau. With two of its divisions, the corps artillery and the 6th cavalry brigade, the commander of this corps would cover Toul and Verdun and would be ready to support either the 20th Corps on its right, or the 2nd on its left. The 12th Division (3rd Division of the corps) would constitute in the Saint-Mihiel-Commercy region a general reserve of the commander-in-chief, superior commander of the coverage.

From the 5th to the 6th day, the coverage would be reinforced:

> By the 3rd Division in northern Woëvre,
> By the 9th Division in southern Woëvre,
> By the 15th Division on the Upper Meurthe.

From the fourth day, the cavalry regiments of the 2nd, 5th and 9th Corps would be in place as reinforcements for the coverage; on the same date, the 1st, 3rd and 5 th Cavalry divisions gathered in the region of Mézières would be at the disposal of the commander-in-chief.

The entire coverage, at first under the direct authority of the commander-in-chief (the covering corps commanders being sector commanders), would pass from the fifth day to the orders of the army commanders.

The *fortification systems* were intended to support the coverage and help protect the concentration; they were also intended to facilitate the entry of armies into operations by ensuring access to the borders.

However, our forts were insufficient, in their current state, to fulfill this last role, none of them being able to fulfill a function similar to that of Metz-Thionville. The situation was therefore to be improved by the organization of improvised works.

Studies had also been undertaken regarding the creation of solid defensive positions on the Hauts-de-Meusae, the Grand-Couronné and at the mouth of the Charmes forest.

Hauts-de-Meuse: the uncontested possession of the Damvillers, Haudiomont, Vigneulles, Apremont front was necessary to allow the security of our deployments and to facilitate an offensive north of the Verdun-Thionville line. The plan was already decided in all its details. The position was to be established and held from the beginning by the covering troops. Around the eleventh day, the coverage would be replaced in this position by reserve divisions.

Nancy bridgehead: In order to guarantee the left flank of the columns moving towards the northeast against Metz, a position had to be established east of Nancy as soon as the covering period started, and kept ready as soon as the strategic transports started. This position was to encompass the plateau of Faulx, the hill of Amance, the heights of Cercueil. The plan had been entrusted to the 20th Corps; the layout had already been decided by the general commanding the 20th Corps in agreement with the army staff, and the engineers had determined the shape of each structure.

Forest of Charmes: It was necessary to secure the opening beyond the Moselle to Gerbéviller and Rambervillers; this opening was to be secured by the occupation of the plateaus of Ortoncourt and Essey; surveys were in progress.

Here ended the list of issues submitted to the deliberations of the Superior Council of the War. With regard to the order of battle, the document read as follows:

> The determination of the order of battle of the armies, of their distribution on the border, of the general plan of concentration, is linked to the plan of operations established by the general in chief under his personal authority. The following data are provided to the Superior Council of War for informational purposes only:
> The Northeast Army Group will include:
>
> 5 armies;
> 2 independent groups of reserve divisions;
> 3 cavalry divisions   } remaining at the disposal
> Heavy mobile artillery   } of the general in chief.
>
> Composition of the armies:
> *1st Army*: 8th, 13th, 14th, 21st Army corps, 6th Cavalry division, in the Charmes-Arches-Darney area.
> *2nd Army*: 9th, 15th, 16th, 18th, 20th Army corps, 2nd and 7th Cavalry divisions, 59th, 68th, 70th reserve divisions, in the region of Pont-Saint-Vincent-Mirecourt-Vittel-Neufchâteau-Pagny-la-Blanche-Côte.
> *3rd Army*: 4th, 5th, 6th Army corps, 9th Cavalry division, 54th, 55th, 56th reserve divisions, in the Montfaucon-Clermont-en-Argonne-Commercy-Louvemont area.
> *4th Army*: 12th, 17th Army corps, colonial army corps, 10th Cavalry division, in the Vavincourt-Void-Gondrecourt-Bar-le-Duc

area.

5th Army: 1st, 2nd, 3rd, 10th, 11th Army corps; 4th Cavalry division, 52nd and 60th reserve divisions, in the Hirson-Rethel-Sainte-Menehould-Mézières area.

Cavalry Corps: 1st, 3rd and 5th Cavalry divisions towards Mézières.

A group of reserve divisions comprising the 58th, 63rd and 66th Divisions in the Vesoul area.

A group of reserve divisions including the 51st, 53rd, and 54th reserve divisions in the Vervins area.

A detachment from Upper Alsace comprising the 7th Army Corps and the 8th Cavalry division.

For the record:
    The 37th and 38th Divisions arriving from North Africa;
    A possible division coming from the Alps;
    The 67th reserve division at the Mailly camp at the disposal of the Minister;
    The 61st and 62nd reserve divisions were initially assigned to the defense of Paris.

With respect to the secondary theaters, the note on the bases of Plan XVII gave the following details:

Southeast Theater: We believe at this time that the Italians, if they engaged in war against us, would not be ready until the eighteenth day and could only attack from the twentieth to the twenty-fifth day; they could aim either at the region of Nice or that of Lyon; in the latter case, the purpose of their operations would be to link their maneuvers with those of the Germans; but they would then have to cross the rough valleys of the Tarentaise, the Maurienne, and the Romanche, which were defended by fortifications.

Under these conditions, we envisage a strictly defensive mission for the army of the Alps for two months. It would use for this purpose the positions of Bourg-Saint-Maurice, Modane, Briançon, Tournoux and Nice, as well as the second line positions of Albertville, Chamousset, Grenoble and Télégraphe. It is to include: four reserve divisions (64th, 74th, 65th, 75th), a territorial division assigned to the coasts of Provence, units specialized in mountain warfare, the garrisons of the positions, that is to say four active regiments (157th, 158th, 159th, 173rd); in the event of declared Italian neutrality, these

Chapter X

active regiments would be used to form the 44th Division.

The southeast region would be divided into five defense sectors:

Sector of Tarentaise (Bourg-Saint-Maurioe);
Sector of Maurienne (Modane);
Sector of Briançonnais (Briançon);
Sector of Ubaye (Tournoux);
Sector of Alpes-Maritimes (Nice).

Coverage would be provided by eight Alpine groups (five in the 14th region and three in the 15th). On the tenth day of mobilization, these Alpine *chasseurs* battalions would be relieved by reserve Alpine battalions, and would be transported to the northeast where they would join the 14th and 15th Army corps. Behind this division, three divisions. The 74th, 64th and 65th would be placed in reserve respectively at Chambéry, Gap and Nice. The 75th would be placed in general reserve at Avignon; the territorial division at Aix-en-Provence.

The headquarters of the army of the Alps would be in Lyon.

Pyrenean Front: In the present state of our relations with Spain, it is only necessary to take surveillance measures, first by reserve regiments, then, after their departure, by two territorial divisions maintained respectively at Perpignan and Bayonne. In the center, a cordon of customs officers and foresters is considered sufficient.

Coastal defense: The defense is entrusted to the French fleet concentrated entirely in the Mediterranean.

The council had to understand:

1. A mobile defense. The coasts of the North Sea and the English Channel, being the most exposed, would be divided into three sectors, including: 1st, the ports of Calais and Boulogne; 2nd, those of Dieppe and Le Havre; 3rd, Contentin. To each of these sectors would be assigned a territorial division stationed respectively in Saint-Omer, Rouen and the Cotentin; a central reserve could, in addition, be provided. For the possible defense of the coasts of Brittany and part of those of the Ocean, a territorial division would be placed at Le Mans or Angers; the territorial division of Bayonne, in addition to its mission facing Spain, would ensure the defense of the rest of the Ocean front.

2. A fixed defense. This defense would be assured by the garrisons of the essential positions: Cherbourg, Brest, Lorient, Bordeaux, Toulon, Bizerte.

Chapter X

The Superior Council of War met in the War Department on the afternoon of April 18, 1913, under the chairmanship of the Minister, Mr. Étienne. Called upon to vote on the question of whether there were grounds for drawing up a Plan XVII on the basis of the presentation report which I have just summarized, the members of the Council voted unanimously in favor, without any objection being raised.

The next day, I left on an inspection tour with Mr. Étienne. We visited in particular Verdun and the defenses of Nancy.

On May 2, the Minister approved the basic plan, which thus became enforceable. The need for it was becoming more and more evident every day; in fact, the preparation of the documents relating to variant no. 2, which had been completed during the month of April, had revealed a certain number of problems attributable to the successive modifications that Plan XVI had undergone; they were such as to make us fear that the operation of the concentration was no longer guaranteed in the conditions of order and regularity which were essential.

I will digress here to report a rather curious fact that was submitted on May 17 to the Superior Council of National Defense.

In the session of January 9, 1912, the Minister of the Navy had expressed the opinion that the control of the sea had to be completely acquired before the transport of troops from North Africa to France could begin; the Department of the Navy considered, consequently, that these transports could only begin on the date prescribed by Vice-Admiral de Lapeyrère; the Minister of War, on the other hand, asked that these transports take place via the vessels of the Mediterranean shipping companies that could sail alone, the first ones leaving on the fifth day from Algiers, Oran, Philippeville or Bizerte for Marseille where their arrival was planned for forty-eight hours later. Now, during the discussion in the session, the President of the Republic stated that it would perhaps be advantageous to accept a proposal by the King of Spain, who agreed to provide us with a naval base in the Balearic Islands, or even to ensure the transport of the 19th Corps through Spain. This proposal was interesting and deserved to be studied. It was decided to undertake, in concert, between the War and the Navy, studies to push this matter to the limit.

Chapter X

The 4th Bureau of the Army Staff (Commission of the Railways of the South) presented the following objections: if the landing of our troops took place in Barcelona, the advantage of the operation would be small; if, on the contrary, the landing took place in the Cartagena-Alicante region, the safety of our troops during the crossing would be easily assured, but the efficiency of the Spanish railroad was low; it ran along the coast for most of its route to France, which made it vulnerable to the enterprises of the enemy; Spain lacked equipment, and, because of the different gauges of the Spanish tracks, it was difficult for us to equip this line of transport; finally, if incidents on the way were to occur, it would be necessary to quarter the troops in the surrounding Spanish localities, which could not fail to cause diplomatic difficulties. For all these reasons, the idea was abandoned. This detail which I have just reported is only useful to show the goodwill which the king of Spain showed towards us in this circumstance.

I now resume my story. The three-year law was passed on August 7, 1913. It would allow us to undertake the reorganization of the army which was the basis of the new plan. The entire summer of 1913 was used to set up this plan, as far as coverage and transportation were concerned. During all this period, I was very much absorbed by the sessions of the House relating to the vote of the three-year law, then, as I said above, by my stay in Russia. On my return, there were the grand maneuvers of the southwest. On my return from the grand maneuvers, I found the preparation work of the 4th Bureau very advanced. We then started to prepare the coverage, but this could not be definitively set up until the end of December, that is to say after the vote of the law creating the 21st Army corps in Épinal.

At that moment, General Pau, who had the eventual command of the main army, the 2nd, in the Superior Council of War, was reaching the age limit. A successor had to be appointed in the Council. On my proposal, General de Castelnau was designated. I then chose as first deputy chief of staff, General Belin, who had worked for a long time with General de Castelnau; I added to him General Berthelot, whose high qualities of intelligence I had appreciated in the Technical Staff Committee. The functions of second deputy chief of the general staff soon became vacant, following the appointment of General Legrand, an energetic general officer, who had given the measure of his value in the preparation of the three-year law, to the command of the recently created 21st Army corps. These functions were entrusted to General Ebener, who had under his command the 1st Bureau, the staff personnel, the accounting offices and the management of Africa, while General Belin kept under his direct action the 2nd, 3rd, and 4th Bureaus, that is to say, the bodies directly concerned with the implementation of the plan. It was thus General Belin who was responsible for the greater part of the plan in its execution, while General de Castelnau worked primarily on the studies that led to the establishment of the basis of Plan XVII.

The first emergency coverage definitively decided in December 1913 only differed from the one expected by the basics of the plan by a few details, in particular the projected assignment of an alpine brigade as reinforcement for the coverage of the Upper Meurthe sector was not carried out. Its transportation would not have been fast enough, and it was deemed preferable to leave the 14th and 15th Corps with their normal composition. On the other hand, the passing of the three years law had made it possible to increase the number of units forming part of the covering troops and the strength of these units. Some of the troops destined to form part of the covering troops garrisoned in the interior of the territory had already been installed in the border zone, which had made it possible to increase the number of sectors by reducing their size. From right to left, the situation of the coverage was now as follows:

Trouée da Belfort and the Hautes-Vosges sector. The 7th Corps was covering in this sector limited on the right to the Swiss border towards Dalle, on the left to the Schlucht. The 14th Division had a brigade at work in Belfort, from the first hours, reinforced in a short time by another brigade. Its mission was to cover the mobilization of the position of Belfort. On its right, the 8th Cavalry Division guarded the approaches between Petite-Croix and the road to Dalle. The 41st Division, in charge of covering the Hautes-Vosges, held the passes with a brigade in place from the very first hours. The other brigade, which landed at the thirty-sixth hour, had its bulk towards Le Thillot.

Upper Meurthe sector. The creation of the 21st Corps made it possible to assign an entire army corps to cover the region between Fraize and Avricourt. The coverage on the Meurthe line, whose importance for the further development of our operations was indisputable, seemed to be assured between Fraize and Lunéville in good conditions; most of the elements of this corps were, in fact, stationed on the Meurthe and the Moselle, and in place from the very first hours. The 6th Cavalry Division was landed on the left of the 21st Corps, in the open part of the sector.

Lower Meurthe sector. The reduction of the sector of the 20th Corps to the zone limited on the left by the Moselle, on the right by the forest of Parroy put this corps in a position to hold solidly with the support of the 2nd Cavalry Division the most important part of the line of the Meurthe in front of Nancy.

Southern Woëvre sector. The limits of this sector were, on the right, on the right bank of the Moselle, the Dieulouard, Port-sur-Seille line, and on the left, the Ornes, Amel, Avril line (north of Briey). Two divisions of the 6th Corps, most of which were stationed on the Meuse, as well as the 1st light cavalry brigade, seemed to be able to cover Toul and Verdun against a sudden attack in the early hours. These elements were reinforced around the fortieth hour by the 12th Division and the corps artillery, then two hours later by the 7th Cavalry Division.

Northern Woëvre sector. This sector belonged to the 2nd Army corps whose 4th Division with three brigades had almost all its elements on the Meuse or further east. This division had a double mission: on the one hand, with two brigades and the 4th Cavalry Division, to ensure at a good distance the protection of the unloading workshops spread out between Verdun and Sedan; on the other hand, to have early towards Givet sufficient forces in a position to occupy quickly the passages of the Meuse from Givet to Namur, at the first news of the violation of the Belgian neutrality by the Germans.

Cavalry Corps (1st, 3rd and 5th Divisions). At the fortieth hour, the cavalry corps was disembarked in the region of Mézières at the disposal of the general in chief.

Moreover, as it was foreseen in the proposals I have already mentioned, it was assumed that the coverage would be reinforced from the fourth day in the evening to the sixth day by:

The 15th Division in the Upper Meurthe sector;
The 9th Division in the southern Woëvre sector;
The 3rd Division in the northern Woëvre sector.

Under these conditions, we anticipated the use of 127 battalions, 24 corps squadrons, 138 mounted battalions, 148 squadrons belonging to cavalry divisions, and 21 mounted batteries.

The overall mission of the coverage was essentially defensive.

As I have already said, until the fifth day, the command of the covering troops was exercised by the corps commanders corresponding to each of the sectors, under my direct authority; from the fifth day the troops of each sector passed to the orders of the generals commanding the armies which its sectors covered.

It seemed necessary to me, as we have already seen, to complete our fortified systems by the organization of positions on which our covering troops would be able to hold for a long time against superior forces: the instructions on the covering were thus completed by orders for the *defensive organization* of the following regions:

1. Nancy bridgehead. A bridgehead position east of Nancy encompassed the Faulx plateau and the four resistance centers of La Rochette, Mont d'Amance, Pulmy-Cercueil and the Rambetant plateau north of Saint-Nicolas.

Part of the work was already in progress. The completion of this position and its defense were to be ensured by the 20th Corps reinforced in cover by two batteries of 120 and two and a half batteries of 155 C.T.R., and later on by reserve divisions. During peacetime, the access roads, the clearing, the concreted redoubts and batteries, the shelters and the ammunition stores were completed.

2. Hauts-de-Meuse. The uncontested possession of the Hauts-de-Meuse was necessary to ensure the security of our deployments and to allow us to maneuver behind the Meuse line.

a) In the Eparges-Hattoncbâtel-Heudicourt region, the organization of three centers of resistance was prepared as early as peacetime, in order to give the 6th Corps a solid base of resistance, on the one hand, and, on the other hand, to allow for a later opening into Woëvre. The organization of these three centers was to be started in peacetime and completed by the covering troops to which reserve divisions would be added from the fifth day. For the defense of this region, the 6th Corps was to have at its disposal four batteries of 120 long.

b) In the region of Haudiomont-les-Blusses, the Verdun garrison

Chapter X

was to hold the Hauts-de-Meuse to the left of the 6th Corps in liaison with it. The Haudiomont position, entirely independent of the defense of Verdun, was already in the process of being organized: batteries with shelters, railroads, clearing of the fields of fire, infantry works at the bottom of the hills.

c) The Ornes-Damvillers region, due to the nature of the terrain, was only suitable for defensive operations; its organization had been foreseen, but was only to be executed upon mobilization, as soon as the first troops of the 4th Army corps arrived (day 7). These troops would have two 120 long batteries. Some work could be started by the detachment of the 4th infantry division in charge of holding the area from the beginning of the coverage.

3. *Montmédy*. The organization of the heights to the south and north of Montmédy had been prepared since peacetime. Its purpose was to:

a) To facilitate the task of coverage at the beginning of operations;

b) To allow an army concentrated on the left bank of the Meuse to break out either in the direction of the east to act in the right flank of the forces which were moving towards Verdun, or towards the northeast to attack the left flank of an enemy army which would have violated the neutrality of Belgium. Part of the work was to be carried out in peacetime; it would then be carried out by the troops of the 2nd Corps and later by reserve divisions during the covering period.

As far as the southeastern border was concerned, we were obliged to take into account the uncertainty in which we found ourselves regarding the Italian decision in the event of a Franco-German war; despite the strong probability of neutrality, we had to assume the case where Italy, at the last moment, would launch a decided offensive. It was therefore essential to ensure sufficient coverage without resorting to large troop movements that could be considered a provocation. To this end, we decided to include in the first emergency coverage only the troops forming part of the garrison of the places, to the exclusion of the units joining the 14th and 15th Corps. These troops, usually staying in the high mountains during the summer, could be put into motion without arousing suspicion and without risking delaying the departure of the 14th and 15th Corps.

As the 21st Corps was created at the end of December 1913,

the coverage plan became enforceable from that moment on.

On the other hand, as far as the new concentration plan was concerned, nothing had been done to implement it. The 4th Bureau had only established its new lines of transport. Its studies led to the following proposals: the concentration of active corps and reserve divisions on the northeast front would be carried out along ten independent transport lines. The distribution of the mobilized formations between the different lines would be regulated in such a way as to make each transport line bear approximately the same load. The proposed lines would be divided into three clusters: three between Belfort and Toul, three between Toul and Verdun, and four between Verdun and Hirson. As I have already indicated, these clusters could be linked together by several shunting transverse lines allowing the making of changes. In particular, the Dôle, Dijon, Paris, Creil, Tergnier transverse line could perform shunts from one line of transport to another behind the regulating stations. A part of the available forces could be brought to any point of this transverse line either by the Paris-Lyon line, or by the Bourbonnais line, or even by the Toulouse-Paris line.

In order to achieve the conditions of flexibility to be given to the debarkations, conditions which had been explained earlier in the basics of the plan, the 4th Bureau also proposed not to regulate in advance the exact method of debarkation; this would be determined by the regulating Commissions and the billeting officers in the zone of action of the regulating stations. The zones of concentration could thus be shaped or advanced at will between the general line Laon-Soissons, Reims, Troyes, Dijon, Besançon and a front marked by the course of the Meuse downstream from Pagny and that of the Moselle upstream from Toul. In addition, in the zone of concentration of their armies, the generals commanding the armies would have the latitude to vary the deployments in such a way as to modify the orientation and articulation of the formation of their army to adapt it to their particular plans according to the conditions set by my own directions.

There was only to approve these proposals and to instruct the various offices of the staff of the army to proceed with the preparation of all the instructions and documents for implementation.

Chapter X

Thanks to the activity deployed by the army staff, very intelligently activated by General Belin, this major undertaking could be completed on April 15, 1914, and on May 1 all the documents were in place. However, General Belin asked me to carry out a general inspection of the territory to make sure that everything was in order. Following this inspection, he reported to me on June 1 that everything was ready.

It is appropriate to pay this tribute to the work accomplished by General Belin and the officers of the army staff. If the act of mobilization and the act of concentration took place two months later without a hitch and in the most perfect order, it must be known that the credit is due to these officers who knew how to set up this considerable work under time constraints that had never been encountered. Among them, I would like to mention Major Poindron, head of the Planning Section, and his direct superior, Colonel Pont, who, after having been deputy head of the Operations Office, became head of this office in March 1914, and distinguished himself there through his intelligence and his methodical spirit combined with a modesty which attracted all sympathy.

However, it was necessary to condense the broad outlines of the concentration into a document intended for the army commanders; it was to be used to direct their personal preparations and the work of their staffs. It was in February 1914 that I had the *Instruction on Concentration* written. It was based on a fundamental idea: the intention of the general-in-chief is to take the offensive when his forces are united. This was the affirmation of a war doctrine that had proven itself both at the Marne in 1914 and during the operations of 1918. Moreover, this *Instruction* has been published and discussed in so many documents that it seems unnecessary to reproduce it here

However, I would like to point out that, in my mind, this *Instruction* was not set in stone. As I have already said, I considered as a firm element of the concentration only the transports up to the regulating stations: beyond that, I considered that a decision should be taken at the time of the conflict, according to the situation, and by modifying, if necessary, the contents of the Instruction.

The *Instruction on Concentration* was not restrictive in my mind; it did not consider all the possibilities; it could not because of the government's directives motivated in large part, as Lord French has very well said, by the enigmatic attitude of Belgium up to the last moment: "It is very regrettable that she could never have been persuaded to determine in advance her attitude in the event of a general war." Our pre-war task would have been singularly simplified: *officially, I could only take into account in a document intended for a fairly large number of people the operations likely to take place outside Belgian territory.* As I was obliged to consider the scenario of the violation of Belgian neutrality, I preferred not to write anything about the plan of operations, contenting myself with a concentration for several purposes. And I made a point of displaying my will to attack in the general direction of the northeast, as soon as the totality of the French forces were united.

This reservation on my part seemed justified at the time I made my decision. It still seems justified to me today.

Let's suppose, for example, that, as a result of particular circumstances attributable as much to the internal state of France as to the skill with which the Germans would have concealed their preparations, we would have been late in our mobilization; it is quite obvious that, in these conditions, it would have been necessary to move back the zone of concentration. It will be seen, moreover, that, in the period of political tension, I had to fear this eventuality.

At the time of its drafting, I was asked to indicate in one sentence that this *Instruction* was far from corresponding to all the possibilities; I refused to do so, preferring to instruct pushing forward the study of the variants intended to concentrate the bulk of our forces in the northern part of the theater of operations. It seemed to me that, such as it was, this *Instruction* was sufficient, by its average solution, to allow the various army staffs to work; I had enough confidence in their flexibility to estimate that, when the time came, they would be able to carry out the modifications that I would order; I considered it dangerous to make known in advance the various maneuvers that I had envisaged.

In fact, it happened that in August 1914 a large part of this instruction was still valid.

It should also be noted that, for the same reasons of secrecy, the text of the *Instruction* is silent on the question of English cooperation, on the role that the Belgian army could possibly play, on the possible use of our troops coming from Algeria, as well as on that of our Alpine troops in the event of Italy's neutrality.

The various variants that I had studied at the army staff came down to the following ideas:

To move the 5th Army northwards, as much as the presence of the English troops would allow it, that is to say, to transport the 5th Army between the Meuse and the Sambre. It is necessary to notice on this subject that the conditions of transport and landing of the English forces had a very particular rigidity: instead of arriving like us, all mobilized and in order of march, it is on the very landing area that the British army corps and Divisions were assembled; as a result it was impossible to vary an organization of transport thus conceived

The movement of the 5th Army could be done on the one hand by means of deployment variants, on the other hand by means of movements on road once the concentration was finished.

To reinforce our left wing with forces taken from the right wing, or with troops coming from Africa and the Alps. I even had to consider to what extent the mission given to the right wing could be modified in case of important withdrawals.

Passage of army corps from one army to another; these changes could not have any serious disadvantage in a period of concentration, since the armies were only assembled at the time of the war. Moreover, during the campaign, this procedure was constantly used; it constitutes one of the means of maneuvering within a group of armies.

Transport to the north of territorial divisions initially planned for the defense of the coast.

Among these variants, motivated, as one can see, by the preoccupations that Belgium caused me, a certain number of them could be carried out even before the concentration; others, on the contrary, had to be delayed; this last case included the variants by land, which could obviously only be carried out once the troops had been debarked, or certain movements parallel to the front, which could only be carried out after the main concentration movements, at the risk of disrupting them. This could result in delays, and the necessity of making a counter-offensive instead of the offensive. The risk was slight, because the space which, on the left wing, separated us from the Germans in this scenario should give us time to see events unfold.

In March 1914, I also had an "Intelligence Plan" drawn up for the Northeast Army Group. I approved it on March 28. It explained all of the information which I judged necessary in order to decide the maneuver to be made; it was to be used as a basis for the "Plan of research of the Special Service of intelligence," for the "Plan of strategic air exploration," and for the missions of exploration to be entrusted to the cavalry divisions of the armies and to the cavalry corps.

This plan is interesting because it clearly indicates the nature of the concerns we had regarding the enemy's maneuvers, and the information that was to be used to support my decision. For this reason, I believe it necessary to give here the main parts.

In order to clarify the goal to be reached, and to increase the clarity of the exposition, this plan was divided into several chapters corresponding to the various periods of the war: political tension, coverage, concentration of troops, period of the great operations. But one should remember that this division should not be taken too literally, nor considered as representing clear-cut stages in the search for information.

Period of political tension. The essential information to be sought and which can only be requested from the Special Service are the following:

Are the Germans preparing for war against us, our allies (Russia) or neutral countries (Belgium, Switzerland, Denmark)?

Are there, on the other hand, preparations by the Belgians, the Swiss, the Danes?

Are the Germans organizing a sudden attack against us with their covering troops, and what is the probable direction of this attack?

The document then listed the details of the various measures

Chapter X

that could be noted as indications of these preparations: suppression of liberties, purchases of foodstuffs, troop movements, restrictions on the freedom of international movement, notices to the press, etc. In particular, concerning the preparations that Germany could make against neutral countries, the note said: "It is important to know if the Germans are preparing a sudden offensive in the direction of *Basel, Liége*, the island of Fionie, with a view to taking control of the straits that separate the Baltic from the North Sea."

Period of Coverage. The essential information to look for is as follows:

On our left wing, are the Germans violating or preparing to violate the borders of Luxembourg and especially Belgium? At which points? With what forces?

On the front, are the Germans preparing a sudden attack with their covering troops supported by fast Divisions, and in which direction?

On our right wing, what obstacles: troops, fortifications, would meet a French offensive in Upper Alsace and in the Vosges between the Schlucht and the Donon?

On the subject of the *violation of Luxembourg and Belgium*, the document stated: "The violation of the border of Luxembourg and *especially of the Belgian border by a German troop of any size should be reported as a matter of extreme urgency to the General-in-Chief, to the commander of the cavalry corps and to the commander of the 5th Army.*" The clues to a possible German offensive through Belgium are as follows:

Deployments in the period from the first to the sixth day of masses of cavalry between Aachen and Saint-With, towards Gerolstein, Prüm, Bittburg (Junterath, Gerolatein, Bittburg, Bleialf); and around Trier: gathering of these masses of cavalry along the borders of Luxembourg and Belgium, west of Trier, west of Bittburg, towards Saint-With and Malmédy... Eventually deployments and cavalry gatherings, further north in the region of Aachen... Concentration of the German VIIIth Corps in the part of its territory situated north of Trier; presence of detachments of this corps along the borders of Luxembourg and Belgium; maintenance in Aachen of the troops of this corps in garrison in this city.

The research of the deployments of troops of all weapons which would be carried out later vis-a-vis Luxembourg and Belgium would be to continue in the zones of quays where the lines of: Goblentz-Trèvae, Remageu-DumpenfeldGerolstein-Lissendorf-Butzenbach-Prüm-Bleral, Cologne-Euskirchen- Gall-Gerolstein-Bittburg, Stolberg-Roeren-MontjoieSaint-With, Neuss or Creufeld towards Aachen. The gathering of forces that could be about to violate the border of Luxembourg and Belgium are therefore to be sought:

> Between Mosel and Saarland north of the Merzig-Sierk line,
> Around Trier,
> In the Bittburg-Neuburg region,
> In the region of Gerolstein, Prüm, Saint-With, Malmédy,
> In the region of Duren, Aachen.

It is essentially important to know:
How far north the large gatherings extend;
Whether they include active formations or only reserve formations.

In particular, the presence of only reserve formations in the region north of Trier, and the establishment of fortification works along the Our and Sure rivers, would constitute a particularly interesting correlation.

Finally, if the enemy penetrates into Luxembourg and Belgium, it is essential to *follow his progress* and to be constantly aware of *the extension of the movement of his northern wing*.

This information will be requested from aerial reconnaissance and the cavalry; but it can and must be cross-checked by the Special Service. In this respect, it would be of interest to be able to spot, as soon as possible, in case of violation of Belgian territory by the Germans, the arrival of the cavalry, and then of columns of all arms on the following crossings:

> Verviers, Stavelot, Diekirch, Remich;
> Liége, Houffalize, Wiltz, Luxembourg;

Chapter X

Huy, Marche, Bastogne, Arlon; .
Namur, Rochefort, Saint-Hubert, Neufchâteau, Virton.

In particular, it would be essential to know if there were or were not enemy columns – of cavalry or of any arm – north of the Marche, Houfialize, Saint-Hubert forest massif.

With regard to the sudden offensive of the German covering troops possibly supported by fast Divisions, and the direction of this offensive, the document stated:

> The German attack seems to be organized in the direction of one of the three following objectives, listed in order of importance: *Nancy, Verdun-Hattonchâtel, Saint-Dié.*
>
> The army corps that can, either immediately or during the period of coverage, participate in this action are: the VIIIth, the XVIth, the XXIst, the IInd Bavarian, the XVth and the XIVth.
>
> Therefore, the information to be sought and requested from the Special Branch and the Air Force is as follows:
>
> Where did the VIIIth Corps gather? The search for the VIIIth Corps north of Trier has already been considered with regard to the violation of Belgium; if this corps is to take part in a sudden German attack, it should be expected, on the contrary, to assemble in the region of Sierck.
>
> As far as the Metz area is concerned, it would be unrealistic to think of obtaining complete information from the Special Service, either on the assembly of the XVIth Corps, or on the state of progress of the works of the fortress or the constitution of its war garrison. We can hardly expect to receive information from the Special Service and from Metz, except during the period of political tension. On the other hand, our airships and airplanes will encounter great difficulties in flying over this stronghold without running great risks. But because of its proximity to our border, Metz can be monitored by airplane, by airship, and even by kites, while remaining above French territory; the observation system should be planned from the period of political tension.
>
> Where does the XXIth Corps gather? Behind its coverage, that is to say in the region of Sarralbe, Gros-Tenquin? On the contrary, is it gathering for an offensive, towards Delme, Château-Salins, Dieuze, or Sarrebourg? As a follow-up, did the troops of Bitche, Wissembourg, Haguenau, leave their garrisons?
>
> Where did the Bavarian IInd gather? In which regions of

Lorraine are Bavarian troops reported? What are these troops? Have the troops of Landau and those of the Vurtzbourg division left their garrisons?

Is the XVth Corps preparing to move through the upper Bruche valley (towards Saint-Dié)? On the contrary, is it preparing to break through at least in part to the west of the Vosges by the region of Phalsbourg, Dabo?

Has the division of the XIVth Corps garrisoned in the Carlsruhe area (28th Division) left its garrisons? In which region of Alsace is its arrival reported?

Finally, are the Germans preparing defensive positions? In which points? On the Delme coast, around Château-Salins and Dieuze, towards Morhange, towards Sarrebourg, between Mutzig, Molsheim and Strasbourg?

The document then drew attention to the difficulties that a French offensive would encounter, on the one hand in Upper Alsace, and on the other hand in the Vosges, between the Schlucht and Donon regions. It stated:

The information necessary in this respect is partly confused with that concerning the XV Corps and the 28th Division. It would have to be completed require by the following information (to be requested from the Special Service and aerial reconnaissance):

Are the Germans creating defensive positions in the Colmar and Schlestadt areas?

Are there any reports of the construction of bridges over the Rhine at Neuf-Brisach and especially at Mulheim and Huningue? Are fortification works being established towards Mulheim, Istein and Huningue? Are preparations being made for the removal of the Huningue bridge?

Are there any deployments at the German station of Basel? (Essential information and of which the General Commander-in-Chief, the Commander of the 1st Army and the Commander of the 7th Corps should be informed as soon as possible).

Are there troop transports on the line on the right bank of the Rhine between Säckingen and Waldshut? Are there any deployments northeast of Basel? Are there any towards Mulheim, towards Freiburg, towards Vieux-Brisach and towards Offenburg?

Are there any preparations or withdrawals in Mulhouse?

Chapter X

Period of concentration (from the seventh to the twelfth day) and period of major operations (from about the twelfth day).

1. The period of concentration will be characterized by *the search for large opposing gatherings*, particularly with regard to the front line armies. This search is to be carried out around the debarkation stations (Special Service) by observing the movements and gatherings that are necessary for the deployments. (Aerial reconnaissance.)

It is certain that we will find important deployments and gatherings in the whole neutral zone between Strasbourg and Trier. Nevertheless, it would be more particularly important to know... if the deployments and the gatherings are carried out in more or less immediate proximity of the border; ...if the Germans do not seem to have the intention to make a relative gap in front of us, in Lorraine, between Metz and the Vosges; ....if the forces that will deploy in the region of Niederbronn, Saverne, Strasbourg remain there initially, if they pass to the west of the Vosges, or if they are directed, on the contrary, towards the valley of the Bruche.

This information is to be requested especially from aerial reconnaissance. It would be interesting, however, if the Special Service could, as far as possible, identify the formations present. It would be, moreover, necessary that it be in a position to collect information at the bridges of the Rhine, as regards the means of transport.

It is also important to continue to search for prepared defensive positions. Apart from the points already mentioned, these positions are to be sought between Metz and Thionville, west of Saint-Avold, south of Saarbrücken.

The main issue during the concentration period will be *the identification of the wings.*

The German right wing has been described in the preceding lines; for the left wing, movements and assemblies are to be sought:

...In the region of Colmar;

...In the plain of the right bank of the Rhine, from Strasbourg to Basel;

...Along the Rhine above Basel

This search, entrusted to both the Special Service and the aerial reconnaissance, should be combined with the surveillance of the railroad junctions of Immendingen and Hintchingen, from where the transport routes can go to Waldshut, Säckingen, or to Donaueschingen, Offenburg, possibly to Donaueschingen, Freiburg.

It is important that any violation or threat of violation of the

Swiss border by the Germans be immediately reported to the commanding general, the commander of the 1st Army and the commander of the 1st reserve division group.

As it is not possible for us to have a large mass of cavalry on our right that could be directed into the northern part of Switzerland, and as it may be in our interest to leave it to the Swiss to defend their own neutrality, the surveillance of German forces that have penetrated into Switzerland should be requested from the aerial reconnaissance and the Special Service. In this respect, the Olten region and the Lanfen-Biel crossing should be observed in particular.

2. At the end of the concentration period and the period of the operations will especially correspond:

...The search for the direction in which the large opposing forces will move.

...The search for second line armies that the enemy could form behind his center or his wings with reserve formations.

Direction in which the large enemy forces will move.

We have already stated our interest in knowing:

...The magnitude of the German movements through Belgium.

...The orientation of the forces deployed in the region between Strasbourg and the Vosges.

In addition, the following information should be pursued:

If the German columns have penetrated Luxembourg without having crossed the Belgian border, did they continue their movement towards the west or did they fall back towards the southwest?

...Are the forces gathered behind Thionville heading straight west?

...Are the forces gathered in the rear of Metz (and which probably constitute the main mass of the German army) heading straight to the west or turning to the southwest?

With regard to the French offensive that would develop between Metz and the Vosges, one senses all the price that would be paid to be able to avoid in good time the counter-attacks likely to intervene on its left wing starting from the region northwest of Metz, on its right wing, starting from the region north of Strasbourg.

The Special Service will undoubtedly be unable to provide information on these matters. Only aerial reconnaissance, and later combat, will be able to provide us with information.

Search for second line armies.

Chapter X

This search for the German second line armies will be continued in the rear of the center and the wings:
...at the railroad junctions of Deux-Ponts and Haguenau,
...to Wesel, to Dusseldorf, Cologne,
...to Mannheim, Carlsruhe,
...on the right bank of the Rhine, near and above Strasbourg.
This will also be done further back:
...around Mainz, Frankfurt, Hanau
...along the railway line Stuttgart, Carlsruhe,
...to Ulm.

It will have to be at the same time investigated if preparations are not made, in these various regions, for transport by rail.

Finally, and in view of a later exploitation of a breakthrough, it is necessary to become aware as soon as possible of the points where the Germans are preparing second line defensive positions, in particular at Coblentz, Mainz, Spire and Gemersheim.

Theater of operations of the coasts and Russia; possible cooperation with the German offensive of the Italians and Austrians; neutral countries.

...The pursuit of intelligence that corresponds to these various issues must be initiated as soon as the period of political tension and coverage is over, and then extended until the end of hostilities.

1. Theater of operations of the coasts and Russia.

In order to be able to confirm the data that we will collect on the German forces, it will be necessary for us to know and identify the forces that they will leave facing Russia and on their coasts.

As far as Russia is concerned, the question will be related to the organization of our communications with her when war is declared. As far as the coasts are concerned, it will be particularly interesting for us to know as soon as possible if they initially leave active troops, in particular the IXth and Xth Corps. These corps could then be considered as formations with reserved transport, intended to play the role of reserves in the hands of their high command. In this case, it would be useful to know the date of their departure.

2. Cooperation with the German offensive by the Italians and possibly the Austrians.

a) Surveillance of Grand St. Bernard, the Simplon, the St. Gothard, the Bremen in order to prevent any Italian offensive through

Switzerland or any transport of Italian troops to north Germany.

This surveillance would be combined with that of the deployment sites in the Po valley (particularly towards Milan and Verona) and in the Veneto region.

b) As a security measure, surveillance of the lines allowing the transport of Austrian bodies to the French border.

More particular surveillance of the corps in Vienna (119 corps) and Presbourg (V corps).

3. Neutral countries.

a) We have already indicated the advantages that the Germans could find in seizing the island of Fionie and in making themselves masters of the Baltic straits.

Eventually, it would be in our interest to know the forces one would commit on that side.

b) Similarly, it is useful to know if there are German deployments on the Dutch border. The question has, moreover, been considered in the search for their right wing.

c) Finally, there remains the question of the measures taken by the Belgians and the Swiss to enforce their neutrality or to join one of the belligerents. In this regard, information will be provided through diplomatic channels, and it will be particularly important that it be transmitted urgently to the General Commander-in-Chief.

From the moment the Germans have penetrated either Belgium or Switzerland, we can seek to enter into relations with the armies of these two powers:

...by sending staff officers,

...via our cavalry and our planes.

But it will certainly be to our advantage to spare them and, particularly as far as the Swiss are concerned, to respect their sensitivities, by not sending, immediately, our planes or our airships to fly over their concentrations.[*]

It is therefore necessary that the Special Service be able to keep us constantly informed of the Belgian and Swiss mobilization and of the military arrangements made between the two countries.

Questions of interest in this regard are as follows:

Belgium – Distribution of Belgian forces between Liège and Givet; forces gathered in Liège, between Liège and Namur, towards

---

[*] We have it on good authority that Swiss troops have orders to fire on aircraft flying over Swiss territory.

Chapter X

Namur, between Namur and Givet. Defense works carried out along the Meuse; preparation for the destruction of the bridges; search for the main assembly points of the Belgians, notably towards Brussels, Landen and Louvain.

Switzerland – ...Troops immediately guarding the French border..., troops occupying the territory of Basel..., troops holding the general line marked by the lake of Neufchâtel and the valley of the Aare. In particular: Yverdon area and south, Neufchâtel (I corps), Olten (II corps), Brugg, Zurich, Wintherthur (III corps).

Indications which could tend to indicate that the intent of the gatherings of the Swiss is directed more particularly towards Germany or towards France.

Where do the Swiss build fortifications?

It remains for me to indicate still some measures which I was led to take in the last months which preceded the Great War, and which had a direct relationship with the subject which I have just discussed in this chapter.

We know that the German mobilization could take place in several stages and was, therefore, very flexible

It was necessary to prepare something similar for us, which would allow us to gradually carry out a large part of our mobilization arrangements, so that we would not lag behind the German mobilization.

Since February 1909, there was an Instruction regulating a series of measures that could be prescribed in case of political tension. I gave the order to revise and update this document. This revision gave birth to two very detailed memoranda, dated April 4, 1914, aimed on the one hand at the measures to be directed to the commanders of the army corps, and on the other hand those to be taken directly by the Minister. One will see in the continuation of this work that, during the period of political tension at the end of July, a whole series of these measures were put into effect; the others seemed likely to give ammunition to our adversaries; they were not applied. I merely note here that Germany did not show the same scruples.

I have already indicated that our system of fortifications, in spite of several deficiencies, was in a state to contribute effectively to the coverage of the concentration and deployment of the field armies; but I also said that our fortified system was insufficient to ensure the passage of our armies. I was led to indicate in what way I had resolved this question by calling upon the resources of improvised fortifications. A well reasoned inventory of the elements of our fortified system appeared essential; moreover, the attention of the public was focused at this time on all that interested our military organization, and polemics were engaged on this subject in the Parliament and in the press. I therefore resolved to review in detail each of our various strongholds, and to determine those among them on which it would be appropriate to concentrate our efforts and the funding which would be granted to us. I had, consequently, a thorough study of the question, the goal being to establish the general basis of the fortified positions in favorable conditions for our operations. This study concerned not only our northeast and north borders, but also the secondary borders of the Alps, the Pyrenees and the coasts.

On February 21, 1914, the result of this study was submitted to me with regard to the northeast frontier; it concluded that there would be an advantage from the point of view of operations:

1. To organize a fortified region including the three major positions of Toul, Frouard and Saint-Nicolas-Tonnoy south of Nancy;

2. To the south of this region, to extend the defenses of the Épinal plain as far as the Durbion, and to rehabilitate the Mont Bart fort south of Belfort;

3. To the north of the Nancy region, to reclaim the Girouville-Jouy complex; to extend the Verdun position as far as Haudiomont by means of an outpost on the Blusses plateau; to create a position at Montmédy to serve as a pivot for the transition that our left wing would have to make if the conditions allowing us to enter Belgium were met.

Improvised positions should be organized in front of the Charmes forest and on the Hauts-de-Meuse.

The forts of the Jura south of Pontarlier, the fort of Longwy, the entrenched camp of Lille were proposed for decommissioning. As far as Lille was concerned, it seemed that, due to its

Chapter X

topographical situation, this city did not lend itself to the establishment of an entrenched camp that could be shot on all sides, and did not allow for any maneuvers.

After a detailed study of the needs of the various positions, I decided to submit this program to the Superior Council of War. Its members were, for this purpose, convened for July 21, 1914 in the office of the Minister of War. The agenda of the session included: the situation of the defense of the great fortifications, the examination of the new siege and fortress artillery materiel, the use of the artillery in the defense and the use of airplanes in the theaters of war.

But already the war was thundering; more immediate concerns were on our minds. It was the same day that the preliminary notices of mobilization were delivered across Germany...

It remains for me to say a word about the members of the Superior Council of War who were to share under my orders the responsibility of the conduct of operations.

At the beginning of 1914, the Superior Council of War was composed of Generals Gallieni, Archinard, Michel (Governor of Paris), Chomer, Laffont de Ladébat, de Langle de Cary, Dubail, Sordet, Ruffey, de Currières de Castelnau; Generals Belin and Legrand, both Deputy Chiefs of Staff, were the reporters of the Council.

I had known General Gallieni, under whose orders I had served in Madagascar, for a long time. During the maneuvers, during the training exercises or on the map, the very favorable opinion that I had of his military talents was confirmed. A methodical approach, a great deal of calm, a great prudence, a luminous intelligence, a very clear understanding of the tasks that were entrusted to him, a concern pushed to the extreme not to interfere in the command of his subordinates, such were the essential characteristics of General Gallieni. In all circumstances, he had given proof that he could be entrusted with the most important commands in complete safety. The confidence that he inspired in me, as well as the confidence that his subordinates showed him, were in my eyes sure guarantees that he would show himself to be equal to his glorious past in all circumstances. No one seemed to me more capable of taking, if necessary, the supreme direction of operations. On my suggestion, he received a letter of service designating him as my eventual replacement in the command-in-chief of the Northeast Army Group.

General Gallieni had been in command of the troops which, in wartime, were to become the 5th Army for three years when he reached the age limit on April 24, 1914.

At my suggestion, he was replaced in the Superior Council of War and in the eventual command of the 5th Army by General Lanrezac, about whom I will speak in my account of the first weeks of the war.

Suffice it to say for the moment that my attention had long been drawn to General Lanrezac by the high qualities of intelligence, activity, initiative, and sense of maneuver that he had demonstrated during the work on the map and the exercises in the field. No one seemed to me better prepared than him for the command of the 5th Army, the one whose maneuver would be the most delicate, the one to which an essentially variable role would devolve according to the circumstances.

The other armies were entrusted:

The 1st, to General Dubail, a handsome, faithful and solid soldier, a disciplined and conscientious leader;

The 2nd to General de Castelnau. He had participated, as I said, in all the studies of Plan XVII, of which he had been one of the principal craftsmen. His reputation as a maneuverer had designated him in my eyes for the command of this army destined to attack in Lorraine between the Vosges and Metz;

The 3rd to General Ruffey, whose reputation as an artilleryman was firmly established. He was a brilliant mind, very imaginative, whose qualities as a technician would be usefully employed in the operations that his army would probably have to carry out in the Metz region;

Finally, the 4th Army was entrusted to General de Langle de Cary. He was an upright and firm character, disciplined, full of authority, animated to a very high degree by a sense of responsibility. He could be trusted with the greatest of confidence. So, when in June 1914, he had to be transferred to the reserve, I ensured that he still kept his letter of command. The noble attitude

Chapter X

and the high qualities that he displayed at the head of the 4th Army in the first months of the war, then as commander of the army group of the center, from the end of 1915 to the middle of 1916, proved that this confidence was well placed.

General Valabrègue, commander of the 3rd Army corps, entered the Superior Council of War to replace General de Langle. He received a letter of command for the group of reserve divisions, which, upon mobilization, was to meet in the Vervins-Hirson region behind the left of our position.

General Sordet, the only cavalryman on the Superior Council of War, was given command of the cavalry corps that was to screen the left of our armies in the region of Mézières.

General Archinard was given command of the group of reserve divisions which was to operate on the right of our armies, and to be concentrated initially in the Vesoul region.

Finally, General Laffont de Ladébat was appointed Director of the Rear.

Part II – 1914: The War of Movement

Chapter I

The last days before the war. July 24 – August 2, 1914.

In the evening of Friday, July 24, 1914, Mr. Messimy, who had become Minister of War again for three months, called me. He seemed preoccupied, and announced to me that the same afternoon the German ambassador, Mr. de Sohoen, had read to Mr. Bienvenu-Martin a note in which the German government approved entirely the Austrian ultimatum addressed to Serbia. This note, marking the very clear will of Germany to support Vienna, was considered worrying by the French government and obliged it to anticipate, added the Minister, that we might have to go to war. The habit of continually thinking about the preparation of the war made me consider this dreaded eventuality without surprise. So, I answered simply: "Well! Mr. Minister, we will do it, if it is necessary."

It is to be supposed that my attitude had the gift of calming the Minister, because he came to me, without concealing his emotion, shook my hand energetically and said: "Bravo!" Then, both of us, as quietly as possible, examined the first measures that would have to be taken if the threat of war became clear.

What made our situation very delicate was the absence of the government: the President of the Republic and the President of the Council, Minister of Foreign Affairs, were in Russia. The members of the cabinet who remained in Paris had a heavy responsibility as a result.

So I am obliged to say that a certain nervousness reigned in the official spheres during these few days.

Saturday, July 25. – So it was that on July 25, at 10:00 p.m., as soon as the Minister of War learned of the rupture of relations between Serbia and Austria, he had his chief of staff, General Guillaumat, send directly, and without consulting me, a telegram giving the order to recall the generals and commanders absent from their garrisons.

Sunday, July 26. – When I learned, the next morning, of this decision of the Minister, I considered it necessary, in order to clarify my responsibilities, to remind the Minister that there was a document fixing in chronological order the various measures to be taken in case of political tension. This document had been carefully considered, composed in a calm manner, taking the question as a whole, in order to protect us from any necessarily faulty improvisation. Also, when, before the Cabinet Council which was held on the 26th at 11:00 a.m. at the Foreign Office, I was received by the Minister of War, I took the liberty of insisting firmly with him on the necessity of putting us in the hands of the strict execution of the various measures foreseen in Annexes II and II bis to the *Instruction on the Preparation for Mobilization.*[*] Mr. Messimy was willing to understand the feeling that impelled me to claim my share of responsibility, and he willingly admitted the need to follow the urgent order of the document of whose existence I had just reminded him. And I can say that from that moment on, the Minister did nothing without consulting me.

During the night of the 25th to the 26th and in the morning of the 26th, disturbing news had reached us. In particular, we had learned that the German officers on leave in Switzerland had been

---

[*] This Instruction, dated February 15, 1909, was updated on April 4, 1914.

recalled by telegraph and that the guarding of major structures had been set up throughout the empire. I asked the Minister to apply all the first precautionary measures planned, namely:

1. To postpone the planned movement of troops;
2. Suspend leave of absence for officers and troops;
3. Recall all officers on leave;
4. Recall all non-commissioned officers and soldiers on leave.

Mr. Messimy left me to go to the Council of Cabinet and to propose the adaptation of these measures. He came out of it at half past noon; he informed me at once that the Council had approved the first three measures; as for the fourth, the Council had estimated that because of the very great number of leaves for harvest that there was then, and of the reaction that their recall would produce across the country, it was appropriate to wait to learn for certain if, as it was announced to us from Switzerland, the Germans had already adopted similar measures.

The staff of the army immediately sent out the orders carrying out the first three measures; I had at the same time urgently recalled to Paris General d'Amade, the eventual commander of the army of the Alps, and his staff, then on a trip of study and inspection in the Alps. The railroad companies and the administration of the State railroads received in the evening a first notice concerning the dispositions to be taken. The Minister of the Interior was at the same time asked to take certain safety measures, and to invite the prefects to act confidentially on the press in order to obtain from it silence and discretion on our military preparations.

Monday, July 27. – The next day, July 27, we received a dispatch from our military attaché in Vienna dated the day before; according to his information, the 7 Austro-Hungarian army corps closest to Serbia and Romania seemed to be fully mobilized; in addition, those in Vienna and Gratz were partially mobilized: in total, 23 infantry divisions were ready for war, without the mobilization order having been issued. On the other hand, Austro-Hungarian military circles boasted about the support of Germany. It seemed as if we were sliding down a slope that would inevitably lead to war.

As far as we were concerned, it was enough to continue to apply the various measures planned, but it was important to take them without delay; now, among these, the recall of the volunteers had not been able to obtain the assent of the government the day before. It was only on the evening of the 27th, at about 6 p.m., that I was able to obtain the Minister's authorization to telegraphically order this measure in the border army corps and in the military government of Paris; around midnight, the measure was extended to the other army corps and to the division of Tunisia. We had just learned that the garrisons of Alsace-Lorraine were consigned and, in characteristic detail, that the "war collections" had been distributed in these garrisons.

Among the measures planned, there was one of a special nature which required a governmental decision: it was to know if it was appropriate to leave all the troops of Morocco, both Western and Eastern, grouped under the command of the residing general, or to withdraw the troops from the borders and attach them to the 19th Army Corps, with a view to their repatriation to the continent. Mr. Messimy submitted the question to the Council of Ministers, which decided that the maximum number of combatants compatible with the security of our North African possessions would be taken from Morocco and Algeria.

The turn that events were taking left me with few illusions: we were going to war and Russia was going to be dragged along with us. My first thought was therefore to tighten the link with our allies, and I asked the Minister that, by all possible means, we insist to the government of Petersburg that the Russian armies, in accordance with our agreements, take the offensive in East Prussia without delay, if the conflict was unleashed. We know the importance of this offensive attitude that we had requested from our allies, and that they had promised us. Our military attaché and, I was told, our ambassador were requested to ask the Russian General Staff if we could count on them, indicating the importance we attached to their offensive in combination with ours. The answer to our request was the announcement, when the war was declared, of the Russian attack.

Improvised lunch in a forest post in the forest of Villers-Cotterets

On the road from Montmirail to Chalons, General Joffre has lunch with his staff officers. To the right, Lieutenant Tardieu.

Tuesday, July 28. – The great concern of the French government was not to do anything that was not, so to speak, replicating a measure taken in Germany. This sort of timidity was largely the result of the absence of the head of the government. However, under the pressure of circumstances, the necessary measures were taken little by little. Thus, during the night of the 27th to the 28th, the order was given to recall by road or by rail the troops of the interior army corps absent from their garrisons.

In the morning of the 28th, we learned successively that the mobilization order had been proclaimed in Austria, and that the first day of mobilization in the Austro-Hungarian Empire was the 28th of July. This information transmitted by the French military attaché in Vienna was confirmed by a telegram sent from St. Petersburg to the Russian military attaché in Paris.

On the other hand, information from various sources confirmed that work was being done on the armament of the fortifications of Metz and Thionville, at least on the left bank of the Moselle (extension of the wire networks, installation of external batteries, distribution of supplies, etc.).[*]

At the same time it was confirmed from various sides that the German volunteers had been ordered to return to their corps; a number of reservists had even been summoned to Alsace-Lorraine.

But the most important piece of information was a dispatch from our ambassador in Berlin, Mr. Cambon, dated July 21 and communicated with an inexplicable delay to the War Ministry: "I have been assured, moreover," said Mr. Cambon in his dispatch,

---

[*] We knew that the German mobilization plan specified that in case of political tension, the delivery of all shipments was subject to the authorization of the commanders of army corps or naval stations, that the transport of certain goods was suspended and in particular that of foodstuffs, ammunition, fuel for cars, etc. Now, we know for sure that, from July 26, the transport of cereals to Switzerland had been stopped by order of the government; similar measures had been taken during the political tension of 1911. The transport of grain up the Rhine to Switzerland had been stopped.

We thus had proof that the German government had implemented the measures expected in the event of political tension regarding restrictions on the free movement of goods, as well as those concerning the withdrawal of railroad equipment, the recall of leave-holders and of troops on the move.

"that, as of now, the preliminary notices of mobilization, which must put Germany on guard during periods of tension, have been sent here to the classes which must receive them in such cases. This is a measure which the Germans, given their habits, can resort to without exposing themselves to indiscretions and without disturbing the population. It is not sensational in character, and is not necessarily followed by actual mobilization, as we have already seen, but it is no less significant."

One can understand the importance of this information. Thus, for at least seven days, the Germans had been applying their plan of measures in case of political tension, without us having been able to know it by our normal means of investigation. In this way, our adversaries were able to achieve an almost complete mobilization, since their army corps were constantly maintained at a strength close to the war footing. We were thus entitled to fear that, suddenly, without declaration of war, in favor of diplomatic discussions, and taking advantage of their advance, they would carry out a sudden strike against our advanced positions. Remember that this fear had been a major factor in the decision taken in France, a few months before, to reinforce the coverage.

Until then, we had only taken passive precautionary measures. Now we had to implement our convergence system. I argued to the Minister that the security of the country required us to take this step without delay. Mr. Messimy considered that we did not yet have sufficiently clear indications to justify such a measure; he thought that it would be interpreted in France and abroad as a bellicose demonstration likely to poison diplomatic discussions; moreover this measure appeared so serious to him that he decided to reserve it and to await the return of the two presidents before taking a decision.

Wednesday, July 29. – Expected in the morning of the 29th, Mr. Poincaré and Mr. Viviani did not arrive at the Gare du Nord until 1:30 pm. It was at the Council of Ministers held at the Élysée from 5:30 p.m. to 7:00 p.m. that the question of the coverage was examined. On the proposal of Mr. Messimy, the government decided to wait a few more hours. But the illusion that some people still nourished to see the things turning in a favorable way was not to be of long duration any more. In fact, that very night, Mr. Isvolsky came to announce to Mr. Viviani that Mr. Sazonoff had received notification of the German decision to mobilize its armed forces the same day, around 3:00 p.m., if Russia did not cease its military preparations. Moreover, a telegram sent by our ambassador from St. Petersburg had come, a short time later, to confirm this news, adding that the Russian government had decided to order the mobilization of the thirteen army corps intended to operate against Austria.

Thus, despite the continuation of diplomatic negotiations, it was obvious to anyone who had not been warned that the situation was suddenly taking on a very serious character. Also, as soon as they received this news, the President of the Council, the Ministers of War and of the Navy went to the Élysée Palace to study in Council "the measures that France would take if Germany mobilized in turn."

For me, it seemed extremely dangerous to temporize thus; the war now appeared inevitable: we had learned on this day, the 29th, that the Austrian transport of its concentration would begin on July 30, and that the forward march of the Austro-Hungarian army would occur probably in the course of the following week; on the other hand the army corps stationed in Bohemia (8th and 9th Corps) were in full mobilization.

In Germany, the series of regulatory measures of political tension continued to unfold: covering measures were taken along the entire border of Alsace and Lorraine, the railroads were militarily guarded in the vicinity of stations and major structures since the evening of the 28th; important requisitions of flour had been made in Metz and Strasbourg, and orders for individual recalls of reservists multiplied. Nothing, however, suggested that an entire class had been recalled; but information from a reliable source made us fear that a sort of secret mobilization was being carried out in the face of Russia.

Knowing the methodical spirit of the Germans was enough to understand that all these measures, which were part of the plan to be applied in the event of political tension, would inevitably lead the German Empire towards this war that William II announced to King Albert in November 1913. One can imagine with what

Chapter I

anxiety, convinced that the war was imminent, I followed the preparations of our possible adversaries, those of our allies, the development of the events, the grouping of the forces, and the slightest indications which reached us.

My anxiety turned more than ever to Belgium. What would its attitude be? King Albert had given too many proofs of his loyalty to the Allied cause for it to be impossible to say today that, because of his family ties and his form of mind, one could fear that he would turn towards our enemies. On the other hand, the powerful Belgian Catholic party was Germanophile. The influence of this party could have a considerable weight on the decision of the Belgian government. It will be the eternal honor of the king to have so perfectly translated the aspirations of his people by siding with us. The fact remains that on that date of July 29, we still knew nothing of the Belgian intentions. However, we learned that all the volunteers had been recalled, that the Scheldt forts were still being armed and that Antwerp was being actively prepared for defence. On the other hand, no special activity was reported either in Namur or in Liège.

From England, we learned by a letter from our military attaché that the War Office had not yet taken any action as of the 26th; the troops were still in camp and the Home Fleet was maintained in Portland, where the naval maneuvers had just ended.

In Italy, it did not seem that the naval army had made any particular provision; on the other hand, the troops absent from their garrisons had received the order to return there; moreover, the rumor began to circulate of the recall of the last two classes.

However, the prospect of war, despite the precautions taken not to alarm public opinion, was beginning to be felt in the country. As proof of this, I need only refer to the approach made to the War Ministry on the 29th by M. Deviès, Head of Service at Creusot. He came, in the name of Mr. Schneider, to make the following communication: "Creusot has artillery equipment ready to be shipped immediately to various powers (Serbia, Italy, Rumania, Greece, Peru); we wish to know if we should delay the delivery of this equipment or accelerate it, or even if the French government would not have the desire to requisition all or part of this equipment. He also wishes to give indications on all the facilities he can place at the disposal of the war. Mr. Schneider, returning to Paris that evening, will place himself at the disposal of General Joffre as of tomorrow."

Thursday, July 30. – On the morning of July 30, Mr. Schneider came in person to the Minister's office, where I was. I remember that in the course of the conversation, I said to the director of Creusot: "Guns will be, indeed, very useful to us; but, above all, we need ammunition. It is necessary that the metallurgical factories start to work immediately." I had, moreover, the impression that my appeal did not produce immediate effects. I will have the opportunity to return to this important matter in a later chapter of these recollections.

The night of July 29 to 30 brought us information that clearly confirmed our predictions concerning the preparation of the Germans for war. On the one hand, the reinforcement of the coverage was certain: in Fontoy, in Moyeuvre, in Saint-Privat, in Verneville and Gorze, in Novéant and in Delme, in Château-Salins and in Dieuze, in the south of Sarrebourg, in the valleys of the Bruche and Oderen, we were informed that the positions were occupied and reinforced by field works; patrols were pushed to the border; in all the fortifications along the border, the various complementary works of mobilization had begun: deforestation, construction of batteries, planting of wire networks; in the rear, troops had come to reinforce during the day of the 29th the garrisons of Cologne, Trier, Sarrebourg and Strasbourg; the railway stations were militarily occupied, the telegraph offices reinforced, the roads leading to France were blocked, travelers were carefully questioned, automobiles circulated only with permits.

In short, we were monitoring step by step, in the very order that we knew about, the course of the precautionary measures that the Germans had planned in a report that had come into our possession. We could not therefore doubt, as far as we were concerned, the fatal outcome of these preparations. It was this certainty that the Germans, with their methodical spirit, were applying their program point by point, which gave me the conviction of the inevitability of war, and showed me the need to

Chapter I

prepare ourselves without delay.

However, in the face of this threatening situation, we had hardly carried out any defensive measures, since the establishment of the coverage had not yet been approved by the government. When I saw Mr. Messimy on the morning of the 30th, I insisted again on the absolute necessity for the government to take this decision. He went to the Council of Ministers where he informed his colleagues of my insistence. The session was very long; after several hours of deliberation, the Minister finally informed me that, for fear of doing a disservice to the cause of peace, the Council had authorized the establishment of the covering troops with the following reservations: only units that could reach their location by road would move; no movement by rail was authorized. No call-up of reservists was to be made for the time being; no recourse was to be had to requisitions; the army would have to obtain the additional horses it needed by informal purchase. Finally, the covering troops were to be kept at 10 kilometers from the border to prevent any contact between German and French patrols.

When the Minister communicated these decisions to me, I protested strongly against the non-convocation of the reservists and against the limitation of the coverage to troops moving by road only; I informed him that this half measure was insufficient to protect us from a forceful strike directed against our border. As far as the 10 kilometer buffer was concerned, I made few objections, understanding the reasons that had motivated it, considering moreover that this measure was not of a nature to compromise either our mobilization or subsequent operations. My objections were without effect; the decision had been taken in the Council of Ministers; Mr. Messimy could not disregard it on his own authority. All that I could obtain was that the troops to be embarked would be brought closer to the stations. In addition, I pointed out that the obligation to withdraw to 10 kilometers from the border was too rigid, and I obtained the authorization to draw myself the line not to exceed.

It was around 5 p.m. that the Minister signed the order to set up the cover assigned to the 2nd, 6th, 7th, 20th and 21st Army corps, shortly after he had learned from the prefect of Nancy of the violation of the border at Xures.

After several reworkings, the order sent out was as follows:

Carry out preparatory measures for operations No. 24 mobilization of the frontier garrisons referred to in Annex II to Instruction February 15, 1909;
This measure will also apply to all garrisons in your corps.
Until further notice, and except in the case of a sudden attack, no call-up of reservists shall be made.
Covering troops moving by rail will be ready to embark. Troops moving by road to provide cover will move to their intended locations without delay in the event of a sudden attack. However, for diplomatic reasons, it is essential that no incident occurs on our part. Consequently, no element or patrol should, under any circumstances, approach the border, nor exceed the line (Hussigny excluded) Mercy-le-Haut, Murville, Mainville, Anoux, Lubey, Abbeville, Labry, Jarny, Friauville, Brainville, Hannonville-au-Passage, Sponville, Xonville, Dampvitoux, Rambercourt-sur-Mad, Villcey-sur-Trey, Pont-à-Mousson, Atton, Sainte-Geneviève, Lixières, Mont-Toulon, Mont-Saint-Jean, La Rochette, Grand-Mont d'Amance, La Neuvelotte, Remereville, Bauzemont, la Neuville-aux-Bois, Blemerey, Domèvre, Bremenil, Allarmont, Moussey, Senones, Saint-Jean d'Ormont, Neuvillers-sur-Fave, Laveline, Fraise, Grand-Valtin, Longemer, la Bresse, Cornimont, Bussang, Saint-Maurice, Ballon de Servance, Giromagny, Etuefont Haut, Saint-Germain, Fontenelle and Charmois.

The information received in the afternoon of the 30th only confirmed the information we already had concerning the establishment of the German cover. At the same time, we learned of the departure of the German fleet from Kiel towards the east. From Austria, we learned that, since July 28, the mobilization of 8 army corps was in full progress and that the first concentration transports were to begin on the 30th. From Belgium, it was confirmed that the volunteers had been recalled and that they were mainly occupied with the defense of Antwerp, without any activity being reported either in Namur or in Liège; finally, the last three classes seemed to have to be recalled. From Italy, we were informed that the spirit of the nation seemed to be opposed to a military intervention on the side of Austria, and that the last events had, on the contrary, brought about a strong movement in our favor. Four classes of reservists were recalled for August 1st.

Chapter I

In short, on the 30th, comparing the measures taken in France and those that we knew had already been taken in Germany (which constituted a minimum), we noted that, if in France and in Germany the volunteers and the troops absent from their garrisons had been recalled and if the major structures were in both countries safe from attack, on the other hand, Germany had taken a strong lead by the following measures:

Reinforced coverage arrangements for the VIIIth, XVIth, XXIth and XVth Corps;
Installation near the border of covering troops engaged in the creation of field fortifications, and installation of batteries;
Armament of the border forts, deforestation, construction of intermediate and external batteries, wire networks, distribution of ammunition, reinforcement of material;
Recall of reservists by individual call-up;
Recall of reservists from classes 1903 to 1911, living abroad;
Summoning of reserve officers:
Stations occupied by the military;
Roads of France blocked and guarded.

The chances of war now seemed so numerous, that I decided to gather, without further delay, the nucleus of my future general headquarters, and, in particular, to gather the officers of the Bureau of Operations; in this way, they could monitor developments from the outset. It was thus on July 30 that I summoned the officers who were to be part of it, and it was the next day, July 31, in the Salle des Maréchaux of the Ministry of War, that it began to function. General Berthelot, Aide-Major in charge of operations, had under his command Colonel Pont and a certain number of officers among whom Maurin, Brécard, Fétizon, Bel, Alexandre and Buat.

Friday July 31. – The whole morning of the 31st was devoted to a long Council of Ministers, which lasted from 9 a.m. to noon; it was only a question of the financial measures envisaged in view of the serious events which one saw approaching.

However, it was obvious that the negotiations were definitely going badly, and I was anxious to see the whole coverage in place at last, while waiting for the total mobilization which could not be delayed any longer. I knew that Mr. Viviani was still hesitating; on the other hand, Mr. Poincaré seemed more determined to make these necessary decisions.

At about 2 p.m., we heard the news of the ultimatum sent by Germany to Russia on July 29 in the afternoon.

Under these conditions, my duty was to clearly inform the government of its responsibilities. I thus wrote a note which stated the last information received; I handed this note at 3:30 p.m. to the Minister of War as he was leaving for the Council of Ministers, asking him to inform the Council of it; the note read as follows:

> The measures taken so far follow far behind similar measures taken by the Germans, especially in the last forty-eight hours.
>
> They are still going on. Not content with having set up the covering elements on the entire border, the bulk of the VIIIth, XVIth, XXIst, XVth and XIVth Corps were brought together near the border; on the other hand, troop movements by rail, coming from the territories of the XIth and XVIIIth Corps, seem to indicate a reinforcement of the coverage.
>
> Calls for reservists have occurred, and horse purchases and requisitions are happening all over.
>
> In the present state of affairs, it is no longer possible for us to proceed with the application of new detailed measures other than those already ordered, without bringing about a profound disturbance in the planned arrangements for covering troops and mobilization, particularly with regard to the railroad service. If the state of tension continues, and if the Germans, under the cover of diplomatic conversations, continue the application of their mobilization plan, the execution of which they continue by avoiding pronouncing its name, it is absolutely necessary for the government to know that from this evening, any delay of twenty-four hours in calling up the reserves and sending the telegram to provide coverage will result in a setback of our concentration, that is to say, in the initial abandonment of a part of our territory from 15 to 20 kilometers per day of delay.
>
> The commander in chief cannot accept this responsibility.

At the same time as I handed in this note, I stressed it strongly to the Minister: I explained to him the repercussions that any delay in the first coverage transports would inevitably bring in the concentration transports; I reminded him that all our information concurred to show that the German troops from the interior were pouring in non-stop towards the border, that the German employees of the stations on the French border were recalled, that the automobiles passing from France to Germany were stopped and seized, that the telephone communications across the border were suppressed, that the railroads were occupied at Pagny, Avricourt and Montreux-Vieux and the French locomotives seized. The Minister recognized that the order to start the coverage could not be delayed any longer, and that the government could only face the facts. I immediately gathered the heads of the offices concerned by this measure, and I gave them my instructions. In particular, all the services of the railroads were to be informed immediately to have to proceed to the assembly of the trains and to their sending to the points of embarkation.

The Council of Ministers met at 5 p.m. and considered my note. This time, Mr. Viviani approved it. This was at 5:15. However, the Council of Ministers decided to grant only half of my requests: while I was finally authorized to send the telegram intended to set up the cover, I was refused the authorization to recall the reservists. In any case, it was exactly 5:40 pm when the telegram was sent: "Dispatch covering troops. The starting time is 9 p.m." I confess that I felt a great relief at that moment.

It was time. Shortly after this telegram was sent, the German ambassador, Mr. de Schoen, went to the Quai d'Orsay and announced to Mr. Viviani that the emperor had decided that very day at noon to declare a state of threat of war. In addition, he announced the general mobilization of Russia, and asked what France's attitude would be in the event of a conflict between Germany and Russia.

On learning this serious news, I insisted once again to the Minister of War that the decision of general mobilization be taken immediately; it seemed to me urgent. Mr. Messimy promised me to persist with the Council which met in the evening.

Indeed, at 9 p.m. a new Council of Ministers – the third of the day – met. While it was taking place, the assassination of Jaurès was discovered. This monstrous attack made us fear unrest, and I immediately received the order from the government to counter-order the embarkation of the *cuirassiers'* brigade of Paris. The First Cavalry Division, to which this brigade belonged, thus embarked for the border with only two brigades. The next day, thanks to the wisdom of the population, it was certain that order would not be disturbed: the approach of danger had restored the unity of all the French. Consequently, it was decided that the *cuirassiers* brigade would embark on August 2 to join its cavalry division.

As for the question that concerned me, that of the order for general mobilization, it was now too late for the first day to be set before midnight on August 2. The Council of Ministers thus resolved to wait a few more hours, while giving me the assurance that, if no improvement occurred in the situation, the order would be given before 4:00 p.m., the extreme limit allowing it to be transmitted in the evening to the most distant districts, and to ensure its execution the next morning. I obtained the authorization of the Minister to send a preparatory order to all the army corps, which left on August 1 at one o'clock in the morning, thus written: "Presumably, the mobilization order will be launched today, August 1, in the afternoon. Proceed immediately with all internal operations of a nature to facilitate mobilization."

Saturday, August 1. – The situation was now so serious that it did not seem possible that things could be resolved. It was thus indispensable now to mobilize the army, that is to say to recall the reservists. I judged it necessary to inform the government of the situation and to make it aware of the responsibilities that it would incur by delaying the call-up of the reservists. I wrote, consequently, a second note that I gave on August 1 at 9 o'clock in the morning to the Minister to inform him of the state of the situation:

> The serious inconveniences pointed out yesterday concerning the delay in the departure of the covering troops become even more apparent if the order for general mobilization is delayed. The German preparations continue, in fact, according to a well established plan, the basis of which we know, according to a report which reached our hands written by the German General Staff. It is said in particular "that one will be able to proceed on simple notice and without waiting

Chapter I

for the order of mobilization, to a discreet mobilization of the personnel and complementary materiel, by convocation of reservists and by purchase or requisition of horses, so as to be able to start the war transports of the army corps of the interior as of reception of the order of mobilization; that the discreet preparation of the mobilization, the arrangements made for the concentration, the transports, the security measures (publication of the law on the requisitions before the beginning of the mobilization) and the rapid execution of the strategic transports, assure us of advantages that it will be difficult for the armies of other nations to achieve to the same extent; that the goal towards which it is necessary to tend is to take the offensive with a great superiority, as of the first days; the provisions adopted in this direction make it possible to hope that the offensive can be taken upon the complete concentration of the army of the Lower Rhine. An ultimatum at short notice, which must immediately be followed by invasion, will sufficiently justify our action from the point of view of the law of nations..." etc.

All of this is becoming clearer from the information received:

Five classes of reservists are called for August 2 at the latest; requisitions and purchases of horses began as early as July 30, perhaps earlier.

We can therefore say that: on August 4, even without a mobilization order, the German army will be fully mobilized, already achieving an advance of forty-eight hours and perhaps three days over ours.

By handing this note to the Minister, I showed him once again the imperative need to order the mobilization. Indeed, our mobilization cannot be done little by little, underhandedly so to speak, as with the Germans: it was done all at once. When I left the Minister, I reminded him that the last deadline for giving the order of general mobilization would expire at 4 o'clock in the evening. Giving me the assurance that he would be my ardent interpreter with the government, Mr. Messimy left to go to the Council of Ministers.

This meeting lasted until noon. While it was taking place, it was learned that the Italian government had decided to remain neutral in case of conflict, remaining faithful to the secret Prinetti-Delcassé convention of 1902. As soon as this important news reached me, that is to say, around 10 a.m., I had additional instructions sent to the 14th and 15th Corps, instructing them that, if general mobilization was ordered, the covering troops of the southeast would remain in their mobilization locations, ready to be shipped to the northeast.

It was also during this Council that Mr. Viviani went to receive the German ambassador, who had brought forward the appointment he had requested the day before. When he returned to take his place among his colleagues, Mr. Viviani did not realize that, despite the vague assurances given by Mr. de Schoen, he agreed with me and was ready, in the presence of the dangerous German preparations, to sign the order for general mobilization. However, in order to preserve the possibility of an arrangement until the last minute, the President of the Council asked the Minister of War to keep this order in his hands until the extreme time limit which would allow the first day of mobilization to be set for midnight on August 2.

The order was signed by Messrs. Poincaré, Viviani, Augagnaeur and Messimy and entrusted to the latter.

At 3:30 pm., the fatal hour having arrived, I sent general Ebener to seek it. At 3:55 p.m., the prepared telegrams were deposited at the central office of the posts and telegraphs of the street of Grenelle and sent immediately in all France: "The first day of the mobilization is Sunday August 2."

Shortly afterwards, I communicated the mobilization order to the 4th Bureau, so that it was immediately transmitted to the network commissions.

Almost immediately afterwards, out of a scruple of conscience no doubt, the Minister asked me to recall the formal prohibition for all detachments to cross the line that I had fixed on July 30. The same evening, around 10 o'clock, on the express request of the President of the Republic,[*] the same recommendation was made again in the most imperative form; it was specified that whoever crossed this line would be liable to the Council of War. It was indeed a question of not giving the English any pretext to withhold

---

[*] It had, in fact, come back to the ears of the President that a squadron of uhlans and a squadron of mounted chasseurs had come face to face in the sector of the 20th Corps.

Chapter I

their collaboration from us.

In this Council held in the morning of August 1st, a question of the highest importance had been raised. It concerned the attitude that we would have to hold towards Belgium in the event of war. The assurance that we would respect Belgian neutrality had been given on the afternoon of July 31 by our minister in Brussels to Mr. Davignon, the Belgian foreign minister. Informed of this declaration by Mr. Messimy, I pointed out to the latter that it was too absolute and that it would be necessary to reserve the case where this neutrality would not be respected by Germany. The Council recognized the validity of this observation and gave the order, on August 1, to the Minister of France, Mr. Klobukowski, to declare to the Belgian government that if the French government intended to respect Belgian neutrality, France, in order to ensure its own defense, could be led to modify its attitude, in the event that Belgian neutrality would not be respected by another power.

On the other hand, the question of respect for Luxembourg's neutrality also arose on that same day of August 1. Indeed, Mr. Eyschen, Minister of State in Luxembourg, asked the French government for an assurance of neutrality similar to that which had been given to Belgium. The French government immediately replied that it intended to respect the neutrality of the Grand Duchy. However, the violation of this neutrality by Germany was likely to force France to be motivated from now on by the sole concern of its defense and its interests.

Thus, on the evening of August 1st, at the moment when our general mobilization was about to begin, we were forbidden to take any measure for the concentration of our armies that could lead one to believe that we intended to violate the Belgian and Luxembourg territories. However, if the Germans were to violate these two neutralities, and under the condition that the French government would authorize us to do so, we had to be able to use these new battlefields.

Thus, the most absolute uncertainty hung over our possibilities at that time. It was therefore sufficient for us, for the time being, to let the first transports take place, as stipulated in our plan, which corresponded precisely to the scenario of the non-violation of Belgium and Luxembourg. Moreover, since the first concentration transports were not to begin until August 6, there were still four full days left before we could take the decision to vary the concentration and to move the left wing of our deployment northward.

Such were my dispositions of mind in this evening of August 1 where we learned first that Italy had declared to the German ambassador that it could not take part in the war, if it occurred, because of the aggressive character which it took on because of Germany and Austria, then towards 11 p.m. the declaration of war of Germany to Russia.

It is at this moment that I became aware of the letter in which General Lanrezac explained to me the way in which he envisaged the execution of the mission which was entrusted to him in case of war. In the midst of the events of that important day, this letter appeared to me to be out of place; indeed, it was premature to discuss with one of the army commanders a strategic situation that was not yet clearly defined. After having assumed as probable the eventuality that the German right wing would be directed towards Sedan, General Lanrezac studied the case where it would march on Givet and further north. In this case, "it is clear," he said, "that once the 5th Army was engaged in the direction of Neufchâteau, it would not be able to deal with this last eventuality, which is considered here only for the record."

It should be noted that in this memorandum written by General Lanrezac on July 31, there was no mention of either the English or Belgian forces. In addition, it is known that if I had not thought it necessary to communicate in writing to the army commanders the various forms that our strategic maneuver could take, these had nevertheless been the subject of in-depth studies. In particular, in the scenario envisaged by General Lanrezac, it is recalled that the maneuver was to consist of leading the enemy columns in the region east of Hirson and Maubeuge, while, by a march northward through Belgian Luxembourg, we would strike a blow in the enemy's position, by threatening the communications of its right wing. But it was still too early to make a decision: the grouping of alliances was not yet specified. If we could hope for British assistance, we were not yet certain of it, and only the non-cooperation of the British army could be such as to make us extend our left towards the north.

General Lanrezac's letter, which was undoubtedly intended to draw my attention to a question whose importance had not escaped me, thus remained unanswered.

Chapter II

Mobilization. – The concentration. – Belgium and England enter the war on our side. – The first meetings in Alsace. – August 2-16, 1914.

Sunday August 2. – During the night of August 1st to 2nd, all the telephone and telegraphic communications with Germany were cut; it caused us serious difficulties in knowing what was happening on the other side of the border: it is thus that the morning of the 2nd, we could not acquire the certainty that the order of mobilization had been issued the day before in the evening by Berlin; it was only rather late that we had the confirmation.

The first reports which arrived to me indicated the good continuation of the cover transports. It was now urgent to determine the mission of the troops thus deployed. The question of the 10 kilometers had complicated the situation, because we had had to abandon positions that we would undoubtedly be obliged to recover later through costly battles. However, the general situation seemed to me sufficiently clear for it to be possible to regain a foothold in this forbidden zone. I explained my point of view to the Minister. But, because of the renewed assurances that the French government had given to the cabinets of Brussels and Luxembourg, as well as the uncertainty of the diplomatic situation, Mr. Messimy considered that it was more necessary than ever to have no border

Chapter II 223

incident; it seemed to him only possible to reduce to 2 kilometers the strip of forbidden border. He promised me moreover to submit the question to the Council of Ministers.

Now, at the beginning of the afternoon, the news reached Paris that the French border had been violated in several places, notably at Longwy and near Cirey; in addition, it was learned that thirty-five German cars loaded with German officers and soldiers had entered Luxembourg. These circumstances no doubt seemed decisive to the French government, because at 2:00 p.m., General Belin received a telephone call from the Minister informing him that the government "gave the General Commander-in-Chief *absolute freedom* of movement for the execution of his plans, even if they led to the crossing of the German border."

It was under these conditions that, on the evening of August 2, I sent to all sector commanders the General Instruction for Coverage: it affirmed my intention to take the offensive only with all forces united and specified, in spite of the authorization given to me, that in order to leave to the Germans the entire responsibility of the hostilities, "the coverage should be limited to throwing back beyond the border any attacking troop, without pursuing it further, and without entering into enemy territory."

On the morning of 2 August, the news of the violation of Belgium had reached Paris: if it was confirmed, it was of particular interest, because it seemed to indicate an extension of the enemy action well north of the Verdun area. From the beginning of the afternoon, we received such details on the German forces north of the Thionville-Verdun line, that the violation of the Grand Duchy could no longer be doubted.

Thus, by the will of the enemy, and in accordance with the very terms of our declaration to Mr. Eyschen, a new theater of operations was opened to us; moreover, the presence of elements of the VIIIth German corps reported in the area of Malmédy could suggest that the battlefield of Belgium would undoubtedly not be long in opening up before us. From then on, I foresaw the possibility of the maneuver through Belgium, which had always seemed to me the most advantageous, and of which I had informed the government as early as February 1912. This probability, and in any case, the possibility of acting through Luxembourg now

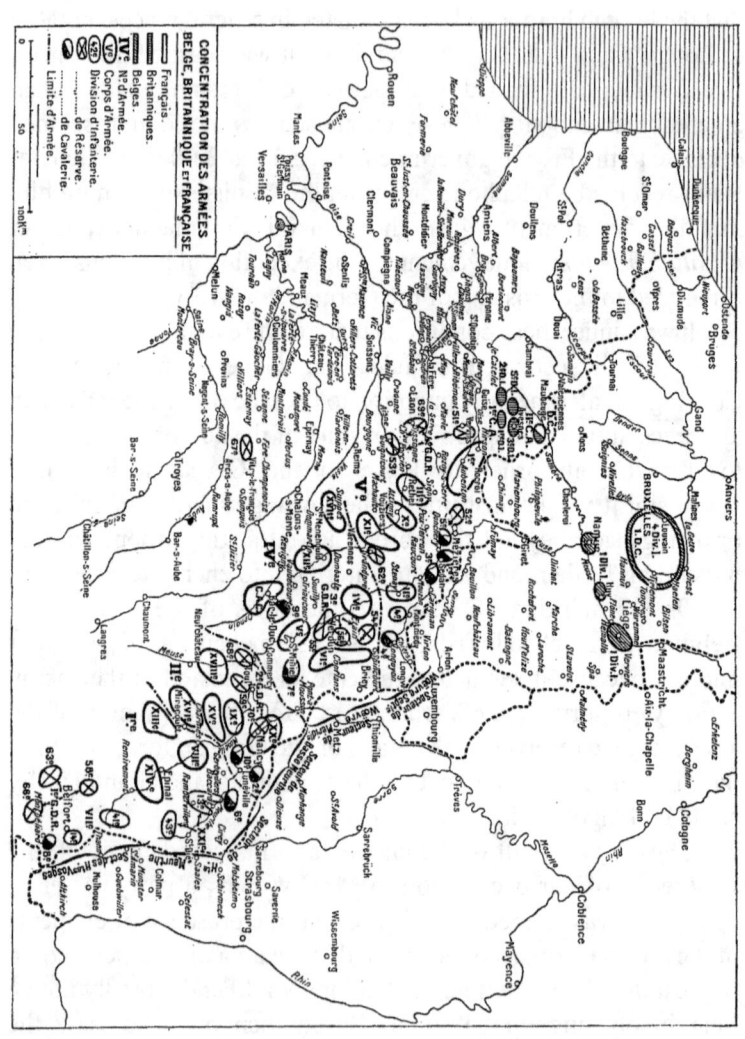

Chapter II

acquired, obviously entailed a modification to the plan of concentration, by moving the center of gravity of our left forces towards the north.

However, it was not possible to move the left of the 5th Army, since it was necessary to reserve for the British the Le Cateau zone which, according to our pre-war conventions, was reserved for them. In these conditions, the only solution, although the concentration transports were not to begin until August 6, was to apply the variant prepared in Plan XVII. The purpose of this decision was, by having the main body of the 5th Army supported on its left, to prepare the entry into the line of the reserve army, the 4th, between the 3rd and 5th Armies, so that it could pass entirely north of Verdun.

From the evening of the 2nd, I gave the order to execute this variant.

This decision had, no doubt, the effect of engaging the use of the main reserve mass at an early date; but, there still remained at my disposal the 44th alpine division and the two Algerian divisions; in addition, the two groups of reserve divisions placed at the wings represented in my eyes available troops; finally, the 67th reserve division remained at the orders of the Minister in the region of Châlons; to increase my reserves, I asked Mr. Messimy for the authorization to dispose of this unit as soon as it was ready: he granted it.

It was again on August 2 that I received a visit from General Galliéni, who had been urgently recalled to Paris. On my recommendation, the President of the Republic had designated him two days before to replace me in case, for some reason, I became unavailable. During this visit, I informed him of this designation of which he had just been the recipient *at my request*, and about which he was not yet aware, telling him my satisfaction of this mark of confidence that he had just received.

Shortly after this visit, the Minister pressed me about the place that General Galliéni should occupy: next to me at the great headquarters or in Paris. I answered that the first solution did not seem to me to be appropriate. I had been Galliéni's subordinate in Madagascar; he had in turn become mine; so that his presence without any definite duties at my headquarters could be awkward for both of us. This did not prevent me from thinking that his firmness of character and his authority over the army commanders would make him an excellent commander-in-chief the day when he would have all the responsibilities of my office and the freedom to choose his advisors. For all these reasons, I made it known to the Minister that I did not want General Galliéni at my side.

Monday, August 3. – The attitude of England never failed to worry us. It seemed that she had promised us the support of her fleet. But how far would this support go? In particular, would our disarmed northern coasts be protected from a landing? This was an important question on which we still had only vague information. So, on the morning of the 3rd, I sent one of my officers[*] to the Ministry of the Navy to get information. He learned that the British fleet had received orders to cover our coasts in the Channel and the North Sea, and that in the Mediterranean, the British fleet, in liaison with ours, was looking for the two German cruisers that had just bombed our coasts in Algeria.

When I received this important news, I no longer had any doubt that England would give us the help we were hoping for, both on land and at sea, for it seemed impossible that, in such a conflict, a country like England would wage war half-heartedly. This was very important to us. Moreover, almost at the same time, I learned of the ultimatum sent the previous evening by Germany to Belgium, as well as the response made by the Belgian government to this insolent threat. It was not difficult to foresee that England would be obliged to intervene in a struggle in which Belgium was thus drawn.

During the afternoon of August 3rd, I gathered the army commanders; they were all present, except for Generals de Castelnau and Ruffey. It was still too early to formally announce my plan to operate in Belgium: too many unknowns remained to be resolved. I limited myself to indicating the main lines of the probable maneuver, that is to say my combination of two attacks, one in Lorraine and the other north of the Verdun-Toul line. In

---

[*] Lieutenant-Colonel Brécard, of the 3rd Bureau of the G.Q.G.

addition, I indicated that the armies on the right and particularly the one destined to act in Lorraine would have as their main mission to hold back as many enemy army corps as possible for the benefit of the action on the left. Finally, I informed the army commanders that, in all probability, the army of Lorraine, the 11th, would have to put two army corps at my disposal to reinforce the action of our left forces.

Tuesday, August 4. – The great unknown was still the international situation, that is to say the consolidation of European forces which was to determine our possibilities of maneuver.

About Russia, we knew, for the moment, almost nothing.

On the morning of the 4th, we learned of the official neutrality of Italy, which was so precious for our transports from Algeria and Morocco. The intervention of England on our side became so probable during the same day that at 5 p.m. the Minister sent instructions to the commanders of Boulogne, Rouen and Le Havre, in anticipation of the landings to be expected in these ports.

On the Belgian side, events were accelerating. The news that the Germans had violated the border had begun to circulate in official circles in Brussels on the evening of the 3rd. But certain reports suggested that the reality of the situation was still being debated, that the supporters of an agreement with the Germans were numerous and powerful in Belgium, and, moreover, it was to be feared that, by means of false news, Germany would try to make us the first to violate Belgian neutrality. The greatest circumspection was therefore still necessary. The rumor was that the Belgians would be just as hostile to our entry into their territory as to the Germans.

If the situation was not yet completely clear on our left, it was not the same on our right. It is known that the directive for the concentration had planned that a portion of the 1st Army would enter Upper Alsace in the general direction of Colmar, and that the order of execution could be given as early as the fourth day of the mobilization. Our maneuver, still undetermined in its form, but already prepared towards the north, was to be helped by this operation in Upper Alsace, which was to have as its goal, if it succeeded, to support the general position on the Rhine and consequently, to allow for an economy of forces on our extreme right as soon as it was covered by the river. It was on the evening of the 5th, that is to say precisely the fourth day of the mobilization, that General Dubail, commander of the 1st Army, was to settle down at his headquarters in Épinal. I therefore signed the order on the evening of the 4th, so that he would receive it as soon as he took command, instructing him to prepare the action in Upper Alsace, which was to be carried out by the 7th Corps and the 8th Cavalry Division; the operation was to be limited first of all to the Thann-Mulhouse front.

Wednesday, August 5. – August 5 was the day set for the opening of the great headquarters and the army headquarters; it was the day when I was to effectively take command of the Northeast Army Group.

On my arrival at the War Ministry, I read the information that had arrived during the night. It seemed certain now that the Belgian border had been violated on the 4th, and that the Germans had reached Verviers. No violation of the border was reported on the Arlon side, while Luxembourg seemed to be completely occupied by the enemy. On the other hand, the mobilization of the Belgian metropolitan forces had been ordered the evening before, the army entering the field under the command of the king; in addition, a series of measures had already been taken in Belgium to slow down the German advance there.

Thus informed, I went to take leave of the Minister at his office; I learned from him that the French planes and airships were authorized to fly over the Belgian territory; the Ministry of Foreign Affairs had just informed him that our cavalry reconnaissances, provided that they were not supported by too vital detachments, could also penetrate Belgium. I immediately took advantage of these authorizations to order the cavalry corps and the 2nd Army corps to intersect as close as possible to the Luxembourg border the roads leaving the Virton-Stavelot front and heading west. Because of the proximity of the German troops in this region, it was indeed urgent to get information on their movements.

Mr. Messimy insisted on accompanying me to Lagny. Near this city, he got out of the car, shook hands with the officers who accompanied me, declared himself optimistic and wished me good luck, without trying to hide his emotion. I left him saying: "Have confidence," and I got back in the car with General Berthelot. At 11 o'clock, we were in Vitry-le-Fràncois, headquarters of the *Grand Quartier Général*.* There I found the officers of my staff who had preceded me the day before by train.

It seems to me useful, given the legends that have been created around the *Grand Quartier Général*, to say a few words about it here.

The *Grand Quartier Général* then had about fifty officers, including all the officers of the services (railroads, quartermaster's office, health, cipher section, mail section, automobiles, command of the headquarters). The bureaus were installed in the college, on the Place Royer-Collard, in front of the church Notre-Dame; I had my office in a study room of the second floor; I was lodged with my orderly officers near there, at the house of a former engineering officer, Mr. Capron, who placed at my disposal his living room in which was installed a cot behind a screen. I took my meals at Mr. Capron's with Generals Belin and Berthelot, Major Gamelin, who was detached to me from the 3rd Bureau, and my two ordinance officers, Captains de Galbert and Muller.

From the beginning, the *Grand Quartier* functioned in the same way as it did throughout the war. There were two briefings per day: the first, called the Grand Briefing, was held in my office in the morning around 7:00 a.m.; the second, in the evening around 8:00 p.m. The Major General, the General Assistants, the Director of the Rear, the heads of the offices and the officers of my cabinet were normally present at the Grand Briefing. At the morning briefing as well as at the evening briefing, I took note of the reports sent by the armies and relating to the events which had taken place in the preceding twelve hours, as well as the information gathered in the same period of time on the enemy. Of course, if important reports or accounts arrived during the day or night, they were immediately presented to me; but, the main interest of the two

---

* Translator's note: This will later be referred to as "G.Q.G." or "General Headquarters."

briefings of the day was to allow us to "take stock." At the morning briefing, the general situation was established, and I often invited the officers present to make their personal observations, after which I fixed my decision.

In these discussions, the personality of General Berthelot did not cease to be emphasized. A powerful mind, an outstanding intelligence, the general had an essential sense of maneuver and organization. However, he himself agreed that difficulties did not always appear to him: "I am so optimistic," he used to tell me, "that I cannot foresee them very well." He also recognized that he had a tendency to mismanage his staff, out of a desire to over-achieve – that is, to do everything by himself.

General Belin was absorbed by the direction and adjustment of the numerous and complex services he was in charge of. The Chief of the Operations Bureau, Colonel Pont, was a conscientious and devoted assistant to us; he was admirably suited to the role he had to fulfill, which consisted essentially in translating into clear orders the decisions I had taken.

Behind these chiefs of staff, there were the bureaus. And I could not, without ingratitude, omit to pay a tribute of gratitude to the officers who composed them: they accomplished a thankless and delicate task, in an atmosphere of absolute work and calm. They had to determine the constantly changing situation of our troops and of the enemy, to organize the execution of the ordered movements, to transmit orders in due time, to ensure supplies of all kinds. They were, in the full sense of the word, good staff officers, that is to say, the helpers of the command; they are entitled to the recognition of the country.

Thursday, August 6. – On arriving at Vitry-le-François, my first concern was to clarify the situation in Belgium. I decided to send to Brussels one of the officers of the G.Q.G., Lieutenant-Colonel Brécard, with the mission of obtaining from the Royal Government the authorization for our troops to enter Belgium, without all the restrictions which were still imposed on us; moreover, he was to advise the Belgian high command that our plan of operations could only be decided upon after our intelligence on the enemy would be sufficient to determine his intentions; from there, it was necessary

Chapter II   231

for us to have as soon as possible a precise estimate of the German forces reported in Belgium. When he arrived in Paris, Lieutenant-Colonel Brécard was to see the President of the Republic, the President of the Council and the Ministers of War and Foreign Affairs in order to inform them of the purpose of his mission.

Hardly had he left Vitry that I received the visit of the Belgian military attaché, Major Gallen; he brought me the news that his government had called the French army to its aid, and that we were given complete freedom to enter Belgian territory. A short time later, a telegram from our Minister of Foreign Affairs confirmed these decisions to me; one can imagine with what satisfaction, after the uncertainties of the preceding days, I welcomed this news. The fog was dissipating and the main maneuver through Belgium, which I had always considered as the most desirable, was going to be able to become a reality. I was anxious to take advantage of the authorization that was given to us. The first information received from Belgium needed to be checked, and I sent, the very same evening, to General Sordet who was in the Sedan area the order to march towards Neufchâteau and to push his exploration in the direction of the east and the northeast up to the main road Laroche-Bastogne-Arlon in order to determine the apparent shape of the enemy and to delay his columns.

At the same time, the diplomatic horizon was gradually clearing up: in the evening, I learned that England had, the same day, declared war on Germany and that the first day of the British mobilization would be August 5.

The reports on the execution of the mobilization and the transports continued to be entirely favorable; for twelve hours, the troops reinforcing the cover had all been deployed without incident. The minister had General Ebener telephone me that the whole country was favorably impressed with the order in which the operations of the mobilization had been carried out: the entire press paid tribute to it, even Mr. Clemenceau.

On the enemy's side, there was nothing clear-cut yet; it did not seem that they were planning a sudden attack at any point. In any case, we had in place now a sufficient cover to give us time to make arrangements, if an incident were to occur.

In Alsace, it did not seem that the 7th Corps and the 8th

Cavalry Division would have to face very serious forces. I therefore fixed the morning of the 7th as the start of our offensive in Upper Alsace. This order seemed premature to the 1st Army; indeed, on the 6th, General Dubail asked me to delay this operation, General Bonneau, commander of the 7th Corps, having expressed fears about his right flank and his rear, and also having reported information indicating the imminent arrival in Alsace of the XIVth Austrian Corps, which had left Innsprück on August 4.

These reasons seemed to me to be of no value: first of all, all the airplane reconnaissance reported an impression of absolute emptiness in the whole Mulhouse-Altkirch-Dannemarie region, while the trains reported on the right bank of the Rhine were all directed towards the north. On the other hand, the information concerning the XIVth Austrian Corps came from Switzerland where the Germans had many agents. Consequently, I sent an order to General Dubail not to modify any of the measures that I had prescribed.

That day, the 6th, was to bring me happy details about the Russian plans. Until then, we had only learned in a doubtful form that Russia intended to put in line the 14 army corps of the Vilna, Warsaw and Moscow districts.

Now, on the 6th in the morning, I received from Mr. Paléologue, our ambassador in St. Petersburg, a telegram in which he informed me that the Grand Duke Nicolas had received him on the 5th, he had been able to insist on the urgency of a Russian offensive, and the Grand Duke had affirmed to him his resolution to attack thoroughly without even waiting for the end of the concentration of all his army corps. He had even fixed August 14 as the probable date for the beginning of his offensive.[*]

This decision was of great importance: in fact, August 14 was precisely the date on which, according to precise calculations, the

---

[*] The next day, I received a telegram from the Grand Duke, in which he expressed his absolute faith in victory and his intention to take the offensive: he asked me to tell the French army commanders that he would have the French pennant that I had given him two years earlier during the French maneuvers he had attended worn next to his Russian generalissimo pennant. He wanted to show how our operations were linked.

strategic deployment of the Germans around their bases should be completed. If therefore, as was probable, except for transportion incidents, our own concentration was itself completed on that date, there would be no need to fear being outpaced by the enemy, and, on the other hand, the synchronization of our attacks with those of the Russians would be assured, all eminently favorable conditions for entering the campaign.

However, in our plans, the English concentration was an essential part of our left. Now, it seemed that the English troops would only be ready to go forward around August 21. As I wished to attack with all our forces together, that is to say, as far as our left was concerned, with the assistance of the English, I was led, from that moment, to consider a staggering of our operations in time: around the 14th, offensive action of our armies of the right and the center; around the 20th, setting in motion the forces of our left wing. All things considered, this difference in date could be favorable to the operations of our left, which, in my mind, were to be the principal ones, because our operations of the right and center would attract on their side a notable part of the enemy forces, would lighten the task of our armies of the left, and would perhaps help deceive the enemy on our true intentions.

The information received in Belgium seemed reassuring; the German troops who had attempted the day before a *coup de main* on Liège seemed to have been pushed back with heavy losses, and to have withdrawn ten kilometers to the east; in addition, the VIIth German Corps having been reported several times in the area of Metz at the same time as in that of Liége, we wondered if the elements reported in Belgium were not simply the 5th Brigade of this army corps equipped in view of a special mission; we were all the more encouraged to do so since important gatherings were reported with persistence and by the best sources on the side of Lorraine.

Friday, August 7. – I was not going to be long in receiving rather complete information on the situation in Belgium. Indeed, Lieutenant-Colonel Brécard was back on the morning of August 7, and informed me of what he had learned on the spot. He had seen successively Mr. Klobukowski, our minister in Brussels, Major

Génie, our military attaché, Mr. de Brocqueville, minister of War, General de Selliers, chief of the general staff; finally, he had been received by King Albert at his H.Q. of Louvain.

He gave details of the situation around Liège; on 5 August, the place, defended by the Léman division, had victoriously repulsed an attack led by two elements of the VIIth German Corps; on 6 August, these elements, reinforced by portions of the Xth Corps, had renewed their attempt and succeeded in penetrating the intervals of the forts and in entering the city. Uncertainty remained about the German strength, due to the contradictions brought by the often suspicious sources of information. The bulk of the Belgian army was concentrated between the Meuse and Brussels, covered by a division in Namur and Huy and by the Léman division in Liège.

On the subject of the general situation and the military projects of our Belgian allies, Lieutenant-Colonel Brécard brought me interesting information: the army was surprised by the war in full reorganization; it was missing cadres. General de Selliers, the new chief of the General Staff, was still recently commander of the gendarmerie. The Belgian public opinion expressed its indignation at the German attitude and its strong sympathy for us. It seemed that the Belgian government, very anxious to preserve its independence, would try to give satisfaction to the national feeling; but the military problem which suddenly arose to him was not without concern, and it seemed that the Belgian army already turned its eyes towards the stronghold of Antwerp, where it would withdraw if Liége were to fall.

From this information gathered on the spot, one could deduce that the Belgian government would hesitate to participate in combined offensive operations with ours, and would limit its action to a purely defensive attitude; it seemed, in particular, difficult to hope that the Belgian cavalry division would cooperate in the operations of our cavalry corps as I would have wished.

On August 7, I asked Major Collon, Belgian liaison officer to the French G.Q.G., to bring to Louvain my point of view on the role to be played by the Belgian army:

In my opinion, the latter could move to the Meuse, contest the passages and thus gain precious time for Allied cooperation. If this

Chapter II

cooperation could be implemented in due time, the Belgian army would seize a favorable opportunity for a flanking attack against the enemy columns marching before it to engage the Franco-British forces. In the event that the disproportion of forces did not allow it to maintain this approach, the Belgian army would have to retreat to Namur and come to link up with the left flank of the Franco-British armies.

Now, a short time after having received the mission report from Lieutenant-Colonel Brécard, a telegram from the Belgian Minister of the War, Mr. de Brocqueville, came to confirm the information which had just arrived: "the Belgian Minister of the War asks the French Generalissimo for the support of the French Army as fast as possible; it is absolutely necessary to make, even if only from the perspective of morale, a military demonstration of support..."

I understood, certainly, the importance of this call; but in the state of deployment of our forces, what support could we give to the Belgian army? Only the cavalry corps could do something immediately. I thus sent to them, in the early afternoon of August 7, the order to move towards the north, by indicating to him that it would be of interest from the double point of view of morale and diplomacy to start from August 8, if he considered the occasion favorable, "a vigorous action" against the enemy.

This action seemed all the more useful and probable as our intelligence organs reported in front of Liège elements of six army corps preceded by large numbers of cavalry in the region of Marche and directed towards Dinant and Givet.

On the other hand, the infantry of the 2nd French Corps held the crossings of the Meuse south of Namur in liaison with the Belgian infantry.

As it stood, that's all we could do.

Soon, the Ministry informed me that an armistice between the Belgian and German armies was being discussed: the President of the Republic requested that I intervene directly with the commander of the Belgian army to give my opinion. I hastened to inform the latter through our military attaché that I considered it necessary to respond with a refusal to the armistice request presented by the Germans.

The feeling of insecurity and anxiety that came from the situation in Belgium, despite the fact that it had become clearer to a certain extent, was aggravated by the difficulty that I had in obtaining information on the events that were taking place there. Here is an example: on the day of August 7, we received the news of the fall of half of the forts of Liége; the information was important and seemed to have all indications of authenticity. The same evening, we learned, this time from a Belgian source, that no forts had fallen and that the fortifications, in an excellent state of defense, promised to hold for a long time. These two pieces of information agreed in reporting that the attacking German troops were very tired, very depressed, and that the Belgian units were taking prisoners in groups of fifty.

While my attention was drawn towards the north, I received in the course of the afternoon the first report on the results we had just obtained in Upper Alsace: without having met any resistance, our troops had reached at 1:30 pm only the Hennersdorf, Pont d'Anspach, Massevaux front, i.e. they had advanced only about five kilometers into Alsatian territory. In the evening, I learned that they had occupied the Saint-Amarin, Thann, Altkirch front.

Saturday, August 8. – The next morning, August 8, I received additional information on the operations of the 7th; at the same time I learned that General Bonneau had "authorized General Berge[*] to maintain his troops in the conquered villages, and to delay the bulk of his forces until daylight."

This way of approaching the situation seemed to me to be worrying, and immediately I ordered the 7th Corps not to retreat under any pretext, to push vigorously on Mulhouse, and to accomplish completely and quickly the mission which had been entrusted to it. I also insisted to General Dubail on the vigor and speed that should characterize an operation of this kind.

Around noon, I learned that the Minister of War had received a telegram directly from General Bonneau, which read: "I report that I am today covering the 7th Corps on the Cernay, Mulhouse,

---

[*] Commander of the 27th Brigade (14th Division).

Altkirch line." In addition to the fact that this direct correspondence between the Minister and the commander of the 7th Corps seemed to indicate the latter had forgotten the hierarchy, it became obvious that General Bonneau had not understood the role he was to play. It was not a question of cover, but of a clearly offensive operation; this extreme slowness and indecision were likely to compromise the success of an operation from which I expected, in addition to an important effect on morale, security for the subsequent maneuvering of the 1st Army in Lower Alsace. I telegraphed the observation to General Dubail, asking him to examine whether the commander of the 7th Corps had the necessary qualities to fulfill his mission. It seemed that, in this whole region, nothing seriously threatened the right flank of the Alsace detachment, whose mission I had been led to broaden in order to bring it within the framework of the instructions given to the armies of the right.

In fact, since the day before, we had received quite a lot of information about the German army corps on the whole front. This was easily explained, since the first concentration transports of our adversaries were, according to our estimates, to begin on the sixth day of the German mobilization, that is to say on August 7. In these conditions, we could assume that this concentration would not be completed before the 13th, a date that we had assumed from the beginning as probable.

Thanks to the first identifications obtained, we could get a first idea of the enemy concentration.

It is important to remember that at that time, we focused our research particularly on the active army corps, believing that the reserve units would only come in the form of second line reinforcements. It seemed to us that if we were able to determine the locations of the large active units, we would thus have clarified the general economy of the enemy's position. This tendency to attribute only a secondary value to reserve units had, it must be recognized, a considerable influence on the development of operations. It derived from the generally accepted idea, in the preceding years, that the war, having to be short and violent, could only be fought in the front line by active units. Consequently, it seemed that reserve units could only be given secondary missions at the beginning of the war: siege operations, holding the defensive front, guarding communications, etc.; it would only be after a certain period of campaigning, when the reserve units had acquired more cohesion, that they could be employed in the same way as the active formations.

To tell the truth, the question of the German reserve army corps had not been completely clarified before the war. We were aware of the new German mobilization plan of October 9, 1913, in which it was stated that "reserve troops are to be employed in the same way as active troops." "But this will only be possible," the document added, "if the units contain a significant number of valuable peacetime officers." Now, it was our understanding that the large German reserve units composed of elements that were not very homogeneous, poorly equipped with artillery (two groups per division), had significant deficits in officers. They did not seem to meet the conditions imposed by the German plan of 9 October 1913.

On the other hand, the study of the same document[*] had shown us that the role assigned to the reserve divisions did not seem to be the same as that reserved for the reserve army corps. Only the latter seemed to be intended for active operations, "the reserve divisions having to serve as second-line troops possibly called upon, for example, to reinforce an army corps for a given operation."

What we knew of the German possibilities inclined us to express doubts on the existence of these army corps; so much so that the 2nd Bureau of the G.Q.G., in a note intended to orient the armies on the German reserve formations, wrote on August 25, speaking of the reserve army corps: "If these corps exist, they are composed of elements that are not very homogeneous, poorly equipped with artillery (two groups per reserve division, including a group of howitzers in some) and have no corps artillery."[†] This

---

[*] Analysis of the mobilization plan for the German army of October 9, 1913, addressed in May 1914 to the Chief of the General Staff by the 2nd Bureau of the Army Staff.

[†] Note about the reserve and *landwehr* formations of the 2nd Bureau of the G.Q.G. dated August 25, 1914, 3 p.m.

Chapter II

explains why, on the date of August 8, we did not expect to find reserve units in the enemy's front line; on the contrary, as indicated in the intelligence plan of February 1914, we believed that the presence of these units on the front line could lead to the assumption that, where they would be engaged, no decisive operations would be conducted.

This state of mind, which I had until about August 23, will make it understandable that in our efforts to establish the enemy's situation, we only took insufficient account of the large reserve units, finding it quite natural that they did not appear on the front during the first days.

It must be confessed: the use that the Germans made in August 1914 of their reserve army corps was a surprise for us, and this surprise is at the origin of the errors of judgement that we made, in particular with regard to the extent of their maneuver towards the north.

In any case, in the early hours of August 8, here is how the enemy's position seemed to be defined:

In Russia, 4 active army corps had already been identified. In Alsace and Lorraine, 6 army corps were recognized; in Belgium, 5 army corps,[*] if we only took into account our own information, 6 corps if we adopted the information transmitted by the Belgians. In total, 15 to 16 army corps were more or less located.

Now, the German army had to mobilize 26 active army corps; there were therefore about 10 of them left, the locations of which were yet to be determined, and which were probably behind the impenetrable Metz-Thionville curtain extended at the time by the

---

[*] Around Liège, elements of the IXth, VIIth and Xth Corps, which in peacetime constituted the inspectorate of Hanover, under the orders of General Oberst von Bülow, and perhaps elements of the IIIrd Corps; to the left of the Xth Corps, elements of the IVth, whose posts were, on the evening of the 7th, on the Ourthe, east of Ferrières.

To our calculations the Belgians added the XIth Corps, to the left of the Xth. In addition, 7 cavalry regiments appeared to have crossed the Meuse north of Liège.

Chapter II

Luxembourg position.[*]

Thus, the bulk of the enemy forces seemed to us to be

---

[*] The information that reached the G.H.Q. during the day of the 3rd confirmed this general view and allowed the 2nd Bureau to send the following bulletin to the armies on the morning of August 9th:

KNOWN GROUPING OF ACTIVE GERMAN FORCES

General distribution	Identified: 17 against France and 4 against Russia (I, V, XVIII, XX). Unidentified: 5

DISTRIBUTION OF FORCES AGAINST FRANCE

1. An army from the Meuse	2 or 3 cavalry divisions (including the 59th), 5 or 6 army corps (IXth, VIIth, Xth, IIIrd, IVth and perhaps XIth).

This seems to have reached its normal composition, with little train movement to Aachen and St. With.

2. A grouping from Luxembourg-Thionville	1 or 2 cavalry divisions (including the 4th) 4 (?) army corps including the 8th and the 18th (certain), perhaps the XIIth Saxon and an undetermined corps.
3. A grouping from Metz and the region to the east	3 cavalry divisions, ? army corps including the XVIth and the IInd Bavarian (certain), the IIIrd Bavarian probable.

Large deployments took place in the area east of Metz, Han sur Nied, Bensdorf.

4. A Strasbourg-Sarrebourg grouping	1 cavalry division, ? army corps, including the XIIIth, perhaps the Ist Bavarian, the XVth.
5. A group from Fribourg	XIVth Baden Army Corps: at least one Bavarian reserve division, elements of landwehr and landsturm.
Untraced Corps	IInd, VIth, XIXth, Guard and Guard reserve corps.

Chapter II

concentrated behind the "Moselle position"; this mass could as well break out towards the west as converge towards the south by pressing on to the area of Metz. As for the army of the Meuse which seemed to us to have reached its normal composition, it seemed destined to prolong the movement of the main mass either towards the west, or in its downward movement towards the south. Finally, the attack on Liège could only be a safeguard taken against the Belgian army, aiming only at the conquest of this important bridgehead.

These were only simple hypotheses; it was still too early to base a plan of maneuver on them. Desiring to make decisions only on the basis of well-established facts, I was led to reserve my orders concerning the use of our armies on the left for the main action.

The situation in Lorraine and Alsace was quite different: our troops were in contact with each other; my intention being to support the right side of my position on the Rhine, it was in my interest to defeat the German forces of Alsace in Strasbourg, in order to obtain an economy of troops by a shortening of our front. In Lorraine, it was in my interest to fix the enemy and to put Nancy under cover while the defense of the Grand Couronne was being carried out; the planned attack against the enemy forces of this region could obtain this result at the same time as it would contribute to relieve the Belgian front, or at least to prevent a shift of the German reserves towards the north. But it was certain, because of the danger posed on the right and left by the positions at Metz and Strasbourg, that this attack could not seek a far-flung goal.

Now, the forces of our 1st and 2nd armies, amounting to 10 army corps, seemed largely sufficient to be opposed to the 6 German army corps identified in this region; it was therefore possible, as I had indicated to General de Castelnau at the meeting of the army commanders on 3 August, to take two army corps from the 2nd Army and to reserve the use of them for the action to be carried out against the Metz and north groups.

Thus, at the end of the first period of concentration, I was led to envisage an action as fast as possible of the 1st and 2nd armies, while it seemed useful to me to limit to simple planning the employment of the major part of our forces until the situation had become clearer on our left.

It is according to these general ideas that I gave, on the morning of August 8, the orders to the armies contained in General Instruction No. 1: it was going to make it possible for army commanders to fix in full knowledge of the facts the stationing of their army corps whose debarkations entered the stage of full deployment. Anticipating moreover that on our extreme left our concentration would be without coverage for a long time, I ordered the fourth group of reserve divisions to organize opposite the Chimay gap, around Vervins, a solid fortified position; I was able moreover, in the course of this same morning, to give all the relevant information on this subject to General Valabrègue, who was designated for the command of this group, during a visit that he made to me in Vitry accompanied by his chief of staff, Colonel des Vallières.

I also received a visit that day from the Chief of Staff of the 5th Army, General Hély d'Oissel, who had come to tell me on behalf of his army commander that he feared that the Germans would execute a movement west of the Meuse in great force. I could only tell him that his fears seemed to me to be at least premature, especially since the maneuver attributed to the enemy seemed, based on our information, to exceed his means, and that, moreover, I had assumed the necessity of reinforcing this left wing, since, for two days, it had been understood that the two excellent African divisions, the 37th and 38th, would be directed towards the 5th Army. Moreover, the 5th Army was covered by the cavalry corps which received the order, if it had to cross the Meuse again, to go to the left of Lanrezac's army towards Marianbourg. In addition, I gave him the Belgian intelligence which depicted the German troops engaged in the region of Liége as strongly depressed and in a bad physical and moral state; a French officer, Captain Prioux, who had arrived the same day from the Belgian G.H.Q., confirmed this optimistic information.

Sunday, August 9. – Instruction No. 1 had considerably expanded the mission of the 1st Army. For it to be achievable, it was essential that the action of the 7th Corps and the 8th Cavalry

Chapter II

Division be carried out with vigor: the imperative order which I had sent to General Bonneau seemed to have produced an effect. During the night of the 8th to the 9th, I received the news that our troops had occupied Mulhouse without a fight. I asked General Dubail to let me know the future intentions of the commander of the 7th Corps; the answer was far from what I expected: the troops of this corps were very tired and unable to take the offensive again for another day or two. However, because of the small distances covered and the insignificant resistance of the enemy, I could only attribute the state of fatigue of the 7th Corps to the hesitations of the command. This half-failure of our action in Upper Alsace seriously compromised the continuation of the operations of the 1st Army, to which I attached particular importance, since they were to allow me, as soon as the rapid conquest of Alsace was completed, to economize on the forces on the right for the benefit of the main maneuver on the left.

The necessity therefore appeared to me to change as soon as possible the organization of the command on our extreme right. Moreover, I learned shortly after that the 7th Corps was attacked at Mulhouse, and I could fear that under the orders of a hesitant leader the affair would turn out badly.

It was then that I decided to form an army of Alsace, and I asked the Minister to appoint General Pau as commander. The great military reputation and the energy of the latter seemed to me to justify such a choice. I decided that this army would include, in addition to the 7th Corps and the 8th Cavalry Division, the 1st group of reserve divisions under the orders of General Archinard, which was to begin deployment on August 18, five Alpine groups which were to arrive from the 13th and the 44th Division from the 15th. Finally, in order to get precise information on the situation of our right, I urgently sent two of my officers to Belfort.

During the night of 9 to 10 August, the unfortunate news of the loss of Mulhouse reached me; the 7th Corps had let 300 men be taken there. According to the first reports, a serious error seemed to have been committed by the commander who had gathered too many men inside the city without any reason.

On the morning of August 9, important information arrived about the English mobilization.

When the British government decided to enter the fight, it had initially set August 5 as the first day of mobilization; consequently, according to our peacetime agreements, the transportation of the expeditionary force on our railroads was to begin on the 11th, thus making the date for commencing operations the 21st. Now, as a consequence of delays in mobilization complicated by certain domestic circumstances, the first day of British mobilization had been set for August 9, so that the British deployment on the Continent could not be expected to move forward until the 26th.

I was therefore faced with the alternative of either postponing until that date the entry into action of the French left, if I wanted the British forces to participate, or of engaging in decisive operations without waiting for the assistance of the latter. The first solution had the double disadvantage of leaving the Belgian army without effective support for too long, and of probably causing us to lose all the advantages of having the lead in the action by leaving the initiative entirely to the enemy. The second solution deprived us of the precious support of the British Expeditionary Force in the first operations.

Of these two solutions, both of which presented serious disadvantages, I chose the second, and I wrote to the President of the Republic to inform him of my decision; but, at the same time, I asked him to inform the British government of the danger that a too great delay in the arrival of Marshal French's army would cause. I indicated, moreover, that the British general staff could perhaps begin the preparatory measures that it had to take.

On the other hand, as I had no news of the German-Belgian armistice project that the President had asked me to discuss on the 7th, I expressed to him, in the same letter, the desire that the Belgian government be told that the moral comfort given by our cavalry corps to its army would not be our only support, but that we would ask it in exchange to continue the action that had been so brilliantly undertaken in the region of Liége.

Monday, August 10. – From this side of the theater of operations, the news continued to not be alarming. Indeed, if the city of Liége appeared to have been taken, the forts were still holding, and the morale situation of the Belgian army was reported to us as

Chapter II

excellent. A series of intelligence reports contributed to confirming our impression that the main German maneuver would not take place in Belgium. Indeed, the German army corps in the region of Liège did not seem to show any more activity, and the Russian military attaché in Brussels reported that these army corps were being relieved by reserve troops who were being organized on the ground. We know what interpretation we had to give to such information. Moreover, on the 10th, an agent arriving from Cologne announced that fortification works were under construction on the Cologne, Bergheim, Erkelenz front, and that the heavy artillery was deployed in support of this front; this same agent declared that there were no gatherings of German troops along the Dutch Limburg.

On the other hand, with aerial reconnaissance coming to confirm our intelligence from various sources, we were led, on this date of August 10, to believe that the Germans were going to undertake a proper siege of Liége, while the movements of troops reported towards Neufchâteau and Bastogne seemed to be the beginning and the coverage of the transport of the northern group of the enemy in the region Bastogne, Marche, Rochefort, Libramont,[*] On the other hand, heavy activity was still reported in Lorraine and in the east of Metz

I could therefore hope that the Belgian army would not soon have to undergo too violent a shock and that we could hope to see it continue to remain on the extreme left of the Allied position. I also wrote down the proclamation addressed three days earlier to his army by King Albert, which contained a fraternal salute to the French army, to thank him and express my hope that his soldiers would march with ours to victory.

The most pressing issue remained that of our extreme right.

Early in the morning, on the 10th, I was informed by the Minister that General Pau had been placed at my disposal, and would come the same day to the Grand Quartier Général to receive my instructions. This notice was accompanied by an energetic

---

[*] Intelligence report no. 31 of August 10, 1914, 5 p.m., from the 2nd Bureau of the G.Q.G.

declaration: Mr. Messimy informed me "that the will of the government was that a general who would not fulfill his duties with sufficient vigor should be brought before a council of war and put to the sword within twenty-four hours."*

The Minister of War, to whose enthusiasm I wish to pay tribute, was perhaps going a little too far. As far as General Bonneau was concerned, if he had shown an inability to pass from the mentality of peacetime to that of wartime, it was an indication that his character was not equal to the circumstances, but that was not a reason to bring him before a Council of War. In peacetime, it is difficult to judge men in terms of character, which in the final analysis is the essential quality of a leader in war. I was expecting to find failures and surprises; my decision was made: I will remove the incapable leaders, and replace them with younger and more energetic leaders.

I received, indeed, as the Minister had promised me, the visit of General Pau. I informed him of the situation and of what I expected from the army of Alsace. In addition, I asked him to send me, as soon as he had made contact with his troops, a report with proposals. Finally, I gave him as chief of staff one of my the officers in whom I had the most confidence, Lieutenant-Colonel

---

* This communication received from the Minister's chief of staff, General Ebener, by General Belin was confirmed to me by a personal letter of Mr. Messimy which reached me on the evening of August 10. Here it is:

Paris, August 10, 1914, 12:30 pm.

My dear General,

I want to repeat what I had Ebener telephone you: If a leader under your command, regardless of rank, shows weakness, pusillanimity, he should be instantly brought before the Council of War and tried. The most severe penalties, including death, should be applied to him. The President of the Republic renounces, in most cases, to use his right of pardon. You will be notified of this. We intend, since war has been declared against us, to wage it in a revolutionary manner as in 1793.

Yours,

MESSIMY.

Chapter II 247

Buat.*

Tuesday, August 11. – During the night of August 10 to 11, the officers I had sent to Belfort returned to the general headquarters; they brought very complete reports: according to these, it was certain that the value of the troops could not be questioned, and it seemed that the loss of Mulhouse could have been largely avoided if the 8th Cavalry Division had been employed in a less parsimonious way. The fault was clear; it was a matter of making an example as soon as possible: I resolved to put the general commanding the 8th Cavalry Division at the disposal of the Minister and to appoint General Mazel† in his place.

For the rest, there was only to wait until General Pau had taken his command and put things in order. However, I decided, in order to calm the emotion that the evacuation of Mulhouse had provoked in the official spheres, to send to the President of the Republic and to the Minister of War one of the officers who had returned from Belfort, so that he could give detailed explanations of all that he had seen.‡ It was all the more necessary to re-establish the truth

---

* General Pau had thought of taking General Roget as his chief of staff. However, Roget was sixty-eight years old and had been out of the army for six years, and General Pau was willing to accept my decision to place under him a chief of staff who was twenty-five years younger than General Roget.

† Following the unfortunate incident at the village of la Garde, which cost us about 2,000 prisoners, and on the report of General de Castelnau, I also decided to replace the general commanding the 2nd Cavalry Division with General Varin.

‡ This officer, Major Maurin, brought me a copy of the letter that King Albert had just sent to the President of the Republic:

Louvain, August 11, 1914.
  Dear and great Friend,
  I thank you from the bottom of my heart for the laudatory appreciation of the conduct of the Belgian troops which you were kind enough to express in the name of General Joffre in your letter of August 9. The Belgian army and I are proud of it and we attach the greatest importance to it. Concerning the cooperation of our soldiers with their French and English brothers in arms, General Joffre wrote to Your Excellency: "We hope that the Belgian army will be willing to continue the action already so brilliantly begun in the north of the left wing of our armies." I

since the Swiss press was announcing a serious French failure in Alsace; it claimed that our killed and wounded had exceeded 20,000 men, that is to say more than we had engaged in combat. The impression produced was very strong, and it was necessary to cut short this short as soon as possible.

It was on August 11, around noon, that I took the decision to fix the 14th as the date for the attack of the 1st Army and the right corps of the 2nd; this date corresponded to the end of our concentration transports. It was also in our interest to facilitate as soon as possible, by an offensive movement to the west of the Vosges, the entry into action of the army of Alsace. In addition, the date I had just chosen was going to coincide with the beginning of the Russian operations, as a new telegram from Mr. Paléologue announced.[*]

Wednesday, August 12. – However, north of the Meuse, the German cavalry had pushed on to Diest and Tirlement; this

---

am responding in a formal way to the wish expressed by the French generalissimo. The French army can count on the absolute assistance of the Belgian army to the left wing of the allied armies, within the limits of its forces and its remaining means and so long as its communications with the base of Antwerp where all its supplies of ammunition and food are stored would not be threatened to be cut off by significant enemy forces.

In order to remain informed about the operations of the great Allied armies and to be able to coordinate our own movements with theirs, I have designated Major Melotte to be attached to General Joffre, after his mission with General Sordet is completed, and Colonel d'Orgéo de Marchovelette to General Lanrezac. On the other hand, I will welcome with great pleasure the officers that you will want to designate to be attached to my headquarters.

Believe, dear and great Friend, in the profound gratitude of the Belgian army and its leader for the fraternal support that the French army lends them in these critical moments and, with my ardent wishes for a common victory, please accept this expression of my devoted feelings.

ALBERT.

[*] Telegram from St. Petersburg of August 9, 1914, 9:16 pm., from Mr. Paléologue, telephoned by General Ebener on August 10, 10:30 a.m. and received by General Belin. This telegram indicated the main lines of the Russian plan of operations; the march of the army of Vilna towards Koenigsberg supported by the army of Warsaw.

Chapter II

progression of the enemy seemed to deeply upset the Belgian command. Indeed, on the morning of the 12th, we received an appeal from the King of the Belgians for the Allies to come as quickly as possible to the aid of his army, announcing that he would bring his army back to Antwerp if the Germans attacked in superior strength; Colonel Génie, at the same time as he communicated this appeal from the King, insisted that the cavalry corps should pass as quickly as possible north of the Meuse.

The intentions of the Belgian government thus manifested were not a surprise to us. I was certainly well aware of the need to support the Belgians. But, first of all, it did not seem that the German cavalry reported north of the Meuse was supported, since on the 12th it suffered a major defeat at Haelen, which was inflicted by the Belgian cavalry division supported by an infantry brigade. On the other hand, it seemed that the enemy forces reported south of the Meuse were more significant than we had believed until now: two new German army corps had just been identified there. Under these conditions, it was difficult to relieve the cavalry corps of its mission to screen the 5th Army. The only thing that seemed possible to me to do for the moment, and which moreover was very necessary, was to establish the continuity of the front by linking via Namur our left army to the Belgian army. To this end, I authorized General Lanrezac, who had asked me for authorization, to bring his left corps to the region of Dinant; in addition, I pushed towards Philippeville the two African divisions which were going to begin their deployments.

But, at that time, there was still great uncertainty as to when the British would be able to enter into action on our side.

On August 9, Colonel Huguet, our military attaché in London, arriving at headquarters, informed me of what had happened in England since the declaration of war. It had been decided, first of all, that mobilization would begin on August 5. Under these conditions, according to our agreements, the transport to the concentration area on our railroads were to begin on the 11th and the disembarked units were to be ready to enter into operations on the 21st. However, during a major Council of War held on Wednesday 5th at Downing Street, everything was called into question: the date of mobilization, the composition of the expeditionary force, the area of concentration. On August 6, Lord Kitchener had been appointed Secretary of State for the War Office, and the first day of mobilization had finally been postponed to the 9th. The British government had expressed the intention of concentrating the forces sent to the continent in an area sufficiently behind the front to ensure them a preliminary rest; for this purpose, it proposed the region of Amiens and planned the organization of a defensive position on the Somme.

In addition to the fact that these proposals completely upset the general disposition of the Allied forces at the most sensitive point of our battle line, they also had the disadvantage of delaying the probable date of the entry into action of the British troops, at a time when, as I have just said, the Belgians were asking us to come to their aid. I said above what solution I had considered, and you have seen that I had asked the President of the Republic to intervene with the English government to point out the serious inconvenience that such a long delay in the arrival of the British troops would have. And to Colonel Huguet, who was returning to London, I gave instructions to insist to the English general staff that the zone of concentration of the army of Marshal French should not be modified, under penalty of ruining our plan.

Thursday, August 13. – Now, on the 13th, I learned with satisfaction that after a discussion which had taken place the day before in Lord Kitchener's own cabinet, the British government had finally accepted our proposals, and had agreed to maintain the concentration zone immediately next to the French armies. This was a very important point to get. But, on the other hand, I learned at the same time that the government, influenced by English public opinion, which lived under the perpetual fear of a landing in England, had found it necessary to maintain two infantry divisions in the metropolis. Under these conditions, the British Expeditionary Force would be reduced to four infantry divisions and five cavalry brigades; the two divisions maintained in England would follow as soon as circumstances permitted.

This solution, without doubt better than the one we had feared, risked putting our left in a critical situation, and I feared that it would be attacked before its concentration was completed. In fact, according to the calculations of the 2nd Bureau, this date of August 13, which we had arrived at, was precisely the date on which the German strategic deployment on its starting point was to end, and it was likely that the Germans would not be long in moving; it was therefore possible that we would not be able to seek battle beyond the Semoy and the Chiers rivers.

In light of this situation I ordered the 1st and 2nd armies, which were ready for action, to attack the next day, the 14th: Dubail towards Sarrebourg with three army corps, flanked on his right by the 14th Corps, Castelnau with his three right army corps, while the 9th Corps and the reserve divisions would protect Nancy. As for the armies on the left, the 3rd, 4th and 5th, I simply ordered a certain number of defensive measures.

However, on the morning of the 13th, I read the report of General Pau, who had arrived during the night: he described our troops as being exhausted and demoralized. The 7th Corps and the 57th reserve division withdrew under the guns of Belfort. General Pau attributed a great part of the responsibility to the insufficiency of command and he concluded by asking me to replace General Bonneau. I agreed immediately and appointed General Vautier to the 7th Corps.

With regard to these transfers, I must say here that I was perfectly aware of the illegality that I was committing by pronouncing them: the general officers from whom I withdrew their employment held their letter of command from the Minister and, legally, only the Minister could deprive them of it. I understood perfectly well that if our affairs went well, I would probably be covered, but that if events turned to our disadvantage, I would not fail to be reproached for these initiatives. Nevertheless, conscious of the responsibilities I had assumed before the country, I did not hesitate to take these measures which seemed to me absolutely necessary and urgent. Since then, I have often been obliged to resort to these disgraceful measures, but I can say, in all conscience, that I have not taken any of them without having the conviction that I was working for the salvation of the country. Many of these actions cost me, and please believe me if I say today, with all the serenity that several years of hindsight give, that I do not believe that I have had to make, in the course of my career, command decisions more difficult and thankless than that which consisted of dismissing perfectly honorable generals, some of whom were among my friends, but whose wartime performance proved that their character was not equal to the task. I must say that if I drew from my conscience the strength to accomplish this difficult duty, I felt in the Minister of War a support to which I pay tribute and which gave me great peace of mind. But ministers are not immortal.

However, late in the evening of the 13th, a great and happy news reached us: the Grand Duke Nicolas Nicolaïevitch informed us through the intermediary of Mr. Paléologue that the armies of Vilna and Warsaw would take the offensive the next morning at dawn. Thus, exceeding all our hopes, Russia joined the fight at the same time as us. For this act of loyal confraternity of arms, which was all the more remarkable because the Russian concentration was far from being completed, the army of the Tsar and the Grand Duke Nicolas are entitled to the gratitude of France.

It should also be noted that the most fanciful rumors continued to circulate about the arrival of Austrians on our front. The intelligence from Swiss and Italian sources was more precise: it was no longer one army corps, but four that were reported to us. It was announced that Austria had requested passage for several army corps through Switzerland and even Italy. But these were only rumors. We did not yet know anyone who had seen an Austrian; reliable correspondents in Basel only believed in the presence of some Tyrolean elements without being able to assess their importance. Finally, the information on Italy was also contradictory; one announced the withdrawal of the troops from Bardonnèche, but at the same time, one spoke about sending Alpine troops and howitzers towards Aosta and the Petit Saint-Bernard.

Friday, August 14. – However, the uncertainty about the German forces and the intentions of our adversaries towards the north remained complete; without doubt, the Belgians seemed to have successes, but, for the first time, we were informed of columns of infantry crossing the Meuse downstream from Liège. We could not yet determine whether these forces were moving against the

Chapter II 253

Belgian army or whether they were proceeding to the total investment of Liége. As for the air force, it did not give any clarity for the moment. Moreover, General Sordet declared to me in a report dated the 13th, which I received on the 14th around nine o'clock in the morning, that he did not know much and that the observations of the airmen seemed to him to be subject to caution. "Certainly," he wrote to me, "I cannot guarantee anything for certain, but my impression is that there were no large masses of infantry on the 12th below the Ourthe-Houffalize-Luxembourg line."

Behind this line, movements were reported. It seemed that the movements that were being carried out under the cover of the Ourthe fieldwork were intended to put in place the army corps destined to form the maneuver mass on the right. By gathering all our information, we estimated at 8 army corps and 4 cavalry divisions the grouping of forces extending between the northern tip of the Grand Duchy and the border of Dutch Limburg.[*] This calculation corresponded to what we had foreseen as deployment possibilities in the German positions along this front. The situation did not seem worrying on this side, since we could field 10 active divisions, 3 reserve divisions, the 6 Belgian divisions supported on the Antwerp-Namur-Liége and Maubeuge system, and, in a short time, 4 British infantry divisions and one cavalry division.

Thus, on the morning of the 14th, we had spotted all the active German army corps, except for the Ist, XVIIth, XXth, Vth and IInd, which we thought were in front of the Russians, and we had the impression that the big German maneuver mass was gathering behind the Ourthe.

However, a very interesting piece of information had reached us during the night of the 13th to the 14th; for the first time, columns of infantry had been reported north of Liège: they were reserve troops. This information was important, but because of the ideas we had about the use of reserve troops by the Germans, we could not yet establish whether these columns of infantry were directed against the Belgian field army or intended to complete the

---

[*] Intelligence report no. 38 of the 2nd Bureau of the G.Q.G., August 14, 6:00 a.m.

investment of Liége.

During this day of the 14th, I received, in order, General Galliéni and General Lanrezac. The first came in the morning, sent by the Minister. I felt that he was trying to approach the question of operations and that Mr. Messimy had asked him to present to me the way in which he believed they should be conducted. One can easily imagine how unpleasant this suggestion was for me, if one thinks of the responsibility I had to bear. So I broke off the conversation rather abruptly.

Lanrezac came to see me at the beginning of the afternoon; he shared with me his fear of seeing the Germans execute a large overwhelming movement by the north of the Meuse. I said that at this date, August 14, the state of our information did not allow for the moment to envisage such a maneuver, and that, on the contrary, the bulk of the enemy forces seemed to be massed behind the Ourthe, to the south of the troops which masked Liége. On the left bank the German forces that were reported to us were reduced to cavalry and a few columns of infantry. On the other hand, the Maubeuge-Hirson region was reserved for the deployment of British troops, and I could not, under penalty of creating disorder in this zone, authorize General Lanrezac to push part of his army there. Consequently, I had to tell the commander of the 5th Army that his fears seemed to me to be premature for the moment, and that, until further notice, his mission was to go to meet the enemy force reported behind the Ourthe and the Houfialize-Luxembourg line.*

---

* Since that time, General Lanrezac has claimed that it was impossible not to see that the German maneuver was developing north of the Meuse; he claims that he saw it without a doubt. This assertion seems a bit exaggerated. Indeed, what we have learned of the German maneuver since the end of the war shows us that it is on August 13 that Kluck's army crossed Aix-la-Chapelle; on the 14th its vanguards reached the Meuse towards Visé; on the 16th they entered Bilsen and Tongres. On the morning of the 17th we could only have known, assuming that our means of investigation were perfect, about the presence of his vanguards on the left bank of the Meuse. To conclude that the entire German maneuver was going to take place north of the Meuse, as General Lanrezac claims to have done, would have required the gift of divination.

However, in reality, for reasons already mentioned, and as we will see in the

Chapter II

As soon as he arrived at his H.Q. in Rethel, General Lanrezac wrote to me to inform me again of his fears and to ask me to prepare from now on the possible transport of his army towards the region of Givet-Maubeuge, by leaving an army corps and two reserve divisions on the Meuse, in connection with the 4th Army.

Saturday August 15. – Now, when this request reached me, we had just received news from Belgium on the enemy forces which were north of Liége: they seemed to be more serious than we had believed at first; during the whole day of the 14th, large German units had crossed the Meuse on four bridges built at Visé. The Belgian army was no longer in communication with the fortification of Liége and was unaware of the German troops besieging it.

This information could lead us to believe that the eventuality that we had until now believed we could rule out was now likely to occur. Were the Germans not going to extend their maneuver to the north of the Meuse? It is in view of this scenario, which for the first time seemed to be taking shape, that I replied to General Lanrezac that I saw only advantages in his preparing the transport northward of two army corps, in addition to the 1st Corps. I pointed out to him, however, that since the threat was still far off and its certainty far from being absolute, the movement would only be carried out on my order.

At the same time, thinking that the enemy forces reported north of the Meuse could come to threaten our rail and river communications in the northern region, I asked the Minister, under whose authority the 1st region was located, to establish with three divisions currently unemployed a barrier from the sea to

---

account of the following days, the information that reached us was always late, incomplete and contradictory. Only the combat of the Belgian army against the German vanguards could have given us information and lifted the veil. The Germans were able to advance their columns behind the curtain of their cavalry supported by some infantry forces. The presence of the Belgian army north of the Meuse in the region of Louvain was sufficient to explain the action of German forces north of the Meuse, without one being entitled to deduce that the maneuver of the bulk of the enemy armies would take place north of the river.

Maubeuge, and to place the 1st region under my authority, in order to allow me to communicate directly with General Percin, who commanded this region. This was the origin of the Amade force.*

This first indication of infantry troops passing north of the Meuse was obviously to be watched carefully. Unfortunately, the day of the 15th was far from bringing us consistent information. At 5 p.m., we received from the governor of Maubeuge the notification that 200,000 Germans were crossing the Meuse between Maëstricht and Visé; he also reported that the enemy, completing the investment of Liège on the left bank of the Meuse, had moved 10,000 cavalrymen with artillery on boat bridges between Flone and Hermalle; these forces were heading towards Waremme. The same evening, new intelligence came to contradict that given by the governor of Maubeuge: the area of Liége, Verviers, Spa, Rouvreux was reported to be empty of troops and the information concerning the passage of elements of all arms north of Liége was declared to be incorrect. On the other hand, numerous troops were reported south of Huy. In the late afternoon, I learned that the 1st Corps in front of Dinant had been attacked by a corps that seemed to be covering the movement of several other corps shifting northwest between Namur and Liège. This attack, coupled with the information we had of large forces in Belgian Luxembourg, seemed to indicate that the enemy was now seeking to make his main effort on his right wing north of Givet.

From all this news, it appeared that it was necessary to push the left of the 5th Army between the Sambre and the Meuse, which would thus reinforce our enveloping position in relation to the German right wing; the latter was going to be caught between the Belgian army, whose situation continued to be portrayed as quite favorable, the place of Namur and the 5th Army positioned behind the Meuse upstream from Namur.

The necessary orders were issued on the evening of the 15th and the morning of the 16th.

---

* General d'Amade was, at the time the war broke out, commander of the army which was to operate on the Alps. The neutrality of Italy had made available, as we know, the troops of this army and their leader.

Chapter II

Sunday August 16. – On the 16th at noon, Marshal French, who had been in Paris since the day before, came to see me accompanied by his chief of staff, General Murray. It was the first time I had seen the commander-in-chief of the British army. He had been received the day before by President Poincaré, and was very favorably impressed by the atmosphere of confidence that he had found in the official spheres. He immediately gave me the impression of a loyal comrade in battle, committed to his principles and eager, while bringing us his assistance, not to compromise his army. He made me understand that the instructions of his government specified that he should consider himself independent and that he could only bring us the collaboration of his army. I understood this point of view very well; it was natural that England would not consent to subordinate its troops to an allied commander. I had never had any illusions on this subject, while at the same time sensing that the lack of unity of command in the Allied forces on the left would be a serious source of weakness. We had to take things as they came and try to make the best of them by working together as closely as possible.

Our conversation then turned to the date on which the English army would be ready to enter into operations. I had counted on August 21, but the marshal informed me that on this date his army could only push forward small detachments which would protect the deployment of the bulk, and that his troops would only be likely to move on the 24th. I explained to the marshal all the disadvantages of this delay: he promised me to reduce it as much as possible.

Then we turned to the analysis of the general situation of the enemy as we saw it at that moment. I stressed the point that we were rather badly informed on the forces which were opposed to the Belgian army on the northern bank of the Meuse, but that, according to our latest information, there seemed to be in this area only cavalry; the significant gathering of forces assembled in the area of Hannut seemed intended to cover on the left bank of the river the movement of German columns reported beforehand around Liége and which seemed to form the principal mass of the enemy maneuver.

We then studied the question of the maneuver to carry out. I indicated to Marshal French that, on the side of the northern wing, the uncertainty regarding the opposing forces was such that I could still define my intentions only in a vague form: my idea was to carry out a general Franco-Belgian action against the group of enemy forces in the north. In my opinion, the assistance that I expected from the British army should consist of moving as soon as possible to the north of the Sambre, ready to march on Nivelles, either on the left of the 5th Army, if it moved towards the north, or in echelon behind the left of this army if it moved towards the east. The Sordet cavalry corps would cover the movement of the English army. As for the Belgian army, I considered that, while covering Brussels and Antwerp, its role should be to act on the outer flank of the German forces, taking them, if possible, in the rear.

Sir John French promised me to give as complete satisfaction as possible to my desires, and he declared to me that he was going to make contact with General Lanrezac, whose maneuvering skills I praised. He left me to go to Reims to sleep.

Chapter III

The Battle of the Frontiers. – August 17-24, 1914.

Monday August 17. – The news that reached us from the armies during the day of the 17th was quite good. The 1st and 2nd armies seemed to be progressing in favorable conditions, and in Upper Alsace there were reports of fairly significant retreats. From Belgium, no new information arrived about the enemy forces: it seemed that only one infantry brigade had passed on the left bank of the Meuse, north of Liège, and that it was reported towards Tongres; two cavalry divisions which had gone towards the Sambre had been stopped and beaten by the Belgian troops; they had withdrawn to Gembloux. The situation thus seemed favorable. So it was with surprise that I learned in the afternoon that the Belgian government had decided to withdraw to Antwerp. It was necessary at all costs to avoid that the army of King Albert followed this movement, and for that, the only means was to make him effectively feel our presence. I renewed the order to General Lanrezac to push the cavalry corps north of Namur to contact the Belgians.

Tuesday, August 18. – All the attention was concentrated on our left. On the morning of the 18th, I learned that the 2nd Army had reached Château-Salins, Dieuze and Marsal, and that the 1st Army had entered Sarrebourg. In Alsace, the XIVth and XVth German corps seemed to have disappeared. Where were the large German units?

We were coming to the end of the concentration period and it was time to decide on our maneuver. But my main preoccupation, the one that never left me since the beginning of the war, was to definitively orient my maneuver only on clearly recognized and identified enemy forces. Moreover, it was necessary that our maneuver remained hidden, in order to ensure the benefit of the surprise. However, our information was still insufficient to determine the extent of the enemy's maneuver and his intentions. On this date of August 18, by studying the question from a rigorously objective point of view, by eliminating all imagination and by using only the information we had at that time, it was impossible to predict the maneuver that the enemy was preparing.

Our information had led us to conceive the enemy order of battle in the following form:

On the left bank of the Meuse, we only knew of the presence of 2 cavalry divisions operating between Jodoigne and Hannut.

On the right bank, between Huy and Liège, under the orders of General von Bülow, a grouping of 4 corps (VIIth, IXth, Xth and Guard) followed in second line by 3 reserve army corps. This ensemble seemed to form the IInd Army; it seemed possible that the Ist Army was the echelon grouped around Liège and in the region of Visé;

Another grouping comprising 4 army corps seemed to be the one that had attacked on Dinant and pushed elements towards Yvoir and Beauraing;

A third grouping seemed to be forming in the Neufchâteau-Recogne area; its advanced elements had not gone beyond the Neufchâteau-Saint-Hubert front. The Arlon area was quite heavily occupied.

This was how our intelligence portrayed the enemy forces on the right.

The unknown was the extent to which the enemy intended to push the movement of his right wing northward; there was obviously in the region of Liège a rather disturbing accumulation of forces. Would the enemy decide to march astride the Meuse between Givet and Brussels? Or, as we had assumed until then, would he engage north of the Meuse only a small part of his forces, by seeking with the bulk of his northern grouping which remained south of the river to attack the left of our 4th Army engaged against the German central grouping from the flank?

In the first eventuality, our 5th Army, operating in liaison with the British and Belgian armies, would seek to outflank the enemy right wing from the north, while our armies of the center, 3rd and 4th, would attack the enemy central grouping from south to north in the general direction of Neufchâteau. I had the right to hope that the 5th Army, enlarged by the fourth group of reserve divisions, the 18th Corps from the 2nd Army, supported by the fortress of Namur, could accomplish this mission. As for the attack of the 3rd and 4th armies, we dedicated, in my mind, 19 active divisions out of 48.

In the second scenario, the Belgian and British armies would probably be sufficient to hold the German forces of the north of the Sambre and the Meuse in check; as for the 5th Army, it would fall back by Givet and Namur towards Marche against the flank of the grouping south of the Meuse.

I informed General Lanrezac of these projects and also communicated them to the King of the Belgians and to Marshal French, sending them Lieutenant-Colonel Brécard, bearer of the instructions that I had just given to the French armies of the left.*

---

* Lieutenant-colonel Brécard arrived in Louvain, the king's headquarters, in the evening of the 18th. There he learned of the retreat of the Belgian army. He had not been able to meet Marshal French when he passed through the British headquarters. The latter answered me on the 19th, without making any objection: "You are considering two hypotheses: the first corresponds to the case where the important mass of 4 to 6 army corps would pass north of the Meuse; you will oppose the forward movement by the 5th Army north of the Sambre and the Meuse with the assistance of the cavalry corps, the British army and the Belgian army which will try to outflank the German attack from the north; or, only one or two German army corps will pass north of the Meuse: then, the 5th Army passing the Meuse between Namur and Givet will flank the German army, while the British, the Belgians and the cavalry corps will protect the flank of the French 5th

Chapter III

However, around 11:30 a.m., Colonel Génie telephoned that German infantry movements were occurring towards the north, causing a great deal of excitement at the Belgian G.Q.G.

In the evening, we learned from Colonel Aldebert, detached to the Belgian G.H.Q., that troops of the Xth German Corps had passed on the left bank of the Meuse by the bridge of Huy, that 8,000 men of the IXth Corps were in Landen pushing detachments on the Gette, in Haelen, in Tirlemont and in Bewerloo. He informed us that the Belgian G.H.Q. had decided at 3 p.m. to withdraw its outposts on the Dyle and to move to Malines.

Thus, it seemed that a certain number of elements of the German forces gathered south of the Meuse had already crossed to the left bank. It was also reported that four bridges had been established at Huy, Ampsin, Ombret-Rosa and Seraing. Finally, in the area of Bastogne-Neufchâteau there were indications of a shift of forces in the northwest direction.

The first of the possibilities that I had foreseen in my morning instructions to the armies of the left thus seemed to have happened. It was important to reinforce the 5th Army, and to this end I decided to send the 9th Army corps to the Sedan-Poix-Terron region, in order to allow the extension of this army towards the north.

On the other hand, in order to allow General Ruffey to devote himself solely to his offensive movement, I decided to create the Army of Lorraine under the command of General Maunoury, with the third group of reserve divisions which was originally part of the 3rd Army, the available 67th Division and the 65th and 75th reserve divisions coming from the Alps. The mission of this new army was to cover the right flank of the 3rd Army against the forces that could emerge from the entrenched camp of Metz, by gradually investing this position from the west. I asked the Minister to put General Maunoury at my disposal to fulfill this task. I had, in fact, a particular esteem for this general, and I had often regretted that the merciless age limit had, at the time of the

---

Army and will take for their objective all the German forces north of the river." At the same time, the Marshal assured me of his most cordial cooperation.

war, kept him from any command.

The minister answered me the next day that he agreed to put at my disposal General Maunoury, whom he had charged with the inspection of the western regions.*

Wednesday, August 19. – The night of the 18th to the 19th continued to bring us details on the passage of German troops from the right bank to the left bank: the regiments reported belonged to the IVth, VIIth and Xth Corps; the German cavalry reached Diest. Our cavalry corps, in liaison with a mixed Belgian brigade, had

---

* Concerning the correspondence that the Minister and I exchanged during the month of August 1914, it is not without interest to quote the following letter. This letter answered both the report that I had sent on the 17th to Paris, in which I announced the capture of Sarrebourg, and a double protest that I had sent against the sending of projectiles and equipment to Belgium and against the order given directly by the Minister to arm the place of Dijon. I had ended my letter by saying that my responsibility was great enough that I could not accept that which would result from decisions made without me. I quote the Minister's reply only to show the tone of sympathy and confidence with which it was imbued.

Paris, 18/8/14. 11 a.m.

My dear general and friend,

1. I was sure of it: I did not say it to those around me, but I had the most ardent and firm confidence in the success of our arms. I do not want to address to the troops the congratulations of the government until the success is definitive. But you, tell them our pride and our joy! Tell them the ardent faith that we have in their heroism, in the intelligence of our officers, in the genius of our race. Let me embrace you;

2. You complain that we have sent ammunition and rifle slings to the Belgians. I understand your protest. It is justified. But really the matter of Liège was of such capital strategic importance that we had an absolute obligation to provide. Given the delay brought to the entry into the line of the Germans in Belgium, we will have after tomorrow evening we will have recovered the 100,000 shells of 75 sent in Belgium;

3. You did well to send us the first flag; its arrival shook Paris with a great thrill of joy and pride. It is at the Invalides... waiting for the others;

4. For Dijon, which is outside the area of the armies, I beg you to notice that I have cancelled the orders, since fortune smiles on us. But I want to insist on this point that Dijon is outside the area of the armies, where I refuse to give instructions or orders."

Affectionately yours.

MESSIMY.

pushed back the reported cavalry at Gembloux, but had encountered organized resistance at Ramillies.

The afternoon brought us a new series of information: first of all, around 4 p.m., Colonel Génie confirmed by telephone that following a battle which had taken place on the 18th before Tienen and into which the Germans had sent troops of all arms, the order had been given to the Belgian army to move closer to Antwerp; on its left, they were even to penetrate the perimeter of the Antwerp forts. By this retreat, our allies exposed Brussels.

But more importantly, we lost all contact with the Belgians and the hope I had entertained that they would actively participate in the envelopment of the German right. Our cavalry corps and the fort of Namur were separated from the main Belgian forces. General Michel, governor of Namur, reported that he had only three brigades and that he was concentrating them to the northeast and southeast of his position: he requested that the Franco-British army cross the Sambre and ensure the security of the northwest and southwest zone. In addition, the Belgians reported that large forces were crossing the Meuse between Liége and Huy; our air reconnaissance had recognized German columns at Hannut and Meeffe marching northwest.

I must admit that this information left me in a state of great perplexity. Either these numbers were small and could only be intended to block the Belgian army, which explained the march of the German columns towards the northwest, or they were large forces, which in this case were intended for a maneuver against our northern wing, and therefore this shift towards the north could only be achieved by weakening the German center in Luxembourg. In this last case, the offensive that I planned for the 3rd and 4th armies would be facilitated. Moreover, it seemed to me that the enemy forces engaged north of the Meuse should not be as considerable as they were said to be, for reasons of supply. Indeed, the examination of the map showed us that the resistance of Liège and the destruction made by the Belgians had to prevent any supply west of the line Verviers-Bastogne-Arlon, and, in particular, the supply of the troops of the area of Huy had to be singularly difficult, as long as the forts of Liège would hold.

At that time, we had no news that these forts had fallen. And

Chapter III

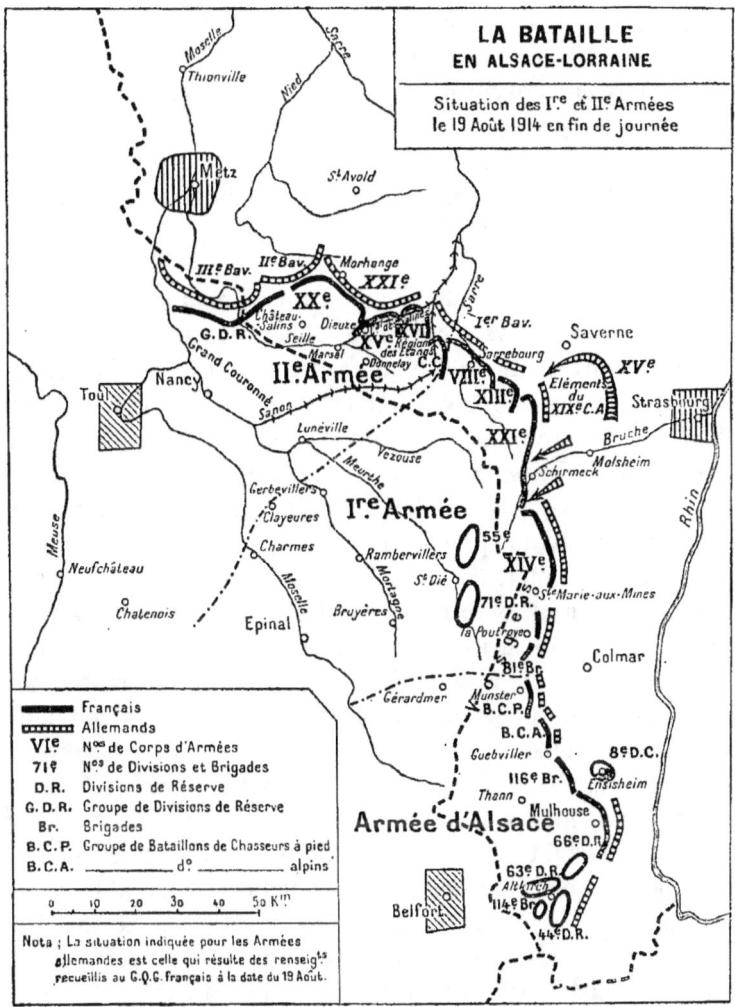

we could not assume that the Germans would find the railroad bridge intact when they took Liége.

Thus, the Belgian army continued to cause me the greatest concern. The day of the 19th ended, however, with the announcement of happy news. Colonel Huguet informed me that a meeting had been held that morning at the British HQ. It had been noted that the arrivals in the assembly area were proceeding without difficulty, and Marshal French, desirous of cooperating as soon as possible in our operations, had studied the possibility of hastening the entry into action of his forces, and he had decided that the forward movement of his army would begin on Friday the 21st.

You can guess with what satisfaction I received this news, which allowed me to hope that our English allies could participate at our side in the first battle.

Thursday, August 20. – The situation, on the morning of the 20th, seemed to me to be favorable on the whole. Indeed, the meeting of the Franco-British forces was completed in good order, before the contact with the enemy. We still had no news from Liège, which we were therefore entitled to believe was still able to resist. Namur was to receive the support of one of our reserve divisions. The 5th Army had slowly gathered between the Sambre and the Meuse, ready to carry out the projected maneuver, whatever the decision taken. In the center, the 2nd Army had occupied Dieuze and pushed vanguards to Morhange and Delme; it is true that we had not been able to break out of the Étangs region. Our 1st Army was in contact with a prepared position that it was preparing to attack beyond Sarrebourg. Finally, the army of Alsace had, after a fight, re-occupied Mulhouse.

I was thus able to send a note of confidence to the Minister, by telegraphing him a report around 8:45 am. This was to be the last good news I would be able to report for a long time. Indeed, shortly after the sending of this telegram, the bad news started to arrive without any break at the G.Q.G. As far as I am concerned, this date is important in my memory, because it marks the reversal of a situation which until then we had been able, in spite of certain incidents, to consider advantageous.

Around 4 p.m., I received from General de Castelnau the news that he was violently counter-attacked on his entire front and that he was obliged to consider a withdrawal to Donnelay, Marsal and the Grand-Couronné; he moved his headquarters to Nancy. At the end of the day, a new telegram was sent: the 2nd Army was going to withdraw during the night and to return to the line indicated.

For his part, General Dubail informed me that his right had been subjected to a severe enemy offensive, and that he was obliged to abandon his offensive plans. In the afternoon, Major Maurin, in liaison with the 1st Army, telephoned that the army had withdrawn but that it hoped to be able to hold onto its new positions to give Castelnau's army time to recover. On the extreme right, the army of Alsace had stopped advancing.

This serious news which arrived to us so abruptly in the evening of the 20th and was confirmed throughout the night was not without surprises to me. Indeed, the numbers of the French right seemed sufficient to stop the opposing left, whose active forces were to include, to our knowledge, only the Vth Bavarian corps, the XXIst, XVth and XIVth army corps, as well as some elements of the XIIIth. I was all the more surprised that, the next morning, the 2nd Army informed me that it had the impression of having only strong rear-guards in front of it.

As a precautionary measure, I judged that it was not advisable to disengage the 2nd Army, and around 6:30 p.m., I gave the order to temporarily suspend the embarkation of the trailing division of the 9th Corps, and to place it at the disposal of General de Castelnau. In addition, I warned General Dubail to take all measures to ensure the security of the right flank of his army.

While these events were taking place on our right, the situation was suddenly becoming clearer on our left.

First of all, the staff at Namur had confirmed important troop crossings on the left bank of the Meuse between Huyr and Liège. Pilots had spotted, on the afternoon of the 19th, columns and bivouacs between Tirlemont, Jodoigne and the Meuse. On the 20th, they reported that on the bridges below Namur, nothing else seemed to have passed during the morning other than the convoys of the German army corps which seemed to be marching against the Belgian army. On the other hand, the retreat of this army to Antwerp continued and was to end during the day of the 20th; to avoid reprisals, the Belgian government had decided that the city guard would not defend Brussels and would also withdraw to Antwerp. In the evening, Belgian and English intelligence arrived which gave us new details: numerous columns had been seen north of the Meuse: they were oriented towards the west, their heads reached the line of Aarschot, Louvain, Jodoigne: they were estimated at least at 4 army corps.

One can judge the importance of this information: it was the first time that we were informed with precision on what was happening north of the Meuse.

First of all, the number of troops turned out to be much larger than we had previously thought. They were obviously too significant to be devoted only to the disabling of the Belgian army. Moreover, the front of the march, the orientation of the columns indicated that this mass was directed against our left wing.

Moreover, this maneuver was much larger than we had envisaged, since it went far beyond Brussels to the north.

Thus, all our previous uncertainties were suddenly dissipated, at the moment when the Franco-British concentration was completed. It seemed that the Germans, behind the curtain of their cavalry, had succeeded in gathering a mass of maneuver on the extreme right.* And the whole of the information allowed us to now form an idea of the plan that our adversaries carried out: it was about a march of the German armies with the right wing in front.

New confirmations during the night of the 20th to the 21st, which reported 5 army corps, 3 cavalry divisions and 2 cavalry brigades north of the Meuse.

Thus, the first of the possibilities that I had envisaged in my letter of August 18, that the enemy would march astride the Meuse between Givet and Brussels, became reality. It was even taking place under favorable conditions. The march of the enemy armies, right wing forward, would allow us to execute the maneuver envisaged: to face the mass in the north with the British and the 5th Army; using the mass of the 3rd and 4th armies, to attack from the south to the north the German forces of Luxembourg, and later to flank the enemy group of the north.

---

* The role of the German cavalry at the beginning of the 1914 campaign as a screen for strategic maneuver does not seem to me to have been studied with sufficient interest until now: it was extremely important and seems to me to be of a nature to change certain ideas regarding the usefulness and use of cavalry. In the shelter of a cavalry curtain, it will always be possible, by night marches, to achieve concentrations that will escape observation and that will be likely to bring about the "event" of which Napoleon spoke.

Chapter III

Already on the evening of the 20th, when I had foreseen the German maneuver, I had given the order to the 3rd Army to begin, on the 21st, its offensive movement in the direction of Arlon. I ordered the 4th Army to begin its march on Neufchâteau, with the Luxembourg forces as its objective, which, moreover, were not reported to us as very important. The 5th Army was given the mission of securing the enemy force in the north, and the British army was asked to cooperate in this action by taking its force in the direction of Soignies.

Friday, August 21. – The orders for the execution of this maneuver were issued in the early hours of the 21st.

In spite of the Belgian retreat to Antwerp, which had broken the circle in which I had hoped to enclose the German right, the situation did not seem bad to me: indeed, the gathering of such a large mass north of the Meuse seemed to be possible only at the expense of the density of another part of the front. However, opposite our right (1st and 2nd armies) the enemy took the offensive; I could conclude that it was in Luxembourg that the German density was the least important; a favorable condition, it seemed, to allow the mass of our 3rd and 4th armies to develop their maneuver.

However, the situation of the armies of the right became rather worrying, although, from that moment, the focus of the operations was shifted towards the north. However, it was necessary that our right wing was not breached.

Then, on the morning of the 21st, I received two reports from my liaison officers, Majors Maurin and de Galbert, who informed me that the fears on this side were quite serious: Dubail regretfully moved his line back to the Vezouse, on account of the retreat of the 2nd Army, although he could have held his positions. As for Castelnau, he hoped to be able to regroup his units under the cover of the Grand-Couronné, but he did not yet know if this reconstitution would be completed in time to allow him to join a new battle. If not, he proposed to continue his retreat towards the upper Meuse, setting up his left in Toul and his right in the Châtenois massif.

I was waiting, understandably, with some impatience, for

information on this part of the front, when around 3:00 p.m., I saw Major Fétizon arrive. He had been present in Nancy, during the whole night of the 20th to the 21st, at the meeting of the 2nd Army staff on the movement of the retreating army corps, and the same morning, around 11 a.m., General de Castelnau had verbally explained to him his assessment of the situation as well as his immediate intentions, instructing him to go to the main headquarters in all haste to report to me. The declarations of the commander of the 2nd Army had seemed so serious to Major Fétizon that he insisted on writing them up immediately and presenting them to the general for his signature. It was this report that he brought to me:

> The enemy is following our retreating columns, and it is to be expected that it will appear before Nancy tomorrow. The Grand-Couronné is occupied by the troops of the 9th Corps and certain elements of the reserve divisions which were not engaged yesterday. In the rear, I am trying to regroup the 15th, 16th and 20th Corps, which are very much exhausted; they will not be in a condition, in general, to be engaged tomorrow or perhaps the day after tomorrow. Finally, the 2nd Cavalry Division was held back by the enemy in the sector of the 1st Army. The 10th Cavalry Division is alone, having just arrived very tired in the Manonviller region. Of the new reserve divisions that had been announced, no more than one element had been received at this time.
>
> I will therefore resist the efforts of the enemy with the only forces available. If I can gain twenty-four hours, I will try to counter-attack with the troops that will have been able, by the day after tomorrow, to regain some measure of strength and cohesion. The situation appears to me to be very serious and I believe I must report to you.
>
> In the event of a new retreat, I will withdraw under the cover of the Toul cannon in the direction of the Upper Meuse.
>
> Another solution would be to free the army from its very critical situation by having the forces disposed north of the Nancy-Château-Salins road diverted to Toul, and towards Épinel, by the left bank of the Moselle, those disposed south of this same road (20th, 16th, 15th army corps). One would thus have some possibility of preserving the whole of these forces and reconstituting them later. If the 1st Army, as I believe, turns its left wing, we could join it.
>
> CASTELNAU.

Chapter III

As one can imagine, the situation thus presented seemed very serious to me. First of all, I could not explain to myself why, so suddenly, this 2nd Army had beaten a retreat, in conditions that looked rather like a rout. In addition, the predictions of the commander of the 2nd Army, envisaging the imminent abandonment of the positions of Nancy and a divergent retreat which would open a breach in our right wing to the enemy, were for me a serious cause for concern. So I immediately telephoned Castelnau that I considered it essential to hold the positions organized around Nancy for at least twenty-four hours, because of the disastrous moral effect that such a retreat would produce in the country, and especially for the very success of our maneuver in the north.

In the evening, a report telephoned in at 5 p.m. informed me that, during the day, no incident had occurred: "I am therefore led," added General de Castelnau, "to envisage for tomorrow, the 22nd, a possible movement only from a rather late hour. The information from the planes will tell me more about this subject." Thus, I could hope that, contrary to the fears of its leader, the 2nd Army could settle on the Grand-Couronné and the Meurthe from Nancy to Lunéville, able to hold the enemy forces that had pushed it back.

Around 10 o'clock in the evening, even better news reached me: "The material and moral situation of the 2nd Army is improving," de Galbert telephoned me from Nancy. "The army is holding, this evening, the Grand-Couronné and the Meurthe from Nancy to Lunéville; the enemy has advanced little; he was, in the evening, about 20 kilometers from the Meurthe. Yesterday he suffered serious losses. All the convoys of the 2nd Army withdrew in very good order. The 20th Corps will be reconstituted rapidly, the 16th fairly quickly, the 15th more difficult. There is no more talk of withdrawing beyond the Moselle."

There was no longer any question of a rout such as General de Castelnau's report had made me fear. Also, when the commander of the 2nd Army asked me to mandate the use of explosives on railroad bridges that evening, I refused, saying that such destruction seemed useless to me.

Thus temporarily reassured about the fate of our army of Lorraine, having made the decision not to pursue any important action in Upper Alsace, I could now turn all my attention to the events in Belgium where all the focus of the maneuver was concentrated.

During the day I had received a visit from General de Morionville, Chief of Staff of the King of the Belgians. He told me in rather pessimistic terms about the situation of the Belgian army, which until now, alone, without support, had had to bear the weight of the struggle. He then explained to me the reasons why the Belgian army had to withdraw to Antwerp, from where it could still threaten the right flank of the enemy masses directed towards the west. On the size of the German forces, I could only obtain from him rather vague information. I informed him of our intentions and assured him that within a very short time the action against the enemy would be conducted by all the Allies.

Chapter III

This approach completed the intelligence that I had received from the head of the French mission to the Belgian headquarters, Lieutenant Colonel Aldebert. The latter had received a letter from Lieutenant General de Selliers, Chief of Staff of the Belgian army, specifying the advantages that the French army had already obtained from the assistance of the Belgian army, and the difficulties in which the latter had found itself in the midst of reorganization, without the support of the French or British forces. He attributed the decision to retreat to Antwerp to the fact that the troops no longer offered any worthwhile resistance for further fighting.

On the morning of the 21st, I had learned that elements of German cavalry had crossed Brussels in the afternoon of the 20th, moving on Ninove and Hal followed by two infantry divisions coming from Louvain. Further south, the enemy columns had resumed their march towards the west. The investment of Namur had begun on the left bank of the Meuse.

In the afternoon, we were informed from Lille that the German cavalry seemed to be approaching Roubaix, Tourcoing and Lille, and that the turmoil was great in these cities.[*]

If the movement of the enemy right wing had a magnitude that we had not suspected, the situation did not seem worrying to me for the moment, because of two things: either the enemy columns would continue their march towards the west and would thus come to present their flank to the 5th Army gathered behind the Sambre and supported at Namur, or they would fall back on the Sambre, and the 5th Army would be able, without a doubt, to force a battle on them lasting long enough to allow the maneuver of the 4th Army to make its action felt north of the Semoy. I thought that General Lanrezac, who had been informed more quickly than I, was on the spot, in liaison with the English, and that he could make the most of the circumstances and play the role that was expected of him.

Also, when, during the evening of the 21st, he pointed out to

---

[*] That same day, General d'Amade proposed to me to entrust General Hermant, commander of the artillery of Douai, with the task of organizing the defense of Lille. I replied around 2 p.m., giving my approval to this proposal.

me that the emergence of his army, from the next day, the 22nd, on the left bank of the Sambre could expose his troops to battle in isolation, and that, to be able to act in liaison with the English army, it was necessary to wait until the 23rd and perhaps the 24th, I answered him that I left it up to him to judge the moment when it would be appropriate to begin his offensive movement, and that I would keep him informed, each day, of the front reached by the 4th Army.

Around 8 p.m., a report from the Belgian headquarters informed us that the German corps operating in the area of Brussels seemed to have made a turn towards the south during the day of the 21st, after having passed Brussels. The 4th Corps, in particular, which had emerged by the Ninove road, had fallen back on Hal. On its right, the 2nd corps, after having marched from Vilvoorde to Aalst, had not yet reached this city at 8 pm.

Thus, it seemed that the German movement would result in a battle facing north on the 22nd or 23rd, in which the 5th Army and the British would be side by side and numerically superior. Indeed, the size of the German forces forming the right wing was estimated, including the troops screening Namur and those who had remained in front of the Belgians, at 6 army corps, 3 cavalry divisions and 2 or 3 reserve divisions. But we were lining up:

For the 5th Army, 10 and a half infantry divisions, 3 cavalry divisions and 3 reserve infantry divisions.[*]

For the British army, 4 and a half infantry divisions and a cavalry division.[†]

The day was calm for the 5th Army, except for an engagement of forward positions at the bridge of Tamines. The bombardment of Namur had started in the afternoon. The 3rd and 4th armies had started their movement without encountering any resistance. To the 4th Army, I confirmed in the evening of the 21st the order to continue its movement towards the north, with the mission to drive

---

[*] 18th, 3rd, 10th, and 1st Corps; 37th and 38th Infantry Divisions; 8th Infantry Brigade; 4th Reserve Division Group (51st, 53rd, and 69th Reserve Divisions); 1st Cavalry Corps (1st, 3rd, and 5th Cavalry Divisions).

[†] 1st, 2nd, 3rd, 5th infantry divisions, a mixed brigade, a cavalry division.

to the Meuse between Dinant, Namur and the Ourthe all the opposing forces which would be in this area; to the 3rd Army, I issued orders to continue to cover the right flank of the 4th against the enemy forces of Luxembourg, by staggering its formation so as to be able to engage easily facing east.

The day of the 21st ended leaving me with high hopes; the battle of Belgium seemed to be going in a favorable strategic direction and the last news of the 2nd Army allowed me to think that, on this side, nothing serious would happen before the matter was settled in the north.

Saturday, August 22. – The day of the 22nd was for me a day of waiting. It was too early for me to intervene in the serious game which was played in Belgium. The floor was given to the players. On this part of the front, my attention was drawn to the Sordet cavalry corps, which seemed to me to be doing a poor job against the German cavalry reported north of Mons. I even wondered if General Sordet was deploying all the necessary activity in this case. On two occasions, at the beginning of the afternoon and around 10 p.m., I made my astonishment known to General Lanrezac, under whose orders he was placed, by asking his opinion on the possible replacement of the commander of the cavalry corps. As far as the protection of the Lille-Tourcoing region exposed to the insults of the German cavalry was concerned, I had Colonel Pellé ask the Minister to put a fourth territorial division at the disposal of General d'Amade.[*]

On the front of the 1st and 2nd armies, the situation seemed to be calming down; on the morning of the 22nd, I sent them instructions to explain their new mission: they had to keep a defensive posture, to last the time necessary for the development of the maneuver started in the North, and to be in a position to take the offensive again.

---

[*] I had known captain Pellé in Madagascar, and I had learned to appreciate his high and remarkable qualities. Also, from the very first days of the war, I asked the Minister to put Colonel Pellé, who was in Morocco, at my disposal. This request was granted and colonel Pellé joined me at the moment when the Battle of the Frontiers began.

The evening brought us new information.

First, as far as the German extreme right movement was concerned, it seemed that it was continuing its large-scale reorganization around Namur, as the Belgian staff had reported to us: the day before, this wing comprised 5 or 6 army corps which seemed to be followed by reserve formations; it was covered towards the west by 3 cavalry divisions. At the beginning of the afternoon, the enemy had crossed the Sambre and attacked east of Charleroi. The 10th and 3rd Corps had to retreat, and this retreat had led to the retreat of the 1st Corps on their right, which had abandoned the crossings of the Meuse. The 18th Corps had not been engaged.

The 3rd and 4th armies had encountered the enemy from the beginning of the day. The 3rd, at the cost of rather serious losses, had established itself on the Joppecourt-Virton front; the 4th had fought successfully towards Neufchâteau and Maissin, but had suffered setbacks towards Tintigny and especially towards Ochamps, which led to a general retreat on the Meix-before-Virton, Jamoigne, Bertrix, Paliseul, Houdremont front. These two armies were to take the offensive again the next day, the 23rd.

On the Lorraine front, only cavalry encounters occurred in the Grand-Couronné region; in the afternoon, the rearguards of the 16th, 15th and 20th Corps were confronted by an enemy that tried to cross the Sanon river, and that managed to enter Lunéville. The left of the 1st Army, attacked in the morning, had retreated towards the Mondon forest and the Meurthe river.

It would have been premature to draw any conclusions from this body of information; it was necessary to wait before forming an opinion and making decisions.

I received that day, towards the end of the afternoon, news from Russia. I had asked that the Russians accelerate their march on Berlin and Vienna. Mr. Paléologue informed me of the result of his efforts. The Russian forces, he informed me, currently formed 10 armies, 7 of which were already engaged against Germany and Austria, that is to say a total of 28 army corps representing approximately 1,120,000 men. Grand Duke Nicholas declared himself resolved to march as quickly as possible on Berlin and Vienna, mainly on Berlin, passing between the fortresses of Thorn,

Posen and Breslau. All his armies had already taken the offensive. In East Prussia, the Russian troops had already advanced 30 kilometers beyond the border; the forces on the left bank of the Vistula were to march directly on Berlin as soon as the armies of the northwest had succeeded in fixing the German army.

From these telegrams I was entitled to conclude that the Germans would soon feel seriously threatened on their eastern front, and I could hope that before long they would be forced to lighten the density of forces engaged against us. However, from a source that seemed reliable, we learned that two active army corps first opposed to the Russian army were being transported to the French front, and that they had been replaced on the eastern front by landwehr formations. I asked the government to insist again to the Russian general staff on the necessity of an all-out offensive towards Berlin.

In Paris, the news of our failure at Morhange had produced some emotion. Mr. Messimy wrote to me on this same date of the 22nd, in that lapidary form that he liked:

> My dear General and Friend,
> The day before yesterday, a success; yesterday, a failure. This is the war. I have full faith in tomorrow's victory. But whatever happens, believe in all my trusting friendship.
> MESSIMY.

Until then, I had been sending a daily telephone report to the Minister on the events of the previous day. On the evening of the 22nd, I received a visit from Captain Tardieu, who was carrying a letter from the President of the Council, Mr. Viviani, who complained that he had been poorly informed. He emphasized the responsibility of the government, which obliged it to take measures to gradually prepare public opinion, and he indicated the need for us to fight against German diplomacy, which sought to deceive world opinion by means of the press. He proposed to me to institute a shuttle of two officers between the great headquarters and the government. The mission of these officers would be to provide the government with information on the course of operations and the manner in which our troops had conducted themselves, without descending in the analysis of events below the actions of the divisions. In closing, Mr. Viviani took the opportunity to "renew to me all the confidence, the affectionate esteem of the government and the whole population which rests on the army, on its leaders and on you." I could not but accept these very legitimate proposals. This was the origin of the institution of liaison officers between the government and the general headquarters, of which I will often have to speak. The two officers who occupied this delicate post during the entire duration of my command were Colonel Pénelon and Lieutenant-Colonel Herbillon; they both showed tact and devotion.

Sunday, August 23. – The hopes that I had nourished concerning the offensive fortunately begun the day before by the 4th Army, and which was to continue on the 23rd, were not to last long. Indeed, in the early hours of the morning of the 23rd, I received from General de Langle the notice that the "disorganized" retreat of the 17th Corps on the left bank of the Semoy and the "disorganization" of three brigades of the colonial corps had resulted in the withdrawal of the 11th and 12th Corps. Thus, a situation was created which imposed on the commander of the 4th Army the necessity of reforming his scattered units on a position of withdrawal. He expected to be able to resist all day on this new position.

This account surprised me. Indeed, according to the information we had, there were only three or four corps in front of de Langle's army. On the other hand, the very words used by the army commander to characterize the attitude of some of his units made me think that there must have been some failure of command. It was essential to act promptly, and I asked General de Langle to inform me immediately of the leaders against whom I should take the necessary sanctions.

In the evening, I learned that the 4th Army had again experienced serious setbacks on several points of its front, and particularly on its right: its withdrawal had been carried out not without difficulty, especially in the 12th Corps and the colonial corps.

Thus, the offensive of this army, which I had counted as the main maneuver, was temporarily halted, and this army was going to be obliged to return to the Meuse and the Chiers. This fact was all the more regrettable that in the 3rd Army, despite the retreat of the right behind the Crusne and the Chiers, General Ruffey hoped to be able to resume the offensive the following day.

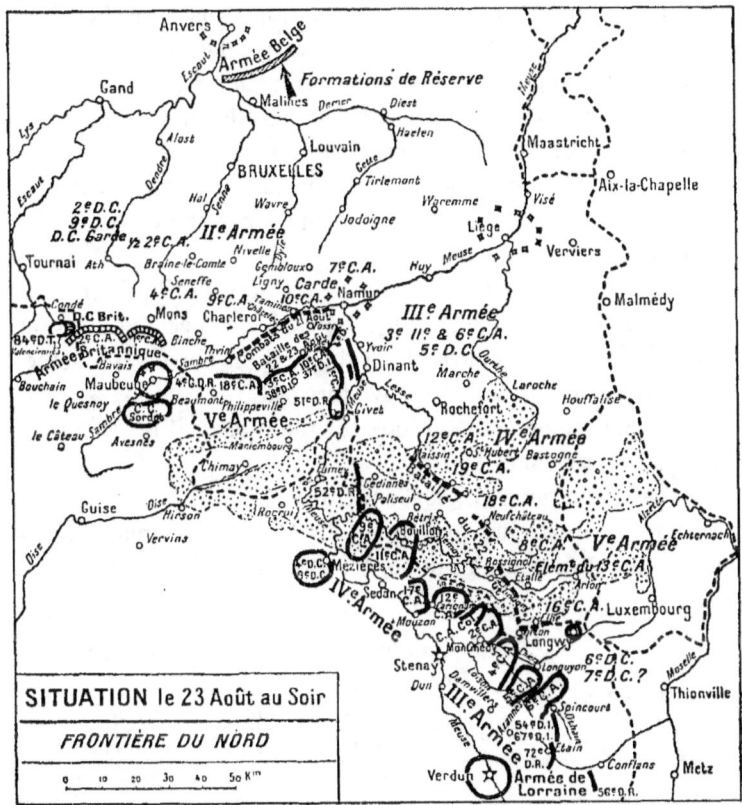

Meanwhile, what happened to the British and the 5th Army?

All day I remained without news. In the evening, I received a telegram from Colonel Huguet, informing me of the situation of the English army that morning: its column heads were at Haulchaim Jemmapes, Saint-Ghislain, the cavalry on the left towards Quiévrain. He informed me that General Lanrezac had asked Marshal French, should the English army not be attacked itself, to attack the flank of the enemy forces which crossed the Sambre. Now, the Marshal had resolved to hold his position from the 23rd in the morning for twenty-four hours; if, after aerial reconnaissance of the German forces to the north and northwest of Mons, the latter did not appear to be too numerous, he would move forward to the northeast, provided that his left flank was not threatened.

Shortly afterwards, I received a report from Lanrezac, whom I had asked to let me know his intentions: his army had been attacked at 11 o'clock in the morning; the 3rd Corps had withdrawn to Valcourt, the enemy was threatening the right of the 5th Army on the Meuse and a German detachment had succeeded in occupying Onhaye. Givet was threatened. Namur had fallen. In view of this situation, and on learning of the failure of the 4th Army, Lanrezac decided to withdraw his army, the very next day, to the Beaumont-Givet front.

The general battle started with a series of failures that endangered the execution of the plan we had conceived. Was this failure definitive, or could we hope that, pulling ourselves together, our armies would be able to move forward?

My first thought was to look for the causes of his failure, in order to find remedies.

What about the numerical superiority?

Here, on this date of August 23, is how we imagined the German order of battle from north to south:

On the Meuse, 2 armies	IInd army: 5 and a half army corps and 3 cavalry divisions.
	IIIrd Army. Presumably on the right bank: 3 army corps and 1 cavalry division.
In Belgian Luxembourg	IVth army: 3 army corps and 1 cavalry division.
In the Grand Duchy	Vth Army: 2 army corps and 2 or 3 cavalry divisions.
In Lorraine	VIth army: 4 army corps and 2 cavalry divisions.

Chapter III

In Alsace	VIIth Army	*North Group*: Elements of 3 army corps and 1 cavalry division. *South Group*: Reserve formations.

Moreover, as far as the German reserve formations were concerned, we only knew that reserve divisions must have been pushed towards the entrenched camp of Antwerp. One of them was reported, on the 22nd, west of Aerschot; no other was reported in the wake of the armies we had spotted.*

On the other hand, we had:

In Belgium	British Army: 4 and a half infantry divisions and one cavalry division. 5th Army: 10 and a half infantry divisions and 3 cavalry divisions; in addition, 3 reserve infantry divisions.
In Belgian Luxembourg	4th Army: 12 infantry divisions, 2 cavalry divisions and 2 reserve divisions. 3rd Army: 6 infantry divisions and 1 cavalry division.
In Lorraine	2nd Army: 7 infantry divisions, 2 cavalry divisions and 5 reserve divisions.
In Alsace	1st Army: 9 infantry divisions and 1 cavalry division. 7th Army: 2 and a half infantry divisions; 1 cavalry division and 3 reserve divisions.

Thus, in terms of manpower, we thought we had a significant numerical superiority over the enemy.

---

* This order of battle was the one established by the 2nd Bureau of the G.Q.G. on August 23, 1914, as it was transmitted to the Armies in appendix to the intelligence bulletin of the same day, 6 p.m.

Was it the strategic implementation that was at fault?

The Allied extreme left wing was held by the British west of Mons; from the state of the intelligence that reached the end of the day on the 23rd, the conversion movement executed by the German corps north of Namur seemed likely to bring them in the evening of that day to the following points

IInd corps:	towards Ath.
IVth corps:	south of Enghien,
IXth corps:	in the south of the zone Soignies Seneffe,
VIIth corps:	south of Pont à Celles,
Xth corps:	and Guard: in front of the right of our 5th Army.

This shift of the German right was covered in the region of Leuze by the 9th Cavalry Division supported by elements of all arms. It thus did not seem that our left was threatened with encirclement: the opposing fronts seemed to coincide rather exactly.

My reflections thus led me to conclude that the fall of Namur, the threat on the right flank of our 5th Army, along the Meuse, perhaps still local failures of the command, had brought about the retreat of Lanrezac's army, and it was to be feared that this withdrawal would involve that of the English army.

Monday August 24. – Indeed, in the morning of the 24th, I received two telegrams: the first, dated 3:45 a.m., came from the English army and announced to me that our allies were also going to withdraw to the Maubeuge-Valenciennes line, the second, sent by the 5th Army, said that the combat had resumed violently during the day of the 23rd, particularly on the front of the 18th, 3rd and 1st corps. "The English army," said General Lanrezac, "informs me that it is withdrawing to the Longueville-Valenciennes line, and that, in the event that it is threatened on the left wing, it will withdraw to Amiens. Please let me know the subsequent direction of retreat."

I received shortly afterwards the situation report of Lieutenant-Colonel Brécard who, the evening before, had found general Lanrezac preoccupied but not discouraged. Lieutenant-Colonel

Brécard shared with me the impressions that the general had asked him to communicate to me about the causes of the failure of his army. Unfortunately, this was not the only news of this nature that I was to receive in the morning. At about 8:30 a.m., de Langle informed me that his offensive towards the north had been "provisionally" halted, and that he considered it necessary to move his army behind the Meuse and the Chiers; he hoped that there it would be able to hold, repair its losses, recover and become capable of taking the offensive again. I knew de Langle and I was sure of the firmness of his character. If he gave me this opinion, I knew in advance that it was the exact reflection of things. Now, this withdrawal of the 4th Army left the German troops, reported in the region of the Lesse and Ciney, free to cross the Meuse.

We had to face the facts. As I wrote to the Minister on the morning of the 24th, our general offensive in Belgium had been definitively halted, and we were condemned to a defensive strategy based on our strongholds and on the great obstacles of the terrain, in order to hold out as long as possible, while striving to wear down the enemy and to take the offensive again when the time came.*

If the initial maneuver had failed, another one had to be prepared. In spite of the painful obligation to abandon a part of the national territory, it was essential first of all to gain ground, in order to reconstitute a mass likely to resume the offensive.

Between half past eight and half past nine, I sent the orders preparing this new maneuver:

> The 5th Army, maintaining liaison with the 4th and with the English, would maneuver in retreat by relying on the position of Maubeuge and the wooded massif of the Ardennes.
>
> The 4th Army would be transferred to the left bank of the Meuse downstream from Mouzon and to the heights of the right bank of the Meuse between Mouzon and Stenay.

---

* The Minister of War, to whom, in the morning of the 24th, I had made known my intention to hold out in order to be able to take again the offensive, when the occasion would present itself, answered me by a laconic message dated the same day, 12:30 p.m.: "We agree, hold out."

The 3rd Army would come to the positions organized on the general front: Montmédy, Damvillers, Azannes, in liaison with the army of Lorraine maintained on the Hauts-de-Meuse in a defensive attitude.

As for the 2nd Army, it did not give me any concern for the moment; the day of the 23rd had passed without any serious combat; the prescribed movements had been accomplished and General de Castelnau had informed me, that very morning, of his intention, if the enemy attempted to invest the southern part of the Grand-Couronné, to attack it during the afternoon.

Finally, the First Army also seemed to be in good shape. The day before, the 21st Corps had been attacked and had easily maintained its positions, while the 8th and 13th Corps had gained positions allowing them to solidly support the front of the 1st Army.

And the army of Alsace had only reserve and landwehr elements in front of it: I considered that in view of the situation of our left wing it was possible to take from this army the greater part of the 7th Corps.[*]

The question which, on our left, worried me the most, was that the envelopping movement of the Germans had seemed to develop. Now, it was the English who alone could oppose this threat, that is to say precisely the army to which I had no right to give orders. I had to content myself with suggesting to Marshal French that he could usefully delay the march of the enemy forces between Valenciennes and Maubeuge, that is to say, on the extension of the Givet-Beaumont line on which I hoped to see the 5th Army hold. At the same time I indicated to him that, if he was obliged by superior forces to withdraw, he could do it in the general direction of Cambrai. Thus, he would link up with the barricade constituted by the three territorial divisions commanded by General d'Amade.[†]

But it seemed to me especially necessary to extend the left of

---

[*] The corps headquarters and one of its divisions.

[†] This barricade had been in place since the 22nd; it included an advanced line between Maubeuge and Dunkirk, and a main line of resistance between Landrecies and the Aa.

the English by French troops to whom I could give orders. Now, two reserve divisions coming from Paris were to be brought during the night to Arras to be put under the orders of d'Amade. I gave them the general mission of covering the English left against any attempt at envelopment.

In addition, I took again under my direct orders Sordet's cavalry corps, which instead of gaining the external wing of the allied armies had gathered south of Maubeuge. I instructed him to pass to the left of the English and to contribute to their safety; but I knew that there was little to expect from him, because of the state of fatigue of his men and his horses.

Once these orders, which had to do with the strategic domain, had been given, it was necessary to investigate why, in spite of the numerical superiority that I believed to have given to our armies, the powerful offensive action attempted from Longwy to the Sambre had tactically failed so completely.

However painful it may be to reveal certain weaknesses, it is necessary to state completely what appeared to us then. Too many of our generals proved to be not up to their task. Among them, some had acquired in peacetime the most brilliant reputation as teachers or as maneuverers on the map, who in front of the enemy showed themselves dominated by the fear of responsibilities. I was told that in some large units there was a total lack of command. In the 3rd Corps, during a whole part of the battle of Charleroi, the orders could only be given by General Rouquerol, commander of the artillery of the corps, who had to replace the commander of the corps when he was nowhere to be found at the most critical moment of the day. In the 14th Corps and in the 5th Corps, the same notable incapacity. In the latter corps, a particularly regrettable event had occurred: a major general, losing control of himself and the feeling of his duties towards his troops, had committed suicide. In the 4th Army, General de Langle blamed the failure he had just suffered on the way the 17th Corps had behaved during the battle. There is no doubt that the purification of the command that I intended to carry out in the course of 1914, if war had not broken out, had to be done without waiting an hour, if we did not want the failure of our first maneuver to turn into an irremediable defeat. As a matter of urgency, I asked that all the generals who had proved to be insufficient be made known to me; as reports arrived, I checked them, then, for the leaders who seemed to deserve this decision, I put them at the disposal of the Minister and I named in their place those who seemed the most worthy.

Upon receipt notice of my initial decisions, Mr. Messimy replied:

24/8/14.

My dear general,

You put at my disposal Generals B... and G... Putting at my disposal is not enough when there has been cowardice as in the case of General G....

You will want, in the future, to bring the officers relieved of their command to the general headquarters by *automobile*, to have them go before the Council of War. I believe that there are no other penalties, as in 1793, than dismissal and death.

You want victory: take the quick, brutal, energetic and decisive means.

In any case, don't send people back inside who will clamor against you and us; lock them up pending their trial.

If necessary, I will ask General Galliéni to preside over this permanent Council of War, which should not sit in Paris but in the armies.

Over to you.

MESSIMY.

It is clear from the terms of this letter that the Minister was even more categorical than I was. The Council of War of which he spoke did not seem necessary to me. I judged that the normal means of the Councils of War which I had at my disposal were sufficient to judge the cases which would come under the code of military justice. For the others, I maintained my decision to send back to the interior those leaders who proved to be incapable.

But inadequate command in a number of units was obviously not the only reason for our setbacks. It was obvious that the principles of offense that we had tried to inculcate in the army before the war had been too often misunderstood and poorly implemented; from all points of the front, I was informed of maneuver errors that had led to heavy losses and sometimes reduced to nothing the offensive and defensive value of the troops. I was informed that the vanguards almost always engaged without the support of the artillery, due to a false understanding of the offensive sense, and fell in massive formations under the blows of the enemy artillery. In other cases, it was a large unit that, advancing without guarding its flanks, was suddenly exposed to cruel adventures. The infantry was almost always launched into the assault at too great a distance from the objectives. The conquered points were never secured before the departure for the conquest of a new objective, so that if this one failed, our repulsed troops lost even the fruit of their first efforts. Above all, the cooperation of artillery and infantry was almost never achieved.

As soon as all these points were known to me, I instructed the armies to regulate with prudence their attacks and, especially, to carry out with the greatest care the coordination of the arms. It was precisely this development of the offensive doctrine that I had taken care of in our training camps that the circumstances imposed on us now with the harsh sanction of the battlefields. Alas! a written order is not enough to instantly transform the mentality of an army; it takes time to create a new state of mind. But in war, experience quickly comes to the aid of the command to reduce the delays.

As Mr. Viviani had invited me to do, I thought I should, in my report to the government, at the same time as announcing the definitive failure of our general offensive in Belgium, indicate the causes of our failure: "Our army corps, I said, have not shown in the open country the offensive qualities that we had hoped for from the partial successes of the beginning, successes obtained especially in mountain operations." Here again, the reaction was strong at the War Ministry. Here is, in fact, the telegram I received in response to my report:

> I receive your telegram reporting failures. Against these, there is no other punishment than immediate death: the first to be struck must be the guilty officers, if there are any. The only law of France, at the present time, is: win or die. I renew my formal invitation to you to bring to the highest functions energetic young men, determined to win at all costs. Eliminate the old men, without pity.
>
> MESSIMY.

General Joffre finds one of his former officers, Bocquet, mobilized in the 54th infantry

If, from a distance, one is tempted to find that the Minister was exaggerating the sanctions to be taken, I want to testify here that I am grateful to him for having constantly given me the impression that I would be supported in all the measures that I would have to prescribe in order to give our armies the necessary vigor.

Monday, August 24 was relatively quiet. I anxiously awaited news from our left. In the evening, and in the night, it arrived rather worse, as one could suppose: Tournai and Condé had been occupied by enemy detachments; then General d'Amade made

Chapter III 289

known that the Germans had arrived at Somain and Valenciennes. Thus, the German right clearly outflanked the English left, and was probably going to be able to freely develop a maneuver which would threaten our lines of communication; that was all the more likely as the withdrawal of the 3rd and 4th armies was going to, undoubtedly, allow the Germans to reinforce their right wing mass.

The danger was serious: it was necessary to consider the probable retreat of all the left, and particularly of the English army. I judged necessary, in anticipation of this eventuality, to fix zones of retreat, intended if necessary to allow the rapid establishment of orders; I determined that for the English army, by directing it towards the southwest, in order to cover the direction of Paris, and to avoid as much as possible the envelopment by the force in which the enemy would find himself extending towards the west. The limit of the English zone on the side of the 5th Army was determined by a line passing through Maubeuge, Le Cateau and Bohain.

At the same time that the overrunning of the English army endangered our lines of communication, it threatened the entire northern region defended only by the territorial divisions of d'Amade. It was high time to stretch the floodgates, and to withdraw the depots near the border. Around 3:00 pm. 30, I agreed by telephone with the Minister on this subject.

As for Lille, I thought that this great city was going to be able to offer some resistance to the enemy, since, as you will recall, I had authorized it to be put in a state of defense. My hope was to be short-lived, because at about 5 p.m., General d'Amade telephoned the general headquarters that he had received directly from the Minister the order not to defend Lille! I was surprised by this decision, which was entirely different from what had been agreed upon on the 23rd. Around 11 p.m., Mr. Messimy confirmed this decision of the government taken on the request of the civilian element of Lille.

From the rest of the front, the news was less bad. The 5th Army had no difficulty in occupying the Marienbourg, Solre-le-Château, Maubeuge line. The enemy had not pursued it. The reports of the 3rd and 4th armies gave me hope. The 2nd Army had seen at least two army corps marching towards Clayeures and

Gerbéville; the 20th Corps and the 70th Reserve Division had counter-attacked them. The first news of this operation was favorable.*

Thus, at the end of that day, all the danger was concentrated in front of the British army; it seemed all the more threatening because, for the first time, the information reached us that the army corps of the IInd German army were probably followed by reserve formations bearing the same numbers as the active corps: the first indication of the presence of reserve units employed in the active operations. This information gave us the explanation of the extraordinary development of the enemy front.

In the midst of the dark hours we were living through, my thoughts frequently went to our Russian allies: I expected that their action would soon ease the pressure that the enemy was putting on us. And that explains the impatience with which I awaited news from that distant front.

I received some the same day. The Russian ambassador had been charged by the chief of staff of the generalissimo of the imperial armies to let me know that "the Russian offensive in Germany was done by large masses and was carried out with all the possible rapidity, compatible with the requirements of safety. In East Prussia, serious strategic problems were being resolved, and as soon as a solution was found, there would be a way to proceed with a more rapid development of subsequent offensive operations. Generally speaking," the document concluded, "the Russian offensive is being pursued with the utmost inflexibility."

All this was still very vague.

---

* Minutes telephoned at 7:40 p.m.

291

Chapter IV

The preparation of the battle of the Marne. – August 25-
September 5, 1914.

*A**ugust 25.* – On the morning of the 25th, it was obvious that the strategic maneuver prepared since the 18th had led to a complete failure for us.

The news of the night could not leave any hope. The forward movement of the German armies in Belgium continued. The British army, attacked during the day of the 24th by significant forces, had fallen back on the Valenciennes-Maubeuge line, and there was every chance that the enemy would start an effective envelopment maneuver against it. Already, in front of the German right wing, Somain was reported as occupied by the enemy, and the German reserve corps reported until now as heading against Antwerp now seemed to follow the tracks of the merchant wing, thus increasing its possibilities of maneuver.[*]

In the belief that the Germans only engaged active corps in their offensive operations, I was led to look for the causes of our failure, not only, as I said in the previous chapter, in tactical failures, but also in the numerical superiority that the Germans had

---

[*] Report no. 59 of the 2nd Bureau of the G.Q.G. (August 25, 1914, 6 hours.)

managed to give to their right wing. This numerical superiority, which our previous calculations were far from allowing us to assume, seemed to me to be attributed to the failure of the main offensive which had been halted from the start: the 4th Army, powerfully equipped with 6 army corps, had been immediately immobilized, and declared that it would hold between the Meuse and the Chiers, but that it would not be possible, because of its losses, for it to produce a new offensive effort before long. In my opinion, the failure of the 4th Army in Belgian Luxembourg had the consequence of allowing the enemy to divert part of the forces operating in this region, to make them cross the Meuse downstream from Givet and engage them against the right of our 5th Army.

I must say that at this point my greatest concern was the attitude of our troops. We had begun with a series of failures. Now, the French soldier is easily impressed; he can lose confidence as quickly as he gets excited. Subjected to this harsh ordeal aggravated by the overwhelming temperature of this late August, would he be able to resist when it was necessary? Indications of weariness and exhaustion reached me, which did not leave me unconcerned: there were frequently bags thrown or abandoned on the back of the ditches, and it seemed that the cadres, whose authority was far from being established, did not always react with enough vigor.

Having indicated these moral concerns, I return to my strategic concerns. It was necessary, without losing an hour, to prepare a maneuver that could stop the enemy movement threatening our left, and pointing in the direction of the Oise valley towards Paris.

First of all, could I hope that our left would resist, leaving me time to prepare a new maneuver? No, the capacity of resistance of our troops and of the English army was too strongly undermined for me to have any illusions in this respect. As painful as this obligation was, I had to admit the necessity to give up ground to give the allied troops time to recover.

Then, what maneuver to consider? During the whole of that long and dark day of the 25th, I studied with my collaborators the various possibilities that could be realized. Berthelot considered that the maneuver begun in Belgian Luxembourg could be taken up again on another ground; he foresaw that the English army, subjected to the overwhelming action of the German right, would not fail to withdraw promptly, accentuating the danger of veing overrun that the left of our 5th Army was running. He claimed that it would then be opportune to take advantage of this situation by launching an offensive on the inner wing of the German right opposite the British. He argued that this solution would be the quickest to implement, and likely to give the greatest results by separating the German right from the main body of the battle.

The solution proposed by General Berthelot did not satisfy me. To be able to consider it, it would have been necessary to be assured that the 5th Army would hold long enough to allow the mass in charge of dislocating the enemy's front to gather behind its front; moreover, if for lack of time, or for any other reason, this maneuver were to fail, we would run the risk of seeing our armies enveloped by the enemy and forced to fight a disastrous battle with reversed fronts.

In spite of the objections which were made to him, Berthelot maintained his point of view. All my preferences went towards a very different solution: the gathering on the German outer wing of a mass likely to envelop in its turn this marching wing.

After having conscientiously weighed the advantages and the chances of success of the two suggestions, I decided, in the evening of the 25th, for the second solution, and I had Commander Gamelin draw up in my cabinet the order which became General Instruction no 2. I signed it and sent it to General Berthelot, asking him to ensure its execution. I must say that, very loyally, in the presence of the decision I had just taken, Berthelot, forgetting all his preferences, did everything possible to ensure the success of this new plan.

In order to have the time to gather in the region of Amiens a mass likely to produce a decisive effect on the enemy's marching wing, it was necessary to allow a retreat of our armies of the left. One could hope that by using the obstacles to stop or delay the enemy progression by frequent counter-attacks, they would not have to exceed the general line of the Aisne extended by the Craonne, Laon, La Fère escarpment. The 3rd Army would take support on the place of Verdun which would be used as a hinge for the general movement of retreat. The 4th and 5th French armies, the British army and the Amiens grouping formed of forces taken from our right wing would constitute a mass capable of taking up the offensive again, as soon as the enemy, emerging from the wooded region of the Ardennes, would find himself with this difficult terrain behind him.

Thus I envisaged an Amiens-Reims battle, with a new army on the extreme left of our line, flanking the British and likely to outflank the German right wing in its turn.

For the success of this maneuver, two essential conditions had to be met:

> First of all, that our 4th and 5th armies resisting every step, combining their retreat with partial resumption of the offensive, counter-attacks, supported by our very efficient artillery against marching troops, leave us time to gather on our left the mass that I had resolved to form.
>
> Secondly, that the British, by a tenacious resistance, would only give up the ground very slowly, so as to avoid that our left wing, by withdrawing too quickly, would favour the enemy's enveloping threat. Moreover, they already had the Amade group to support them, to which the 61st and 62nd reserve divisions, currently deploying at Arras, had been added.

The obligation to convince the English command of this necessity seemed so urgent to me that I organized a meeting with Marshal French in the evening of the 25th at his headquarters in Saint-Quentin for the next morning. I took advantage of this to summon General Lanrezac, with whom it was important to reach an understanding in the presence of the English commander-in-chief.

In order to form the Amiens group on our extreme left, I needed to take large units from the entire front. Already my resolution to stop the operations of the army of Alsace, which had become secondary, had allowed me to take part of the 7th Corps from this army; the dissolution of the first group of reserve divisions of General Archinard was going to free the 63rd Division and make it possible for it to embark for Picardy. As for the 1st and 2nd armies, they were engaged in a joint action which, according to the latest news of the evening of the 25th, seemed to succeed;

Chapter IV

there could therefore be no question of reducing their numbers for the moment.

That left the 8th Army, the Army of Lorraine, commanded by Maunoury. The day before, I had informed Maunoury that the situation required that he stick to the defense of the Hauts-de-Meuse, north and south of Verdun as far as Toul. Maunoury had answered me[*] that the circumstances seemed to him to be able to lead to a success, if he was authorized to use part of his reserve divisions, to support the attack that the 3rd Army was leading, on the basis of a German order of operations taken that very morning, against the German forces marching on Verdun by Conflans and Jeandelize. In the evening, I only learned that at the end of the day the attack of the 3rd Army was progressing and that at 2 p.m. the army of Lorraine had counter-attacked in conjunction with the 6th Corps.[†] This operation, as advantageous as it was, could only appear to me as secondary, and without any significant results being expected. Indeed, according to the German order, it was against an enemy army corps flanked by an infantry division and a cavalry division that this action was engaged. Faced with the necessity of urgently reinforcing our troops in the north, it was necessary to know how to choose and not to attack everywhere; it was enough to maintain a defensive attitude on the Hauts-de-Meuse. I resolved to order the army of Lorraine to put at my disposal two divisions, ready to be transported by rail. On the morning of the 25th, I sent Major Bel, liaison officer of the 3rd Army, to the main headquarters of this army, bearing orders for the 35th Army and the army of Lorraine to stop the battle, to return to the Hauts-de-Meuse and to take a defensive position. On the 25th, around noon, Bel informed me that two intact divisions were directed towards Dugny and Saint-Mihiel. That same evening, Maunoury reported to me that, linking his movement to the retreat ordered for the 3rd Army, he had in turn broken off the fight.

Thus, at this time, I conceived the mass of the extreme left as

---

[*] Telephone conversation between General Maunoury and General Belin (August 25, 10 h 30).

[†] Report of the 3rd Army of August 24, 20 h 30.

having to be formed of the 7th Corps and a division coming from Alsace, of two divisions coming from the fortified camp of Paris and of two divisions taken from the army of Lorraine. The request for the transport of these last two units had been addressed: to the Minister on August 23; on August 24, the army of Alsace had received the order to embark, as of the 25th, in Belfort and Montbéliard, the staff of the 7th Corps and a division of this army corps; on the 25th, the order to embark the 63rd reserve division. Finally, on the morning of the 25th, the army of Lorraine knew that it had to return two reserve divisions to me; on the 26th, at 11:25 a.m., it was advised that the transport of these divisions to Compiègne would begin on the 27th.

This is how I formed the group that was to become the 6th Army.

Now, on August 25, around 9 p.m., I received the following order from the Minister:

> If victory does not crown the success of our arms and if the armies are reduced to retreat, an army of at least three active corps will have to be directed on the fortified camp of Paris to ensure its protection. An account will be given of the receipt of this order.

The reading of this telegram produced a sharp surprise to me. Indeed, I saw in it the threat of a governmental intervention in the conduct of the operations, an intervention which would risk, if the envisaged eventualities were carried out, hindering considerably my freedom of maneuver at the moment when it seemed to me more necessary than ever.

Moreover, the idea of confining three active army corps in the fortified camp of Paris, at a time when we needed all our resources in the open country, seemed to me to be fraught with danger. It should be noted, on the other hand, that there was no link between forming a maneuver army in the region of Amiens, which was my idea, and sending three active army corps to guard the fortified camp of Paris, which was the Minister's own decision.

Fortunately, the Minister's order was in itself a corrective, in that it was not imperative, since it began with the words: "If victory does not crown the success of our armies, and if the armies are reduced to retreat...." Now, as I have just said, I was in the process of organizing a maneuver which, in my mind, was to lead to a battle on a front marked out by Amiens, Laon, the heights of the north of the Aisne and Reims.

The very terms of this order therefore seemed to authorize me to wait until this battle had been fought before carrying out the Minister's instructions.

I therefore considered myself entitled to provisionally suspend the execution of these instructions, reserving the possibility of acting in due course, depending on the circumstances.

Moreover, however worrying the situation was, it did not yet seem so serious that we were obliged to consider the defense of the capital immediately, and, in any case, if it came to that, we would still have time to carry out the government's decision.[*]

---

[*] The minister's order was accompanied by a letter in two parts, the first dated 7 a.m., the second at noon.
Here is the letter:

MINISTRY OF WAR
THE MINISTER –
No. 19 Min.   Paris, 25/8/1914, 7:00 morning.

My dear general and friend,

1. I am very surprised and, I will say more, dissatisfied with the role played by Sordet. The German cavalry corps roams the northern region ravaging everything, pushing the territorial troops around: Sordet, who has fought little, sleeps. This is inadmissible.

If you want cars for the infantry, there are a large number of them available in Paris. Provided you have the gasoline to refuel them, at least 60 carrying 500 men can be immediately available for operations with the cavalry. But this is only a secondary issue.

2. It seems clear to me that the theater of operations in the north is going to take on real importance, strategic importance overall, moral importance because of its proximity to Paris. An army must be formed to fight there. In my opinion, this is necessary, given the lack of resistance from the territorial troops who are not holding out.

3. I adopt the principle of the promotion system. But I do not want this decree to allow for the advancement of staff personnel at any cost: a captain is worth a colonel in a headquarters. I will not ratify, I warn you, the nominations made for staff personnel, unless there are quite exceptional circumstances: it is to ensure the command of the troops that I admit this

August 26. – On August 26, I left early in the morning for Saint-Quentin accompanied by Berthelot and my orderly, Captain Muller.

I attached great importance to the meeting that I was going to have with the commander of the British army, the first since he had come to see me in Vitry when he took command. It was a question of agreeing with him on the execution of the new plan of operations concerning the Verdun-Laon-Amiens battle that I had decided upon. I knew, moreover, what difficulties I was going to encounter; I could fear, indeed, that the Marshal was not entirely free of his decisions, because I knew that Kitchener was frequently tempted to intervene in the direction of the operations of the

---

revolutionary procedure.

4. Herewith, finally, an order whose capital importance will not escape you: order to give to Paris a minimum garrison of three active corps, in good condition, in case of failure. It goes without saying that the line of retreat of the rest of the army should be quite different in the center and the south of France. We are determined to fight without mercy.

Affectionately yours, MESSIMY.

August 25, 1914, noon.

My dear general,

5. The impression produced by the incursions of the German cavalry corps on our left is so strong that I am keeping at my disposal the 3rd Algerian division in the process of being mobilized at Perpignan-Carcassonne. If necessary, it could be transported to Chantilly or Beauvais in forty-eight hours. The overflow from the left is a fact whose strategic importance should not be exaggerated, but it has an effect on opinion in proportions that you cannot imagine.

Sordet's inaction appears to me to be more and more culpable: I consider that he has seriously failed in his duty. Besides, I do not recriminate; I beg you to believe in my complete confidence.

6. Finally, I beg you personally and in the most urgent manner to authorize Paymaster Caillaux, accompanied by Corporal Ceccaldi, to join Sarrail's staff, who accepts them both on his staff, I know.

Neither you nor I have any interest in creating political difficulties for ourselves; I ask you in the most formal way to authorize this assignment. With peace restored, or even sooner, you and I might create real enemies if it were not done.

My very cordial friendship.

MESSIMY.

English army.

On the other hand, I knew that there was already some tension between the Marshal and the commander of the 5th Army.

I arrived in Saint-Quentin at about half past ten. D'Amade had already arrived. He was informing me of the difficult situation of his group when Lanrezac arrived in his turn; he had received my instructions of the previous evening concerning the battle of Amiens-Reims-Verdun. He told me that he understood my intentions very well, raising objections only concerning the limit of the zones attributed to his army and to the British army; he pointed out that our allies, ill-prepared to maneuver as a whole, seemed to take little account of the directives intended to coordinate the actions of neighboring armies. As I insisted on the necessity for his army to observe an attitude of constant counter-attacks in order to gain the time necessary for the constitution of the extreme left mass, he assured me that he intended to take again the offensive as soon as his army corps would be released from the covered ground of the region of Avesnes, where his artillery could not do anything, and that moreover the favorable state of his troops authorized him to take this approach.

At this point French entered accompanied by General Murray, his chief of staff. I expected to find the calm man whom I had met a few days before. To my great surprise, the English commander-in-chief told me in a rather lively tone that his army was violently attacked, that the previous evening, General Haig's corps had been obliged to withdraw to Guise and the cavalry corps to Bohain, that is to say, in the middle of the zone assigned to the 5th French army, that his 2nd corps and General Snow's 4th Division were marching under the pressure of the enemy towards Catelet; He explained to me that since the opening of hostilities his troops had been subjected to such hardships that he could not envisage for the moment a resumption of the offensive and that he considered the situation to be very delicate. On several occasions, he raised complaints against the manner in which the 5th Army, his neighbor, had behaved, which he accused of having broken off the combat by leaving him completely isolated.

I answered Marshal French that all the allied troops had been equally subjected to the vigorous enemy effort and that it was not reasonable to believe that the English army had the sole privilege of the harsh conditions of war. I also drew the attention of the Marshal to the interest that I saw in his conforming his maneuver to the general instructions that I had given to our armies, and in particular, that he should endeavor to respect the zones of march reserved for each army, in order to avoid disorder. I indicated to him that, the first conceived maneuver having failed, I urged him to put all in work to allow the execution of the new envisaged battle. To his astonishment, I understood that he was not aware of my intentions and I asked him if he had received the copy of my instruction of August 25 that I had sent him. He was not yet aware of it: it had remained in the hands of General Murray.

I then explained the plan of the new maneuver which I proposed to carry out, by indicating in detail the role which the English army would have to play there. French immediately raised objections; in spite of my insistence, I had the impression of not convincing him: he was thinking especially of withdrawing to Saint-Quentin. I promised him to give orders to Sordet, so that not only would he cover the English left, but also intervene in the battle with the greatest energy and with all his forces. In addition, on the request of the Marshal himself, I immediately gave the order to d'Amade to push his two fresh reserve divisions on Bray, in order to support the British army. On the other hand, I asked Marshal French if he hoped to receive reinforcements from England soon, and especially the 6th Infantry Division, because it was necessary, in the present situation, to make use of all the allied resources.[*] French informed me that the Secretary of State for War was considering sending this division to Belgium, in support of the Belgian army. I represented to the Marshal how dangerous such a solution would be; I told him my conviction that the decision could only be obtained on the French front, and that all the efforts that England could provide had to be accumulated without delay towards the left of our battle line. On this point, I had the impression to be in agreement with my interlocutor.

---

[*] In his letter to which I have already alluded above, General de la Panouse informed me that Kitchener was very reluctant to send a division to the continent.

Chapter IV

When, at the beginning of the afternoon, I left the British headquarters, I carried with me the impression of the fragility of our extreme left, and I wondered with concern if it would hold out long enough to allow me to carry out the new grouping of our forces. On the other hand, I was impressed by the misunderstanding that I felt was developing between Marshal French and the commander of the 5th Army: two temperaments, two mentalities so essentially different that, in the harshness of the difficulties of battle, they could not seem to agree.

I returned to my headquarters in the evening. The information I found on the whole front was not very comforting. From the 4th Army, Colonel Paquette had reported a pessimistic impression: the 17th Corps in particular seemed to have collapsed; the other corps had suffered heavy losses in the sustained fighting in the wooded area where they had been engaged. The 4th Army was now withdrawing to the left bank of the Meuse, blowing up all the bridges. The 3rd Army was still holding on the right bank with difficulty. But, from everywhere, the word was coming back of failures that made me fear the collapse of the morale of the troops: discouragement was beginning to be felt in all spheres of the army and even at the main headquarters.

The attitude of the British also caused me serious concern; during the day we had intercepted two German radio transmissions which indicated that the right grouping of the German forces was to march during the day on the Cambrai-Le Cateau front; at 9:10 a.m., the leading elements of this grouping was to attack on the whole front. I was not without concern about the way our allies would have withstood this German thrust, during this particularly critical day; upon their resistance was going to depend in great part the possibility of carrying out our new maneuver. However, I received, late in the night, a very pessimistic telegram from Colonel Huguet, dated from Noyon, giving me the worst news on the results of the day: "Battle lost, he said to me, by the British army, which seems to have lost all cohesion; it will require, for its reconstitution, to be seriously protected; the English headquarters will be, this evening, in Noyon."

In order to avoid fearing the most serious events, it was necessary, in the presence of this situation, to organize on the left a solid command, equipped with all the organs allowing him to make his action felt. I then thought of General Maunoury, who seemed to me to be the most suitable to take this heavy command in these difficult circumstances. Thus, after having decided to dissolve the army of Lorraine, I organized, in the first part of the night, the 6th Army, which I placed under the orders of General Maunoury, who had the staff of the army of Lorraine. He would take command of all the forces transported to the west of the general disposition of the French and English armies, that is to say, of the 7th Corps, of the 61st, 62nd and 63rd reserve divisions, of the 55th and 56th reserve divisions, with General d'Amade retaining the direction of the four territorial divisions. As for the four remaining reserve divisions of the army of Lorraine, I transferred them, under the orders of General Paul Durand, to the 3rd Army. I had General Maunoury invited to go as soon as possible to the main headquarters to take my orders.

At the same time, I deemed it necessary to dissolve the army of Alsace. The remaining forces of this army, from which I had just taken part of the elements destined for the 6th, were divided into two groups subordinated to General Dubail.

It was in the midst of the serious events of that night that I learned from Captain Tardieu that a ministerial crisis had just occurred, that Minister Messimy had resigned and was going to be replaced by Mr. Millerand. I was delighted to learn that the latter, in whom I had the greatest confidence and for whom I nourished the most lively friendship, was going to take over the direction of the ministry in these difficult hours; his seriousness, his tenacity, his patriotism were for me the certainty that he would be able to face all the necessities.

The next day I received the following letter from Mr. Messimy:

Paris, August 27, 1914.

My dear general,

I was "unloaded" by the President of the Republic for having treated the public authorities and the press too harshly.

But Millerand replaces me, in whom you can have full and complete confidence.

I *need* for the future a personal letter from you protesting against

Chapter IV 303

the official statement that had been taken* from me: "There were only 'territorials' in the northern region." This is a revival of the article in Le Temps in August 1870.

I will go in five or six days to my position as a commissioned battalion chief at the general headquarters, as my letter of service tells me. I request to be assigned to the 2nd Bureau.

In the meantime, my hand; I have confidence in France and in you.

MESSIMY.

From the information which had reached us on the English army, it appeared that instead of taking the general direction of Cambrai which I had indicated to it on 24 August, it had retreated towards the zone of march reserved for the 5th army, thus facilitating the envelopment which the German right wing was obviously seeking. The concentration of the 6th Army had not yet reached a sufficient point to protect the British withdrawal, and to allow the Marshal's forces to recover. In these conditions, the solution which seemed to me to be the most profitable consisted in having the 5th Army execute, at the heights of Guise and Vervins, a vigorous attack on the enemy forces, from the south to the north, by carrying the density of its forces to its left wing.

On the morning of August 27, around 6:00 a.m., I learned that the 5th Army had continued its retreat, and that the intention of its leader was to settle behind the Oise and the Thon. This attitude was not at all in conformity with the one I expected General Lanrezac to adapt: the day before in Saint-Quentin, he had expressed to me his intention, as soon as he would be out of the wooded area where the use of his artillery was difficult, to push the German troops who were following him by a vigorous counter-offensive. Nothing was more in line with my intentions which were, I repeat, to gain the time necessary to reunite the 6th Army. In addition, the situation of the English army required that we hold back the greatest possible number of German corps by an aggressive attitude. Moreover, General Lanrezac had assured me

---

* The original word was "snatched"; this word has been crossed out and replaced by "taken."

that the state of his troops and their morale were excellent. Now, the region in which the 5th Army was arriving seemed particularly favorable to an operation of this nature. I therefore invited General Lanrezac to take advantage of these circumstances, representing to him that there was no reason to take into account what the British were doing on his left, and that if he did not act as I told him, he would diminish the morale of his army by the continuing of a retreat which would look like a defeat and which might compromise the result of the campaign.[*] At the same time, to give some appeasement to colonel Huguet who had depicted to me in a very dark light the situation of our allies, I made him aware of the orders given to general Lanrezac, which had the intention of allowing the English army to carry out its withdrawal methodically; in addition, I sent Lieutenant-Colonel Brécard to Noyon, accompanied by Major Clive, liaison officer of the British army with me, with the mission to inquire about the situation and to give Marshal French the assurance of our assistance.

Brécard had hardly left when Colonel Huguet phoned me. He had just seen Marshal French and had informed him of the instructions given to Lanrezac. French had replied that a feeling of bitterness and regret would not fail to arise in England, when the conditions under which the British army had made contact with the enemy were known. The Marshal suggested that a telegram sent by me recognizing the great services rendered to the common cause by the English army would be likely to calm this state of mind.

I hastened to satisfy this desire by expressing to Marshal French the gratitude of the French army for the courageous help that his troops had given to ours.

However, Lanrezac, upon receiving my instructions of the morning, informed me that he would stop his troops at the point of Vervins, and would be ready to attack any enemy who would open up south of the Oise. I could therefore envisage that the enemy's march against the British would be slowed down, and that they would take advantage of this to stop, when, at about 2 p.m., I

---

[*] Message telephoned on August 27 at 6:30 a.m. by Lieutenant-Colonel Alexandre of the G.Q.G. to Major Schneider of the 5th Army staff.

learned that our Allies were evacuating Saint-Quentin to withdraw to the south. Thus, they discovered Lanrezac's left just as he was about to counter-attack and they put him in a delicate situation. I asked for confirmation of this information, and insisted that Marshal French slow down the retreat of his army; I presented all the disadvantages of this maneuver in the present circumstances, and I argued that the situation of our allies was in no way critical since we had two reserve divisions at Bertincourt and Bapaume, the entire Sordet cavalry corps in front, and that new forces were deploying in the region of Chaulnes. It was necessary to mark a time of pause to allow the counter-attack of the 5th Army to occur; this counter-attack would not fail to relieve the pressure which was exerted against the English.

In the meantime, I received a visit from General Maunoury, who had been summoned to headquarters to take instructions concerning the army he was to command in the Amiens region. I instructed him to arrange his forces in such a way as to be able, when they were reunited, to act offensively on the enemy right wing, thus covering the left flank of the English army that I hoped to see stopped on the Ham-Tergnier front; I also indicated to him that later on, the resumption of the offensive would begin with the 6th Army, in order to improve the envelopment of the enemy right wing.* It was agreed that the headquarters of the 6th Army would initially be stationed at Mareuil.

No sooner had Maunoury left me, taking my instructions with him, than serious news came to me that everything I had planned and prepared for the battle of Amiens-Laon-Reims was close to collapse. At about 6 p.m., Huguet reported to me the arrival of a German cavalry division at Péronne† and described the situation as "extremely serious"; it was to be feared that the retreat of the army would turn into a rout. For his part, Lieutenant-Colonel Brécard returned from Noyon at about the same time and brought me rather pessimistic news; the day before, four German army corps had

---

* Special Instruction no. 19 given to General Maunoury in the afternoon of the 27th, during his visit to the G.Q.G.

† This information was later recognized as erroneous.

Chapter IV

given battle to our allies, and in the evening, at about 6 p.m., they had suffered a costly defeat: two divisions out of five were almost annihilated, and the others were in rather poor condition. General Wilson had told Brécard that, for eight days, the British troops would be unable to fight, and the British command had only one concern: to move towards Compiègne to gain ground and to recover.

Thus, at the moment, when I had in my plans the English towards Ham, they had already turned their eyes towards Compiègne. The situation became particularly anguishing. It appeared to me as impossible to count on the assistance of the English to gain the time necessary for the constitution of the 6th Army. Would it even be possible for the rest of the front to maintain it? Would it be necessary to give up defending the line of the Aisne? And an immediate question arose: what would be the consequences of the English retreat on the attitude of the 5th Army? It will be remembered that the very morning I had ordered it to counter-attack towards the north. Now its left flank was completely uncovered.

At the same time, a German radio intercepted revealed that the First German Army would act in isolation while the Second would invest Maubeuge.[*] It therefore seemed probable that on the front of the 5th French Army the enemy thrust would slow down considerably. From then on, it became useless to consider an action of Lanrezac's troops towards the north, while an offensive directed towards the northwest would have the advantage of slowing down the march of the elements of pursuit launched against the English. From all points of view, the operation seemed necessary and possible.

Also, around 7 p.m., I decided to modify the orders previously given to Lanrezac, and I telegraphed him that because of the information indicating that a part of the forces which were opposed to him remained in front of Maubeuge, he had to move his left the next morning between the Oise and Saint-Quentin; he had to attack

---

[*] Intelligence report no. 63 of August 27, 1914, 6 p.m., of the 2nd Bureau of the G.Q.G.

all the enemy forces marching against the English army which he had to disencumber at all costs.*

However, Lieutenant-Colonel Alexandre, who was at Marle, Lanrezac's headquarters, at the time this order reached him, informed me by telephone that the commander of the 5th Army had serious objections to this new directive. Also, at 10:15 p.m., I again informed General Lanrezac of all the importance I attached to the execution of my orders. At the same time, I resolved to go to Marle myself, the next morning.

All this news which had so profoundly aggravated our situation reached me during the visit that the new Minister of War, Mr. Millerand, made to me. He had arrived at the great headquarters, not only to pay me a courtesy visit, but also and especially to inquire about the situation. He was accompanied by Mr. Messimy, who had put on his battalion commander's uniform.

While I was in conference with Mr. Millerand, Major Gamelin, whom I had sent that morning to liaise with General de Langle, entered my office and gave me an account of his mission: the day before, enemy units had crossed the Meuse downstream from Sedan, and the commander of the 4th Army intended to counter-attack them on the 27th. Major Gamelin had been present at the beginning of this operation. The staff of the 4th Army had seemed a little nervous to him at the news that, in the morning, the enemy had established itself in force on the left bank of the Meuse, from Donchery to Autrécourt. On the other hand, the calmness and confidence of General de Langle and his chief of staff, General Maistre, had impressed him deeply. De Langle had ordered his corps to combine their efforts to drive the enemy back into the Meuse. On leaving the headquarters of the 4th Army, Gamelin

---

* The telegram no. 2500 mentioned here arrived at Marle at 8:20 p.m., i.e. shortly after General Lanrezac had just given me an account of the orders which he had given for the 28th in execution of my instructions of the morning, namely: to tighten his front towards the left and to be ready to attack any column which would cross the Oise. Lanrezac's report arrived at G.H.Q. around 9 p.m. To avoid any confusion, General Berthelot insisted in a new telegram sent to the commander of the 5th Army at 9:45 p.m., to confirm order n° 2500, specifying that Lanrezac's left should attack any enemy force marching centered on the British between Saint-Quentin and the Oise.

went to La Besace, the headquarters of General Roques, commander of the 12th Army corps; there again, he admired the order and confidence that reigned in the command, and before leaving for Vitry, he was able to witness the start of the counterattack, which was expected to succeed.

Around 10 p.m. we received a message from the 4th Army confirming the satisfactory results of the day; de Langle asked, in order to consolidate his success, that the 3rd Army attack, in its turn, and relieve the 4th Army from holding part of its front.

From the 1st and 2nd armies, equally good news reached us: these two armies, reduced in their means, had given in a series of fights, for fourteen days, an example of tenacity and courage that I had been happy to bring to the attention of the other armies. In the evening, we learned that the 1st Army was continuing its offensive on the battlefield of 25 and 26 August, and that everywhere, on the reconquered ground, it had found signs of the heavy losses suffered by the Germans.

This news impressed the Minister favorably. However, I did not hide from him that all my preoccupations were currently shifting to my left. At 10 p.m., Colonel Huguet telephoned me that, the next day, the English army would move to the rear, between the Oise and La Fère. This withdrawal completed the exposure of the left of the 5th Army, at the same time as it isolated the right of Maunoury's army. Almost at the same time, I received from Colonel Huguet a letter dated Noyon at 5:30 p.m., which confirmed my fears. Here it is:

> I have the honor of confirming to you my telegram of yesterday evening, the 26th, giving you an account of the defeat suffered yesterday by the English army; from the new information which has just reached me, it appears that its situation is most critical. It is, for the moment, only a beaten army, incapable of a serious effort. The column on the right (1st and 2nd Divisions), which is retreating on Origny-Saint-Benoît, still presents a certain cohesion, as well as the 4th Division; but the 3rd and 5th Divisions, extremely tested, having lost considerable numbers of men, part of their artillery and their crews, and having been subjected to the most violent artillery fire for nearly thirty-six hours, no longer form anything more than a disorganized herd unable to offer the slightest resistance or reappear

on the battlefield before having rested and having been completely restored. Fortunately, the pursuit is not active; it is hoped that this evening the divisions will be able to reach the front: Reisel – 4th Division, Vermand. -3rd Division, north of Saint-Quentin. – 5th Division, Mont-d'Origny. – 1st and 2nd Divisions. (No news yet of the cavalry division); and tomorrow the 28th, the general line: Ham – 4th and 3rd Divisions, Saint-Simon – 5th Division, Jussy and La Fère – 1st and 2nd Divisions. Under these conditions, the English army no longer exists for the moment; it will not be in a position to resume campaigning until it has had a long rest and has been rebuilt, that is to say, for at least three divisions out of five, not before a delay of several days or even a few weeks.

The wound received by British pride will be sharp: already, recriminations and reproaches are manifesting themselves; it is important to prevent them from spreading by addressing, from now on and without delay, gratitude to the English army and nation for the great sacrifice they have just consented to make in our favor; this is why I addressed to you the telephone message of this morning requesting, on behalf of Marshal French, that thanks be addressed to his army by the French general-in-chief; it would be appropriate for the French government to take the same initiative.

I have informed General Lanrezac and General Sordet of the situation in which the English army finds itself, the former so that he may be aware of the dangers which could threaten it on its left, the latter so that he may continue to ensure the security of the English retreat on its rear and towards the west. According to the indications given this morning by Colonel Brécard, I have informed General Sordet that his mission is to ensure this service until the English army is in complete security behind the Somme, and then to maintain himself in the region of Saint-Quentin until he has received your instructions.

It is not yet possible to specify, for the moment, where and under what conditions the reconstitution of this army will be carried out; but, it could be that the English government requires that it all be transported back to its base of Le Havre, until the moment when, rebuilt, rested and reorganized, it would be in a state to resume campaigning. There is no doubt that this halt will only be temporary; the will remains just as firm and even more unshakeable than in the past, to enter into action again as soon as it is possible.

There is thus no longer any reason to count on the English army for some time; it is obvious that, under these conditions, the tactic of envelopment which has been carried out for the last eight days and has brought upon the left wing of our line a sufficient mass to overwhelm it, will continue and will be carried out under conditions all the easier as our line will be less extended. The left of General Lanrezac, constituted by the reserve divisions and the 18th Corps, thus seems to be in a few days very seriously threatened, and the movement will thus continue to extend from the left to the right.

The only way to face such a certain and dangerous threat seems to be to create on our left a new and very strong army composed of all the active corps that it will be possible to take back on the rest of our line (at the sacrifice even of the security of certain parts of the territory) to transfer all our effort to our left. It is there that the decision will be made in a very short time. Lieutenant-Colonel Brécard had, this morning, on this subject with General Wilson, a most instructive and conclusive discussion, which he will have already reported to you when you receive this letter, and which I failed to mention to you as being of great interest.

I did not conceal from Mr. Millerand the seriousness of the situation of our left wing; I told him that the maneuver planned on the Amiens, La Fère, Laon, Craonne and Aisne line was going to be compromised; the state of the English army made it uncertain whether it would be possible to complete the deployments of the 6th Army. Our duty was to firmly consider the most serious consequences. In particular, it was necessary to inform the government that in four or five days perhaps, the German cavalry would appear in front of Paris. It was urgent to prepare the public opinion for this eventuality, and to make everyone understand that, in our will to carry out our defense to the end was the insurance of the final victory. Our goal was to know how to hold on and resist the time necessary to organize a new maneuver. And if this one should fail again, to know to expect another one.

Mr. Milleraud and I studied the general situation and particularly that of the Russians. The news that reached us from this front was favorable. The offensive of our allies was going on well: a German corps, enveloped on its left flank by our allies, had to abandon Osterode. It was therefore to be hoped that, if the Russian successes continued, the enemy would be obliged to bring back from the French front large numbers of troops to oppose our allies, and within a fortnight, we should expect to see the pressure

Chapter IV

on our front slow down. We must not forget that the Germans had pinned all their hopes on the swift destruction of the French armies. But the French armies were not defeated and were still capable of vigorous efforts, which we would have to ask of them when a favorable opportunity presented itself.

We came to speak about the situation of Paris. I told the Minister the confidence I had in Galliéni to organize the defense of the capital.

At this point, I informed Mr. Millerand of the order that Mr. Messimy had sent me two days before, to send three active army corps to the fortified camp of Paris to take part in the defense of the capital. I explained to him my point of view, which was that it had to be defended in open country, by the operating armies; all our manpower resources had, without restriction, to take part in the maneuver and the battle which would decide the fate of the country; any unit withdrawn from this task, even if it was devoted to the defense of Paris, would be badly employed. The minister represented to me the necessity of defending the capital, and of agreeing for that to the necessary levies.

I informed Mr. Millerand of the visit I intended to make the next morning to Marle to urge General Lanrezac to accomplish the operation I had prescribed, and which seemed to me more and more necessary. This visit would allow me to study on the spot the possibility of carrying out the battle envisaged for the beginning of September.

Mr. Millerand, after this long conversation, spoke with a certain number of officers of my General Staff. He slept that night at the great headquarters and left the next morning at 5:30 a.m., just as I myself was getting into an automobile to visit Lanrezac.

August 28. – On August 28, in the morning, before leaving for Marle, I took note of the intelligence that had arrived during the night. Among these, one of them particularly caught my attention: in the region of Chimay an aerial reconnaissance had signaled, in the afternoon of the previous day, movements of columns marching southward, as well as large gatherings in the region of Chimay and Rocroi. This threat, obviously directed against the left of the 4th Army and against the fragile weld that united this army to the 5th, seemed to be linked to the action of the enemy forces against which General de Langle had fought in the region of Donchery. Because of the size of the German forces reported, it was to be feared that this movement would succeed in breaking our lines. The link between the 4th and 5th armies needed to be reinforced and it was necessary to provide for any eventuality on this side. I therefore decided to form a group of forces whose mission would be to ensure the link between de Langle and Lanrezac.

Consequently, I gave General Berthelot, who remained at the main headquarters during my absence, the order to urgently summon General Foch, commander of the 20th Army corps, to receive instruction of the mission that I wanted to entrust to him,[*] and to direct General de Langle to begin without delay the withdrawal movement that I had ordered him to do by the Instruction of August 25, commanding him to move to the rear of the Aisne

I arrived at Marle around 8:30 am. As soon as I saw Lanrezac, I was struck by his physical state: he wore on his face marks of fatigue: yellow complexion, bloodshot eyes. Immediately, with gestures that reflected his nervous state, he objected to the orders he had received the day before, to the fatigue of his troops and the threat that the enemy was going to make on him in the northern direction. I explained to him again the situation of the English, which he could not ignore, and told him that it was necessary, because of the circumstances, to attack in the direction of Saint-Quentin. The tone of the conversation having risen, I had to remind Lanrezac that the grievances of Marshal French with respect to the French army were mainly attributable to him: on the Sambre, he had withdrawn at the moment when French had made known to him that he was attacking, and the day before, he had allowed the English to be crushed without giving them any help.

At the end of his arguments, Lanrezac told me that he had not received a written order to attack; I then told Gamelin, who had

---

[*] When I summoned Foch to the G.Q.G., I ordered him to bring with him Colonel Weygand, whom I wanted to give him as Chief of Staff. Weygand had made a name for himself shortly before the war at the Center for Advanced Military Studies as an outstanding officer.

Chapter IV 313

accompanied me, to draw up one immediately; on the corner of a table, with General Hély d'Oissel, chief of staff of the 5th Army, he drew up the following order, which I signed: "The 5th Army will attack as soon as possible the forces which were engaged yesterday against the English. It will cover itself on the right with the minimum of forces and will escape from this side at a great distance." General Lanrezac declared himself satisfied and ready to obey; he told me, moreover, that he had already given orders in the morning in the direction I indicated to him.

As this conversation was coming to an end, I received General de Mas-Latrie, commander of the 18th Corps, who was passing through the headquarters of the 5th Army. He was suffering from dysentery, and seemed to have lost some of his strength. I showed him the seriousness of the situation and ordered him to demand the maximum effort from his troops; the salvation of the country was at stake. Then, I saw General Hache arrive, exhausted with fatigue, after the hard fighting of the 40th Division. Having the highest esteem for this valiant and intelligent soldier, I had appointed him to take command of the 3rd Corps, on the recommendation of General Lanrezac. Hache missed his beautiful division, and begged me to let him have it. I could only maintain my decision, appealing to his selflessness and devotion.

So painful had been the impression that I brought back to the great headquarters, that I decided to return the next day to Lanrezac to control the execution of my orders.

My presence at Vitry-le-François was essential on the one hand to coordinate the operations of the 5th Army with the British movements and those of the 6th, and on the other hand to take all the measures required by the threat detected in the region of Rocroi by our air force, and in particular, to give Foch my instructions for the mission I was going to entrust to him.

On arriving at Vitry-le-François, I was given an account of the news received during the day from the cavalry corps and the 61st and 62nd reserve divisions; Sordet, the day before, had used his divisions separately: they had engaged in good conditions north and east of Péronne, after which he had brought them back to billet on the south bank of the Somme; the two reserve divisions had acted on the left of the cavalry corps, and seemed to have had successful engagements. I asked Maunoury by telephone what his first impressions were, as well as his intentions. The commander of the 6th Army answered that he intended to hold the Somme, from the same evening, in the region of Péronne with the 61st and 62nd reserve divisions,* and between Saint-Simon and Saint-Christ with elements of the 55th and 56th reserve divisions, which would have completed their disembarkation that same evening at midnight; he would then push the 7th Corps towards the Somme.

These conditions seemed favorable to me, since, in the 5th Army, the 3rd Corps and a reserve division were to come, in the same day, to border the Oise upstream from Moy. To obtain the continuity of the front and thus ensure the development of the attack of the 5th Army towards Saint-Quentin, it was sufficient that the English army agreed to stop its rearguards on the Crozat canal, between Saint-Simon and Tergnier. I asked Marshal French if his army could play this role of liaison between the 5th and 6th armies and I sent Colonel Brécard on a mission to the English, the Maunoury army and the Sordet cavalry corps, to help them link their actions. I could thus, towards the end of the afternoon, hope to have finally achieved a favorable defensive situation on our left, behind the big obstacle of the Somme, the Crozat canal and the Oise; under these conditions, the offensive of the 5th Army, launched the following day on Saint-Quentin, would bring the necessary respite to complete the constitution of the 6th Army and to allow it to envelop in its turn the German right.

Unfortunately, my hope was short-lived. Indeed, at about 8:30 p.m., I received from Colonel Huguet the following telegram: "The Marshal regrets not being able to cooperate in the general action to the extent desired by you. The tired troops require at least one day of rest in the locations occupied this evening. The day after tomorrow, they will be able to occupy the Crozat Canal line, if necessary. If later the French army is victorious, the marshal will place his troops at your disposal as a reserve."

Shortly afterwards, a telephone call from the 6th Army,

---

* The 61st and 62nd Reserve Divisions had just come under the command of General Ebener, previously Chief of Staff of the Army under Mr. Messimy.

Chapter IV

confirmed a moment later by Commandant Maurin, who was the liaison between Maunoury and the main headquarters, informed me that the fate of the 61st and 62nd reserve divisions was unknown, and that General Ebener, who had been appointed to take command of them, had been looking for them in vain all day; He assumed that they had had to withdraw to Amiens in front of reported enemy columns marching from east to west, in the region of Péronne, from where the sound of a heavy cannonade could be heard. Around midnight, we learned that the 61st Reserve Division had been pushed back to Amiens; there was still no news of the 62nd.

Thus, not only was the defensive front of the Somme not held, but also the deployment zone of the 6th Army seemed to be seriously threatened by the enemy advance. In the present state of affairs, I could only hope for a happy change in the situation through the success of the 5th Army. Also, I felt the need to insist again to General Lanrezac that the action of his army be as energetic as possible.

During the afternoon of the 28th, when I had made my efforts to stabilize the situation of our left and prepare the offensive of the 5th Army, I had to worry about the threat that was being prepared in the region of Rocroi against the left of the 4th Army. But, while I had been obliged to insist on several occasions to General Lanrezac to bring him to stand up to the enemy, General de Langle, ardent and determined, was stubborn in not wanting to abandon the ground to the enemy. Under his tenacious direction, the 4th Army, after having fought on all the cuts of the ground, stubbornly defended the positions of the Meuse; it had made the enemy pay dearly for the few advances he had made on the left bank.

However, the execution of the plan conceived on August 25 to create a battle front based on the Somme and the Aisne required that the 4th Army not linger on the Meuse, especially since the threat reported towards Rocroi could threaten its left at any moment.

When I returned to the main headquarters after the visit to Lanrezac, I learned that the 4th Army was fully engaged with the objective of driving the Germans back into the Meuse; the morale of this army was excellent, despite the losses it had suffered. Under these conditions, it found it painful to give up its advantages and to retreat when it felt victorious. I cannot emphasize enough the admirable behavior of General de Langle; around 5:00 p.m., he informed me that his situation was good, especially in the wings, and that before obeying, with a heavy heart, the order to retreat that I had given, he wanted to warn me and waited for a new order before doing anything. I could not hesitate, and, while paying homage to such an energetic attitude, I had to tell de Langle, in the general interest of the maneuver, that I authorized him to remain on the Meuse to affirm his success, but that, as of the next morning, he should redeploy his large units to the heights to the southwest of the river and then resume the withdrawal movement prescribed by the Instruction of the 25th, by linking his movement to that of the two neighboring armies.

Moreover, if the efforts of the 4th Army had had happy results, it was almost certain that it had almost reached the limit of its forces, and it was to be feared, as General de Langle informed me that very evening, that it would not be able to resist for long on the Aisne line.

However, the threat from enemy forces concentrated in the Rocroi region had not become clearer during the day. So much so that in the evening, around 7:00 p.m., when General Foch presented himself at the main headquarters, the problem had changed. The 4th army, which had been so powerfully reinforced for its first offensive mission, had become too cumbersome for the maneuver we were about to undertake. To lighten it, I decided to form with the left of this army (9th and 11th Corps, 52nd and 60th reserve divisions and 9th Cavalry Division) a grouping under the orders of General Foch, which would be under the command of the general of the 4th Army. It was agreed that this grouping would eventually cover the bulk of de Langle's army against the opposing forces that would emerge from the Rocroi region and would ensure the liaison between the 4th and 5th armies.

Finally, the situation of the 1st and 2nd armies remained to be settled. These armies, hastily put back in order, had, that very morning, resumed the offensive. Towards the end of the afternoon, General de Castelnau had asked me, as his own right and the left of the 1st Army had been forced to retreat, if it was a question of "lasting or continuing the offensive?" I immediately told him and General Dubail that it was only a question of their two armies "lasting" while fixing the enemy forces which were opposed to them and remaining linked between them.

In fact, until September 3rd, the front of these two armies did not change much. General Pau, whose army had been disbanded, passing in the afternoon to the main headquarters confirmed to me that in Upper Alsace, a state of equilibrium had been reached.

Thus, at the end of the 28th, the situation looked quite favorable on most of the front, while on the left the formation of the 6th Army seemed compromised.

Would the offensive of the Fifth Army, the next day, restore our fortunes sufficiently on this part of our line of battle to allow the hope of fighting the battle in the form I desired? That would be tomorrow's secret.

The last hours of the night of 28-29 August brought more bad news: it seemed that the German 1st Army had advanced between Péronne and Saint-Quentin. At Péronne, the French forces had been forced to retreat and the deployment zone of the 6th Army was more and more compromised. It seemed that nothing could stand in the way of the German right wing's victorious march toward Paris, which it was likely to take as its objective. Under these conditions, it would be impossible to carry out the offensive that I had assigned to the 6th Army if, as the intelligence led me to believe, it was caught in the act of deployment; it would be necessary to postpone the new battle front, perhaps as far as the great cut of the Seine: on the left, the 6th Army towards the Lower Seine with the British, whose eyes were turned towards Rouen, the 5th Army in the region of Paris, the 4th Army in the region of the Middle Seine and the 3rd Army between the Seine and the Meuse. It was with this idea in mind that I warned General d'Amade that if, after having defended the Somme and blown up the bridges of this river, he was forced to retreat, he should take his line of retreat towards Rouen.* It was also with this in mind that I warned the

---

* Telegram no. 2666, dated August 29th, 1914, to General d'Amade.

Minister of War that the garrison of the fortified camp of Paris would be completed, if necessary, by a part of the Lanrezac army.*
Moreover, in order to give the fortified camp of Paris the means to push forward the preparation of its defenses, I prescribed that the 45th Division coming from Algeria would be directed to the region of Paris.

If it was my duty to foresee this scenario, I still hoped that the offensive of the 5th Army on the right bank of the Oise would restore the situation. This shows the importance I attached to this operation.

However, the state of mind in which I had found General Lanrezac the day before made me fear that the commander of the 5th Army was not up to the capital task that he was going to have to fulfill. I had already decided, as you will recall, to go to his headquarters and assist in the operation. I was even resolved, if the thing seemed necessary to me, to replace General Lanrezac in his command, in spite of all the disadvantages that this change could cause in the middle of the battle. What was appropriate at the present time was a man of energy and will. I was thinking of General Franchet d'Esperey, whose command at the head of the 1st Army corps had confirmed precisely his qualities of character. It was in this frame of mind that, having left the main headquarters at about 7:30 a.m., I arrived at Laon at about 9:00 a.m., where the 5th Army had moved its headquarters.

I had the satisfaction of finding General Lanrezac infinitely calmer than the day before and especially more in control of himself: I assisted during the whole morning, in his office, to the dictation of his orders, and I had the impression that he directed his battle with authority and technique. Unfortunately, the first information was not very favorable. Instead of a battle facing northwest, we were engaged in an action facing north against the forces coming out of the Nouvion forest where our air force had been unable to discover them. On the Oise front, our troops were almost everywhere stopped, when I left Lanrezac to have lunch at

---

* Situation report no. 2671 of August 29th, 1914, 8:20 a.m., to the Minister of War.

the buffet of the Laon station. It was there that Lieutenant-Colonel Brécard, passing through Laon, came to give me an account of what he had learned that morning in Montdidier, at the Maunoury headquarters and near the Sordet cavalry corps.

Maunoury, whose calmness had impressed Brécard, found himself in a very delicate situation: the 65th Division had only five battalions and two artillery groups in position; the 56th Division did not yet have any elements that had arrived in the concentration zone of the army; the 63rd reserve division had only just begun to arrive; the 61st was not rallied; as for the 62nd, its whereabouts were still unknown. In these conditions, General Maunoury feared an attack by the enemy to which he could only bring the 7th Army corps.

Lieutenant-Colonel Brécard then visited the cavalry corps, and found it very tired: the mounted elements were no more than the value of a single division; as for Lieutenant-Colonel Serret's battalions of *chasseurs*, which were attached to it, they had suffered a very serious setback the day before at Péronne; there were only scattered elements left. Fortunately, the German attack on the line of the Somme was not very biting.

Before leaving Laon I returned to the headquarters of Lanrezac. I learned there that the situation did not seem to improve, and it was to be feared that, following the attack which it underwent in the region of Guise, the 5th Army could not make its action felt on the side of Saint-Quentin, as I had hoped.

Leaving Lanrezac, I went by Soissons to the castle of Compiègne where French had moved his headquarters. I had the desire to meet again the commander in chief of the British army. The rumor had come back to me that he and his government were turning their attention to their maritime bases, and I feared that, in his desire to get closer to them, the Marshal would leave our line of battle for a long time, which would have made any resumption of the offensive impossible. I thus explained to French the general situation of our left wing, and more particularly that of the left of the 5th Army where the reserve divisions of General Valabrègue were in a difficult position. I stressed to him the interest that the English army had in maintaining contact with these two neighbors, in order to avoid opening a breach in the Allied battle line. I insisted on the results that the Russian offensive would not fail to produce, by forcing the Germans to withdraw from our front some of the forces they had committed there. Under these conditions, I added, the enemy pressure would soon become less strong on our front. If, therefore, the British could keep up with us until the moment when the 6th Army was definitively constituted, there is no doubt that the circumstances would then become favorable for a general resumption of the offensive. In addition, the Crozat Canal offered the British army an obstacle behind which its resistance would be easier.

French did not yield to my entreaties. Moreover, while I was speaking, I could see his chief of staff, Sir Archibald Murray, pulling the marshal by the hem of his tunic, as if to prevent him from agreeing to my requests. So much so that all I could get from him was: "No, no, my troops need 48 hours of absolute rest. After I can give them that, I will be willing to participate in what you want to do, but not before." Murray went out for a moment and returned with a paper containing information reported during the day by the air force: enemy gatherings were reported in front of the English front. From that moment on, I understood that nothing would succeed in shaking the will of the Marshal. I had to leave him without having obtained any result. I must admit that when I left Compiègne I was in a rather bad mood, because it was now certain that the Amiens-Verdun maneuver was becoming unfeasible and that it would be necessary to set up another one.

While returning to the great headquarters, I was crossing the square of the cathedral of Rheims, when I saw the car of General Wilson stopped in front of the statue of Joan of Arc; the general waiting for some unknown person was pacing in front of the square of the cathedral. I immediately made the car stop, and I went to him. He told me that he was coming back from Vitry. We began to talk and, without trying to hide from him the impression that I brought back from my meeting with his boss, I explained my point of view. Wilson saw very clearly the gravity of the situation; he promised me to work to bring Marshal French back very gently from the idea in which he seemed for the moment to be obstinate. Our conversation lasted about ten minutes. I then went back up in the car to join Vitry where I only arrived at 9:30 in the evening.

Chapter IV 321

Berthelot was waiting for me to give me the information of the day. First of all, he informed me that the 6th Army had been attacked at 10 o'clock in the morning,* from Bray-sur-Somme to Ham by forces estimated to be at least two army corps; in the presence of this attack, Maunoury had asked for orders in case of failure; he had been told to withdraw eventually to the Avre and later to Saint-Just-en-Chaussée, avoiding any contact that could be decisive. But around noon the enemy had abruptly stopped its attacks, and even marked a withdrawal movement. In these conditions, the 7th Corps, the only one engaged during the day, had, in turn, suspended its retreat, and occupied the Avre river from La Neuville-Sire-Bernard to Guerbigny. Almost at the same time, the French and British air forces had reported that the numerous German columns that had come down towards the Somme had turned back, and seemed to be heading north. This information was of great interest, although it was not yet possible to interpret it.

From the English, no recent news.

From the 5th Army, a whole series of reports had reached the main headquarters: between the Oise and Saint-Quentin, our troops, who had reached the Urvillers, Mesnil-Saint-Laurent, Marcy line, around 3:30 p.m., had seen their left pushed back toward the Oise by columns coming from the west; Valabrègue's reserve divisions, on the extreme left, had even risked being cut off for a moment from the Saint-Gobain massif. In the evening, while the 3rd Corps was engaged on Guise, the right of the 5th Army had won a success by pushing back to the north of the Oise the German Guards and the Xth corps by inflicting severe losses on them.

In summary, if the attack of the 5th Army had not completely restored the situation as I had hoped, it had undoubtedly drawn towards it the Allied columns that were marching on Péronne, and thus cleared the front of the British army and the 6th Army.

From then on, given that I had not been able to obtain any slowing down in the speed of the English retreat, that, on the other hand, the attack carried out against Valabrègue's divisions risked

---

* That is to say, shortly after Lieutenant-Colonel Brécard had left Montdidier.

compromising the situation of the 5th Army, I decided that there was no longer any reason to maintain it on the Oise, and I prescribed to him to transfer his forces behind the Serre, by blowing up the bridges of La Fère, Coudren and Chauny.[*]

The link between the 4th and 5th armies, already delicate because the latter had made an oblique turn to the left, was further compromised by the turning of this army towards Saint-Quentin. General Foch, who now had the mission of re-establishing this link, had spent the morning at the main headquarters settling the organization of his unit; he had left Vitry at the beginning of the afternoon to go to Machault to take command of his troops; when I arrived at the main headquarters, there was no news from this part of the front.

From the 4th Army, the news that reached us was good: the orders of retreat had been executed without difficulty, the enemy having not appeared anywhere, and weak enemy detachments being reported on the left bank of the Meuse.

In anticipation of the reinforcement of the armies of the left and the center, I had sent Commander Bel to the headquarters of the 3rd Army the previous afternoon to warn General Ruffey of my intention to take away from him the 6th Corps that I proposed to transport from August 29 to our left. Now, on the morning of the 29th, I received a letter from the commander of the 3rd Army informing me that he expected to be attacked incessantly; in these conditions, he insisted that the 6th Corps not be taken from him. Faced with his fears, I gave in, unwillingly, and decided that only the 42nd Division would be transported to Guignicourt, where it would be part of the Foch detachment. In the evening of the 29th, the staff of the 3rd Army telephoned that, until 3 p.m., no attack had occurred, but the commander of the army persisted in foreseeing one on his left. My attention had been drawn for some

---

[*] As a result of a serious error committed in the mail service of the G.Q.G., the order in question was not immediately transmitted to the 5th Army. This omission was only discovered the next morning at about 6 o'clock, when General Lanrezac telephoned to ask for instructions. As a result, the telegraphic order to withdraw behind the Serre, signed by me on the 29th around 10 p.m., did not reach the 5th Army until the following morning around 7 a.m.

time to the state of mind that prevailed in the staff of this army. I knew Ruffey: I considered him to be a very intelligent officer, but inconsistent in character and overly imaginative.

What aggravated this situation was that the chief of staff of this army, General Grossetti, that magnificent soldier who covered himself with glory a few weeks later in Champagne and Flanders, did not seem to be at his best in the functions he fulfilled with General Ruffey: wanting to do everything by himself, making poor use of his personnel, unfortunate delays, and even more unfortunate oversights in the transmission of orders were attributable to him. As a result of all this, there was a malaise in the staff of the 3rd Army, which Major Bel, with his fine conscience and his uprightness, had echoed to me.

At this point, when my attention was drawn to the serious events on our left, it was necessary for me to have no concern for our armies of the right and center. The 1st and 2nd armies seemed to be on the right track and even seemed to be gaining ground. I promised myself to personally ascertain the situation that was reported to me in the 3rd Army. And if it was as I had been told, I was determined to entrust the command of this army to General Sarrail, who had just shown himself to be a calm and energetic leader in command of the 6th Corps. As for Grossetti, thinking that he would be more useful at the head of a division, I proposed to replace him with Colonel Leboucq, deputy chief of staff of this army, whom I considered to be an officer of great value. I postponed the final decision until the next day, after I had been able to see for myself the necessity of these changes.

Finally, during the night of August 29-30th, another question came to my mind: that of moving my headquarters. Whatever the events to come, given the retreat of our armies of the center and the left, it was obvious that Vitry was going to become inconvenient for my communications with the army headquarters. I therefore ordered that searches be made without delay at Bar-sur-Aube. It should not be forgotten, in effect, that the setting in state of the electric communications of an organization such as a large headquarters requires a very important development of the existing networks. This news spread, in spite of the precautions taken, to all the staff personnel, accentuated the excitement that I noticed around me. Rare were the officers who, at the great headquarters, had been able to preserve their calm and their composure. In the midst of these events which were unfolding so rapidly, we were going through such extremes of hope and discouragement that everyone's nerves were put to a severe test. Berthelot's unalterable optimism fortunately stood out against the general anxiety and nervousness.

August 30. – On the morning of August 30, the situation appeared to me in the following manner:

The Somme had been crossed by the enemy upstream from Amiens; part of the First German Army was reported near Chaulnes, Lihons and Rozières; the Sixth French Army, in the midst of deploying, had to withdraw behind the Avre; the Lanrezac Army had to be ordered to move back behind the Senre, because of the dangerous situation in which the English retreat had left it. Finally, following my meeting on the afternoon of the 29th with Marshal French, I no longer had any hope of keeping our allies on the planned line of battle; they were preparing to withdraw to the area of Compiègne and Soissons, thus creating a most dangerous gap between our 6th Army in formation and our 5th Army. Moreover, if I had still been able to preserve some illusions on this subject, Marshal French took it upon himself to destroy them, by letting me know at the beginning of the afternoon of the 30th that the English army was not in a position to take its place in the first line before ten days.

Obviously, the offensive battle that I had conceived on the 25th was no longer possible in the form in which I had envisaged it. It did not seem, for the moment, that we could oppose the German right wing with sufficient forces to stop an enveloping movement that would logically lead our enemies to Paris.

But it seemed possible to carry out a maneuver facing, as a whole, the N.N.W., and allowing to renew under more favorable conditions the rupture of the communications of the German right wing; in other words, it was a question of repeating the initial maneuver that we had tried facing the N.E. while emerging from the Meuse. General Berthelot was very much in favor of this maneuver, and after having discussed it at length with him, I charged Colonel Pont, head of the 3rd Bureau, to study its preparation. Here is the full text of the memorandum that he drew up as a result:

GENERAL HEADQUARTERS
OF THE EASTERN ARMIES
        Staff   at Vitry, August 30, 1914.
        3rd Bureau

MEMORANDUM

The movements to be carried out later by our armies must allow us to:
    Last without exposing our field armies to destruction, so as to wait for the right time to resume the forward movement,
    take advantage of any favorable opportunity to teach the enemy a lesson, if possible, and to maintain the morale of the troops,
    finally, to direct the march of the armies in order to create a situation that would allow the offensive to be resumed at any moment.

How to produce this offensive?

    It no longer seems possible to oppose the German right wing with sufficient forces to stop its enveloping movement that could bring it to Paris.
    But the presence of our armies in Lorraine, Argonne and Champagne forces the German army to establish its corps in a huge circle from Verdun to Paris. If it shifts its forces constantly westward, it may be forced at some point to see its communications pass almost entirely through Belgium.
    We can take advantage of the possession of the Hauts-de-Meuse line, first of all, and of the presence of the 1st and 2nd armies in Lorraine, secondly, to establish a constantly covered and supported position *on the right, facing north-northwest on the whole*.
    We can start from this position to renew, but on better ground and, undoubtedly, in a better position, the break that we tried to make to the northeast by emerging from the Meuse.
    In the final analysis, it seems that we can consider, for the moment, as the terminal location of our armies in the center, the Seine and the Aube (*from Bray-sur-Seine to Arcis-sur-Aube*) for the 5th

Army[*] and the detachment of the 49th Army,[†] the Marne (from Vitry to Bar-le-Duc) for the main part of the 4th Army, and the region north of Bar-le-Duc for the 3rd Army.

A strong mass of cavalry, established from Ramerupt to Vitry-le-François, would form a link between the two army groups.

On the extreme left, the 6th Army would enter into the composition of the garrison of Paris; the English army, bypassing Paris by the north and the east, would establish itself behind the lower Seine.

On the right, the group of reserve divisions could either remain on the Hauts de Meuse, or withdraw to the Commercy region, linking up with Toul and the entire Lorraine army.

In this case, the 3rd Army would establish itself south of the Ornain to the east of the 4th Army; but as long as it would be possible, it seems that it would be in our interest to keep our right as far north as possible in order to force the German position to bend and consequently to weaken.

In other words, the general movement would be a pivotal movement around the 3rd Army holding the Verdun-Bar-le-Duc region.

Without hoping to give any precision on this point, we can indicate as successive stages, maintaining the possibility of a partial tactical success or a resumption of the offensive, the following general lines:

5th ARMY (minus 2 units in Paris).	DET. 4th.	C. C.	REST OF 4th	3rd
Laon	Château-Porcien	"	Attigny	Montfaucon
Soissons	Bourgogne	"	Monthoir	Varennes
Château-Thierry	Épernay	Suippes	Valmy	Dombasles-en-Argonne

---

[*] Minus one or two army corps directed on Paris.

[†] This detachment could form an independent command.

Chapter IV

La Ferté-Gaucher	Vertus	Châlons	Dommartin	Souilly
Provins	Fère Champenoise	Vitry	Heiltz-le-Maurupt	Vaubecourt
Behind the Seine	Behind the Aube	Between the Aube and the Marne	Behind the Ornain	Bar-le-Duc area

The deduced marching areas of the movements indicated above could be:

Between the 6th and 5th armies. – The main road from Villers-Cotterets to Meaux and Paris (the Villers-Cotterets main road by Nanteuil being however reserved for the corps of the 5th Army directed on Paris).

Between the 5th and the 4th Army (detachment). – Craonne, Dormans, Montmirail, Nogent-sur-Seine.

Between the 4th Army (detachment) and the cavalry corps. – Beine, Vertus, Fête-Champenoise, Arcis-sur-Aube.

Between the C. C. and the 4th Army. – Suippes and Vitry.

Between the 4th and 3rd armies. – Sainte-Manehould, Revigny-aux-Vaches.

As can be seen, the situation in which we now found ourselves led me to abandon the maneuver on the enemy's outer wing and to return to the plan of an offensive action which would have as its objective to separate this wing from the rest of the enemy's battle line.

This decision explains all the orders given on August 30 and the following days until the moment when the enemy, against all expectations, avoided Paris, allowing me again to return to the plan of August 25, aiming at assembling a mass that would overrun the enemy's marching wing.

Also, when in the evening, on my return from Varennes, headquarters of the 3rd Army, I became aware of the desire that Marshal French had communicated to me to postpone his troops behind the Seine to reconstitute them in the Mantes, Poissy, Saint-Germain area, I informed him that I accepted his proposals with the only reservation that he withdraw first of all to the east of Paris, that is to say behind the Marne between Meaux and Neuilly-sur-

Marne, except for transferring then to the west bypassing Paris by the south.

In the 6th Army, Paris was indicated as the general direction of retreat, while General d'Amade, who had made it known that his territorial divisions were unable to hold the campaign any longer, was given Rouen as the direction of retreat.

The 5th Army received the order to withdraw behind the Serre, and to lead a corps to Paris, partly by rail, partly by road.

The Foch army detachment, after a very hard day, had passed in the evening on the left bank of the Aisne, its vanguards remaining alone on the right bank.

At the beginning of the afternoon of the 30th, as I had resolved, I went to Varennes to see General Ruffey; I found him in a state which proved that all that I had been told was true: he was very irritated and venting bitter words against the majority of his subordinates, especially against General de Lartigue and General de Trentinian who, he said, had had his division massacred at Ethe, lost a part of his artillery and showed an absolute worthlessness as commander of division. The exaltation of the commander of the 3rd Army was so great that I felt that we could no longer rely on his assessments. Thus, after having, on the previous day, claimed that the 4th Corps was indispensable to him in order to counter imminent threats of attack, he now declared that the enemy was no longer showing any activity, and that the 4th Corps was going to be pushed forward.

In these conditions, I judged it imprudent to leave the command of his army to General Ruffey any longer, and I informed him that he had to hand it over to General Sarrail.[*] At the same time, I informed General Grossetti that I was entrusting him with the command of the 42nd Division, which he would join as soon as Colonel Leboucq had taken up his duties as Chief of Staff.

On leaving Varennes, I went to Monthois to see General de Langle. As much as I had been negatively impressed by the state of mind of the commander of the 3rd Army, I was happily

---

[*] General Ruffey accepted without apparent regret this decision. He dined the same evening at my table, in Vitry-le-François.

impressed by the calm, the self-control and the firm attitude of the commander of the 4th. In the morning, the latter had informed me that he could not continue his withdrawal without damaging the morale of his troops who were only too willing to fight; he announced that he intended to leave his current positions to resume the offensive towards the north. During our afternoon meeting, I authorized him to carry out this action in agreement with the one that the 3rd Army was preparing to the northwest of Nouart. This offensive attitude was, in my mind, to contribute to the relief of General Foch, who was engaged on the left of the 4th Army against significant forces.

The conduct of the armies was not the only question that occupied my mind at that time.

First, there was the question of Paris.

In the morning, General Galliéni had already telephoned Vitry-le-François to explain the situation of the fortified camp, and to ask that active troops be placed at his disposal for the defense of the capital. I told him that my intention was to direct the 6th Army to Paris, composed mainly of reserve formations, to which an army corps taken from the 5th Army would eventually be added.

Shortly after my departure for Varennes, Colonel Pénelon, of the military house of the President of the Republic and liaison agent between the government and me, arrived at Vitry charged by Mr. Millerand to draw my attention to the advisability of providing the fortified camp of Paris with a sufficient quantity of active troops. In addition, he had the mission of determining my opinion on the possibility of transferring the seat of government to Bordeaux. On my return to the main headquarters, I received a telephone call from Mr. Millerand: after having informed him of the situation and having made known to him my decision to withdraw our forces, I did not hide from him that Paris was seriously threatened, and that, under these conditions, in order to facilitate its defense and not to bring any obstacle to the maneuver, I saw only advantages in the departure of the government for Bordeaux. I informed him, moreover, that orders had been given for the 5th Army to direct, as of the next day, an army corps with two divisions on Paris. Finally, I told him that I had decided to make other withdrawals from the 1st and 2nd armies for the benefit of our left.

Our Russian allies brought me, at the end of the day, concerns that added to all the other ones I was facing. I have said on several occasions the interest that I attached to the Russian operations. The favorable information we had received so far made me hope that the Germans would soon be obliged to transfer to the east part of their forces which they had committed against us. This was our main reason for trying to hold on, believing that before long the momentum of our opponents would be broken on our front. Now, towards the middle of the night, we learned that in Belfort a German radio had been intercepted saying: "The success of the battle of Tannenberg is even more complete than we thought at first: three Russian army corps are completely annihilated; 70,000 prisoners; part of the 6th and 1st Army corps are on the run; the 2nd Russian army no longer exists."

What credence should be given to his news? I don't hide the fact that I couldn't help feeling a dark foreboding.

And yet, in spite of this catastrophe, the Russians had just rendered us the service that I expected from them. As I learned the next day, when the sad news of Tannenberg reached us, two German army corps had just left our front to go to East Prussia.

August 31. – As often happens in war, the general situation on the morning of August 31 seemed to me to be more favorable than on the day of the 30th of which I have just spoken.

Indeed, a German radio intercept seemed to indicate that the enemy corps engaged on the 29th against our 5th Army had suffered a real failure: "Hide from the troops our failure on the left flank," said the radio.

But above all, the most important news I received was that German troop transports from the west to the east were reported in Belgium, and had been spotted as they passed through Berlin; these were thirty-two troop trains that obviously appeared to be headed for Russia.

Thus, the reaction of the Russian offensive on our front began to be felt; the pressure that the enemy exerted on the Allied forces in the west would decrease.

On receiving this favorable news, I thought it would be useful

Chapter IV

to insist on the need to give up only the strictly necessary ground, by resisting every step of the way:

To the 6th Army, I recommended giving way only under the pressure of the enemy, and to stop its retreat as soon as it would be certain not to be caught by superior forces.

To Lanrezac the same recommendation, at the same time as I ordered him to guard the 18th Corps intended the day before to be directed towards Paris, and to make his troops rest.

Finally, with French, I was most urgent; I explained to him that our 5th and 6th armies, which had received, because of the information which had just reached us, the mission to give up ground only under the pressure of the enemy, could not fulfill this task unless there was no gap between them: I therefore asked the commander-in-chief of the British armies "to withdraw the British army only if we ourselves were obliged to give ground, and at least to maintain the rear-guards in such a way as not to give the enemy the impression of a marked withdrawal and a gap between our 5th and 6th armies.

In the evening, I received the Marshal's reply: "In deference to the desire I had expressed to him, the English army would withdraw the next day only to the line Fontaine-les-Corps-Nuds, Nanteuil-le-Haudouin, Betz, and it would remain there as long as the 5th and 6th armies occupied their present positions, which were both a strong step forward of the line indicated by Marshal French." If these two French armies retreated, the English army would follow suit: it could not move forward until it was reinforced and reorganized.

Certainly this was not the answer I wanted; this systematic withdrawal of the English line one step backwards uncovered the left flank of our 5th Army. Now, a German radio intercept in the morning had informed us that a German cavalry corps had succeeded in crossing the Oise at the Bailly bridge, which had been left intact by the English detachment in charge of destroying it. This mass of cavalry was reported to be marching towards Soissons, that is to say, on the rear of the 5th Army, and it appeared to be followed by two army corps. We had asked the English to intervene against this maneuver, which risked transforming into disaster the withdrawal of the 5th Army by cutting its communications. We have seen how the Marshal refused me in the evening. I was also very worried about the fate of Lanrezac until I learned that, thanks to the precautions taken by him, the German cavalry had been kept out of the marching zone of our columns.

While I was thus preoccupied with the situation of the 5th Army, I had to make an important decision concerning our forces in the center. It will be recalled that, the day before, I had authorized General de Langle to attack the enemy on the 31st. His action was to be combined with an offensive by the 3rd Army and the Foch detachment, astride the Aisne. However, while the 4th Army declared itself ready to restart its attack the following day, General Foch, whose personal opinion I had sought, informed me that, in a great hurry, he would have difficulty in holding out against the enemy who was opposed to him without any serious support, due to the nature of the Champagne battlefield, the fatigue of his troops and the low density of the artillery of the 9th Corps. In these conditions, it seemed to me that the continuation of the offensive of the 4th Army could have as a consequence to create between this army and the Foch detachment a gap similar to that which the English retreat had just produced on the left wing of the 5th Army. Also, I decided, in the evening, to end the fighting of the 3rd and 4th armies, and I ordered them to withdraw on the Reims-Vouziers line. This was the beginning of the general movement of retreat of our front which I had decided the day before.

Other worries came to me that day, from the interior. Mr. Messimy, who had just received a command on the front, came to the main headquarters and had lunch with me. He brought me the news of what was happening in Paris: a wave of pessimism had been provoked by the evacuations and the announcement of the departure of the government; within the government itself, some were thinking, it is said, of making peace at all costs. Also, taking advantage of the fact that the withdrawal of German troops from our front could give hope of a lull, I telegraphed the Minister of War that, because of the situation, the departure of the government for Bordeaux could be postponed at least until September 2. I hoped that this would bring a little calm and hope to the Parisian spheres.

Chapter IV 333

September 1. – The information we had received on the 30th about the crossing of the Oise River upstream from Compiègne by German forces had been communicated to General Maunoury. He had thought he had to conclude that the First German Army, preceded by cavalry divisions, was moving eastward, abandoning the direction of Paris, and that it was content to mask the Sixth Army with part of its forces emerging from the Saint-Just-Montdidier region. With a correctness of vision that did him the greatest honor, Maunoury had understood the risk that the 5th Army was running, and judging that his army, although only just formed, had an important role to play, he offered to attack from the 1st of September in the direction of Clermont towards the northeast.

This way of seeing things corresponded entirely to the directives I had given to Maunoury on August 27, when I had informed him that the resumption of the offensive would begin with his army in the general direction of the northeast. But the general situation had changed. Since August 30, I had had to give up the overall battle under the conditions in which I had envisaged it on the 25th. The mission of the 6th Army, in the new plan that I had conceived, was to cover Paris, avoiding any failure which, in the present conditions, could have particularly severe consequences, by the repulsing of Maunoury's forces far from the fortified camp, separating them from the English army.

Also, after having congratulated General Maunoury for his correct assessment of the situation, I informed him on the morning of September 1st of his new mission, which consisted of withdrawing to the capital and immediately establishing liaison with the military governor.

Thus, at the beginning of the day of September 1, I envisaged that the defense of Paris would be assured by the Maunoury army reinforced by an active army corps; in my forecasts, the forces destined to defend the capital would amount to two active army corps and five reserve divisions,* the active units having to form

---

* The transport of the 18th Corps that the 5th Army had been ordered to direct on Paris had been made impossible by the advance of the German cavalry corps towards Soissons; I had thus decided to replace this corps by the 4th withdrawn

the mobile defense, and being able to be called upon to participate in the overall operations of our armies. As for the English, in spite of the little success I had obtained with their commander-in-chief, I remained convinced that their situation would improve more quickly than they thought, and I did not despair of seeing them participate in the maneuver that was beginning to appear in my mind.

The direction taken by the enemy columns of the extreme right seemed to move them away from Paris: it was thus possible to consider a combination of the maneuvers of the main body of the army with those of the troops in charge of the defense of the capital, and the possibility of taking advantage of the fortified camp for the benefit of the maneuver.

In any case, if, as the change in direction of the enemy columns seemed to suggest, the Germans avoided Paris, it was necessary that the fortifications and the garrison defending the capital be placed directly under my orders. This is why I asked the Minister to give me authority over the fortifications of Paris, in order "to be able, if necessary, to involve the mobile garrison with the operations of the campaign."[*]

By gathering all the information which had reached us, the whole of the German armies seemed to us, this morning of September 1st, to occupy the following situation:

> The Ist Army, under the command of General von Kluck, composed of 4 active corps and 1 reserve corps, was moving southward past the Compiègne region;
>
> The IInd Army, commanded by General von Bülow, with 3 active army corps and 2 reserves, had reached the region of Laon;
>
> The IIIrd Army, under the command of General von Hansen, comprising 2 active corps and 1 reserve corps, had crossed the Aisne between Château-Porcien and Attigny;

---

from the 3rd Army, which was to be concentrated on September 3 and 4 in Paris. The two divisions of this corps were to, with the division of the 7th Corps and the 45th Division, bring up to four active divisions the forces responsible for the defense of the capital.

[*] Telegram No. 3168 of September 1, 9:05 a.m. to the Minister of War.

Chapter IV

The IVth and Vth armies commanded respectively by the Duke of Wurtemberg and the Imperial Kronprinz, with 6 active and 4 reserve corps, were in contact with our armies between Verdun and Vouziers;

Finally, from the vicinity of Nancy to the approaches of Belfort, the VIth and VIIth armies, with 6 active army corps reinforced by numerous reserve and ersatz formations, were entrenched in front of our right, under the orders of the Kronprinz Rupprecht of Bavaria and the general von Hoerigen.*

In front of the large enemy movement against our left, it seemed obvious that we could not accept the battle immediately. The engagement of one of our armies would inevitably lead to that of all our forces. The 5th Army would find itself in a situation that the march of the 1st German army, facilitated by the incursion of the enemy cavalry corps, made most perilous. The slightest failure would run the risk of turning into an irremediable defeat. Moreover, our troops, who had been constantly fighting and marching, were tired and needed to fill the gaps in their ranks.

As I have already said, our position in the coalition made it our duty to last, holding back the maximum of German forces in front of us, to wear down the enemy by offensives taken at every favorable opportunity, and to avoid any decisive engagement until we had in our hand the greatest chances of success.

This is how the general situation presented itself to me, on September 1, around 9:30 a.m., when I left Vitry-le-François for Bar-sur-Aube, where I had decided to move my headquarters.

I arrived in Bar at about 11 o'clock in the morning, and while the General headquarters was setting up in the boys' school, I studied with my collaborators the various possibilities that the situation seemed to involve. Opinions were very divided. Berthelot proposed transporting three army corps to our left; it was easy to show him that this option would require too much time, and that the situation was too urgent to allow such a maneuver to be considered. After careful reflection, I concluded that the most

---

* German order of battle drawn up on the evening of August 31 by the 2nd Bureau of the G.Q.G.

(Photo Rale, Bar-sur-Aube.)

The garden, in Bar-Sur-Aube, where General Joffre transported his G.Q.G. during the preparation of the Battle of the Marne (September 1 to 5)

advantageous option in the present state of our affairs consisted in taking back the field necessary to avoid a general clash in poor conditions. It was, in short, the plan that I had assumed as early as the 30th, and had a memorandum written by Colonel Pont: the whole of our formation was to pivot around its right in front of the outflanking movement carried out by the enemy against the left wing. In this way, the 5th Army and the British army could escape the threat of envelopment, and when this first step would be achieved, the whole of the 3rd, 4th and 5th armies would resume the offensive.

For this movement to be possible, it was necessary that the 3rd Army, which was to serve as a pivot, was solid. Also, the head of the 3rd Bureau, Colonel Pont, insisted that this army, already weakened by the sending of an army corps to Paris, should be reinforced. I envisaged that the reserve divisions of this army, which were currently holding the Hauts-de-Meuse, could abandon this position when the time came, in order to take part in the general offensive; in addition, I proposed to make withdrawals from the 1st and 2nd armies up to the extreme limit of security; on our right wing, in fact, the enemy no longer showed any activity, and our situation had particularly improved there.

In the establishment of this plan, I was led to consider a limit to the retreat that I had ordered, without, in my mind, this limit necessarily having to be reached; it was necessary, indeed, to be ready to exploit any favorable opportunity which would come to be presented. On the 1st of September, since it seemed necessary to gain a sufficiently large battlefield, and to establish a solid line as a starting point for the future offensive, I set this limit at the Aube and the Seine.. It seemed to me that it would be possible to realize a maneuver assuming the cooperation on our left of the English army and the mobile forces of the fortified camp of Paris. By creating a sort of pocket marked out by Verdun, Bar-le-Duc, Arcis-sur-Aube, Nogent-sur-Seine and the fortified camp of Paris, it seemed that we would achieve a favorable strategic situation.

These were the bases of the general instruction no. 4 that I had written at Bar-sur-Aube, at the beginning of the afternoon of September 1st, and that I sent to the armies of the left, to the English army and to the military governor of Paris.

Throughout the morning of September 1, the 5th Army continued to preoccupy me. The threat of German cavalry on its left flank called for protective measures on my part: I was thus led to form a new cavalry corps on the left of Lanrezac under the orders of General Conneau, whom I urgently ordered to the general headquarters. When Conneau arrived in Bar, I was pleased to learn that the 5th Army had been able to cross the Aisne without difficulty and that the German cavalry had been stopped without being able to compromise the withdrawal of the reserve divisions south of the Saint-Gobain massif. However, I was aware that this retreat could only be carried out at a very low speed due to the congestion of the roads and the great fatigue of the troops who were subjected to an overwhelming heat. If the 5th Army managed to withdraw between the Aisne and the Vesle, the fear of seeing this army enveloped was rekindled by the information we received in the evening, which made me want to see Conneau's corps in place as soon as possible: in fact, reconnaissance flights by French and English aircraft carried out during the course of the day all pointed to enemy columns marching south-southeast. A very important piece of information was sent to us at the end of the evening by the 5th Army: a map had been found on a German officer wounded in a car and taken prisoner during the day near Coucy-le-Château; this map bore indications relating to the movements of the First German Army, and gave with precision the objectives that the various corps of this army had to reach; the whole of these movements clearly showed that von Kluck's army had crossed the Oise river and was bending its general direction of march towards the southeast.

If the intentions of the enemy revealed by this bundle of information seemed to threaten Lanrezac's army, on the other hand, it seemed that von Kluck was now giving up on marching on Paris. Nothing could be more advantageous for us, since this movement would have the effect, if it continued, of placing our 6th Army in a position similar to that which I had envisaged, on 25 August, for the Amiens-Laon-Verdun battle. One can guess with what interest we were preparing to follow von Kluck's movements.

Almost at the same time that this important information reached us, I received the following letter from Mr. Millerand:

Chapter IV

September 1, 1914.

My dear general,

I would have liked to have been able to discuss with you, by direct wire, the enclosed note. It was written in front of me, at the end of a conference of more than two hours, by Marshal French who had come to Paris today.[*]

Without wishing in any way to encroach on your freedom, which must remain complete, as must your responsibility, I believe I must tell you that the government is unanimous in wishing that you consider it possible to accept the proposal of Marshal French. In the first place, it seems more favorable to the defense of Paris. On the other hand, your acceptance would have the result of bringing the two headquarters closer together and of opening the way to a more intimate cooperation between the two leaders.

I would blame myself for insisting. You know our feeling. Let the leader that you are weigh and decide.

Believe, my dear general, in the new assurance of my affectionate and devoted sympathy.

MILLERAND.

P.S. – If you agree, I need not emphasize the extreme urgency of notifying Marshal French, and getting the work started.

Here are the Marshal's proposals that the Minister of War transmitted to me:

Paris, September 1, 1914.

Proposals of Marshal Sir John French.

It seems to me that the present situation requires that we set a plan that is well understood by all, so that we can all cooperate in its realization.

I would like to see a line of defense chosen on the Marne River extending for a few kilometers west and northwest of Paris. The length of this line should be determined according to the number of troops that would be likely to occupy it, sufficiently dense in depth to

---

[*] Marshal French had had an interview the same day at the British embassy in Paris with Lord Kitchener, who had arrived from London in the morning. Messrs. Viviani and Millerand were present at this conference.

permit both local and general counterattacks.

I would prefer that the elements of the general counterattack be concentrated behind the left flank and formed as strongly as possible.

If a position of this kind is prepared, I am ready to hold on my present line, that is to say, at Nanteuil, as well as to the east and west of this point, as long as the situation requires it, provided, however, that I do not run the risk of seeing my flanks exposed to an attack.

I am prepared to do my utmost to cooperate in this plan, but I cannot, under any circumstances, place the English army, under the inferior conditions in which it now finds itself, in a position where it is liable to be attacked by superior forces without the certainty of being supported and rescued.

If this plan is to be accepted, it would be advisable not to lose a moment to begin the defense of the position with all the means at our disposal."

September 2. – These proposals reached me after the sending of General Instruction no. 4. They could all the less call into question the solution adopted since the news received from the Marshal during the night of September 1 to 2 seriously limited the possibilities of action of the English army: in fact, we received on September 2 at about 3:00 a.m. from the head of the French mission the following telegram: "English troops obliged to retreat are withdrawing this night to the line north and west of Nanteuil-le-Haudouin. Tomorrow, September 2, they will withdraw to the Dammartin line, the 3rd to the Marne."

To deliver a defensive battle on the Marne was not a solution: the course of this river offered a parallel obstacle to the general front of our armies only in the region of Châlons; it was to leave our two wings in the air and to allow the Germans, establishing themselves in a defensive position on the northern bank, a free hand to deal with the question of Verdun and Paris; it was to give up the enveloping formation which the French armies, supported by the fortifications of Verdun and the fortified camp of Paris, were taking little by little in their retreat. Such a resolution could have had the most serious consequences. On the other hand, the transport of troops from our right wing to the center and the left

Chapter IV   341

wing* was not finished. It was this question of the conditions of the concentration in view of the battle which seemed to me to have to be invoked to push back the suggestion of Marshal French, in order, on the one hand, to spare his susceptibility, and, on the other hand, not to reveal yet the definitive form which I intended to give to the maneuver.

It should be noted, moreover, that the river Marne played only an episodic role in the battle. The name "Victory of the Marne" was given afterwards by the French high command, because the action took place in a general way in the valley of the Marne and its tributaries (Ourcq, the two Morins, Ornain) and that it seemed the best way to synthesize the theater of the battle.

After reflection, I concluded that Marshal French's proposals could not lead me to modify the orders already given, which were to place our troops in a position that would allow them to take the offensive at short notice. I continued to think that, barring favorable events, the stopping position should be on the Seine and the Aube, from which our forces would start forward again. If the British were willing to cooperate effectively, it would be in the defense of Paris that our allies would play the most useful role, on the Seine front between Melun and Juvisy.

On the morning of September 2, I answered in this sense to the Minister of War and to Marshal French.

Moreover, the question of the defense of the capital was not without concern for me. At noon, in fact, Galliéni had had a long telephone conversation with General Pellé, in which he drew my attention to the fact that the fortified camp of Paris was in no condition to defend itself: "If General Maunoury cannot hold out, we are in no condition to resist," he said *verbatim*, and he concluded that it was necessary for the armies in the field to help him in the defense of the northern and eastern fronts. This situation had not escaped me, and on the morning of September 1, a few

---

* 55th and 56th reserve divisions, and 4th Army corps taken from the 3rd Army for the 6th; one division of the 9th Corps coming from the 2nd Army for Foch's detachment; 21st corps coming from the 1st Army for the 6th; 15th Corps coming from the 2nd for the 3rd; 3 cavalry divisions coming from the 1st and 2nd armies to form the cavalry corps between Lanrezac's and French's armies.

hours before the telephone conversation that I have just recounted, I had made known to the Minister of War that it seemed to me necessary for the government to leave without delay.

This is why, also, on the morning of September 2, I had General Galliéni tell me that it was essential that the distribution of forces on the defensive positions be carried out as soon as possible, the important thing being to be in Paris before the enemy. I was also in a hurry to see that the 6th Army did not linger in its withdrawal movement. This movement was linked, moreover, to the one I had ordered to the 3rd and 4th armies, which was executed without being hindered by the enemy. I had recommended to the army commanders to make it clear to all levels that this was not a forced retreat, but a movement to prepare for future operations.

During the night of September 1 to 2, we received confirmation of German troop movements to Russia: elements of the VIIth Corps, the IXth Corps and the IIIrd Corps had embarked in Belgium for the Eastern Front.

On the other hand, while the day before the Ist German Army seemed to want to avoid Paris, the information that reached us on the morning of September 2 seemed to indicate that von Kluck was heading for the capital. I had no illusions about the fate of this city, if the enemy attacked it.

Finally, the withdrawal of forces to the eastern front seemed to me to constitute favorable circumstances, which I anxiously wondered if there would not be cause to exploit by a very prompt resumption of the offensive. The question arose as to whether we should extend our retreat to the limit that I had indicated the day before as being able to become the starting point of our forward movement. All in all, our withdrawal had left our troops more or less intact. We had not yet fought the great battle that would decide the fate of the war. We had only had partial encounters which had turned some to our disadvantage, others to our advantage. To continue this retreat without ceasing, we would end up taking the appearance of the vanquished, before the decisive game was played. Finally, this retreat delivered to the enemy a large part of our territory, and it was our duty to limit this painful sacrifice to what was strictly necessary. Was it possible to hasten the date of the general resumption of the offensive?

At the main headquarters, opinions were divided on this question. The 3rd Bureau and its chief were in favor of trying everything to resume the forward movement as soon as possible. Berthelot, on the contrary, was very much in favor of a withdrawal behind the Seine: the troops were so tired from their retreat from the Sambre that they were incapable of any effort. Indeed, General de Langle had sent his deputy chief of staff, Lieutenant-Colonel Dessens, to inform me that his army needed respite before being able to begin any operation: the 12th Corps, in particular, was in a state of fatigue which obliged us to provide the transport by rail of part of its infantry.

Berthelot felt that, under these conditions, it was necessary to remove the troops from the pressure of the enemy, to allow them to breathe under the shelter of an obstacle such as the Seine, before fighting a battle on which the fate of France would depend.

Belin thought that our essential duty was to hold out, to reserve our forces for the moment when the Russians would have made their action more fully felt, and that this prudent attitude was the best way to frustrate the German plan, which was undoubtedly to finish off the French as soon as possible.

After much reflection, I found that Belin's advice was wise: it was necessary above all to last. Moreover, the state of our troops reported by the army commanders was such as to incline me towards this solution: we had just learned that the columns of the IIIrd, IVth and Vth German armies were on the march towards the south, starting from the region of Rethel. Their mass, of at least a dozen army corps, was likely to come up against the tired corps of Foch, de Langle and Sarrail. The latter would find themselves in a very inferior numerical situation. Was this a set of favorable conditions for the decisive battle? No.

Consequently, I decided to stop again, and to move the front a few steps back. This solution offered, in addition, the advantage of allowing me to modify the distribution of my forces, by making new levies on the 1st and 2nd armies for the benefit of the center and the left wing.

On the evening of the 2nd, I sent an order to the armies

indicating that the purpose of the current withdrawal was to tighten our position in order to prepare for the resumption of the general offensive, the signal for which I reserved to give in a few days. In the meantime, it was important to replenish our staff and personnel, and to take the most drastic measures to ensure complete order in the withdrawal movement. At the same time I indicated to the armies the broad outlines of the plan that had been decided upon, which was, in short, only the continuation of the maneuver described by Instruction no. 4 of the day before: it was a question, I told them, of withdrawing the armies from the pressure of the enemy, by establishing them on the general line: Pont-sur-Yonne, Nogent-sur-Seine, Amis-sur-Aube, Brienne-le-Château, Joinville, to reinforce our armies of the center by two army corps taken from the two armies of the right wing, and to pass then to the offensive. As for the garrison of Paris, I already foresaw that it would have to act in the direction of Meaux, and I informed Galliéni.

In fact, as far as the capital is concerned, various interesting information reached me during the afternoon of September 2.

First of all, the Government had taken the decision to leave Paris, and relocate to Bordeaux. On the other hand, I received, around midnight, a letter from the Governor of Paris in which he reminded me with particular insistence that the capital would have an absolute impossibility of resisting, if the garrison was not reinforced by at least three active army corps. I knew it: neither the forts which dated from the time when I was lieutenant of engineers, nor the abatis made in haste were able to stop the enemy. But it was not in this way that I envisaged the defense of the city; it was by an active cooperation of the mobile defense to the general operations, in direction of Meaux, as I had instructed, i.e. by an overall action against the outer wing of the enemy. This was very different from the conception that General Galliéni seemed to have.

Concerning Galliéni, I would like to express here the great respect that I have for his memory. With his great uprightness as an honest soldier, he was for me during this tragic period a devoted and clear-sighted collaborator, as our correspondence of the time testifies.

Telegram from General Joffre to Colonel Huguet of the G.Q.G. detached to Marshal French. (The last two sentences are in the hand of the general)

To complete the account of this day of September 2, I must also mention that it brought us news from the Ministry of Foreign Affairs that we had been dreading for two days: in Eastern Prussia, the Russians had suffered a serious setback that the great Russian headquarters seemed to want to hide as much as possible. On the other hand, we learned with satisfaction that in Galicia a great victory was reported to have been won by the Allies over the Austrians.

On the Serbian front, it was announced that the Serbian general headquarters had decided, following the victory it had just won on the slopes of the Tser, to take the offensive in Syrmy in the first days of September.

September 3. – On the morning of September 3rd, the situation on our left seemed less unfavorable than one might have feared. The 6th Army had been able to withdraw without being seriously troubled. The English had established themselves on the Dammartin-Saint-Soupplets-Étrépilly front, without being more pressed; one could hope, according to the advice of Galliéni, that they would not cross the Marne.

One point was still unclear to us: on September 1st, the Ist German army marching south-southeast had reached by its right corps Saint-Just-en-Chaussée, and by its other corps, the Verberie-Vivières front and the region west of Soissons. But on the 2nd, some of von Kluck's corps had again appeared to be heading southwest. What was to be concluded from this? Yes or no, would Paris be attacked? On the other hand, we were without information from the IInd German army.

These hesitations in the march of the adversary, his lack of bite in the pursuit, the persistence of intelligence on the transport of enemy troops from the west to the east imposed themselves with force on my mind and seemed to determine a circumstance favorable to the resumption of the general offensive which remained my dominant concern. In spite of the decision I had taken the day before, I wanted to know the moral and physical state of Foch's troops, who would obviously have to play an important role in the general offensive. I therefore decided to consult him.

At the same time, and always in anticipation of this return to

Chapter IV

the offensive which would require of all, command and troops, the maximum of will and tenacity, I mentally reviewed all the great leaders who would be called to participate in it. The day before, I had indicated in a general order that the salvation of the country depended on this offensive, and that all had to stretch their energy in view of the final victory. In the course of the previous days, as the information I had requested had reached me, I had replaced a fairly large number of generals, who had proved to be inferior to their task, with officers who had shown qualities of character and command.

In this order of considerations, I had a serious question to solve: that of the command of the 5th Army. Since the battle of Guise, where, as you will recall, I had found General Lanrezac very much in control of himself, whereas the day before I had been impressed by the state of physical and moral depression in which I had seen him, since that battle, I say, the leader of the 5th Army had not ceased to discuss the orders he had received and to raise objections to everything he was told. His physical fatigue had exasperated the critical side of his mind, which had always been one of his characteristics. He had become hesitant and pusillanimous. Under his failing leadership, his staff was deeply divided. And his personally bad relations with French had compromised the collaboration of the English army with the French armies.

I could not help but think of his brilliant peacetime career. Like all those who had been his pupils, I, who had had him under my command as a colonel when I was in command of the 6th Division, had been captivated by his high and brilliant intelligence; on the exercise map, he had been marvelous in his clarity, lucidity, judgement and spirit of appropriateness. It is precisely because I had the highest esteem for his intelligence that I had made myself the architect of his military fortune, and it is to me that he owes it to be at the head of the most delicate army to lead.

But, if I compared what I had expected from him before the war with the way he behaved in the presence of realities, I was, in spite of my deep sympathy for him, obliged to conclude that the responsibilities crushed him: a brilliant military critic of operations in which he would not have been an actor, he had collapsed morally before the hard circumstances of the beginning of this campaign. Now, war is only fought with men who have faith in success, who, by their self-control, know how to impose themselves on their subordinates and dominate events. Perhaps, in a happy war, he would have done wonders; in the difficult conditions in which we found ourselves, his presence at the head of the 5th Army was a weakness, and I can say that the same conviction was shared by all those who were called upon to see Lanrezac during those dark days.

From then on, what was my duty? However painful it might have seemed to me, however reluctant I might have been to deprive one of the most esteemed leaders of the army of his command, I thought it necessary to replace him at the head of the 5th Army, if I wanted to be able to engage without second thoughts, with the conviction of having done all I could to succeed, in the offensive that was being prepared.*

Once this decision was made, it was infinitely painful for me to carry it out. All the details of that late afternoon of September 3 have remained engraved in my memory: I felt that it was my duty to act in this way and, however, I feared at the last moment that I would not have the courage to accomplish it. As if to put myself in front of a *fait accompli*, I resolved to summon Franchet d'Esperey to ask him if he would accept the command of the 5th Army, and only then to see Lanrezac and to announce my decision to him.

I had given an appointment to Franchet d'Esperey at the entry of Sézanne, at a crossroads, near a small farm. I found him there at 4 pm. I told him point-blank: "The 5th Army is not marching according to my wishes, especially in view of the upcoming offensive. I will be obliged to replace Lanrezac: I thought of you. Do you feel capable of commanding an army?"

"Just like anyone else," replied the commander of the 1st Corps.

---

* It has been said, written and repeated that I had never forgiven Lanrezac for having broken off the fight after Charleroi and Guise. Nothing could be further from the truth. These resolutions were taken in perfect agreement with me. Not only did I approve Lanrezac's resolution after Charleroi, but it was the starting point of the new maneuver conceived on August 25.

We then spoke about the state of his corps, that of his neighbors, and, having asked him his opinion on the possibility for the 5th Army to resume the offensive, he answered that this decision seemed to him premature, because of the state of fatigue of the troops.

Our conversation lasted about half an hour. Franchet d'Esperey left me to go to his headquarters where I was to send him my orders.

On my side, I continued my way to Sézanne, where the headquarters of the 5th Army was installed in the school. Lanrezac was in his office. I entered and remained alone with him. Our conversation was brief: "My friend," I said to him, "you know that I have always supported and encouraged you in your career. But, you are tired, hesitant; you must leave the command of the 5th Army. It is painful for me to tell you this; but I am obliged to do so."

Lanrezac thought for a moment, then answered me: "You are right, my general." And against all expectations, he appeared to me as if delivered from a crushing burden, and his face literally lit up. I announced to him that I was going to put him at the disposal of Galliéni and that, in this situation, he would render, I was convinced, the greatest services.

I then sent for Franchet d'Esperey at his headquarters. I waited for him, pacing back and forth in the schoolyard. When the new commander of the 5th Army arrived, I confirmed my decision to him, and I left Sézanne to return to the general headquarters.

It was nearly 8 p.m. when I arrived there. The answer to the question that I had asked Foch in the morning was waiting for me there. It was Captain André Tardieu who had brought it to me; the general's opinion was clear: because of the material situation of his army, still in the process of being organized, he considered it premature to resume offensive operations before a few days.

Lieutenant colonel Bernard of the staff of the 4th Army had come, on his side, to ask, in a precise way, for the transport by railroad for one or two stops, of the infantry of the 12th Corps, literally at the end of its breath: this corps, under the skillful command of general Roques, had behaved very well since the beginning of the campaign, and it had arrived at the extreme limit of human strength. It was necessary to give satisfaction to this request, and the directorate of the railroads was going to accomplish this difficult problem.

From the 6th Army, the news had arrived that no engagement had taken place on its front, and that it had been able to occupy without difficulty its new locations: it even seemed that it had no one in front of it.

As far as Galliéni is concerned, we remember that, during the night of the 2nd to the 3rd, I had received a rather worried letter from him in which he declared himself unable to defend Paris, unless he was reinforced by 3 active army corps. I had answered him on the morning of the 3rd, specifying the forces at his disposal.[*]

During my absence, two letters from the governor of Paris had arrived at my address, one official, the other handwritten and of a more personal character.

The first one was as follows:

Q. G. OF THE ARMIES OF PARIS
        no. 622   *Invalides, September 3, 9:10 a.m.*

The Military Governor of Paris to the General Commander-in-Chief of the Northeast Army Group.

I have just received from the Minister of War an order informing me that the fortified camp of Paris is placed under your orders under the conditions provided for by article 144 of the Instruction on the conduct of large units and article 151 of the Decree on the service of the places, in order to allow you, if necessary, to associate the mobile garrison of the place with the operations of the armies in the field, without this garrison being able to be moved away from the place to a distance too great to compromise its safety.

    I have the honor of asking you, consequently, to kindly give me instructions on the role that you intend to assign to the fortified camp

---

[*] These forces were the following: Maunoury's army (7th Army corps and 3 reserve divisions), the 45th Division (coming from Algeria), the 4th Army corps (which was to disembark from the 3rd at midnight to the 5th), Ebener's group (61st and 62nd reserve divisions), the territorial divisions.

of Paris and to the army of Paris in the overall operations. On this subject, allow me to remind you that the garrison of Paris includes a considerable proportion of territorial troops whose maneuver value is very low, and who are only very imperfectly equipped as field troops. They have neither a combat train nor a regimental train, and I am working to provide them with embryos of these trains. Furthermore, these troops are poorly provided with artillery and ammunition. They have no depots, no convoys, no ambulances.

Unless you order otherwise, I will endeavor to hold in Paris as long as possible. But, because of the weakness of the defense, particularly on the northeast side, we are exposed, I insist on this point, to see this front forced, if you do not intervene, at the proper time, by a diversion.

GALLIÉNI.

To this letter was attached another one, handwritten:

MILITARY GOVERNMENT
    OF PARIS
       Governor   *Paris, September 3, 1914.*

General Galliéni, military governor of Paris and commander-in-chief of the armies in Paris to General Joffre.

My dear Joffre,

I have just received from the Minister the letter placing me under your orders. My full support is given to you. I insist only on the situation of the fortified camp: works, old-fashioned artillery equipment, insufficiency of ammunition, insufficiency and poor quality of the territorial troops, etc... This is simply to indicate to you that our capacity of resistance and especially of offensive resistance is rather weak, for the moment at least.

General Maunoury will be this evening on his positions in front of the northern front. On the other hand, the English are presently moving back from the Marne, no doubt to obey your intentions.

I have come to ask you to tell me as exactly as you can, by a note, the role that you want the fortified camp of Paris to play, at the different moments of your operations, in the conditions in which it is. We will do our best to cooperate with you or to assist your operations.

I have sent you information regarding the steps I had taken. This information will bring you up to speed on what we can do.

I would be grateful if you would not forget that the Government, by leaving me alone here, has given me the responsibility of maintaining tranquility among the Parisian population, which learned suddenly of the departure of the Government and the military situation, while it was expecting successes because of the previous communiqués presented in a favorable light. I would therefore ask you to take this consideration into account.

This population is thirsty for information and news, if we want to maintain it in the good dispositions in which it is today. But it is essential that you send me, every day, through our liaison officer and whenever you deem it useful, by telegraph, by telephone, etc., the communiqués on the general situation of the Franco-English army, on the events which occur in the other theaters of the war and especially those which in a general way can interest them.

Always faithfully yours.

Signed: GALLIÉNI.

In response, I wrote him the following two letters.

The first official one was written on September 3, shortly before midnight.

General headquarters
OF THE EASTERN ARMIES
    Staff
        3rd Bureau   At the G.H.Q., on September 4, 1914,[*]
        No. 3636   2:55 p.m.

The general in command of the Northeast Army Group to the military governor of Paris.

In reply to your letter n° 622 of September 3, 1914, I have the honor of informing you that it is not my intention to associate the territorial troops of the fortified camp of Paris with the operations of the field armies in the vicinity of the position, because of the weak maneuvering capabilities of its troops.

On the other hand, I reserve the right to ask you for the participation of the active and reserve troops of the garrison in these

---

[*] This date and time are those of the departure of the letter, when it was sent by the G.Q.G. mail.

Chapter IV

operations, particularly to act in the direction of Meaux, at the time of the resumption of the offensive provided for by Instruction No. 4 and note 3463, of which I am sending you a copy herewith.*

JOFFRE.

To this first letter, I attached another handwritten one, thus written:

At the G.Q.G., September 4, 1914.

My dear comrade,

I am sending you in an official letter the instructions concerning the military action of the forces under your orders. You will receive, at the same time, a copy of a letter that I am sending to Marshal French, which will enlighten you on the same subject.†

From now on, part of General Maunoury's active forces can be pushed eastward as a threat to the German right, so that the English left will feel supported on that side.

It would be helpful to let Marshal French know and to maintain frequent liaison with him.

I have placed at your disposal General Lanrezac who commanded the 5th Army. His hesitations and lack of decision were a danger for this army. His pessimism, which made him see all the risks of an operation and which paralyzed any initiative in him, must not be given free rein. He is a remarkably clear mind who discusses all military questions admirably, but who, in action, does not draw the necessary conclusions from his discussions. He is a remarkable teacher who does not meet in time of war the expectations that one had founded on him.

I put him at your disposal, you can do what you want with him.

Yours faithfully and cordially

J. JOFFRE.

---

* General Instruction 4 had been sent on September 1 to the military governor of Paris at the same time as to the armies concerned. Note 3463 was a personal and secret note sent on the evening of September 2 to the army commanders in which it was specified that the garrison of Paris, at the time of the resumption of the offensive, should act in the direction of Meaux.

† The letter in question here, bearing the number 3675, was written in the middle of the night of September 3 to 4; it left the mail of the French G.Q.G. for the English G.H.Q. on September 4 at 8 o'clock in the morning.

This last letter, written in the last hours of September 3, requires some explanation.

Remember that on the morning of the 3rd, we were not sure about the general direction of the march of the First German Army, because the day before, it had appeared that some of von Kluck's corps were heading back towards Paris.

However, on the evening of the 3rd, various pieces of information, all concordant, revealed that the entire First German Army was moving towards the southeast. Around 7 p.m., from Raincy, Maunoury telephoned that the German forces opposed to him seemed to have marched during the day of the 3rd towards the southeast, in the direction of the Marne, and that the reconnaissance carried out at the end of the day had not revealed any troops west of the main road between Louvres, Senlis and Verberie. At 9 p.m., the military government of Paris informed us that airplane reconnaissance had recognized the march of a column 15 to 16 kilometers long, passing through Étrépilly and oriented towards the southeast. At about the same time, Colonel Huguet wrote the following: "From the very reliable and concordant information of English aviators, it seems that the whole of the I°st German army except the IVth reserve corps (i.e.: IInd, IIIrd, IVth Army corps and XVIIIth Division) is moving towards the southeast in order to cross the Marne between Chateau-Thierry and Ferté-sous-Jouarre, in order to attack the left of the 5th Army. Its column heads will probably arrive on the river this evening."

Shortly thereafter, a telegram from Huguet reached us confirming that the British air force had reported that the march of the First German Army southward was now turning southeast. "At 5:00 p.m.," he added, "it seems that there is no force left in front of the British army's front, and that the entire Ist German Army is going to cross the Marne between Ferté-sous-Jouarre and Château-Thierry to attack the left of the 5th Army."

Finally, at about 10 p.m., a new message telephoned by the head of our mission to the British army said that it was possible that Marshal French, whose troops were receiving their first reinforcements, would march on the 4th in the evening in the direction of the east, "especially if the 6th Army, which seemed to have no one in front of it, began, on that same day, a similar movement which would carry it to its left."

It is conceivable that in the presence of such clear, affirmative information, in the presence of this threat of envelopment of our 5th Army, there could be no question of leaving Maunoury's forces under the cannon of Paris. On the contrary, since the English seemed to be willing to participate in this maneuver, it was appropriate to direct all the active and reserve forces of the entrenched camp eastward.

These were the considerations that led me to send Galliéni the instructions that we have just read.

September 4. – The day of September 4 was to usher in a decisive crisis in the strategic situation. Indeed, the change of direction of the enemy columns seemed to be confirmed and accentuated. On the other hand, Marshal French had informed me that he had received General Instruction no. 4 and the note of September 2 for the army commanders, and, a crucial point, added that he fully understood my projects and the part I wished to see the British army take in their execution.

Thus, a happy change had just occurred in the attitude of the English commander in chief. The adventurous situation of the enemy held all my attention, and I wrote to Marshal French on September 4 at about 8 a.m. to take advantage of his new dispositions:

> In the event that the German armies should continue their movement south-southeastward, thus moving away from the Seine and Paris, perhaps you would consider, as I do, that your action could be carried out more effectively on the right bank of this river, between the Marne and the Seine; your left, supported by the Marne, buttressed by the fortified camp of Paris, would be covered by the mobile garrison of the capital, which would go forward to the attack in an easterly direction along the left bank of the Marne.

Then, I went to the office of the chief of the 3rd Bureau, Lieutenant-Colonel Pont, and I found there a whole group of officers of this office, who were hotly discussing in front of the large map on which the situation of our troops and that of the enemy had been plotted, the latter according to the latest information received: present were commanders de Partouneaux, Bel, Alexandre, and Lieutenant-Colonel Mangin, liaison officer of the Paris Military Government.

The situation was striking:

Our troops stretched along the Verdun-Sainte-Menehould line, and on the Marne River, which they crossed between Epernay and Château-Thierry, to reach the general line of Montmort, La Ferté-Gaucher. The British army was south of the Marne from Ferté-sous-Jouarre to Lagny. The 6th Army was fortifying itself on the Mareil-en-France, Dammartin, Montgé front. Thus, our front formed a vast circular arc enveloping the enemy. This arc, oriented to the south-southeast, reached the Marne between Château-Thierry and La Ferté-sous-Jouarre.

While our 5th Army, escaping the envelopment maneuver directed against its left, was going to be able to approach head-on the enemy columns crossing the Marne upstream of Ferté-sous-Jouarre, the British army and the mobile forces of Paris were in a good position to attack in flank the German troops that had just bypassed Paris.

It seemed, therefore, that the result sought by General Instruction No. 4 of September 1 was about to be realized and that it was not necessary to extend the retirement to the positions set as a limit on that same date.

Wishing to discuss this with General Berthelot, I went to his office, which was adjacent to the operations office. To my great surprise, I found the general staff aide in a rather different frame of mind than I had expected: in his opinion, it was preferable "to let the Germans sink further into the mass"; the 6th Army, he added, was not yet complete as a result of the delay that had occurred in the transportation of a division of the 4th Army Corps; Berthelot saw the main offensive starting from the region of Arcis-sur-Aube with the right of the 5th Army and the entire 9th Army, then extending in a northwesterly direction between the Seine and the Marne, while the British army, helped on its left by Maunoury, would take the offensive south of the Marne, its left wing supported at this river.

This idea, which was so different from the one that had first

Chapter IV

occurred to me, was based above all on the difficult situation of the 5th Army, which prevented it, Berthelot thought, from making a sudden U-turn in the open country to resume the offensive; it seemed preferable to him to withdraw this army to a solid front, in this case the bridgehead of Nangis, which Commandant Maurin was in the process of reconnoitring.

The disadvantages of the solution envisaged by General Berthelot did not fail to appear to me: to wait a few more days was to risk not taking advantage of the opportunity which was offered to us and to see the Germans sniffing out the danger and maneuvering to avoid it. Who could, in fact, ensure that our enemies would continue to neglect Paris? The idea of an immediate concentric action on the German right wing was reinforced in my mind during this discussion.

It was still going on, when at about 10 a.m., I was informed that Galliéni's chief of staff, General Clergerie, had just telephoned Pellé to inform him of the shift of the whole of the Ist German army towards the southeast: considering that this movement was dangerous for the 5th Army, Galliéni proposed to push the Maunoury army towards the east, reinforced by all the available elements of the entrenched camp; "under these conditions," he added, "it would be necessary for the English army to shift towards Montereau."

This proposal proved to me that Galliéni had received my personal letter and note 3636 that I had sent him the previous night, and that he understood perfectly the role that could fall to the active part of the troops in the defense of Paris; he had definitively abandoned his idea of devoting the totality of his forces to the passive defense of the fortified camp.

Berthelot again raised objections to this conception of the battle, finding that we were going to reveal our intentions to the enemy too early; he continued to insist on an operation whose main element would be an offensive leading from the region of Arcis-sur-Aube to the northwest. Without dwelling further on these suggestions, I had Galliéni reply that I had learned that the Maunoury army was marching eastward. On receiving this indication, Galliéni informed me that he was in the process of coming to an agreement with Maunoury, who would put his army on the march in the evening of the 4th, ready to operate according to the circumstances either to the north or to the south of the Marne: the governor of Paris asked which of these two solutions suited me best.

From that moment, I was tempted to answer that the 6th Army would develop its action north of the Marne. But Berthelot insisted so much that I gave in to his arguments: in any case, the 6th Army could not, on the day of the 4th, cross the Marne, and there would always be time, if the situation allowed a faster counter-offensive, to direct it by the north of the river; moreover, it was to our advantage not to push the 6th Army too early towards the east in order not to reveal our maneuver to the Germans, before we could involve our armies on the whole front.

So I had General Clergerie reply, around 1:00 p.m., that of the two operations he had told me about regarding the use of General Maunoury's troops, I considered the one that consisted of bringing the 6th Army to the left bank of the Marne south of Lagny to be the most advantageous.[*]

My goal, in answering thus, was not to modify prematurely the maneuver in progress; my decision was, in fact, not yet made. I could not fail to attach some importance to certain objections of Berthelot, especially with regard to the possibility of asking the 5th Army to turn around in the open country to leave for the attack. I thus decided to consult Franchet d'Esperey by telegram: "Circumstances are such," I said to him, "that it could be advantageous to give battle tomorrow or the day after tomorrow with all the forces of the 5th Army, in concert with the English army and the mobile forces of Paris against the Ist and IInd German armies. Please let me know if you consider your army in a position to do so with a chance of success."[†]

At the same time, I sent Lieutenant-Colonel Paquette to General Foch to inform him of the general situation, of which he

---

[*] This telegram was not received at the Military Government in Paris until 2:50 p.m., that is, after General Galliéni had left for Melun. He was not aware of it until the evening, when he returned to Paris, at about 7:30 p.m.

[†] Telegram no. 3704 of September 4, 12:45 p.m., to the 5th Army.

was unaware, and to ask him what his capabilities were.

In addition to the uncertainty in which I was able to ask the 5th Army for a return to the offensive, another circumstance inclined me to reserve my decision: it was the attitude of the English army. Galliéni had seemed, by proposing to have it support Montereau, to assume that it would not participate in the action; I could not accept such a scenario. However, towards the middle of the day, I was informed by Huguet that, under the influence of the advice of prudence given to him by his chief of staff, General Murray, French, who had been very anxious the day before to march eastward, had modified his decisions; his troops were to have rested on the 4th, and to be ready to resume the retreat in order to go in three stages behind the Seine.

The afternoon was spent waiting for the answers I had requested from Foch and Franchet d'Esperey. The heat was overwhelming. And we were all thinking about the suffering endured by the troops, and we wondered if they would be in a condition to carry out the maneuvers we were planning.

At about 2:00 p.m., we received intelligence that the cavalry corps covering the left wing of the Fifth Army was going to be forced, under pressure from three German columns of all arms that had crossed the Marne at Château-Thierry and downstream, to pass south of the Petit-Morin. This information led us to believe that, even if the battle could be envisaged in the short term, it would not be on the north bank of the Marne that the enemy's right wing would have to be sought, but on the south bank.

On the other hand, as the decision to be taken concerning the form to be given to the battle depended essentially on the answer that we would receive from Franchet d'Esperey, it seemed to us that the threat of envelopment directed against his left would diminish the opportunities of this army. Berthelot did not need so much to come back to defend the advantage of the maneuver that he preferred: the central attack in direction of the northwest. In any case, to prepare for the upcoming battle, he asked me to modify the order of battle as well as the limits of the zones of action of the 4th Army. It was about 3:30 p.m when I signed the General Instruction no. 5 which specified these various modifications, at the same time as it ordered the 3rd Army to maintain itself on the flank of the enemy, to be able at any moment to pass again to the offensive facing the northwest. Whatever the decision taken, whether I decided on the immediate battle, or whether I took, upon receipt of the reply from the 5th Army, the resolution to delay the moment of the decisive action for five or six days, this modification to the zones of action, and this orientation given to the 3rd Army were useful.

It was also in the course of this afternoon that I took the decision to relocate the next day my headquarters once more to the rear: Bar was becoming, in fact, too close to the front for the ease of my communications. I chose Châtillon-sur-Seine.

However, all the information of the day clearly established that the Ist German Army, neglecting Paris and Maunoury's forces, in front of which nothing was visible, continued its march towards the Marne, upstream from Ferté-sous-Jouarre. It could have been 4 p.m. then. I had just received a telegram from Colonel Huguet: he informed me that, as I had asked Galliéni in my letter of the night of the 3rd to the 4th of September, the governor of Paris had gone to see French and had informed him of my order to bring the 6th Army east. French had replied to Galliéni that he would remain in his present position south of the Marne as long as possible, ready to cooperate either with the 5th or the 6th Army, or with both together, as the situation required. Huguet also informed me that French was to meet Franchet d'Esperey at 3:00 p.m.; the positions of the English corps were to be modified to allow the army to move forward to the east.

This telegram had a very great influence on my decisions: it arrived in the tense atmosphere of that afternoon of the 4th when I was anxiously awaiting an answer from Franchet d'Esperey in order to make a final decision. While Berthelot, during these hours of waiting, continued to defend with persistence his point of view, this message brought me the proof that Galliéni had succeeded in convincing the English to participate in the battle, as I had asked him; moreover, it allowed me to believe that Franchet d' Esperey, in front of the agreement carried out between Galliéni and French, would rally to this maneuver, like Foch, whose answer had just arrived and who declared himself ready to attack.

However, the night was coming on, and I was anxious to

decide. Once again, I ordered Belin and Berthelot into my office where the three officers of my cabinet were already present: Gamelin, de Galbert and Muller. I invited the major-general and his aides to give me their opinion once again. Berthelot held to his position; Belin hesitated. After having considered everything, I decided that it was necessary to maintain the maneuver that *I had* envisaged the day before, and which would allow us to exploit the overwhelming position of the 5th Army; it was advisable to also benefit from the good intentions of the English. However, in order to take into account the objections that Berthelot had been making since the morning to this maneuver, I set the beginning of our offensive for September 7. This had the advantage of letting the Germans penetrate further into the heart of our enveloping maneuver, and of allowing the troop transports coming from the east to be completed.* This additional day of waiting would make it easier for the armies to switch from the retreat to the attack. Moreover, the orders for retreat would, without doubt, have already left the army headquarters for the day of the 5th, when my order reached them; by wanting to attack too suddenly, perhaps we risked creating disorder. Finally, it was still necessary to allow for a certain delay in order to achieve complete concordance with Marshal French in due time. These were the reasons which convinced me to start the battle only on the 7th. Gamelin was with me at that time. During the day, we had studied, several times together, the implementation of the maneuver which I had just decided upon; I charged him to write a draft of orders on the bases which I have just said, that he would submit to Colonel Pont.

It was then 6:30 p.m. I had invited Major Clive and two Japanese officers to dinner that evening. Not wanting to keep them waiting, we went to dinner at my private residence, leaving Major de Galbert in charge of my personal office. The dinner was nearing its end when the door opened and Major Maurin, one of the officers of the 3rd Bureau who had been sent to Nangis by General

---

* 15th and 21st Army corps, 2nd Division of the 9th Army corps, Conneau's cavalry corps, 4th Corps. Unfortunately, these transports were jammed because of the evacuations that the Military Government of Paris, without asking for authorization, carried out in part through the city of Lyon.

Berthelot to reconnoiter positions there, entered; on his return from his mission, he had passed through Bray-sur-Seine, where he had seen General Franchet d'Esperey leaving a conference with General Wilson. The commander of the 5th Army had asked Maurin to let me know that the English agreed to stop, and that, under these conditions, he was ready to attack as of the 6th. I could not hide my *satisfaction*. Almost at the same time, de Galbert telephoned from the general headquarters that important documents had just arrived from the 5th Army. So, the end of the meal was rushed. I apologized to my hosts and returned quickly to the headquarters.

We found two notes of Franchet d'Esperey, which constituted the answer to the question I had asked him. The first one, dated Bray-sur-Seine 4 p.m., was thus written:

> I. – The battle cannot take place until the day after tomorrow, September 6.
>
> II. – Tomorrow, September 5, the 5th Army will continue its withdrawal on the Provins-Sézanne line. The British army will make a change of direction facing east on the Changis-Coulommiers line and further south, provided that its left flank is supported by the 6th Army, which would come on the Ourcq line north of Lizy-sur-Ourcq, tomorrow, September 5.
>
> III. – On the 6th, the general direction of the English offensive would be Montmirail, that of the 6th Army would be Château-Thierry, that of the 5th Army would be Montmirail.

The second note, completing the previous one, said:

For the operation to be successful, it requires:

> 1. The close and absolute cooperation of the 6th Army emerging on the left bank of the Ourcq to the northeast of Meaux, on the morning of the 6th.
>
> It must border the Ourcq tomorrow, September 5, or the British will not march.
>
> 2. My army can fight on the 6th, but is not in a brilliant situation; we must make no reliance on the three reserve divisions.
>
> In addition, it would be good for the Foch detachment to participate in the action in an energetic way, towards Montmort.

Chapter IV 363

Bray, 4 September 4:45 p.m.

These two very complete answers filled me with joy. They do the greatest honor to their author. Franchet d'Esperey had just taken, barely twenty-four hours ago, the command of an army in retreat, quite adrift. It was to be feared that the fighting capacity of this army, weakened by the terrible heat of the summer, would be considerably diminished. With an intelligent audacity that is found only in the soul of true war leaders, understanding the situation admirably, Franchaet d'Esperay did not hesitate to answer "yes" to a question that would have made many others back down. I could not help but think that if his predecessor had still been at the head of the 5th Army, the answer I would have received would most likely have been different. In addition, the initiative of the new commander of the 5th Army had succeeded in restoring the harmony between his army and the British at the Bray interview. The role of Franchet d'Esperey in the day of September 4, 1914 deserves to be underlined in the eyes of history: it is he who made the battle of the Marne possible.

Since the agreement between the commander of the 5th Army and the excellent representative of Marshal French seemed complete, it seemed that there was not a moment to lose to accept the suggestions contained in Franchet d'Esperey's two notes; I had no objection to the directions of attack on which we had agreed at Bray.

I therefore instructed Gamelin to take back the draft order he had written before dinner, and to modify it in accordance with the prepositions of General Franchet d'Esperey.

Gamelin was in the process of writing the new draft, when I was informed that Galliéni was asking for me on the telephone. Having always had little taste for telephone calls myself, I asked Belin to go to the telephone. But, Galliéni insisting on having me myself on the phone, I accompanied the major general into the phone booth.

The governor of Paris had just returned from his headquarters. He had found my telegram ordering him to bring the 6th Army on the left bank of the Marne south of Lagny. This instruction modified the orders that Galliéni himself had given to Maunoury for the next afternoon. I reassured him by letting him know that, since the sending of my telegram of 1 p.m., I had taken the resolution to engage in a general offensive in which the 6th Army was to participate; moreover, I added, the orders were in preparation, and provided for the action of the Maunoury army on the north bank of the Marne as Galliéni wished.

After this telephone conversation, I returned to my office. Gamelin and Berthelot were finishing the drafting of the order: it was established, according to my intentions, for the resumption of the offensive on September 7. But I thought that, in spite of my preference for this date, it was appropriate to bring it forward by one day, because of the arrangements made by Galliéni, which made it possible to anticipate an encounter of the 6th Army with the enemy as of the afternoon of the 5th; Maunoury's entry into the line would undoubtedly have the effect of revealing our maneuver, and, on the 7th, we would find the enemy on his guard. Moreover, Foch and Franchet d'Esperey had accepted the date of the 6th, and by being diligent, we could send the orders in time to allow the armies to establish theirs in due course. I therefore decided that everyone would go on the offensive on the 6th; consequently, I had the dates rectified, I signed the minute of the order which was immediately taken to the Department of Ciphers.

I must say that it is with reluctance that I brought to these instructions this modification in the date for the beginning of the offensive; I was and I remained convinced that if the battle could have been engaged only on the 7th, the results would have been appreciably superior, because we would have seized the enemy in a situation more disadvantageous for him than that in which we found him. It is the haste brought to the maneuver of the 6th Army that forced me to make this regrettable modification to my initial draft.

It is not necessary to give here the text of this General Order no. 6: it was frequently published. It indicated the plan to be carried out on the 5th in the evening, as well as the directions of

Chapter IV 365

attack of the allied armies of the left.*

At 9:30 p.m., I gave the order to call on the telephone the staff of the military governor of Paris to make known to him the front lines of attack of the various armies for the battle of the 6th.

Things were thus settled, when, around 10:00 p.m., Lieutenant-Colonel Brécard, returning from a mission with Sordet's cavalry corps, came to report to me that he had passed in the afternoon to the headquarters of Galliéni and in Melun to the headquarters of Marshal French. At the latter point, Brécard had seen Galliéni coming out of a conference with French and Maunoury; my liaison officer brought me the conclusions of this conference, which completed the impressions that Galliéni had given us on the telephone at 8:30 p.m., to Belin and me. The resolution of the British commander-in-chief did not seem as formal as I had thought it would be following Huguet's telegram and the notes that Franchet d'Esperey had sent me after his meeting in Bray with Wilson. This contradiction seemed to stem from the fact that Wilson, who was very understanding, had thought he could commit himself in the name of his chief, while the latter placed a certain number of restrictions on his cooperation: from Brécard's report, it appeared that the two agreements, that of Bray between Wilson and Franchet d'Esperey, and that of Melun between French and Galliéni were not identical.

Moreover, at about the same time, a telegram from Huguet announced to me that because of the continuous changes in the situation, Marshal French preferred to study it again before deciding on further operations. Undoubtedly, there was a misunderstanding, and all the agreement that I believed had been reached for the now decided battle, was called into question.

There was only one course of action to take, given the already advanced hour of the night: to send an officer to Melun, bearing the dispatch of the order intended for the Marshal, and who would explain to him the capital importance that I attached to his adherence to our plan. Major de Galbert, very aware of my

---

* General Order No. 6 was sent to the various armies in the form of an encrypted telegram; written confirmation was carried by officers in their cars.

intentions, was chosen for this mission. He left the great headquarters in the middle of the night of the 4th to the 5th of September, in order to be at the English headquarters at dawn.

September 5. – The uncertainty which hung over the English decisions was, at this decisive hour, particularly distressing. I felt that it was necessary to obtain at all costs the assistance of the English army. If it was refused to me, I saw the victory which I foresaw fleeing. The necessity of new talks made me fear that I would once again be obliged to go back on the date I had set for the resumption of the offensive.

I impatiently awaited the return of Galbert. While waiting for him, it occurred to me to ask for diplomatic support to put pressure on the Marshal and, in spite of my deep reluctance to speak in advance of my plans for the operation, I tried to explain to Mr. Millerand, in whose tact and patriotism I had such complete confidence, the exact state of my decisions and the necessity of a governmental intervention which would come in addition to mine with Marshal French. In a personal letter, I explained to him that the strategic situation had become excellent and that I had decided to go on the attack; I did not hide from him that the struggle that was about to begin could have incalculable results in case of success, on the other hand, in case of failure, the consequences would probably be very serious. I was determined to commit all our troops fully and without reserve. But to achieve victory, it was essential that the English army do the same: "I count," I added, "that you will want to draw the attention of the Marshal by diplomatic means to the decisive importance of an offensive without ulterior motives; if I could give orders to the English army as I would give them to a French army positioned on the same ground, I would pass immediately to the attack."

Then, I had two orders written, intended respectively for the 3rd and 4th armies, to complete the general order no. 6 addressed the evening before to the armies of the left. I had just signed the orders, when Galbert arrived. It was about 9:30 a.m. He returned without having been able to see either Marshal French, or any of the officers around him. He had left the order with Colonel Huguet, who had informed him that our allies had again taken advantage of the night to evade the enemy, and that the state of mind of the general headquarters seemed to have become unfavorable to the resumption of the offensive. Believing in these conditions that he would not have enough weight to make the Marshal change his decision, he had very rightly thought that he should, at full speed, return to the general headquarters to report to me, and to let me know that, in the opinion of all, I ALONE could succeed in perhaps overcoming the resolutions of the English Commander-in-Chief.

My decision was immediate: I telephoned Melun to say that I was going to the general headquarters to see Marshal French, and I left taking with me Lieutenant-Colonel Serret, Major Gamelin, my orderly Captain Muller and Major Clive.

At Sens, we were stopped interminably at a level crossing; it was the transports of the 4th Army corps which continued slowly because of the congestion of the lines by the evacuations of the military government of Paris. We stopped for lunch. The mayor of the city, Senator Cornet, hearing of my visit, came to see me, very moved by the advance of the Germans; he asked me if it was appropriate to start the evacuation of the inhabitants of the city towards the interior. I reassured him, and announced to him that our troops had so far accomplished only a long maneuver by the retreat, but that now the hour had come for them to turn back. Sens would be saved. A little reassured, Mr. Cornet left me, shaking my hands effusively. Then, by Fontainebleau, we arrived at Melun a little before 2 pm.

Huguet was waiting for us at the British general headquarters. He led us to the castle of Vaux-le-Pénil, where we found the Marshal surrounded by officers of his staff, and in particular by General Murray and General Wilson. These represented in my eyes the two tendencies which existed in the English command: in Wilson that which was favorable to us, in Murray that which I feared.

I immediately took the floor. I put all my soul into convincing the Marshal; I told him that the hour was decisive and that we could not let it pass: we had to go to battle, all forces united and without second thoughts. "As far as the French army is concerned, my orders are given, and whatever happens, I am decided to throw my last man into the balance to win the victory and save France in whose name I have come to solicit with all my strength the British assistance. I cannot doubt that the English army will come to take its part in this supreme struggle; its abstention would be severely judged by history."

At the end, carried away by my conviction and by the gravity of the hour, I remember striking the table beside me with a pummel and saying, as I finished, "The honor of England is at stake, sir Marshal."

Until then, French had listened impassively to the translator who reported my words to him. But at this moment he blushed strongly. There was a short, impressive silence, then he murmured with emotion: "I will do all I possibly can."*

Not understanding English, I asked Wilson what the Marshal had just said. He answered simply: "The Marshal said: yes."

I had felt the emotion of the English commander-in-chief; I had especially heard the tone with which he had spoken. To me, as to all the witnesses of this scene, it appeared that these simple words were equivalent to a promise under oath.

Then, tea was served, which was already prepared; French then accompanied me back to my car. I left Lieutenant-Colonel Serret with Huguet, in whose energy and knowledge I had full confidence, and I went to Châtillon-sur-Seine where, during the day, the great headquarters had been moved. The staff offices had been installed in a former convent of Cordeliers. My office had been placed in an old monk's cell. It is from there that I followed the battle of the Marne, and it is there that the following day, at 7:30 am, I signed the order of the day to the troops:†

At the moment when a battle is being waged on which the fate of the

---

* Translators note: In the original French, this sentence is written as: "I will give all my possible." In the absence of this sentence in any English language account of this meeting, I have deferred to T. Bentley Mott's correction of it in his translation of these memoirs.

† This order was transmitted to all army headquarters between 8 and 9 am. The written confirmation was sent to the armies on September 6 at 6 pm.

country depends, it is important to remind everyone that now is not the time to look back; all efforts must be employed to attack and drive back the enemy. A unit which cannot advance any further must, at all costs, hold the ground conquered and be killed on the spot rather than retreat. Under the present circumstances, no failure can be tolerated.

On my return to Châtillon, I found a telegram from the Minister of War in response to the letter I had sent him in the morning to announce the imminent resumption of the offensive, and to ask his help to bring about Marshal French's resolution. In his message, the Minister informed me that he had no objection to my plan, and that the Minister of Foreign Affairs was going to the British ambassador to ask him to approach his government with the request I had made. We have just seen, moreover, that the visit which I had just made to Marshal French had in the meantime clarified the situation, and that I knew I could count on the cooperation of the English forces in the decisive battle which was about to begin.

On my arrival at Châtillon, I had also found the reports sent by the armies: all the ordered movements had been carried out everywhere without difficulty.

Chapter V

The battle of the Marne.

At the moment that the battle on which the destiny of the country depended was about to begin, the military situation was looking infinitely more favorable than I would have dared to hope a few days before.

The 3rd, 4th, 9th and 5th French armies, supported on the right by the fortified camp of Verdun, were deployed on a front of about 250 kilometers marked out by Sermaize, Vitry-le-François, Sommesous, the marshes of Saint-Gond, Esternay, Courtacon. On their left, forming an advanced echelon, were the British army and the French 6th Army, the former to the southwest of Coulommiers, the latter covered on its left by the Sordet cavalry corps, northwest of Meaux. The whole of this line formed a vast pocket into which five German armies seemed to want to rush. The information gathered during the day of September 5 had shown us, in effect, that the enemy was continuing its march southward.

Von Kluck's army (Ist Army) had reached the region of Coulommiers; it had left some elements on the right bank of the Ourcq that were entrenched facing west.

Von Bülow's army (IInd army) had crossed the Marne between

Chapter V 371

Dormans and Épernay in the morning of 5 September; its column heads were reported at midday on the Champaubert, Étoges, Bergères, Vertus crossroads.

From von Hansen's army (IIIrd army), the XIIth corps had been identified on September 4, at Condé-sur-Marne, between Épernay and Châlons.

The Prince of Wurtemberg's army (IVth Army) had reached the Châlons, Francheville, Bussy-le-Repos crossing on September 5.

Finally, the army of the Imperial Kronprinz (Vth Army) moved southward, on both sides of the Argonne.*

Thus were finally realized the strategic conditions that I had envisaged on August 25. One remembers that due to a series of circumstances I had been obliged to give up the envelopment maneuver conceived on that date, to try another one, and now, thanks to the movements of the adversary, the maneuver planned on August 25 appeared to be feasible again.

But, however advantageous the overall situation was, especially now that I could count on British cooperation, it is conceivable that I was nevertheless beset by heavy concerns.

In spite of the assurances given to me on September 4 by Generals Foch and Franchet d'Esperey, this offensive, suddenly launched with armies tired from an exhausting retreat, represented a problem full of hazards. I said in the preceding chapter that, in order to give the troops time to recover and organize themselves, I would have preferred not to engage in battle until the 7th; we have seen the reasons why I was obliged to give up this short delay which would have been so useful to our armies. Nevertheless, not for a moment did I doubt that our soldiers and officers were morally equal to the task I was going to ask of them. The reports showed that the troops and the staffs, astonished by this long retreat of which they did not perceive the necessity, only asked to march forward again. In a word, thanks to the precaution I had taken a few days before to warn the army commanders of the reasons which pushed me to continue the movement backwards,

---

* G.Q.G. intelligence bulletins dated September 5 and 6, 1914.

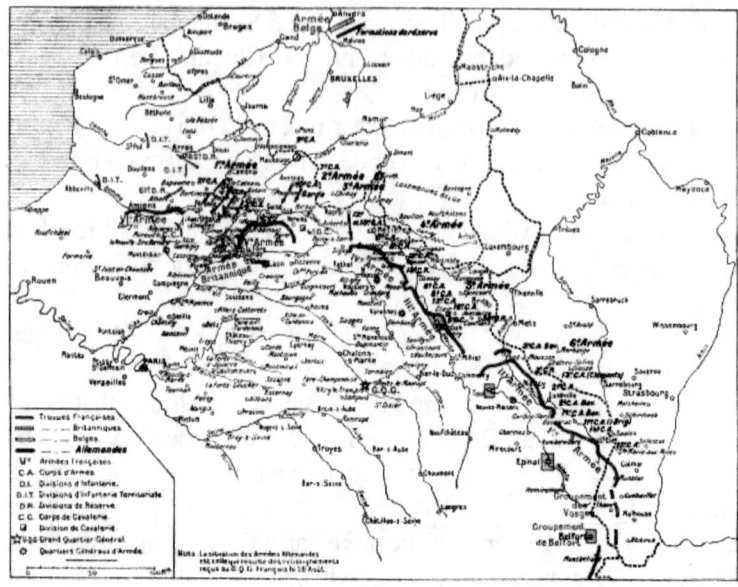

Situation on the evening of August 28 (eve of the Battle of Guise)

Situation on the evening of September 1

Chapter V

Situation on the evening of September 5

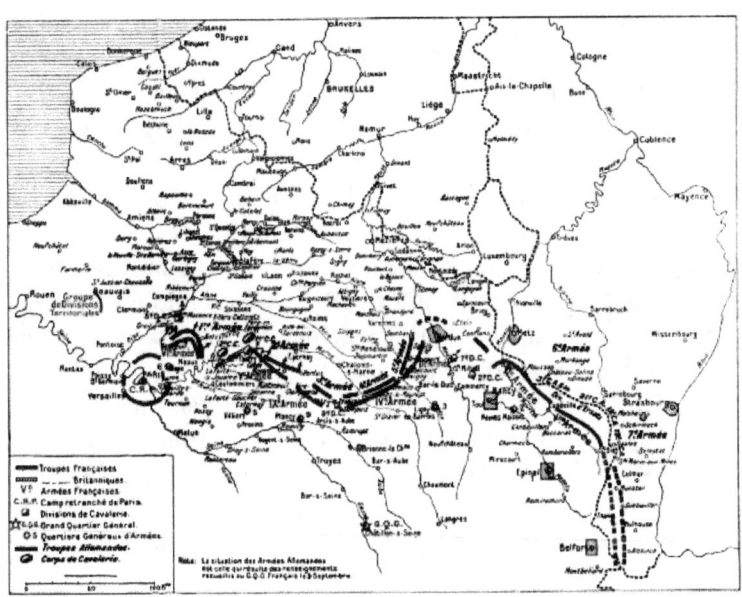

Situation on evening of September 9 (beginning of the German retreat)

our troops had the mentality not of a defeated army, but of an army which was maneuvering. Moreover, the reinforcements coming from the interior had made up for the heavy losses in our ranks at the beginning.

If I believed I could count on the morale of our soldiers, and if I was sure I would be understood by them by explaining that the fate of the fatherland was at stake, I thought, on the other hand, that the morale of the enemy must be at its highest level. But, if we think about it, this was far more dangerous for our adversaries than for ourselves; we could count on the element of surprise that our sudden offensive would not fail to produce on them at a moment when they believed they only had to sweep away the debris of an army in rout.

On the other hand, the army corps that were to come and reinforce the sensitive points of our battle line were still being transported, notably the 15th destined for the 3rd Army, the 21st that was going to reinforce the 4th, and a division of the 9th that was joining the 9th. And this consideration made me regret even more the obligation to engage the battle on September 6.

Finally, since September 4, the battle had resumed with a new violence on the Lorraine front. There, the enemy tried to seize Nancy, while leading in Woëvre an action threatening the rear of our 3rd Army; on the front of the 1st Army, they fortunately showed less activity, but because of the reduction of his numbers, General Dubail had to limit himself to holding his positions. The German attacks began in the afternoon of the 4th and continued throughout the day of the 5th on the Gerbéviller and Champenoux Forest fronts. In the evening of that day, General de Castelnau reported to me that the superiority in numbers, the power and the range of the enemy artillery, whose siege crews had appeared on the front, did not allow us to expect prolonged resistance from the 2nd Army. "In the event," he said, "that I am strongly pressed, I can resist on the spot as long as I can... or evade, in due course, first on the positions of the Haye Forest, Saffais, Belchamps, Borville, then on another, trying to last, and continue to cover the right flank of the army group."

Now I needed, for the success of the maneuver that I was going to undertake, to be assured of the solidity of our two right wing

Chapter V

armies. We will see, in the pages that follow, that the 2nd Army was for me, during the battle of the Marne, the source of serious concerns.

All our forces, as I had written to the Minister, were now in the line or about to arrive there. The only troops available were the 2nd Moroccan division, of which one brigade (General Cherrier) had just arrived in France, and the other (General Gouraud) was not to complete its deployments until September 12.

From this point of view, the Germans were in a more precarious situation than we were. Their deployment had long since been completed; our air force reported no forces in the wake of their armies, which confirmed my belief that the opposing command must have none available. Better still, the information I mentioned earlier about large German troop movements through Belgium, moving from the west to the east, gave us hope that the enemy had weakened before us. To tell the truth, we did not know to what extent this weakening was advantageous to us, for we only learned later that this weakening had been precisely on the German right against which I was preparing to make our maximum effort.

It has sometimes been said that, in modern battle, the general-in-chief, after having put his forces in place and given his initial orders, has only to wait for the results of a game whose course he cannot control.

This theory was the one that the Germans had inherited from Marshal von Moltke.* History shows, in fact, that if the victor of Sadowa and Sedan had led his armies to battle with great application and method, the direction of the battle had always escaped him, without him even attempting to make his will felt. This manner corresponded to the temperament of the Marshal, who was undoubtedly reluctant to direct events which, by definition, thwarted forecasts: he assumed that the conduct of the battle was the responsibility of the subordinate command. The wars that he had led had not contradicted this doctrine, von Moltke having had the rare fortune to meet as opponents only generals like Bénédeck

---

* Translator's note: Here Joffre is referring to Moltke the Elder.

and Bazaine, whose inertia and passivity were, one might say, absolute. The Germans having noted the results acquired by this method agreed that it was good. They stuck to it, and General von Moltke, the nephew of the Marshal, who led the German armies in the first weeks of the war, was not unwilling, as far as one can judge, to modify a formula that must have secretly pleased his self-effacing temperament. In fact, it is clear from the documents that we have today that the German high command, from its distant headquarters in Luxembourg, knew almost nothing of what was happening on the battlefield of the Marne, and conversely, it only made its action felt on its army commanders in fits and starts, it did not orient them on the overall situation, and it only gave them its directives late and incompletely.

In France, we had another understanding. We assumed that the modern battle, by the extension of the fronts, by the size of the masses to be moved, by its duration, does not lend itself any more to the sudden inspirations, but requires on the other hand a greater spirit of foresight than the battles of which the general in chief could follow the events in the field of his telescope. But we thought, nevertheless, that the battle, in spite of its difficulties, can and must be conducted. However intelligent and energetic the army commanders may be, they know only a small part of the action; the events that unfold before their front take on a shape that distorts them; only, by the overall perspective that he has on the battle, can the general-in-chief give events their exact weight. Moreover, the situation is constantly changing; only the leader is able to give, as they unfold, the orders that allow the exploitation of events.

The Battle of the Marne highlights what I have just said. It began when we succeeded in concentrating around the German right a mass that gave us on this part of the battlefield the double advantage of numerical superiority and position. Nevertheless, if we had tried to apply brutally a formula of envelopment at all costs, which was not in my mind, we would have played into the enemy's hands. But our means were such, and our system was flexible enough that the inevitable reaction of the enemy did not catch us off guard. Kluck was only able to counter the threat on his right by opening a gap between his army and Bülow's army, which became bigger and bigger. Thus, the Battle of the Marne had, from the second day, the character of an action to break the enemy's position, a break that the German supreme command had neither the means nor the time to avoid.

Such an approach to the conduct of battle, under the conditions of the extent of modern combat fronts, requires not only a complete unity of doctrine, but also sure and rapid connections between the commander-in-chief and his subordinates, by means of the telegraph and the telephone, and also through the intermediary of officers who are, strictly speaking, the embodiment of the thought and will of the supreme commander. The mission of these officers was certainly a sensitive one; they have sometimes been accused of having given themselves powers beyond their rank. It is possible that mistakes were made by these liaison officers who may have been the target of grudges motivated by dismissals that I had to make in the interest of the country.

Nevertheless, during this battle, being obliged to remain at my post* to make decisions at any time of the day or night, I was able to command armies whose right was supported by the Vosges and whose left, by the divisions of General d'Amade, extended to Rouen.

With the courage and tenacity of our armies, it is the French method of command that triumphed at the Marne.

It is not my intention to recount the battle of the Marne. The story has already been told many times. I will limit myself to demonstrate in the following pages what my action was.

Maunoury's army had established itself, as of September 5, between the Ermenonville forest and the Marne, from Meaux to Ver. From that day on, his right had some contacts with the enemy, notably at Penchard, Monthyon and Saint-Soupplets. Its objective for the 6th was the Ourcq, from Lizy to Neufchelles. But it

---

* I forced myself during the whole battle of the Marne, and during the delicate phase which followed it (to be precise, from September 5 to 20) not to leave my headquarters. I only left my office to walk 2 to 3 kilometers every day to get some fresh air, to have my meals, and to go to sleep every evening at the "Marmont" castle that Colonel Maitre had put at my disposal.

immediately came up against fierce resistance from the IVth Reserve Corps, supported shortly afterwards by the IInd Army Corps, which, forced to march from Coulommiers, tried to overrun our left through Étavigny. On the evening of the 6th, the 6th Army was stopped on the Chambry, Marcilly, Puisieux, Betz front, which means that it was still far from its first objective. Nevertheless, the first results of the 6th Army's entry into the line soon became apparent to me.

In fact, the 5th Army had emerged on the morning of the 6th from the Sézanne, Villiers-Saint-Georges and Courchamps fronts, and around noon it came up against the enemy. Conneau's cavalry corps, north of the forest of Jouy, covered its left and ensured its connection with the English army. The latter had left on the morning of the 6th, not from the Changis-Coulommiers front which had been assigned to it by General Order no. 6, but from a line located 15 kilometers to the southwest, marked out by Pézarches and Lagny; on the evening of the 6th, it came without difficulty to border by its left the western bank of the Grand-Morin, while its right, which had been opposed to the enemy, remained in the region of Pézarches.

On 7 September, at 11 a.m., Franchet d'Esperey reported to me that the Ist German Army was "in full retreat towards the north on the Esternay-Courtacon front..." and that the 5th Army was continuing its forward march. In the evening, while its corps on the right (10th Corps) supported the 42nd Division of Foch's army towards Soizy-au-Bois, its center and left reached the Morsains, Tréfols, Moutils line, while Conneau's cavalry corps arrived at La Ferté-Gaucher. As for the British army, it reached the Choisy, Coulommiers, Maisoncelles line in the evening of the same day, without having encountered any significant resistance.

On the other hand, our 6th Army tried in vain to reach the Ourcq river; the enemy was reinforcing in front of it, and appeared to be trying to envelop it through Betz, as Maunoury was trying to do against Kluck's right.

On the evening of the 7th, the situation of the enemy in front of our left appeared to us in the following way:

To face Maunoury's attack, which had obviously surprised him, Kluck had formed a detachment on the Ourcq comprising the

Chapter V

IVth Reserve Corps, the IInd Active Corps and the IVth Cavalry Division, while with the rest of his army he fought south against Franchet d'Esperey's left. Between these two sections of the Ist German army, a gap had just opened, in front of the English; this gap was masked by important German cavalry forces, but too weak nevertheless to stop our allies.

It was therefore a question, on the one hand, of hooking up with Franchet d'Esperey's left the part of the Ist German Army that was facing him, of pushing the English army into the void I have just indicated by making it cross the Grand-Morin, the Petit-Morin and the Marne, while at the same time accentuating Maunoury's all-encompassing movement, no longer directed at Château-Thierry, but further north on the right bank of the Ourcq. It was in this spirit that I sent a directive to the three armies on the left, in the afternoon of the 7th, informing them of my intentions.*

During this time, the battle presented itself under less favorable auspices to our center and our right.

The left of Foch's army, solidly supported by the right of Franchet d'Esperey's, contained all the assaults of the enemy in the region of Soizy-au-Bois and Mondement; but, on the other hand, its right had been losing ground since the beginning of the battle: it lost Fère-Champenoise, and on the evening of the 8th, it was on the line of Semoine, Gourgançon, Corroy, which represented a retreat of twelve kilometers. This was serious, especially because it increased the already large gap that separated Foch's right from Langle's left. I had called the attention of the commander of the 4th Army, as early as the 6th, to the necessity of keeping strong reserves behind his left, in order to be able to counter-attack the enemy forces that would try to overrun Foch's right wing. It was

---

* Incidentally, in order to better coordinate the actions of the 6th Army, which was moving further and further away from Paris, I had a telegram sent to the Governor of Paris on the morning of the 7th to let him know that I would henceforth address my orders directly to General Maunoury. A duplicate of my instructions to the 6th Army was to be sent to the Governor of Paris. This decision was necessary. I had already been led on several occasions, in order to save time, to send orders directly to the commander of the 6th Army, in particular General Order no. 6 of 4 September ordering the general resumption of the offensive.

with this in mind that I had placed at the disposal of General de Langle the 21st Army corps, which was to be available on the 7th in the Wassy, Montiérender region. Unfortunately, since the morning of the 7th, the 4th Army was in the grip of the IVth German army reinforced by part of the von Hansen army (IIIrd); and precisely, by a combination of circumstances that were not attributable to General de Langle, the left of his army, contrary to my orders, was precisely the weak point of his line: the infantry of the 12th Corps, which had had to be evacuated by rail during the previous days to the region of Chavanges, lined up south of Vitry-le-François only a few battalions that framed the artillery of the corps as best they could, and the 17th Corps, also very tired, had reached the Aube with its large troops towards Ramerupt, and was just beginning to move forward east of Mailly.

It was all the more difficult for General de Langle, during these first days of battle, to reinforce his left, since on his right, where the fight was very lively, a gap existed, marked by the Trois-Fontaines forest, between de Langle and Sarrail. The latter complained about it strongly, and demanded an energetic action of the 2nd corps (right of the 4th Army) on Revigny or Contrisson, while waiting for the 15th Corps, coming from the 2nd Army, to be able to concentrate northwest of Bar-le-Duc between the Saulx and the Ornain.

Thus, I feared for a moment of seeing the center of my position dislocated by a double rupture occurring at the two wings of the 4th Army.

Fortunately, this was not the case.

Von Hansen's army, engaged in front of Foch's right and against the left of de Langle's army, was unable to penetrate the 40 kilometer gap that existed between these two armies, a gap that was imperfectly masked by our 9th Cavalry Division. From the 8th, the infantry of the reformed 12th Corps came to reinforce the front of the 4th Army, and the 21st corps arrived the same evening at Sompuis, ready to support the left of this army, but too late, however, to obtain a tangible result as of that day.

As for the 3rd Army, I addressed to General Sarrail, during the day of the 7th, two orders which were to complete the orientation of the 3rd Army,[*] in which I ordered him to work for the benefit of the 4th Army, as the latter should work to support the 9th. Moreover, on the evening of the 8th, the 15th Corps, after having weakened between the Saulx and the Ornain under the pressure of the enemy, was able to move forward, ensuring the link between the 3rd and 4th armies.

But a new danger threatened Sarrail: enemy detachments marched towards the Meuse in the direction of Saint-Mihiel, and on the 8th, in the evening, the fort of Troyon was vigorously cannonaded by the Germans. To counter this threat, General Sarrail had the bridges over the Meuse destroyed, and placed the 7th Cavalry Division on guard along the river.

In fact, the situation of the 3rd Army became delicate because its leader felt obliged to maintain contact with the place of Verdun. On the 8th, at 8 p.m., I sent him an order authorizing him, if necessary, to withdraw his right to ensure his communications and to give more power to the action of his left wing. By doing so, I indicated to him that I attached more importance to the linkage of the 3rd Army with the 4th, than with the place of Verdun, which, in fact, was quite capable of defending itself by its own means.

The day before, to reassure Sarrail and relieve him of his task, I had ordered Castelnau to direct the 2nd Cavalry Division towards the Woëvre on the 8th, to ensure the rear of the 3rd Army. And on the 8th, in the same vein, I approved the transport by rail to Commercy of a mixed brigade taken from Toul.

While the battle grew in violence on the whole front and now extended beyond the Meuse to the Woëvre, I did not neglect the armies that operated between Nancy and the Vosges. I had drawn from these two armies very important forces, and I proposed to draw others if the situation required it. But I had to be sure that their capacity to resist would not be compromised, otherwise the enemy would have taken the initiative in the operations that we had just taken away from them.

I said at the beginning of this chapter that, on the evening of September 5, General de Castelnau had expressed his intention to

---

[*] One at 8:30 a.m., the other at 4:15 p.m.

abandon the Grand-Couronné and Nancy, in case he could not hold his positions without compromising the future. On the 6th, at 1:10 p.m., I sent him a telegram to let him know that, while I approved of his intentions in the event that he would be obliged to abandon the Grand-Couronne, I considered it preferable that he maintain his current positions until the outcome of the battle that had just begun.

In fact, the commander of the 2nd Army managed to stop the enemy attacks that day, and he was even able to resume the offensive. But on the 7th, the situation on his front worsened again. General de Castelnau, who was deeply affected by the death of one of his sons, and learning that the battalion in charge of defending the butte Sainte-Geneviève had evacuated this position, gave his chief of staff, General Anthoine, instructions to retreat, and he was ready to order the civil authorities of Nancy to evacuate the city.

This decision was serious. We did not need, at such a moment, the enemy to be able to announce his entry in Nancy. From a strategic point of view, the retreat of the 2nd Army would put the 1st Army in the following situation:

Either it would follow the 2nd in its retreat by linking up with it, and this would mean the abandonment of Franche-Comté and the probable envelopment of the right wing of the French armies; or it would resist by relying on the positions of Belfort and Épinal; but then it would be the rupture of our two right wing armies with the prospect of seeing Dubail's army being cornered in a short time at the Swiss border.

Fortunately, before sending these orders, the seriousness of which he was aware, General Anthoine telephoned the general headquarters to announce the decision that had just been taken. I immediately had General de Castelnau on the phone. This memory is all the more vivid in my mind as I rarely phoned anybody myself during the campaign. The commander of the 2nd Army gave me a very dark picture of the situation of his army: there had been serious defections in one of his corps; troops had broken away. "If I remain on my positions," he added, "I feel that my army is lost. It is necessary to consider my immediate withdrawal behind the Meurthe."

"Don't do anything," I replied. "Wait twenty-four hours. You don't know what condition the enemy is in. Perhaps he is not in a brighter situation than you. You must not abandon the Grand-Couronne, and I give you the order to remain on your positions."

Then I immediately sent Commandant Bel on a mission to confirm to General de Castelnau the order I had just given him orally, to postpone the execution of the retreat that he was preparing to begin, and to hold on to the front of Nancy at all costs.

It turned out, moreover, that if the butte Sainte-Geneviève had been evacuated, it was not because of the enemy but because of a bad maneuver. This position was immediately reoccupied. From that day on, the German attacks gradually decreased in violence and on September 11th, the enemy abandoned its attempt on Nancy, at the moment when our victory of the Marne was completed, and marked a significant withdrawal in Lorraine, which was accentuated in the following days.

As for General Dubail, throughout this period he maintained an unalterable confidence, his morale never wavered, and he always punctually executed my orders.

Let us return to the armies of the left that we left on the evening of the 7th, guided by the directive that I had sent them.

On the 8th, General Maunoury found himself grappling with an enemy who had become even stronger during the night, and who, by a bold maneuver, was trying to regain the initiative of the operations by enveloping our extreme left. Fortunately, the 4th Corps, which I had previously withdrawn from the 3rd Army, had begun to land in Paris on September 5.

During the night of the 7th to the 8th, General Galliéni directed one of the divisions (7th) of this corps towards Maunoury; he used all means of transport (railroads, requisitioned cars) to expedite the movement of this division and to place it in a relatively fresh state at the disposal of the commander of the 6th Army. As for the other division of the 4th Corps (8th), General Galliéni, in agreement with Maunoury, felt obliged to engage it south of the Marne, to support closely the movement of the British army. This division was, to tell the truth, completely useless in this region, and on the morning of the 8th, it was still on the Petit-Morin, where it did not show any activity. This is why I pointed out to Maunoury that day, around

9:00 a.m., the usefulness of withdrawing this division from his right and moving it to his left where it could be used advantageously, and where it would find the other elements of his corps.

In the morning of the 8th, I learned the unfortunate news that Maubeuge had died the day before. I had just mentioned the governor, General Fournier, for his good defense, but the radio had arrived after the surrender of the place. This event came at a bad time: the Germans were going to recover at least one army corps, which could be quickly transported to Montdidier or Anizy. Also, at noon, when I announced this news to Maunoury, I invited him to detach Sordet's cavalry corps to act against enemy communications, particularly in the direction of Soissons and Compiègne.

At the end of the day, the 6th Army, far from having succeeded in advancing, resisted with difficulty on the spot, and prepared to deny its left in the face of the growing pressure of Kluck. Fortunately, the 5th Army continued its victorious advance: while its right solidly supported Foch's left, its center, overcoming the resistance of the enemy rearguards, reached the Petit-Morin, and its left corps (18th) arrived at Marchais-en-Brie.

Between Maunoury and Franchet d'Esperey, the British army did not advance as quickly as I would have liked. Certainly, the results achieved were already appreciable. On the 7th, I had expressed to Lord Kitchener, through the Minister of War, my warm thanks for the constant support given to our armies by the British forces, and I had sent French a personal letter to state my gratitude. French replied the same day, thanking me for my message: the situation now appeared to him in a favorable light, and he congratulated me on the "happy arrangement" that I had just achieved. Nevertheless, I was impatient to see the British army accelerate its advance. On three occasions, during the day of September 8, I pointed out to the British commander-in-chief the importance I attached to his offensive; I insisted on the necessity of marching as quickly as possible to relieve the 6th Army, which was now carrying the full weight of the Ist German Army, and I expressed the hope of seeing the British at the end of the day break through north of the Marne.

Chapter V

But the Marshal informed me that he was stopped by rearguards on the Petit-Morin, and in the evening he took ground only on the heights north of this river.

On the evening of the 8th, the situation appeared to me as very favorable, quite different from the one I had expected to achieve a few days before.

From the Vosges to the Meuse, all the German attacks were under control, despite the numerous withdrawals that I had made from the 1st and 2nd armies.

The frontal combat of the 4th and 9th armies now gave me the hope that the enemy would not succeed in dislocating our center. The right of de Langle's army was now supported by the 15th Corps which had just entered the line to the left of Sarrail. It is true that Foch's right had lost ground again, and this did not fail to worry me, because de Langle was not yet in a position to bring him effective relief. But the high morale and unshakeable confidence of the commander of the 9th Army assured me that the weakening of his line was only a local accident whose repercussions would not be felt in the overall operations.

It is only fair to pay tribute here to the exceptional merits of General Foch during this battle in which he gave his full measure. Admirably assisted by his chief of staff, Colonel Weygrand, at no time did his activity slow down or his morale falter.

Finally, on our left wing, the maneuver that we had conceived changed entirely in character. General Maunoury had to give up enveloping his energetic adversary. But the latter had only succeeded in parrying our maneuver against his right by opening between his left and Bülow's army a breach into which penetrated like a wedge the left of Franchet d' Esperey, and into which I endeavored to rush the British army. Informed by the aerial reconnaissance and the battle identifications, I felt all the possibilities of action that this new situation opened to me. It is with the aim of orienting the three armies of the left on the maneuver to be carried out that I addressed to them at 7 p.m. a Special Instruction[*] of which here are the essential passages:

---

[*] Special Instruction No. 19.

Chapter V

Faced with the combined efforts of the Allied left wing armies, the German forces fell back in two separate groupings:

One, which seems to include the IVth reserve corps, the IInd and the IVth active corps, fights on the Ourcq facing west against our 6th Army, which it attempts to overrun from the north;

The other, comprising the rest of the Ist German Army (IIIrd and IXth active corps) and the IInd and IIIrd German armies, remained facing the 5th and 9th French armies.

The meeting between these two groups seems to be ensured only by several cavalry divisions supported by detachments of any army opposite the British troops.

It seems essential to put the German extreme right out of the way before it can be reinforced by other elements that the fall of Maubeuge could make available.

Therefore, I asked:

The 6th Army to keep the enemy forces in front of it;

That the English army cross the Marne between Nogent-l'Artaud and La Ferté-sous-Jouarre, and to move on the left and the rear of Kluck's army;

The 5th Army, while covering the right flank of the British with its left in conjunction with Conneau's cavalry corps, and continuing to support Foch's left, which was preparing to take the offensive, to march northward with the bulk of its forces, driving the enemy back beyond the Marne.

The first paragraph of this Instruction depicted the situation in a way that one can recognize today as exact with only one difference: the IIIrd and IXth German corps had just been identified in the combat of the day, and this Special Instruction still places them in front of the 5th Army; in reality, they were already on the march towards the front of the Ourcq.[*] The breach opened

---

[*] Here, in fact, is the radio sent by Kluck on September 8 at 6:30 p.m., which was deciphered a few days later by the Cipher Section of G.H.Q.:

> The army found itself engaged today in a difficult combat against superior enemy forces west of the Ourcq, on the Antilly (3 kilometers east of Betz) - Congis (south of Lizy) line. The IIIrd and IXth Corps, moved by night to the right wing, will attack tomorrow morning by an enveloping movement. On the Marne, the Lizy, Nogent-l'Artaud line will be defended by the IInd

between Kluck and Bülow was thus even wider than I had imagined.

The day of September 9 seems to have marked the supreme effort made by the enemy to get out of the situation in which he found himself.

The 6th Army succeeded at first in holding its positions; the enemy even showed a slight retreat in the region of Batz, and evacuated this village. But, in the afternoon, the IIIrd and IXth German corps, coming from the northeast and the north, forced the French left to withdraw to the Chèvreville, Silly-le-Long front. Maunoury immediately recalled the 8th Division, as I had invited him to do, and led it on a night march to the left of his army. For my part, I had taken care in the morning to withdraw from the 5th Army an infantry division that I ordered to be directed urgently by rail to Dammartin-en-Goële. In notifying General Maunoury of the arrival of this reinforcement, I set out the attitude to be observed: "While awaiting the arrival of reinforcements that will allow you to resume the offensive, you must avoid any decisive action, by withdrawing your left, if necessary, in the general direction of the fortified camp of Paris."

Moreover, at no time, in spite of the violence of the attacks to which he was subjected, did General Maunoury lose sight of his mission, and he did not abandon the intention of resuming the offensive, as the telegram he sent me after his left had withdrawn testifies: "...I will have the 8th Division near Silly-le-Long, and I will then give the order to attack. Very heavy losses during the four days of fighting. Morale remains high. Cavalry dispatched far away."

The stubbornness of the battles fought by the 6th Army, the efforts imposed on the troops, the tenacity and composure of its leader achieved the immense result of making the victorious progression of French and Franchet d'Esperey relatively easy. I personally expressed my satisfaction to General Maunoury and his army. The Grand Cross of the Legion of Honor was awarded to the

---

Cavalry Corps and a reinforced infantry brigade against attacks coming from the direction of Coulommiers.

commander of the 6th Army to show how much I valued the service he had just rendered to the country.

In the report from which I have just quoted a few lines, Maunoury alluded to a new task entrusted to the cavalry corps.

This mass of three divisions was admirably placed on our extreme left, and should have rendered us the greatest services. Unfortunately, when the war had barely begun a month before, Sordet's cavalry corps had fallen into a worrying state of exhaustion. The almost useless raid that it had carried out in Belgium, then the retreat to the southwest of Paris, had already imposed enormous fatigue on it. But events were not the only ones responsible for this ruin; the command at all levels had a great deal to do with it. Thus, on September 7, General Sordet, after having engaged his cavalry corps in the region of Batz, decided, at night, under the pretext that the region in which he was operating lacked water, to bring his divisions back to Nanteuil-le-Haudouin, where they arrived only at midnight. Upon learning of this retreat, General Maunoury ordered Sordet to move forward, and the cavalry, after a rest of barely an hour, had to retrace the already useless path it had just covered.

On the recommendation of the commander of the 6th Army, I decided to relieve General Sordet of his command and to replace him with General Bridoux, commander of the 5th Cavalry Division. I had a great esteem for Sordet, and he had seemed to me, before the war, to justify all my confidence. Without doubt, he was a victim of the fact that his branch of the service had not evolved sufficiently in the years preceding the war. As for General Bridoux, he was full of energy, and he would have made his cavalry corps render the greatest services, if he had not been unfortunately killed almost the day after he took command: while carrying out a trip by car at night, an error in the itinerary made him and his staff fall into an enemy post; he was mortally wounded and several of his officers killed or wounded with him. It was a misfortune.

General Maunoury tried, as I had ordered him on the 8th, to detach the cavalry corps, both to threaten the right flank and the rear of Kluck, and to delay the entry into action of the enemy forces freed by the fall of Maubeuge. Unfortunately, the state of our cavalry did not allow it to realize this mission. At the most, the division of General de Cornulier-Lucinière managed to cause some trouble in Kluck's rear and failed by a small margin, it seems, to capture the commander of the German Ist army and his staff.

During the same day, the British army, after having been stopped in the vicinity of Ferté-sous-Jouarre by the breaking of the bridge, succeeded in gaining a foothold in the evening north of the Marne between this locality and Château-Thierry, which was held by the 5th Army; this advance threatened the left of Kluck's army, which was attacking Maunoury:

Franchet d'Esperey, for his part, had continued to advance on his left. His 18th Corps was oriented on Viffort, halfway between the Petit-Morin and Château-Thierry. I activated it towards the Marne by an order telephoned at 2 p.m.: "It is essential that the 18th Corps cross the Marne this very evening in the vicinity of Château-Thierry, so as to effectively support the English columns...." On the evening of the 9th, this corps did indeed manage to set up its outposts north of the river. On its left, Conneau's cavalry corps also had a brigade on the right bank. The rest of the 5th Army was stationed at the end of the day south of the Surmelin between Condé-en-Brie and Baye. The corps on the right (10th), placed at Foch's disposal by Franchet d'Esperey, relieved the 9th Army, which was under great pressure on its entire front. In his report at the end of the day, the commander of the 5th Army declared himself ready to start an action in the flank of the Germans who were attacking the 9th.

On the whole, if the maneuver prescribed for the 9th for the three armies on the left by my Instruction No. 19 had not yet been completely carried out, its development was well underway. The retreat of the left of the 6th Army was not serious. Its commander retained all his confidence, and he would soon have new means at his disposal to go back on the offensive. The British army and the left of the 5th Army began to break through north of the Marne, penetrating like a wedge between the First and Second German armies.

In a new Special Instruction,* I specified in the evening of the 9th the results obtained and the maneuver to be pursued: the 6th Army, its right supported at the Ourcq, would push Kluck towards the north, while the British forces supported by the 5th Army would gain the Clignon and complete the separation of Kluck from his neighbor on the left.

During this time, the battle at the front had continued.

We know the maneuver that General Foch carried out that day: at the request of Franchet d'Esperey, the latter had given him the complete control of the 10th Corps and the 51st reserve division. The commander of the 9th Army directed the 10th Corps west of Champaubert between the Petit-Morin and Fromentières, and used the 51st reserve division to relieve the 42nd which formed the left of the army; having thus reconstituted a reserve, he brought the 42nd Division to the rear of his center, with orders to prepare to attack in the direction of Fère-Champenoise. And at 4 p.m., he gave the order to attack on the whole line. The 11th Corps merely began the movement; the 42nd Division arrived too late to engage before nightfall; only the 10th Corps, passing north of the Saint-Gond marshes, began to push back the enemy, while the 77th Infantry Regiment took back from the enemy the important stronghold formed by the Château de Mondement.

In the 4th Army, the situation was also improving. The violence of the attacks in front of its right and its center was visibly weakening; west of the Marne, the entry into action of the 21st corps and elements taken by General de Langle from his two right corps would allow him to begin an action towards the northwest in support of Foch the next day.

Finally, at Sarrail's Army, the fight continued without the enemy succeeding in gaining ground; and on the left of this army, the 15th Corps progressed in connection with the right of de Langle's army. During the night of the 9th to the 10th, the Germans launched a violent attack on the front of the 6th Corps; this offensive, which was stopped on the morning of the 10th, marked the end of the German efforts on the front of the 3rd Army.

---

* Special Instruction no. 20 of September 9, 1914, 10 pm.

Chapter V

On the Meuse, the enemy continued his vain attempts: Troyon did not let himself be intimidated by the bombardment, and the curtain stretched by the 7th Cavalry Division, the presence of the 2nd Cavalry Division on the right bank towards Saint-Mihiel and of the mixed brigade, carried by Castelnau de Toul towards Commercy, succeeded in covering the rear of Sarrail's army.

Thus, on the whole, the situation appeared to me on the evening of the 9th in a favorable light: on the left, the success was accentuated, while in the center and on the right the enemy thrust seemed to be definitively stopped.

Victory was even closer than I had hoped.

On the morning of the 10th, as the 6th Army was attacking in execution of my directive of the previous evening, it suddenly felt the enemy resistance give way before it, and it gained about fifteen kilometers during that day, almost without a blow.

On its right, the British army reached the Clignon, without encountering any resistance, and came to station itself at the end of the day south of the Ourcq, from Ferté-Milon to Neuilly-Saint-Front.

As for the 5th Army, it was crossing the Marne from Château-Thierry to Dormans, and General Franchet d'Esperey reported to me that, in front of him, the retreat of the enemy was rushing partly to the north, partly to the east.

On the front of the 9th Army, the success was also taking shape: the general offensive that Foch had outlined the day before was now developing and everything showed that, there too, the enemy had made a hasty retreat during the night. On the evening of the 10th, Foch set up his headquarters in Fère-Champenoise, which the Prussian Guard still held in the morning.

In front of the 4th and 3rd armies, the situation remained stationary. Instead of, as I had hoped, General de Langle's left being able to work for the 9th Army, it was the latter that was in a position to work for its neighbor on the right. In front of Sarrail, the enemy's activity was still slowing down, and the 15th Corps, having completed the clearing of the Trois-Fontaines forest, was holding on to the right corps of the 4th Army.

It was now a question of developing the success of our left and our center, and of dominating the resistance which still stopped the two armies of our right.

Consequently, I sent that day a series of orders that were to give a new impetus to the battle:

To Maunoury and French, I asked them to push on both sides of the Ourcq, straight north, while on the extreme left, Bridoux's cavalry corps would seek to constantly worry the enemy's lines of retreat, and on their right the 5th Army would put itself in a situation "to act facing east in the direction of Reims, against the columns that were retreating in front of the 9th Army";[*]

To General Foch, I pointed out the interest that the action of his army on the bodies opposed to the 4th Army (2) presented for the outcome of the battle;[†]

To General de Langle, I ordered a push by his left and to attack vigorously;[‡]

Finally, I asked General Sarrail only to hold on and to last longer.[§]

In addition, I endeavored to threaten both wings of the retreating enemy:

On the right, by ordering General Coutanceau, governor of Verdun, by radio to attack the enemy convoys crossing the Meuse north of Verdun with all his forces.

On the left, pushing the territorial divisions of General d'Amade into the region of Beauvais.[**]

Finally, I telegraphed to the 1st army to embark the 13th Army corps in Épinal for the north of Paris, because all my attention was now concentrated on the necessity to prevent the enemy from recovering, and for that, I wanted to reinforce again the army of

---

[*] Special Instruction No. 21 of September 10.

[†] Special order of September 10 morning.

[‡] Special order of September 10, 10 a.m.

[§] Special order of September 10, 10:10 a.m.

[**] Special order of September 9.

General Maunoury, which I considered as the main piece of our maneuver.

That evening, without yet being able to measure the full extent of the victory, I was certain of it, and I informed the Minister of the first results: the enemy in full retreat in front of my left had already withdrawn more than 60 kilometers, the German center was bending in front of Foch, and the opposing left was not yet shaken but seemed to be out of breath.

On September 11, the victory was confirmed on all fronts.

The 6th Army reached the Pierrefonds-Chaudun line; the English crossed the upper Ourcq; Franchet d'Esperey, chasing weak rearguards in front of him, carried his column heads south of the Vesle between Chéry and Ville-en-Tardenois; his right corps, the 10th, which had contributed so powerfully to Foch's success, went up from Vertus to Épernay, while the 9th Army itself came to border the Marne between Sarry and Tours. The 4th Army was now progressing, too: its left reached the Marne during the night, downstream from Vitry; on its right, the colonial corps occupied the passages of the Saulx and the 2nd corps those of the Ornain in connection with the left of the 3rd Army, which crossed this last river. The rest of Sarrail's army was not yet advancing, but at the end of the day the staff reported to me that an "impressive calm" reigned on its entire front.[*]

That evening, I telegraphed the Minister:

"The Battle of the Marne ends in an unquestionable victory."

Before writing this victory bulletin, a question arose: what name should we give to the battle we had just won?

In the past, battles took their name from the place where they were fought, or from the point where the decisive action took

---

[*] I must say that this report of the 3rd Army which was telephoned, if my memories are correct, by colonel Leboucq, chief of staff of this army, in person, plunged me into astonishment, and caused me great discontent. At a time when the enemy was assuming that it was beaten on the whole line, the 3rd Army, so well placed to achieve victory, was content, fearing some kind of trap, to note that calm reigned on its entire front. I immediately ordered it to pursue the enemy energetically.

place. The modern battle, with its immense fronts on which multiple equally important actions are engaged simultaneously, can no longer be characterized by the name of a locality. Already in Manchuria, the belligerents had been led to name several battles after rivers whose valleys had served as the scene of the struggle. The battle that the Allied forces had just fought from Verdun to the outskirts of Paris had taken place in the valley of the Marne and its tributaries: Ourcq, Grand and Petit-Morin, Saulx and Ornain. This is what convinced me to give this battle the name of "the Marne," which evoked at the same time the idea of a front and of an extended region.

As I said at the beginning of this chapter, the Battle of the Marne, which had begun on our side with a maneuver of envelopment of the enemy right wing, had ended with the dislocation of the opposing position in which two gaps had opened, one between the Ist and IInd German armies, the other between the IInd and IVth armies, the IIIrd Army having itself broken into two sections which had been joined respectively to the left of Bülow and to the right of the Prince of Wurtemberg. Of this unforeseen situation, we had taken advantage; and this confirms what I said above about how dangerous the doctrine is which consists of abandoning strategic control of the battle to those carrying it out..

On the other hand, if one compares the battle of the Marne to that of the borders, one sees that they are closely related. If, on the Ourcq, Maunoury had given in as our left armies did on August 22nd, if Foch had given in at Fère-Champenoise as our 3rd and 4th armies did from Audun-le-Roman to Paliseul, my plan would have collapsed a second time. If success met my expectations on the Marne, it was largely because our armies at the beginning of September were no longer those of the first days of the war. Educated by the hard experience of the battles fought on the frontier, the infantry, although having lost many of its cadres, made better use of the terrain, used its tools more willingly, whose value it now understood, and no longer engaged without the support of the artillery. It is also true that many of the leaders whose inadequacy had been suddenly revealed by the war had given way to others who were more capable: from mobilization to September

6, I had had to relieve two army commanders,* nine army corps commanders,† thirty-three generals commanding infantry divisions,‡ one cavalry corps commander and five generals commanding cavalry divisions.§ If I had not gone as far as the radical measures recommended by Mr. Messimy, which consisted in having the incapable ones shot, one can say that these changes in the command had already purified and rejuvenated it.

As for the English, they had, in parallel to us, taken advantage of the hard lesson of this beginning of the war. Since Waterloo, they had only fought in Europe during the Crimean War. The leap was abrupt. If they did not march as fast in the Battle of the Marne as I would have liked, and they probably could have done so because of the small forces the Germans had left in front of them, they held a place worthy of their military traditions in that battle and played the role I expected of them. This loyal soldier, Marshal French, was now showing full confidence since the success of our maneuver at the Marne had been confirmed. Unfortunately, he was divided between two influences: one represented by General Wilson, a man of very keen intelligence who understood all situations admirably, who was moreover accustomed to our methods and who knew France very well, for which he had deep sympathies, and the other by General Murray, Chief of Staff of the expeditionary forces, who spent his time giving advice of prudence to the Marshal. It was a great relief to us when, a few months later, General Murray was recalled to England.

---

* The commanders of the 3rd and 5th armies.

† Out of twenty-one army corps.

‡ Twenty-three commanding generals of active divisions out of forty-seven (including the two colonial divisions) and ten commanding generals of reserve divisions out of twenty-five.

§ Five out of ten generals commanding cavalry divisions.

Chapter V

The Pursuit After the Marne

On the evening of September 11th, the enemy gave way on the whole front, leaving us wounded, equipment and supplies. In front of the 6th Army and the British army, he evaded to the north, obviously trying to place the Aisne between him and his victorious adversaries; the German VIIth Corps, which formed during the battle the right wing of Bülow's army, was reported on the Vesle between Fismes and Braine, facing the 5th Army; in front of the 9th and 4th armies, the enemy withdrew to the north of the Marne and the Saulx.

Berthelot, back to the optimism that had abandoned him for a moment at the end of August, already saw the German armies in disarray. In his opinion, the only way to exploit the victory was to push forward brutally on the whole line. I did not share this opinion. We had just won an unquestionable victory over the German supreme command, which had made essential mistakes. But the enemy armies were not routed, and we had to expect to find them reformed somewhere beyond the Marne, behind the Aisne, or perhaps behind the Meuse. It was thus a question of mounting without delay a maneuver to prevent the Germans from recovering. By taking, as I said above, new forces from our armies on the right, I resolved to reinforce the 6th Army to put it in a position to overrun the German right wing; in addition, the 5th Army was well placed to exploit the crack that had occurred in the enemy center, by maneuvering according to the circumstances, either with the French-Maunoury grouping, or with the Foch-de Langle pair of forces.

I made my intentions known to the armies of the left by a Special Instruction that I addressed to them on September 11. The next day, I pressed General Maunoury, reminding him that his zone of march was not limited to the west, and that, in the event where the enemy would make headway on the Aisne, it was necessary that we immediately have forces which would go up the right bank of the Oise; I added that the 13th Corps placed, as we have seen, recently at the disposal of the 6th Army seemed to be very well suited to play this essential role. The same day, September 12, I emphasized my orders to the 6th Army. I requested that General

Chapter V 397

Maunoury widen his outflanking movement towards the west, leaving only a strong detachment in connection with the British army, and to gradually bring the bulk of his forces to the right bank of the Oise.

For the other wing of my line, it was important to provide an energetic boost to bring it out of its lethargy. On September 12, I instructed General Sarrail on the maneuver I expected from him: "...It is to be presumed that the enemy forces in front of the 3rd Army will not be long in withdrawing themselves under the pressure of the 4th Army. In the presence of this eventuality, you must arrange your forces in such a way as to be able to begin an energetic pursuit northward through the open ground between the Argonne and the Meuse, supporting yourselves at the Hauts-de-Meuse and at the place of Verdun."

I am obliged to say that the execution did not meet my intentions.

On the left, General Maunoury did not understand my thinking. He had encountered on the plateaus north of the Aisne a resistance that immediately absorbed his attention and his forces; he did not know how to give his left wing sufficient strength or means, and he soon fell into a fruitless frontal combat.

Franchet d'Esperey, for his part, did not exploit the favorable situation in which he found himself. The maneuver to be executed was based on a rapid march beyond the Vesle, which would have largely cleared Reims and forced the Germans to abandon the Chemin des Dames where they were putting up energetic resistance to the British. The 5th Army was certainly tired, like all the others, and as armies always are after a hard-fought victory. Without ignoring the difficulty he was facing, I must say that Franchet d'Esperey lost time. The hole that existed in front of him in the enemy line and which had allowed elements of our cavalry to push on to Sissonne closed and the enemy front stabilized in the immediate vicinity of Rheims, whose slow destruction began.

Finally, on our right, Sarrail did not understand, either, the decisive role that his army could play in these circumstances. More occupied with personal matters than with the operations of his army, he did not make his drive felt with energy. And on the afternoon of September 13, I had to order him to make an inquiry to determine how the enemy had been able to break away for forty-eight hours in front of his army, without his having been informed of it.

A serious question began to arise: that of artillery ammunition. It is known that we had started the campaign with a total supply of about 1,400 rounds per 75 mm gun. The consumption of ammunition, which had only amounted to about 200 rounds per gun during the first month of the war, had increased considerably during the battle of the Marne, where certain divisional artilleries had fired 300 rounds per gun per day. As early as September 14, I was led to take measures to react against the unfortunate tendency that was spreading to constantly use explosive shells while neglecting bullet shells, a tendency that threatened to rapidly exhaust our stocks. I will come back later on to this ammunition crisis, which started to occur at the same time with our adversaries. For the moment, what I want to say here is that the stabilization of the Germans was not due to our shortage of ammunition, which was only really felt after the enemy had embedded himself in fortified positions; the essential cause of this stabilization was the lack of maneuvering skill and the slowness shown during this short period of exploitation of the victory by the two armies on our wings and the 5th Army.

Even if the victory of the Marne did not give all that I expected, it seems to me legitimate to mark, however, in few words the essential results.

The month of August 1914 had given the Germans the first round of the game: the Belgians driven back to Antwerp, the French-British towards the Seine, our left wing threatened with encirclement and Paris with being taken; undoubtedly, at this moment, the Germans saw a renewed Sedan on a gigantic scale. The plan of our adversaries was based on a quick victory in the west. The necessity of winning the war before the resources of Russia were brought to bear, was now all the more imperative as the British Empire had thrown itself into the war on our side. As I have said several times in the preceding pages, it would have been to play into the hands of the enemy to risk the destiny of the country at a time when our primary concern was to last. It was this consideration that allowed me to wait for an ever possible return of fortune, at the price of the sacrifice of a part of our soil that I hoped would be momentary. In the absence of a total defeat inflicted on the Germans, the patiently awaited opportunity had just allowed us to push them back on the whole line and our victory forced them to bury themselves in the trenches! What a disappointment for people in a hurry!

But this result, which was the main cause of the final defeat of the Germans, was not fully appreciated at the time.

Among the Allies, and particularly in France, public opinion, after having felt an immense relief at the removal of the threat which, in the first days of September, made people fear all kinds of disasters, saw only one thing a few days after the victory of the Marne: that the mass of the German armies was encrusting our soil. The Minister of War, instead of showing to the public the happy reversal of the situation, made mitigations in the publication of the communiqués that I had addressed to him following the battle. Mr. Millerand, to whom I made known the somewhat saddened feeling that I had experienced in observing these mitigations, wrote to me on September 15:

> I am the only one guilty, and I would not want there to remain in your mind a shadow of doubt as to the considerations which led me to mute the expression of our joy.
>
> It seems to me good to spare the nerves of this country, and I have preferred to run the risk of underestimating the truth, than of exaggerating it.

Mr. Millerand's patriotism was too sincere, and his sympathy for me too loyal, to allow us to attribute to him here the slightest ulterior motive. Nevertheless, I am not far from thinking that the Minister was too modest in the expression of our victory. Enemy propaganda acting with violence covered the voice of victorious France among neutrals and even among ourselves. For some, the Marne seemed like a kind of miracle, for others like a happy and unforeseen chance. For those who took their inspiration from the enemy press, it was even reduced to a maneuver of the German command, which, in the absence of a strategic result that escaped him, used, from that moment on, the easy excuse of the "war card."

Fortunately, the essential fact was there: the enemy was defeated 80 kilometers north of Paris, and one can say that it was definitively stopped. We took a breath and regained confidence.

Chapter VI

The autumn campaign. – The stabilization of the Western Front.

On September 14, the armies reported that the enemy was beginning to make headway on a front marked by the heights north of the Aisne, those overlooking Reims to the north and northeast, and by a line passing through Saint-Hilaire, Souain, Ville-sur-Tourbe and Vienne-la-Ville.

The next day, the resistance of the Germans increased. The 6th Army, whose advance was essential to force our adversaries to continue their retreat, was stopped on all of its front; more seriously, its left (4th Corps and 37th Division) was engaged on a difficult terrain in a confused fight which, in the evening, left us in close contact with the enemy, while a division of the 13th Corps, which had just landed, went up the right bank of the Oise, in direction of Noyon.

That day, I had the distinct impression that the Germans were going to accept a new battle on the line where they had just held their resistance. In my mind, there could be no thought of starting a general action which would have cost us many casualties and exhausted all our ammunition. My intention was, while observing an aggressive attitude which would keep the enemy under constant threat of a general attack and would prevent him from taking forces for the benefit of his right wing, to initiate, by means of units which I would withdraw from my armies of the center and the right, a powerful action of my left against the German right.*

But already, the lack of importance given by Maunoury to the maneuver of his left wing no longer left me with any illusions about the results I could expect from this army. And, as early as September 17th, I was led to consider the creation, on the left of the 6th Army, of a new unit to which would fall the mission that I had previously entrusted to Maunoury.

For the success of this maneuver, it was necessary that the armies at the front continued to show great activity and that they ensured, in spite of the levies that I was going to make on them, the integrity of their positions. And it is really from this moment that the question of the ammunition became worrying.

Towards the end of September, the total endowment of the armies fell to 400 rounds per piece; the echelons of the regulating stations were empty, the warehouses had only a weak reserve: 30 batches (that is to say 45 rounds per piece). The daily production was at this time only 8 to 10,000 rounds per day.

The minister, to whom I sent a letter on September 20 asking him to increase the daily production to 50,000 rounds, answered me the next day:

> My dear general,
>
> I am no less concerned about the production of 75 ammunition than you are.
>
> I had, before I received your letter, met with you on the necessity of a daily manufacture of 50,000 rounds.
>
> It is impossible under the current conditions.
>
> Also, I gathered last night the representatives of the War, the Navy and private industry (Saint-Chamond, Creusot, railroads, automobiles, etc.), to see how we would achieve this production.
>
> It will not be convenient, because it takes time and a lot, in spite of an indisputable competence and good will, to gather personnel, material, and put everything in motion.

---

* Special Instruction No. 29 of September 17.

Chapter VI

I don't despair, however, of reaching 30,000 rounds in three weeks, four at most.

In any case, the irons are on the fire. We will have a second meeting, on Saturday, of the industrialists who are going to use their week to secure the indispensable assistance.

On your part, I urge you to take all measures to avoid waste as much as possible.

I insist on the necessity to have the shell casings collected by drudgery or by the inhabitants, for a fee, on the battlefield.

I will ask for the ammunition data for the British and Russians.

You will have received prior to this letter the answers to your various communications. I hope you will be satisfied with them.

My thoughts are unceasingly with you, and our admirable troops, and my confidence is without reserve.

Affectionately yours

A. MILLERAND[*]

While waiting for the realization of the program that the Minister announced to me, I took immediate measures:

I reduced the armies' supplies to 200 rounds per piece. The remainder of the supplies constituted a reserve at my disposal, which I could use to deal with unforeseen situations.

I repeatedly urged the armies to avoid wasting our precious ammunition.

I took extra 75 mm ammunition from the supplies of the eastern cities, Le Havre, Dunkirk and the fortified camp of Paris.[†]

These measures allowed us, together with the sending to the armies of older model batteries, to ensure as well as possible the supply of the armies, while facing the needs of the battle which developed little by little from the Oise to the Somme and, through Flanders, was soon going to reach the edge of the North Sea.

But it is certain that this shortage of ammunition occurring at such a time considerably hindered our operations: to feed the battle in the north, it was necessary to put large areas of the front in semi-

---

[*] Strictly personal file of the general in charge of the Eastern Armies. Book 1. Room 45.

[†] This measure allowed us to recover about thirty lots. (1 lot = 6,000 shots.)

dormancy. The enemy was able to work at leisure on his defensive positions; behind this front, which was becoming more solid every day and which it was possible to hold economically, it was easy for him to draw forces for the benefit of his right wing, which, in parallel with our left wing, extended towards the north. It was also possible for him to carry out reinforcements intended for local actions directed against sensitive points of our front.

In this respect, the Vth German army started a powerful offensive on both sides of Verdun on September 21. Although it did not give our adversaries all the results they were expecting, it had very unfortunate consequences for us.

Following the departure of General de Castelnau, the staff of the 2nd Army, and with the 20th Army corps called, as I will say later, to a new theater of operations, I had to proceed with a new distribution of forces and missions between the 1st and 3rd armies.[*]

While fulfilling their defensive mission, which consisted in "ensuring the security of the right of our position," the 1st and 3rd armies had to "maintain contact with the enemy in the region east of Metz."

On September 20th, following information reporting enemy forces gathering in the Jonville-Dampvitoux-Essey-Beney-Thiaucourt region, I telegraphed General Dubail, commanding the 1st Army, to use the 16th Corps that he had in reserve on his left, "with a view to attacking in the flank the enemy troops that would attack the Hauts-de-Meuse or the Commercy Gap." At the same time, I informed General Sarrail, commander of the 3rd Army, of these dispositions, and ordered him to take measures to repel the enemy attack head-on if it occurred.

That same day, the 75th Division, which held the Hauts-de-Meuse in the Hattonchatel area, was violently bombarded. The next day, it was strongly attacked. After an insufficient resistance, it gave way and the enemy gained a foothold in Hattonohatel and Creue.

On the 22nd, another German attack, vigorously pushed by two

---

[*] Special Instruction No. 30 of September 18, 1914.

army corps, took place west of Verdun, in the Argonne and on the eastern edge of this massif, in the Varennes region. This new offensive took place at the poorly established junction between the 3rd and 4th armies, and at a point where our defense line was still poorly established. While the Germans were attacking in the Argonne, their progression continued towards Saint-Mihiel. In the presence of this situation, I placed at the disposal of General Sarrail the 8th Corps that I had previously taken from the right of his army and sent towards Sainte-Menehould, where it was to constitute a reserve to oppose any enemy movement by the west or the east of the Argonne. This army corps was immediately transported, partly by rail, partly by road, from the Sainte-Menehould region to the Saint-Mihiel region, and was available from the 24th to reinforce the right of the 3rd Army, which seemed to be more strongly threatened.

On the 24th, the enemy's advance south of Varennes was halted, while on the right bank of the Meuse, the Germans reached the outskirts of Saint-Mihiel. Also, in the evening, I ordered the commander of the 1st Army to devote as many forces as possible to his offensive in Woëvre in order to relieve the 3rd Army.

On the 25th, some elements of the IIIrd Bavarian Corps, which had gained a foothold on the left bank of the Meuse, were repulsed at Chauvoncourt. Because of the difficulties of communication of the 3rd Army with those of its units operating on the right bank, I subordinated to General Dubail all the troops which were east of this river.

Our offensive continued over the following days. It stopped the German thrust but did not succeed in regaining the lost ground.

In this affair, the command of the 3rd Army had lacked foresight and activity: foresight by neglecting the intelligence that signaled important gatherings in Woëvre, and activity by not knowing how to use the 6th Corps, of which a division stationed in peacetime at Saint-Mihiel knew the terrain admirably. This corps remained almost useless during the whole time of this crisis, a few leagues from the battlefield.

The consequences of this German attack were serious. It put in the hands of the enemy at Saint-Mihiel the road, the railroad and the canal that allowed the supply of Verdun; it placed under the gun of the Germans the railroad near Commercy, and the line from Châlons to Verdun near Aubreville. As a result, Verdun was only supplied by a single one-meter gauge railway line from Bar-le-Duc, the "Petit Meusien." The danger of this situation became apparent when the Battle of Verdun began in February 1916.

Nevertheless, in order to take into account the difficult position from which the 1st and 3rd armies had just emerged with, it must be admitted, little means, I expressed my complete satisfaction to these two armies via order no. 33 of October 1.

On September 26, the main headquarters, which I found too far from the front since the German retreat, was moved, on my order, to Romilly.

On the 28th, I went to the headquarters of General Franchet d'Esperey. To get there, I crossed the battlefield of the 9th Army. It was a spectacle of desolation. Almost all the villages were destroyed by bombardment or the fire that the Germans had set when they left. The road from Père-Champenoise to Châlons ran through a huge cemetery. In the woods along the railway line, near the small station of Normée, one saw as far as the eye could see large graves all white with quicklime: kepis, jackets, weapons were hung on hundreds of small crosses at the foot of which pious hands had placed flowers from the fields. Between Épernay and Reims, the roads were smashed, the milestones and the telegraph poles torn up; carts, cars of all kinds, even carriages that had come from who knows where, lay disemboweled with their wheels in the air, car frames formed huge heaps of scrap metal; only the vineyards, by who knows what chance, seemed to have suffered little. To the east of Reims, I visited some batteries. The city was still almost intact, but the cathedral, which the enemy had, in violation of the law of nations, savagely bombarded on September 19, had been set on fire, and had already suffered irreparable damage.

The war had hardly begun two months before, and already it was possible to measure the accumulation of ruins that our victory over Germany would bring.

I have just said that, on September 15, the resistance in front of the 6th Army became more pronounced. In vain, on the 18th, General Maunoury withdrew the 4th Corps from his front to bring it to the

Chapter VI

left of the 13th, which was operating on the right bank of the Oise. The failure of the maneuver, for lack of strength, was obvious, and our forces on the left fell, like our other armies, into a fruitless frontal struggle in which our lack of ammunition left me with no illusions as to the success of the operation. As I said, this situation led me to form a new army west of the Oise. The Special Order no. 31 of September 18th named it the 2nd Army. I called upon General de Castelnau to command it. My choice was guided by the following considerations:

First of all, General de Castelnau enjoyed a justified military reputation in the army: he was gifted with a keen intelligence, with a widespread military education; he had managed, to his credit, to get through the difficult circumstances in which he had found himself in August and early September. His energy and his calmness had probably not been equal to his intelligence during the affairs around Nancy, but I had the right to think that in the mission that I was going to entrust to him, requiring activity and a developed tactical sense, he would be able to fully display the maneuvering qualities that I recognized in him.

On the other hand, events had gradually led me to move the 2nd Army towards the Woëvre, and to narrow its front. Now placed before the southern front of Metz, it could only fulfill a defensive mission. It was this army that it was easiest for me to withdraw from my battle line. I entrusted most of its sector to General Dubail, commander of the 1st Army, and the rest to General Sarrail, commander of the 3rd. And the 2nd Army, just as it was being reborn in Picardy, on September 20, was disbanded in Lorraine.*

Originally, the new 2nd Army included:

> The two left corps of the 6th Army: 4th and 13th Corps;
> The 14th Corps, transported by rail to the Clermont-Beauvais

---

* The Special Instruction no. 30 disbanded the former 2nd Army; the H.Q., the army components, and the 20th Corps were transported west of the Oise; the components remaining in the east were attached partly to the 1st Army, partly to the 3rd.

area;

The 20th Corps, also transported by rail in the Poix-Grandvillers region;

Conneau's Cavalry Corps (1st, 3rd, 5th and 10th Cavalry Divisions).

General de Castelnau's mission was defined by Special Instruction No. 32 of September 19th:

> The 2nd Army must act against the German right wing to relieve the 6th Army and allow it – and consequently our forces as a whole – to resume forward movement.
>
> This action will be perceived as a withdrawal on the enemy's right wing, but this withdrawal movement will always be limited in time so that the 2nd Army can recover and always keep, whatever happens, a direction of march that is overwhelming in relation to the new units that the enemy could put in line.

The deployments and the reunion of the elements of the 2nd Army were masked and covered by a group of four territorial divisions[*] placed under the orders of General Brugère. This group was to move in small stages to the region of Beauvais, then Corbie; secondarily, it was to put an end to the requisitions and acts of robbery in which the enemy was engaged in the northern region.

The 2nd Army had to enter the line as a matter of urgency. On the 20th, because of the situation of the 6th Army, which was strongly attacked on the Aisne, I sent an order to General de Castelnau to "hold the bridges of the Oise around Compiègne and those of the Aisne as far as Rethondes... and to make this action felt as soon as possible." He gave an account of his intention to direct the 13th Corps on Noyon the next day and the 14th on Lassigny and Guiscard. But the situation of the 6th Army improved in the evening and I ordered the commander of the 2nd Army to widen his movement to the left.

On the 21st, the 13th Corps took Ribécourt, but failed in front of Lassigny; the 4th Corps reached Fresnières and Le Plessier (northwest of Lassigny) without resistance, while the Bridoux

---

[*] 81st, 82nd, 84th and 88th territorial divisions.

Chapter VI

cavalry corps circled around Péronne.

The activity of the German T.S.F.,* which was one of our most precious sources of information, showed us that day that the enemy command was paying particular attention to its right wing. There were indications that a VIIth Army, under the command of General von Heeringen, was being formed to operate on the right of Kluck's Army.† And, as if to confirm my impression that the enemy effort was shifting, the front of our 6th Army remained that day in a calm that contrasted with the activity of the previous days.

During the following days, the 2nd Army continued its movement towards the northeast and the north, pivoting around the 13th Corps, which remained on the Ribécourt-Fresnières front. But on the morning of the 24th, General de Castelnau informed me that all his corps were already in contact with the enemy: the 4th Corps in the Roye area, the 14th in the Lihons-Foucaucourt area, while the 20th arrived at Corbie. And the next day the situation became clearer: a violent battle was now joined between the Oise and the Somme. And the German forces that were opposing the advance of Castelnau's army were already extending north of the Somme on the Feuillères-Bapaume-Marquion line in contact with our cavalry corps, whose action did not obtain an appreciable slowing down of the enemy columns.‡ As for the territorial divisions which I had

---

* Translator's note: This is a term for the wireless telegraph.

† I do not know if this information was inaccurate, or if, being true, the Germans were led to modify their plans; in any case, the VIIth Army which operated in Alsace was indeed withdrawn from the front, but engaged between the Ist and IInd German armies to fill the vacuum which had occurred between them.

‡ General Bridoux, commander of the cavalry corps, had been killed on September 17. I had temporarily replaced him with General Buisson, who commanded the 1st Cavalry Division. I had to relieve him on 30 September and replace him with General de Mitry. If the cavalry did not produce great leaders at that time who knew how to handle a mass of three or four divisions, it is fair to say that the division generals did not facilitate the task of their leader.

General de Castelnau reported to me daily that the cavalry divisions remained for entire days without sending information, and without even making known where they were. These errors were confirmed to me by Lieutenant-Colonel Brécart, my liaison officer with the Maunoury army, a cavalryman, however, who

ordered, on the 24th, to move towards Arras and Bapaume to cover the left of the 2nd Army, they withdrew during the night of the 26th to the 27th to the west bank of the Ancre, where they entrenched themselves from Aveluy to Miraumont with a division at Bucquoi.

The rapidity with which General de Castelnau's army was caught on all of its front showed that the enemy was trying, by a movement symmetrical to ours, to seize and envelop our marching wing.

It was necessary, without dismay, to begin a new phase of the maneuver, by means of new forces brought back in haste towards our extreme left. Unfortunately, we did not have at that time the powerful automobile service which reached its full capacity only in the last year of the war. A few troops were able to move by land; for all the others, the railroads had to be called in. Their task was a difficult one, for many of the tracks were out of order, and the convex shape of our front forced us to travel in an arc of which the Germans held the tether.

The following schedule gives an idea of the importance of the transports that the railroad service had to face in the last days of September and the first days of October:

> The 11th Corps, taken from the 9th Army, embarked on 25 September for Amiens.
>
> The 10th Corps, taken from the 5th Army, embarked on 28 September for Amiens.
>
> The 77th Division, taken from the 1st Army, embarked on 28 September for Arras and Lens.
>
> The 70th Division, taken from the 1st Army, embarked on 28 September for Arras and Lens.
>
> The 8th Cavalry Division, taken from the 6th Army, moved by land to Montdidier.
>
> The 4th Cavalry Division, taken from the 5th Army, embarked on 30 September.
>
> The 21st Corps, taken from the 9th Army, embarked on

---

was very humbled by the reports that his honesty obliged him to give me.

Chapter VI

October 1st for Lille.

The 45th Division, taken from the 6th Army, was transported by car to Compiègne and embarked by rail for the north.

As, on the other hand, the Germans seemed to have brought in front of our left the major part of the forces which were in Belgium, I suggested to the Minister of War that "the moment had come for the Belgian army to act on the enemy's communications." I must say that this cooperation of the Belgian army in the battle we were now waging in Picardy and which was approaching Flanders, also appeared to me as a means of bringing our allies out of the dangerous isolation in which they found themselves under the walls of Antwerp. My proposal, as we will see later, was not taken into consideration at that moment, and it took the imminence of a catastrophe to bring the Belgian forces back to our side.

In any case, in the last days of September, the battle, by the entry in line of new forces, extended little by little to the north of the Somme. On our side, the 11th Corps, supported on its left by the 20th, came up against already solid enemy positions on the Thiepval plateau.

On October 1st, probably to reduce the pressure exerted by our left wing, the enemy launched violent attacks between the Oise and the Somme. Because of the fragility of his front, which was still not well established, the distension of his army corps, and the signs of weariness shown in some places by the local command, particularly in the 4th Corps, General de Castelnau appeared to be very worried about these attacks and, as his reserves were naturally oriented towards his left, he asked for support from those of the 6th Army. This request seemed justified to me: the enemy had weakened in front of the Maunoury army. Consequently, I ordered the latter to "bring all his available reserves and all those that it would be possible to constitute, on the west bank of the Oise to support the 2nd Army."* In execution of this order, the 56th and 62nd reserve divisions were brought to Compiègne on October

---

* Order sent on October 1st at 5:15 pm.

2nd, where they were placed under the orders of General de Castelnau, who used them to shore up his defensive front between the Oise and the Somme.

But the extent of the front on which the 2nd Army was now fighting, the increase in the number of troops engaged north of the Oise, the very different role that fell to the troops of this army depending on whether they were in line north or south of the Somme, all these causes now made the command of the 2nd Army all the more onerous, as I foresaw the need to reinforce and extend the action of my left wing. It was with this in mind that, on September 29th, I placed General de Maud'huy at Castelnau's disposal, to exercise, under the orders of the commander of the 23rd Army, the direction of the 10th Corps and the elements placed on its left.* And by an order of September 30, I created a large cavalry force on the extreme left of my position, including:

Conneau's cavalry corps (1st, 3rd and 10th Divisions), and a corps formed under the orders of General de Mitry with the 5th Division already on site, and the 4th and 6th Divisions brought in by rail.†

If we take into account that the 2nd Army had the 6th Cavalry Division and the detachment of Maud'huy on the 7th, we can see that four fifths of the French cavalry were now north of the Oise.

The mission of the cavalry corps was determined in the following way:‡

Conneau's Corps operating south of the Scarpe under the direct orders of General de Maud'huy had the mission of contributing to the overrunning of the enemy right wing;

De Mitry's Corps, activated by General de Castelnau, had to operate north of the Scarpe river, to prevent enemy reconnaissance

---

* The army detachment of Maud'huy was transformed into the 10th Army on October 3, 1914.

† The 4th Cavalry Division was taken from the 5th Army, the 6th Cavalry Division from the 4th Army, which had received it from the 9th Army on September 17th.

‡ Special Instruction of October 1st.

Chapter VI

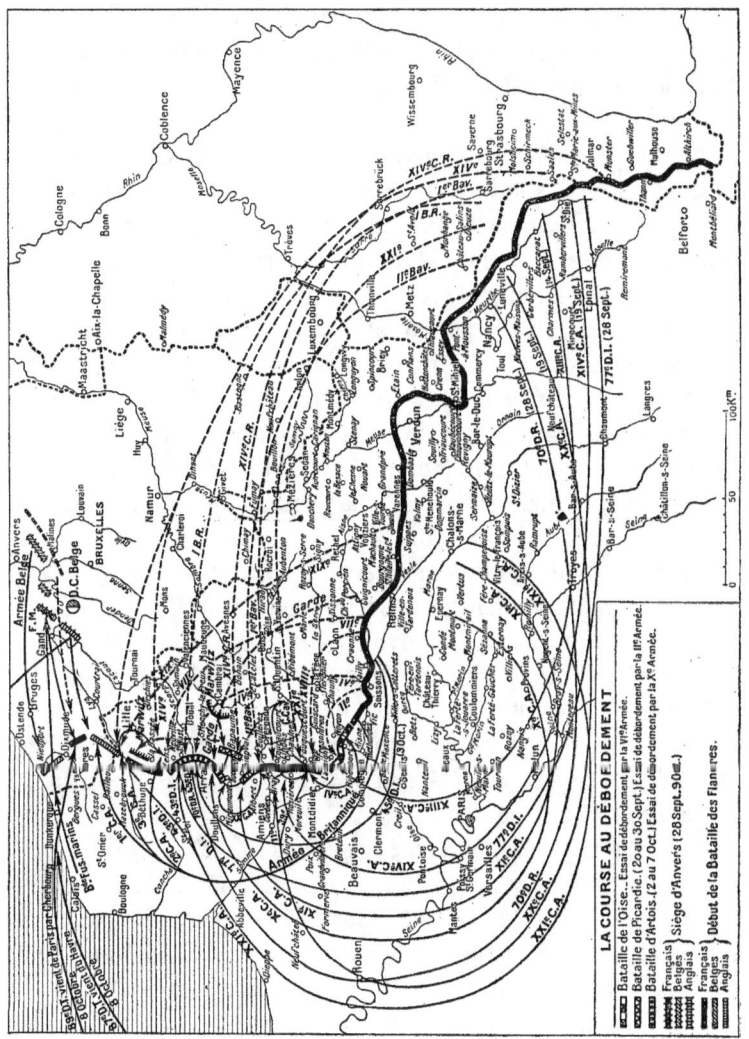

from penetrating our outposts, to try to attack the enemy's communications, and to try to link up, on the one hand, with the troops of the Dunkirk garrison, who had been pushed to Douai, Orchies and Mouchin, and on the other hand, with the Allied troops operating in the Lille region on Belgian territory.

These arrangements had hardly been made when, on October 2nd, the situation in the north suddenly seemed to take on a serious aspect.

At the detachment of Maud'huy, while the 10th Corps attacked without success south of Arras, Barbot's (77th) and Fayolle's (70th) divisions which had just arrived were violently attacked by German forces coming out of the Douai region. Barbot lost Monchy-le-Preux, Fayolle resisted with difficulty to the southeast of Lens; to his left the territorial troops of the Dunkirk garrison abandoned Liétard and the 7th Cavalry Division withdrew to Lens.

Now, on October 3, the deployments of the 21st Corps were to begin, in the region of Lille or immediately to the west, at a distance "sufficient from the left wing of the army detachment to allow it to outflank, in any case, the German forces that would be engaged against the 2nd Army."

The day before, a telegram sent at 12:20 p.m. from the 2nd Army informed me that the current situation in the Lille-Douai region did not allow the deployment of the 21st Corps as far as it was planned. The staff of the 2nd Army proposed the region of Béthune to carry out the projected deployments.

At 2:50 p.m., a message from General Anthoine, Chief of Staff of the 2nd Army, came back and insisted that the deployments be postponed to Béthune.

These repeated calls seemed ominous to me.

First of all, they showed that the command of the 2nd Army considered the possession of Lille and its powerful industrial resources as compromised, and perhaps its loss as imminent. Above all, they showed that we no longer seemed to be in the lead, and that the enemy, on the contrary, was getting ahead of us and tending to impose its will on us.

Also at 5:20 p.m., I telegraphed to General de Castelnau "that in case of absolute impossibility of a deployment in Lille, the 21st corps would be stopped on the Armentières-Hazebrouck sector...

Chapter VI 415

this result would be extremely unfortunate. Do not give up Lille except at the last extremity...."

And I immediately sent Major Fétizon, my liaison officer with the 2nd Army, bearing an order clarifying this decision.

On arriving at Breteuil, headquarters of the 2nd Army, Major Fétizon was immediately received by General de Castelnau and his chief of staff, who explained to him the risks that the deployment of the 21st Corps at Lille presented to them. And the army commander, in order to make my liaison officer aware of the situation, added that not only could he not think of deploying the 21st Corps in Lille, but that he was even considering withdrawing the left wing of his army behind the Somme downstream from Amiens, because of the violent attacks of the enemy who threatened to envelop us.

Fétizon tried in vain to fight this outlook, so contrary to my intentions. He understood very quickly that he would not be able to change the mind of the commander of the 2nd Army. Rightly measuring the seriousness of the consequences that such a decision would entail, he returned that very night to the main headquarters and reported to me, on October 3rd at 6:30 a.m., on the mission that he had just accomplished. He added that when he got into his car at about one o'clock in the morning, Major Jacquand, head of the 3rd Bureau of the 2nd Army, had assured him that, in his opinion, the situation was not as serious as he had just been told, and that the withdrawal behind the Somme had to be and could be avoided.

I do not need to say that the news reported by Commander Fétizon caused me great discontent. The decision envisaged by General de Castelnau was the loss of the rich regions of the north, of our coal basin in particular, the loss of our coasts up to the mouth of the Somme, and, in the short term, the total collapse of the Belgian army. Without hesitation, I resolved to go to Breteuil, where I arrived at about 12:30 p.m. I immediately showed Castelnau and his chief of staff that the situation was not as bleak as they saw it, and I made them understand the absolute necessity of holding on at all costs without considering the slightest retreat that could compromise the success of the maneuver I had been pursuing tirelessly for three weeks. Castelnau also complained about the failings of certain generals, but he excused them because of the seriousness of the circumstances in which they were placed. I replied that this was not the time for pity, that the greater good took precedence over all other considerations, and that those who were not capable of exercising their command should be ruthlessly removed. And I concluded by stating once more my determination not to allow any talk of withdrawal. Then I hurried back to the general headquarters where I arrived at about 7 p.m., and where other worries awaited me.

Those first days of October left me with bad memories. The maneuver that I was pursuing encountered difficulties that I could not deny: the enemy, as I said, was maneuvering along the tether of the arc on which we were operating. In spite of the dedication of the railroad service, we were not able to outflank the German right, which rose northward parallel to my extreme left. The attack on Saint-Mihiel had barely been halted, and I had every right to wonder whether, on this immense and still fragile front, a new offensive would not compromise its solidity at some sensitive point.

The fate of the Belgian army in Antwerp caused me great concern.

Finally, Marshal French requested to leave the Aisne front to take over the left of the French armies. This was a new problem added to the others. I will come back to the operations of the Belgian and British armies in a moment.

For the time being, and without letting myself be stopped by growing difficulties, it was important to give the operations of my left wing a new impetus.

If the capacity of our railroads, and the obligation to take forces from the rest of the front only sparingly, limited the arrival of troops in the north, it was possible for me to exert immediate action on the local command that I had just seen falter.

It was then that I called on General Foch.

Already at the end of September, I had thought of appointing him to be my deputy. I had, for this purpose, sent the following telegram to the Minister of War on September 24:

> General Galliéni is currently designated as my eventual successor.

But among the army commanders, General Foch has asserted an unquestionable superiority from the point of view of character and military skill. I ask that a letter of service be issued to him, designating him as my eventual replacement. In the event that the government accepts this proposal, I will take General Foch with me as an *ad latus*[*] to relieve me of part of the daily heavier task that falls to me, and I will name his successor in the command of the 9th Army.

J. JOFFRE.

The minister had agreed to my request, without however wanting to give general Foch a letter of service accrediting him in the functions that I reserved for him.

On October 4, I decided to send General Foch to the north, as "deputy to the commander-in-chief," with the mission of coordinating the action of Castelnau and Maud'huy's armies and of General Brugère's group of territorial divisions.

Foch left immediately. His army was disbanded on the 5th, and its elements distributed between the 4th and 5th armies.

During the day of October 4, the news from the 2nd Army continued to get worse.

Around 4 p.m., General Anthoine warned that the situation was getting worse, and that General de Castelnau was preparing to take "serious decisions" that very evening.

I immediately answered by telephone:

> An encrypted telegram is sent to you. Do not, until you have received it, make any decision of the nature referred to by General Anthoine in his telephone communication of 4 p.m.

And the encrypted telegram sent at 5:35 p.m. said:

> I cannot allow a withdrawal that would give the impression of a retreat and remove any possibility of further maneuvering.

But shortly afterwards a new message arrived by telephone

---

[*] "At the side."

from General de Castelnau:

> General de Maud'huy tells me that his mission was to envelop, and that it is rather he who is enveloped.
>
> He made it known that his situation, in spite of the lost ground, is good on the front, but he is pressed on both wings, especially the left. He believes that he can still hold on tomorrow, but he fears that his situation will not be as good and does not know what the day after tomorrow holds for him.
>
> He just asked me:
>
> 1. If it is to hold again tomorrow;
> 2. Which direction should he take in case of a possible withdrawal: Saint-Pol or Doullens?
>
> Saint-Pol seemed more difficult to him, his left wing being the most threatened and this direction distancing him from the main body without ensuring its connection with the 21st corps.
>
> As far as he is concerned, General de Castelnau persists in thinking that Doullens is preferable in the greater good, the situation today being the one feared by General de Castelnau the day before yesterday and explained to Captain Fétizon.
>
> According to the telegram which has just reached the headquarters of the 2nd Army, General de Maud'huy has ceased to be independent of the orders of General de Castelnau;[*] it is up to him to decide without his intervention, but before giving him back his independence, which releases his responsibility, General de Castelnau considers it his duty as a man of honor to transmit to the general headquarters a statement of the situation.

To this new call, I made answer by encrypted telegram:

> General Foch, designated as deputy to the commander-in-chief, was delegated to coordinate the actions of the 2nd Army, Maud'huy's army and General Brugère's group of territorial divisions. General Foch will be returning tomorrow morning, October 5, to the headquarters of the 2nd Army.

---

[*] We have seen above that General de Maud'huy's army detachment had been transformed into the 10th Army.

Chapter VI

And on my order, Lieutenant-Colonel Pont telephoned:

> Lieutenant-Colonel Pont informed General de Castelnau that a telegram following the one he had just received announced the arrival of a general officer who would be qualified to give General de Maud'huy useful instructions. It is decided that while awaiting the arrival of this general officer, General de Castelnau will order General de Maud'huy to hold again tomorrow.

On the 5th, the situation seemed to be stationary.

But on the 6th, the situation worsened again. Our troops engaged between the Oise and the plateaus east of Arras maintained their positions on the whole, but with difficulty; in the Roye area, they lost a whole series of villages; further north, some strongpoints were evacuated under the pretext that they were too far forward, or that the positions in the rear seemed more advantageous.

At 5 p.m., General Anthoine telephoned:

> 4th Corps yields more and more, and we are concerned about it. Everything is spent. The 2nd Army appeals to the general headquarters: it has the impression that the line is going to break down somewhere.
>
> 53rd Division only arrived in part this evening, but its men are in a sorry state, having become drunk at Compiègne.
>
> General Foch cannot be reached by the current communication as of yet. Encrypted telegram has been sent to general headquarters.

This message did not worry me too much. I was beginning to be sure of the state of affairs of the command of this army. Moreover, the information sent by Maud'huy's army showed that to the south and east of Arras, the enemy was unable to penetrate our positions; further north, the two divisions of the 21st Corps were respectively at Neuville-Saint-Waast and at Lens, linked by five cavalry divisions, and had made slight progress.

Also, I answered at 6:20 p.m. by encrypted telegram to general Anthoine's message:

> Situation is getting better and better in the north; must absolutely hold

on at all costs. Strengthen yourselves as much as possible on all your fronts. Act with all possible energy. We are working on ways to bring reinforcements.

And to Foch, at 6:40 p.m., the following message:

I have received the following message from the 2nd Army...: (see above). It seems to me absolutely necessary that you raise the morale of this army.

And in the evening (at 9 p.m.), back to the 2nd Army:

Ask General Gough, on behalf of the commander-in-chief of the French armies, to lend you his support momentarily. Marshal French is notified of this request.[*]
On the other hand, I request that the commander of the 6th Army give you, if it is possible, the support of a brigade. Arrange directly with him the conditions of transport.

On the morning of October 7, Marshal French ordered Gough and Allenby's cavalry divisions to lend their support to the 2nd Army until the arrival of the French reserve troops. The 6th Army, for its part, placed at the disposal of General de Castelnau the 138th brigade, which was transported by car to Compiègne.

The 53rd Reserve Division from the 5th Army had been directed on the 4th to the same position (it was to this division that General Anthoine had alluded in pessimistic terms in one of the messages I quoted above).

Finally, the 58th Reserve Division, taken from the 1st Army, deployed on the 8th in the Montdidier region and was immediately attached to the 2nd Army.

All these reinforcements succeeded in consolidating the front, which was henceforth to be substantially maintained between Oise and Somme.

This did not prevent the 2nd Army from telephoning on the

---

[*] We will see later that the English cavalry division of General Gough was at that moment moving overland behind the front of the 2nd Army.

7th, at 7 am:

> Nothing new this night. Fouquescourt has been evacuated as too far forward... No change in the north.

I then telegraphed to General Foch at 9:35 a.m:

> By telephone message, 2nd Army reports that Fouquescourt was evacuated last night as being too far forward. Please call the attention of the commander of the 2nd Army to the disadvantage of these rearward adjustments of the front which can give the enemy the impression of success and are likely to demoralize our troops. It is the third adjustment of this kind which has been carried out in the 2nd Army. I hope that it is the last. When one wants to adjust, one must do it by attacking forward.

In this crisis, the dangers of which I did not ignore, and on which I have only elaborated by letting the official documents speak for themselves, General de Castelnau showed once again that his tenacity and his will were not equal to the brilliance that I liked to recognize in him. Unfortunately, while at the Grand-Couronné his chief of staff Anthoine had preserved his composure and lucidity in the difficult hours, at Breteuil he lost these indispensable qualities. The reports that he sent me are proof of this.

I immediately resolved to change this. I called upon Colonel Duchêne, Chief of Staff of the 20th Corps, in whose energy and will I had great confidence, to replace him. I must say that Castelnau, who at the time had only reluctantly accepted this transfer, soon welcomed it. The day after it occurred, Major Fétizon went to Dury[*] where the 2nd Army had just moved its headquarters, and Castelnau confessed to him, "This is the first night for a long time that I have slept peacefully."

On the other hand, Foch, from his arrival, had closely supported my action. He had several rather stormy meetings with Castelnau. To tell the truth, the character of these two men was

---

[*] Near Amiens.

very different. At the beginning of the war, Foch was Castelnau's subordinate. And, during the operations of August, there had been quite violent tug-of-war between them; the mission that I had just entrusted to Foch in these first days of October, and which he fulfilled to my utter satisfaction, could only amplify the conflict.

Relief and Transport of the English Army

If I attached so much importance to the inviolability of my front between the Oise and Arras, it was because new tasks were demanding my attention. I want to speak of the problem that Marshal French had just created, by expressing the desire to see his army transported to the north, and of the critical situation in which the Belgian army found itself, which ran the risk every day of being captured in Antwerp or of being rejected on Dutch territory.

At the end of September, Marshal French expressed to me the desire to see his army corps relieved on the Aisne front and transported to the left wing of the French armies.

On the 29th he developed his point of view in a note addressed to me:

> Ever since our position in the French line was altered by the advance of General Maunoury's 6th Army to the River Ourcq, I have been anxious to regain my original position on the left flank of the French Armies. On several occasions I have thought of suggesting this move, but the strategical and tactical situation from day to day has made the proposal inopportune. Now, however, that the position of affairs has become clearly defined, and that the immediate future can be forecasted with some confidence, I wish to press the proposal with all the power and insistence which are at my disposal. The moment for the execution of such a move appears to me to be singularly opportune.
>
> In the first place, the position of my force on the right bank of the River Aisne has now been thoroughly well entrenched.
>
> In the second place, I have carefully reconnoitred an alternative position on the left bank of the River Aisne, and have had this position entrenched from end to end, and it is now ready for occupation.
>
> The strategical advantages of the proposed move are much

Chapter VI

greater. I am expecting to be reinforced by the 7th Division from England early next week.

Following closely on this reinforcement will come the 3rd Cavalry Division from home, and then the 8th Division from home, and simultaneously with this last reinforcement will come two Indian Divisions and an Indian Cavalry Division.

In other words my present force of six Divisions and two Cavalry Divisions will, within three or four weeks from now, be increased by four Divisions and two Cavalry Divisions, making a total British force of ten Divisions (five Corps) and four Cavalry Divisions.

All through the present campaign I have been much restricted both in initiative and in movement by the smallness of my Army in face of the enormous numbers of the enemy.

With an Army of five Corps and four Cavalry Divisions my freedom of action, field of operation and power of initiative will be increased out of all proportion to the numerical increase in Corps, more especially as almost half my total force will then consist of fresh troops and will be opposed by an enemy already much worn by the severity of the previous fighting.

Another reason of a strategical nature for changing my position in the line is the great advantage which my forces will gain by a shortened line of communication, an advantage which falls almost equally on your railways.

It appears to me, therefore, that both from strategical reasons and from tactical reasons it is desirable that the British Army should regain its position on the left of the line.

There remains the question of when this move should take place. I submit that *now* is the time.

We are all sedentary armies, and movements and changes are easily made. Once the forward movement has been commenced, it will be more difficult to pull out my Army from the line of advance, and a further delay in the transfer of my force from its present position will lead to great confusion both at the front and on the L. of C., and a great loss of power and efficiency in the coming campaign.

It is for these reasons that I advocate the transfer of my force from its present position to the extreme left of the line, and I advocate that the change should be made now.[*]

J. FRENCH.

---

[*] Sir John French, *1914*, p. 164-167.

The arguments of the Marshal developed in the note that we have just read were, from his point of view, irrefutable. For my part, I admitted the validity of them. Where our opinions differed, it was especially on the advisability of immediately making this change which would bring an enormous disturbance in the execution of my left wing maneuver. When Marshal French stated that we were "in a sedentary situation," this was true for the front of the British army and the French armies that flanked it, but he did not seem to fully appreciate the importance of the actions committed to the wings.

I sent a note to the English commander-in-chief on September 30, in which I explained in detail my point of view and the solution I was advocating:

G.Q.G   At G.Q.G., September 30, 1914.

STAFF   NOTE

3rd BUREAU   from General Joffre, Commander-in-Chief, to Marshal French, Commander of the British Army.

N° 8095

Marshal French was kind enough to draw the attention of the commander-in-chief to the particular interest he had in seeing the entire English army take back the position it had originally occupied on the left of the French armies.

Because of the ever-increasing numbers of English forces, this position would have the great advantage of relieving the French railroad service by reducing the length of the English line of communication, and above all of giving Marshal French's army a freedom of action and a performance far superior to that which it now possesses.

The increase in power that the English army will soon benefit from following the arrival of the 7th and 8th Divisions, a cavalry division, two Indian divisions and an Indian cavalry division, fully justifies the Marshal's request.

The commander-in-chief shares this view and is convinced that if this movement had been possible it would have been very advantageous for the allied armies. But, until now, the general situation has not allowed it to be carried out. Is it possible at this time to envisage its next realization?

His Excellency Marshal French considers that the moment is now particularly favorable to his project. Before the front of the British army, as well as before the front of the 6th, 9th and 4th armies, the situation is, so to speak, unchanged; for nearly a fortnight, the armies in the center have been clinging to the ground without any appreciable progress. But the commander-in-chief believes he must point out that the situation is far from being the same on the wings. In fact, on the right, the 3rd Army and part of the 1st Army had been fighting for several days in the Saint-Mihiel region, in a stubborn battle whose outcome was not in doubt, but whose results had not yet been felt. On the left, the 2nd Army, which today constitutes the extremity of the system, has been subjected for three days to furious attacks which show how much the enemy is interested in crushing our wing. Will this army always constitute the left of the French forces? One should not think so, since the fact that a fragment of an army was formed on the date of today will undoubtedly lead the commander-in-chief to create a new army there. The transport of forces required by the creation of this army, made up of elements taken from the front without creating gaps in our lines, will inevitably make our situation somewhat delicate for a few days: if the French command has considered the possibility of withdrawing a certain number of corps from the front without modifying the front, it has never considered transporting an entire army, the removal of which would create a vacuum that would be impossible to fill.

Since September 13, we have been in battle: it is important that during this period of crisis, which will have a considerable influence on the continuation of operations, everyone maintains his situation without thinking of modifying it, so as to be ready for any eventuality. Now, the movement foreseen by His Excellency Marshal French would necessarily entail some complications, not only in the situation of the troops, but also in that of the convoys; it could perhaps bring about a disturbance in the general disposition of our armies, the extent of which it is difficult to measure.

For the reasons set forth above, the Commander-in-Chief cannot agree with Marshal French's views as to the time at which this movement can be put into effect. On the other hand, it would seem that it could be initiated today by a number of arrangements detailed below:

1. The English army could operate like the French army: it is

today solidly entrenched in the positions it occupies. While maintaining the integrity of its front, it would undoubtedly be possible for it to recover a certain number of divisions (first of all a corps), which would gradually be transported to the left;

2. The British cavalry division is currently unused on the front line: it could, as the 11th, 10th Corps and 8th Cavalry Division did, be transported overland to the extreme left to serve as a link between the Belgian army and the French troops;

3. The 7th and 8th divisions, which will arrive soon, could be landed in the region of Dunkirk; they would then act in the direction of Lille. Their action would be immediately felt on the right flank of the German army, which is receiving new reinforcements every day. They would be reunited with the divisions withdrawn from the front;

4. The Indian divisions, as soon as they were in a condition to enter into operations, would join by rail the English contingent transported to the northern region and would constitute the nucleus to which the other English divisions would join as soon as it was possible to transport them;

5. As soon as the forward movement can be resumed, the front will be tightened: it would then be possible to make the English army halt for a while and to make it move backwards to transport it to the left of the line while the 6th and 5th armies would press one towards the other; the movement will be all the easier as the number of units remaining to be transported would be more reduced.

In summary, the commander-in-chief shares Marshal French's view of the advisability of having the entire English army on the left of the French armies: he cannot completely agree with him as to the time at which this movement will be put into effect.

The Commander-in-Chief would be grateful to His Excellency Marshal French to let him know if he shares his views on the above proposals.

Marshal French immediately accepted these proposals.

The 2nd British Corps, which occupied the center of the British front, was relieved on October 1st by the extension of the two corps that were surrounding it, and directed to Compiègne where it started on October 5th to embark for Abbeville-Étaples

On October 3, French, through General Wilson, conveyed to me the desire to see the entire English army follow the movement of the 2nd Corps.

Chapter VI

Agreement was reached on the following points:

The 69th reserve division (coming from the 5th Army) arrived on October 5th in the Soissons area at the disposal of General Maunoury, in order to relieve the British left corps (3rd).[*] This corps, relieved on the 6th and 7th, moved towards the Compiègne-Pont-Sainte-Maxence area, where it started its deployments on the 9th.[†] Gough and Allenby's cavalry divisions were to move by land. As for the 1st Corps, it would be relieved later, i.e. as soon as I had an available element to put it in its place.

But I drew Marshal French's attention to the following point: "Since the current maneuver requires a constant reinforcement of our left wing by withdrawals from the various parts of the front, and since the transport of the British army prevents any movement of French troops for nearly ten days, it is of capital interest for the continuation of the operations that all the movements carried out towards the north concur *immediately* to the same goal, the stopping of the German right wing and its outflanking." Consequently, I requested that the Marshal not wait to employ his transported elements until all his forces were united.

Marshal French accepted these proposals in a letter addressed to me on October 5.

But the same day, in spite of the established agreement, he asked that his last Army corps be relieved in the night of the 6th to the 7th. It was impossible for me to grant this request. Nevertheless, he came back to the demand again during the day of the 9th and the 10th of October.

I finally gave him satisfaction by having the 1st Corps relieved by a brigade of the 6th Army and by some elements of the 32nd

---

[*] In fact, the 69th Reserve Division was, at that moment, the only reserve of the 6th Army, which had, as we have seen above, placed all its available troops under the orders of General de Castelnau. The 3rd British Corps was relieved of its positions by the mixed Klein Brigade, which included the non-divisional elements of the 7th Corps, i.e. a total of eight battalions.

[†] It arrived in the region of Saint-Omer.

Division.*

I am obliged to say that the haste with which the English army was relieved on the Aisne had the effect, as I had announced, of interrupting almost completely for ten days the transport of French troops to the same theater of operations. The definitive loss of the rich region of Lille was due, in my opinion, to this maneuver that I had executed only with regret.

It had another consequence:

The three British corps had been relieved on the Aisne by two French divisions, one of them a reserve, and a mixed brigade of eight battalions. On October 30th, following a violent artillery preparation, the left brigade (137th), which was holding the Rougemaison plateau, was pushed back to the left bank of the Aisne by the Vailly and Chavonne bridges, where some enemy units even managed to slip through. On November 2nd, also following a powerful preparation by artillery fire, the 138th Brigade, which held the right of this new sector, and which had been able to hold its positions on October 3rd, was attacked and pushed back from the Cour-Soupir plateau into the Aisne valley.

The Siege of Antwerp and the Exit of the Belgian Army

The Germans had begun the siege of Antwerp on September 30.

Because of the importance that the Belgian staff attached to this place, which was reduced to the defense of the kingdom, an importance that was increased tenfold by the fact that the government and all the active forces of our allies were now gathered there, the government of King Albert "begged" the French government to take into consideration the services that Belgium had rendered to the cause of the Allies, and asked for help and protection.

I had not waited for this moving appeal from our loyal allies to do everything I could on their behalf.

---

* The 1st British Army Corps finished its deployment in the Hazebrouck area on October 18th.

Chapter VI

On September 26th, General Brugère's group of territorial divisions, which was heading for Bapaume, together with Conneau's cavalry corps, was in contact with elements of the detachment of the Dunkirk garrison, consisting of six battalions, two batteries and a squadron, which occupied Douai, Orchies and Tournai.

The governor of Dunkirk was ordered to try to establish contact on the upper Scheldt, even by simple patrols with the Belgian cavalry which, starting from Ghent, went up the valley of the Dender, in the direction of Valensiennes.

On 27 September, the link was established between the Dunkirk detachment and the Belgian cavalry.

It is at this moment, as I said above, that I wrote to Mr. Millerand, Minister of War, to point out to him the advantage of "an energetic action of the Belgian army on the communications of the enemy." To facilitate this operation, I ordered the governor of Dunkirk "to send light detachments in the direction of Ghent, transported by car or by rail... and to announce in Belgium the imminent arrival in the region of important Anglo-French forces." With the same aim, the garrison of Dunkirk was reinforced by the arrival of a brigade of marine fusiliers, which embarked by rail in Paris on October 7, and by the 89th territorial division, which was transported on October 8 from Versailles to Cherbourg, where it embarked.

But it was not my intention to go with an army to the aid of our allies, as the Belgian staff and government urged.

I have said how difficult our own situation was in the first days of October: Castelnau's army clinging to its entire front, and its leader expecting from one moment to the next to see his line broken somewhere, Maud'huy's army giving up ground in places, and its leader having the impression that instead of enveloping the enemy, it was he who was enveloped.

On October 1st and 2nd, I exchanged numerous telegrams with Bordeaux to explain my ideas. In my opinion, it was impossible to distract French troops from the general action underway, 150 kilometers as the crow flies from my left. The sending of a territorial division to Antwerp would have a more moral than material effect. It seemed to me indispensable that the Belgian field army leave the place, that immediate measures be taken for the evacuation of the transportable material and the disabling of the rest. Anglo-French forces were being formed in the northern region that would act in liaison with the Belgians, and provide security for their flank should they decide to retreat to Bruges and Ostend. Once this arrangement was in place, the Belgian army would be on the wing of the Allied armies, and in close contact with them.

In the same vein, I opposed with all my might the idea that the English reinforcements arriving on the continent should go to Antwerp. Without wishing to imply (as Marshal French thought) that Lord Kitchener wanted to create the embryo of a new English army that would have escaped the authority of the Commander-in-Chief of the British Expeditionary Forces, I found it dangerous that Allied troops should go astray in a divergent theater of operations, when their place was in the battle that was growing every day in Flanders.

This is what I explained in a telegram to the Minister of War, dated October 2, 1914, (5:40 p.m.):

> Response to encrypted telegram 745.
>
> You confirm telegrams 203, 332 and 353, October 1 and 2. General situation and maneuver in progress do not allow at present to divert active division to Antwerp. As already said, territorial division landed Ostend will be only useful from the moral point of view. Place Antwerp can be defended only by its garrison.
>
> I see a serious disadvantage to adding to this garrison the entire Belgian field army and an English division, on the contrary a serious advantage to gather all these troops away from the place. The territorial division of Le Havre and the fusiliers marines brigade of Paris could be transported by sea to Calais or Dunkirk, and from there by rail, the fusiliers marines to Antwerp, and the territorial division to Ostend.
>
> I also insist particularly on the interest of not transporting the 7th English division to Antwerp. Have asked in agreement with Marshal French that 7th and 8th Divisions be directed to Boulogne from where they would be transported to the north as well as the English forces withdrawn from the front.
>
> Moreover, the maneuver in progress which includes the meeting of important forces in the Courtrai-Lille-Hazebrouck area is the best help we can bring to the Belgian army. From there, we will enter in

liaison with it towards Ghent.

Will see only advantages to sending general Pau on mission through my headquarters.

On October 5, General Pau left on a mission to the Belgian government with my instructions in which I said:

> He is qualified to give to the superior command of the Belgian armies all the necessary information to ensure a cooperation, as complete as possible, of the Belgian and French armies.
>
> In particular, the Belgian forces exiting Antwerp will have to receive all the information allowing them to continue their efforts towards the southwest of the position with the allied forces.*

Unfortunately, my plan, based only on the military possibilities of the moment, was shared neither by the Belgians nor by the English.

The former were very reluctant to move away from Antwerp, which General Brialmont had made the core of Belgium's defense. History – ours, in particular – shows, however, by what disasters the operations of an army riveted to a stronghold result.

For the English, it is a traditional dogma not to allow Antwerp to be in the hands of a great continental power. It is nevertheless surprising that the government, the War Office and the Admiralty assumed with such stubborn unanimity that, in the situation in which we found ourselves, we could save the place and the Belgian army by sending directly to their rescue the feeble means which we and the British Empire had at our disposal at that moment.

As early as September 7th, Mr. Winston Churchill, First Lord of the Admiralty, had addressed a memorandum to his Prime Minister, Sir E. Grey and Lord Kitchener, in which he insisted on the importance of Antwerp, particularly from a naval point of view:

> The Admiralty view the sustained and effective defence of Antwerp as a matter of high consequence. It preserves the life of the Belgian

---

* Mission order of October 5th, 1914.

nation: it safeguards a strategic point which, if captured, would be of the utmost menace.*

On October 2nd, Lord Kitchener wrote to Sir John French:

> The German attempt to besiege Antwerp has created a very serious situation. There is a danger of Antwerp falling before very long.
>
> We are informing the French Government that, if Joffre cannot launch a decisive action in France within three or four days, we cannot hope that Antwerp will hold out, unless he is able to send some regular troops there to co-operate with all those we can despatch, that is to say, the 7th Division and a cavalry division.
>
> If you leave your present positions, would it be possible to suggest to Joffre that, if he can send some troops, you would rejoin the 7th Division and all the other troops which we are able to send from here, with such part of the force now under your orders in France as might be judged necessary for saving Antwerp? In the meantime, the remainder would continue the move to the new positions.†

It is probably not rash to believe that this telegram contributed to increasing the desire manifested by Sir John French to see me liberate, as I have related above, his army from the position of the Aisne.

On the same day, Sir E. Grey stated the same thesis, in almost identical terms, in a telegram addressed to the English ambassador in Bordeaux:

> Unless the main situation in France can be decided favourably in a short time, which would enable us to relieve Antwerp by detaching a proper force, it is most desirable that General Joffre should make an effort and send regular troops to region of Dunkirk, from which post they could operate in conjunction with our reinforcements to relieve Antwerp.

---

* Winston Churchill, *The World Crisis Vol. I*, 1938 edition, p. 299.

† Translator's note: In the absence of a more direct source on hand for the English version of this document, I have reproduced Mott's version in his original translation, page 307.

Chapter VI

We can send some first-line troops, but not sufficient by themselves to raise the siege of Antwerp, and we cannot send them to co-operate with any but French regulars.

If General Joffre can bring about a decisively favourable action in France in two or three days the relief of Antwerp may be made the outcome of that, but if not, unless he now sends some regular troops the loss of Antwerp must be contemplated.*

To send significant forces to the aid of Antwerp, as would have been necessary to obtain decisive results, was not in my power, because of the number of enemy forces that we had on our hands, and of the difficult maneuver that I was carrying out at this moment. As for sending to our allies "a few regular troops" as the War Office and the English Foreign Secretary had suggest to me, it seemed to me not only useless, but dangerous, because it would have been a temptation for the Belgians to prolong a situation that I was trying to change.

One point is worth noting:

Colonel Dallas, whom Marshal Kitchener had sent to Antwerp on 29 September, announced that the German siege army consisted of the IIIrd Reserve Corps, a marine infantry division, an ersatz division, a landsturm brigade, two engineer regiments, a siege artillery regiment, i.e. about 90,000 men, to which were added on the part of the Belgian military government a landwehr brigade and some landsturm elements. On the other hand, the Belgian field army numbered 80,000 men, to which were added 70,000 men who constituted the garrison of the forts. If we take these figures as accurate, we are led to note once again that an army that has locked itself into the perimeter of a fortified place no longer plays a role that is suited to its numbers.

In any case, the English had directed 8,000 "Marines" to Antwerp. Then, to judge the situation on the spot, they sent the first lord of the Admiralty. Mr. Winston Churchill, who upon arriving offered to take command of the British forces operating in Antwerp. This proposal was not accepted by the government in London. But Mr. Churchill says in his book that he, by his personal

---

* Churchill, *The World Crisis, Vol. I*, 1938 edition, p. 304-305.

action, delayed the fall of Antwerp by five days. Perhaps he also delayed the departure of the Belgian army, whose retreat to the Yser was made more difficult by this.

As for the brigade of French fusiliers, which had for a moment had been considered to be pushed on to Antwerp, it was stopped by General Pau as it passed through Ghent.

General Rawlinson, who commanded the British forces stationed in Ostend and Zeebrugge (7th Division and 3rd Cavalry Division) set up his headquarters in Bruges.

Antwerp succumbed on October 9.

On the 11th, the Belgian army, whose exit had been slowed down by hesitations and counter-orders, arrived in the Ostend-Nieuport-Dixmude-Thourout area. Its retreat had been covered by General Rawlinson's troops and the French marine brigade.

Thus, on the left wing of the Allied Western Front, in mid-October 1914, the Belgian army, French troops, and the entire British expeditionary force were now united. This new situation, which in itself had undeniable advantages, required an authority to direct the efforts of the Allied forces towards a common goal.

As far as the English leadership is concerned, although there was nothing changed in the form of my relations with them, I said that the victory of the Marne had created an atmosphere of confidence between the English commander-in-chief and me that never wavered. I will say later what service I had the opportunity to render to Marshal French, and how his esteem for me increased. Moreover, General Foch, who represented me in Flanders, was able to ensure a fruitful liaison with our British allies by his energy, by his communicative spirit, by his tact, by the personal relations which united him to General Wilson, deputy chief of staff of the English army.

Vis-à-vis the Belgian army that King Albert commanded in person, my situation did not fail at first to be rather delicate. The difficulties were smoothed out thanks to the magnanimous selflessness of the king. It was agreed that the Belgian army would remain on its territory under the command of His Majesty who agreed to receive my directives in the same way as the English army.

While respecting the freedom of the Belgian army, I estimated

Chapter VI 435

that it was necessary to give it a vigorous impetus. I was informed of the sad state in which it was. The retreat from Antwerp had subjected it to a severe ordeal, during which it had had the impression of being abandoned by its allies, which was certainly not our intention. It was necessary to overcome this situation as quickly as possible and to put the Belgian army in a position to cooperate in the maneuver against the German right wing. This maneuver, by the influx of allied forces in Flanders, was going to take on a new magnitude, but it was also going to, by the entry in line of new German forces,* be bristling with new difficulties.

On October 16th, General Pau came to report to me on his mission. The Belgian army seemed to him momentarily incapable of any effort. He did not hide his impression that even if the men showed calmness, courage and endurance, the cadres presented deficiencies as always happens to armies which have just experienced a long period of peace. Now, Belgium had been at peace with her neighbors since her birth, and in this happy and rich country, almost nobody believed in war before August 1914.

All the information which arrived to me had, before the return of General Pau, confirmed me in the impression that it was necessary to act without delay to help our unfortunate allies to overcome this crisis. To establish with them a solid and durable liaison, I decided to detach to the Belgian general staff a mission placed under the orders of Colonel Brécart.

Colonel Brécart left without delay. On October 17th he returned from Furnes to report to me on his installation and his first contacts with the Belgian command. He too reported impressions that corroborated those of General Pau. But the Belgians were already pulling themselves together.

For his part, General Foch went, without delay, to make contact with the Belgian army. Accompanied by Colonel Brécart, he was received by the king on October 16. Foch was moved and saddened by the state in which he had just found the allied army. The king, forced to withdraw with his army and his family to the

---

* We know that the enemy threw into the battle of Flanders, in addition to the forces he brought back from the other parts of the front, newly formed corps and the troops that the fall of Antwerp had just made available.

only part of Belgium that was not in the hands of the enemy, bore the marks on his face of the anguish he had just suffered and the worries that the future seemed to hold for him. In the course of the conversation, Foch tried to show King Albert the hopes that should sustain us and unite us during the terrible trials that we would still have to endure.

While trying to cooperate in the restoration of the Belgian army, I was concerned with supporting it solidly. What I considered essential was that the Yser line be maintained at all costs.

To this end, I decided to organize a group under the command of General d'Urbal, with a group of territorial divisions, all the cavalry, the garrison of Dunkirk and all the reinforcements that I would send later.[*]

In the same vein, I had telegraphed to Lord Kitchener on October 16th: "Now that the Operations extend to the North Sea coast between Ostend and the forward defenses of Antwerp, it would be important for the two Allied navies to participate in this operation by protecting our left wing, and by acting with long-range guns on the German right wing. The commander of the naval forces would therefore act in liaison with General Foch through the governor of Dunkirk."

And Mr. Winston Churchill, who quotes this telegram in his book, *The World Crisis*, adds:

"This duty we instantly accepted."[†]

Then, as soon as it was possible, I decided to go in person to King Albert and his army. The services rendered by the Belgians to the common cause and the hard trials they had just endured made them doubly worthy of our interest and affection.

On October 19th, I paid a short visit to General Sarrail in Verdun; on my way back, I stopped in Châlons with General de Langle, commander of the 4th Army.

On the 20th, in the evening, I left by rail for Amiens. On the

---

[*] This group, named Belgian Army Detachment on October 20th, was transformed into the 8th Army on November 16th, 1914.

[†] Churchill, *The World Crisis, Vol. I*, 1938 edition, p. 331.

Chapter VI 437

morning of the 21st, I found General Foch waiting for me. As usual, he was full of energy and life. We left together for Gagny, headquarters of the 2nd Army. I had a brief talk with General de Castelnau, whose positions were now stabilized. I then passed through Doullens, headquarters of General Foch and General Brugère's group of territorial divisions. At Saint-Pol, where I stopped afterwards, I saw General de Maud'huy at his headquarters, where General d'Urbal, who had just taken command of the Northern Group, and General Conneau were also present. I then made a short visit to Marshal French at his headquarters in Saint-Omer.[*] Finally, via Dunkirk, I arrived in Furnes around 4 pm. I was immediately received by the king at the Hôtel de Ville. The calm physiognomy of the sovereign reflected an inexpressible sadness. I expressed to him my satisfaction to see his army come out of the dangerous isolation in which the events had placed it during the first months of the war, and I affirmed to him my conviction that the victory would come to crown our efforts and would reward the immense sacrifices supported for the common cause by Belgium.

As I was leaving City Hall, at the end of my visit, a moving incident occurred that deserves to be reported here:

The day before, the glorious 42nd Division, commanded by that admirable soldier, General Grossetti, had arrived in Dunkirk and had driven the 16th Battalion of chasseurs to Furnes. The arrival of this beautiful troop, alert and disciplined, in the city, at nightfall, had produced a very comforting impression on the Belgians. While leaving with the king of the City hall as I have just said, Colonel Brécart informed me that the 16th battalion of chasseurs was gathered in the vicinity for an inspection. I immediately gave him the order to parade in front of His Majesty. The passage of this splendid troop, hardened by three months of campaign, was a magnificent spectacle: it seemed that the chasseurs, guessing my intentions, wanted to show to the king of the Belgians the resolution and the ardor of which the whole of

---

[*] As I entered Saint-Omer, I came across some magnificent units of the Indian Corps that were arriving.

France was animated. The Belgians, who do not usually show their feelings noisily, let their enthusiasm burst, and King Albert seemed to me suddenly all warmed by this scene whose poignancy I still feel today.

At 5 pm, I took leave of the king.

I had dinner in Calais where I was received by Mr. Sartiaux, chief engineer of the Compagnie du Nord. To the words that he addressed to me at the end of the dinner, I answered by a tribute to the magnificent effort that the railroads had accomplished since the beginning of the war. The staff of the Compagnie du Nord, in particular, was doing a prodigious job at the moment. It is only fair to repeat here once again the gratitude that France owes to her railroads in the many crises she has gone through during this war.

The same evening, I got back on my train. On the 22nd in the morning, I found my cars in Creil and I returned to Romilly.

On October 12th, a general offensive was planned for the following day.

The 10th French army had to march by its left on Lille.

The English army, on its right, would pass north of Lille and march on Tournai, while its left would follow the Bailleul-Courtrai axis, supported by the Rawlinson corps.

The Belgian army, supported on its right by the French marine brigade, had to face the German forces arriving from Antwerp via Ghent.

The entry in line of fresh German troops (newly created corps and the siege corps of Antwerp) did not allow hope that this offensive could obtain decisive results. However, if executed with vigor, it would have allowed us to inflict a serious defeat to the enemy right, to reoccupy Lille, and to preserve from German occupation a larger part of the French and Belgian territories.

Unfortunately, this was not the case. I have already indicated the causes:

The 3rd British Corps, which had reached the Eecke-Pradelles front (northeast of Hazebrouck) on October 12th, was only engaged on the 20th, after the completion of the transports of the 1st Corps and the Lahore Division. During these eight days, the 2nd Corps remained alone in the region of La Bassée.

Chapter VI

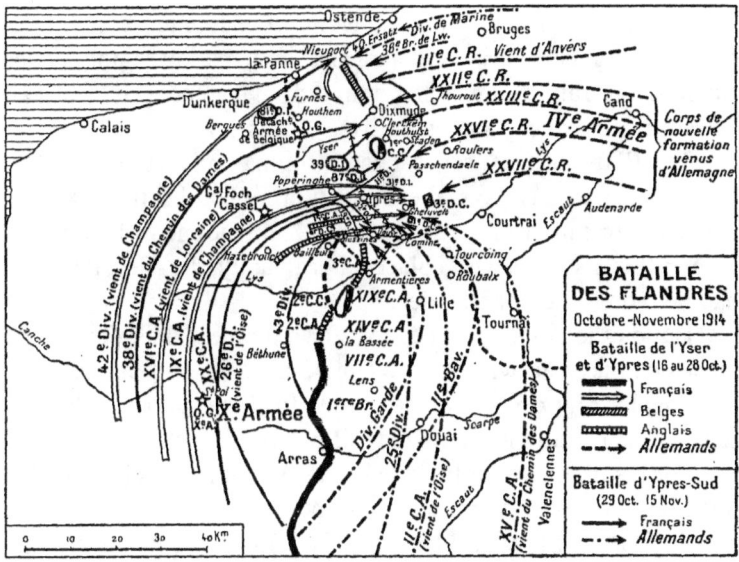

The state in which the Belgian army had joined us did not allow it to make the efforts required by the tense situation in which we were.

Finally, on the French side, the troops engaged in the north were of a very diverse nature. Alongside excellent active corps and elite units, there were cavalry divisions that were perfectly recruited and trained, but whose performance in foot combat was poor, mainly because of their armament,* and territorial divisions that were sometimes rather poorly trained.

On the other hand, from mid-October the Germans launched two strong attacks in the northern region.

The first was led by the Prince of Wurtemberg, who had previously commanded the IVth Army in Champagne. It aimed at forcing the Yser and putting the Belgians out of action.

The second and more powerful one was led by the Kronprinz of Bavaria, who had until then commanded the VIth Army in Lorraine.

---

* It should be remembered in particular that the cavalry had no bayonets. Some dragoon regiments carried their lances into the trenches.

It was, in short, an immense battle of encounter, which took place with diverse variations, in a flat, low, muddy region, under a continuous rain, and which required from the engaged troops an extraordinary energy and an untiring constancy.

The Battle of the Yser reached its climax on October 26th.

In the previous days, the Belgian army had been weakened, which became more pronounced on the 25th; the enemy had started to cross the Yser in several places. Fortunately, the 42nd Division had held on to Lombaertzyde.

But on the 26th, our allies lost for a moment the railway line on which they had withdrawn. The 42nd Division reinforced by two cavalry regiments, and the marine fusiliers supported by two Senegalese battalions, clung to their positions.

For his part, Grossetti made it known that he was holding his positions firmly, and that he would be on the railroad track that evening, no matter what. He kept his word. History has already immortalized Grossetti sitting on a chair in the middle of a bullet-ridden crossroads, from where he directed the battle of his division with admirable calm. This man was, on that day, the center of crystallization of the resistance.

The evening fell without the enemy having made any significant progress. The Belgians were radiant. The catastrophe was averted.

On the 27th, the order was given to flood the area between the Yser and the railroad. On the 26th, the flooding developed, and on the 29th, the Germans were forced to withdraw part of the troops that had started to advance beyond the railroad. Thus relieved, the French troops were able to resume the offensive and, on October 30th, Ramscapelle, which had been lost by a Belgian detachment, was brilliantly recaptured by elements of the 42nd Division, who took many prisoners.

On November 1 and 2, the Germans were forced to retreat to the right bank of the river, leaving many wounded and much equipment mired in the flooded land.

In the following days, the German attack gradually decreased in violence, and then, after a few jolts, stopped.

The Germans, in this offensive along the coast, had entirely failed: they had neither succeeded in reaching Calais, nor in putting out of action the Belgians who remained clinging to their soil.

Meanwhile, the battle of Ypres was raging.

On October 16th and the following days the offensive of the Allied forces progressed at first, although rather slowly.

But soon the entry in line of fresh German troops represented by newly formed corps stopped our advance, and I had to immediately send reinforcements to General Foch, to allow him to support this new shock.

On October 20th, I placed at his disposal the 9th Cavalry Division and the 31st Division of the 16th Corps, which I had placed in general reserve at Compiègne. Almost immediately afterwards, I sent the brigade of Senegalese riflemen to the north. I have already said that it was at this time that I formed, under the orders of General d'Urbal, the "Belgian Army Detachment," which included, at the beginning, the 42nd Division, the brigade of marine fusiliers, the 87th and 89th territorial divisions, the cavalry corps of Mitry (4th, 5th, 6th and 7th Cavalry Divisions), the 9th Corps and the 9th Cavalry Division.

Then, in the following days, General Foch received 16 regiments of cavalry from corps temporarily taken from our right and center.

On October 25th, despite the importance of the reinforcements sent to the north, I had to note that our offensive was turning into a defensive one. The increasing violence of the German attacks forced Foch to engage in battle the troops he received as they landed. The Germans were overexcited by the presence of the Emperor, by the idea that they were making "the decisive effort against the French left wing" and because they were told that they were thus going to "decide the fate of the great battle that had been going on for weeks."[*]

So, in the following days, I continued to bring in new reinforcements to the north.

On October 27th, Foch received two units of the corps artillery of the 6th Corps, immediately followed by the 38th Division and the headquarters of the 32nd Corps that I had just formed under the

---

[*] Proclamation of the Kronprinz of Bavaria.

orders of General Humbert.*

The same day, I placed at the disposal of General Foch the 32nd Division and the E. N. E.† of the 16th Corps. (This corps was formed in the north).‡

On the 28th, I gave the order to the 2nd Army to withdraw the 20th Army Corps from the front and to place it in general reserve, ready to be removed at the first signal.

The situation seemed to get worse in the following days.

On October 31st, the enemy effort intensified in the region of Messines, which the British lost, but which they immediately recaptured. On November 1st, the attacks were renewed with a new violence. The English lost Messines again, but the situation improved again the next day.

These costly and fruitless shocks that the enemy was putting on our front showed that the battle had reached a period of balance. And it was to be feared that the German command, realizing the vanity of its efforts, would seek, by a sudden attempt on another part of the front, to mask and repair the failure it had just suffered. Railroad embarkations reported at Ostend and Thourout, an unusual activity on the front of the 1st, 5th and 6th armies confirmed my intuition.

Also, on November 4th, I addressed a letter to General Foch in which I pointed out to him the advantage of "reforming the army reserves, all of which have been directed towards the north, so as to be able to stop, if possible, enemy attempts as soon as they occur, until the day when the situation of our ammunition will allow us to take the offensive energetically in suitably chosen regions."

In the following days, General Foch's operations were mainly aimed at consolidating the situation around Ypres. Nevertheless, on the 6th, the German attacks redoubled in violence north and

---

* The 42nd Division was part of this new army corps.

† E. N. E. elements not in divisions.

‡ We have seen above that the other division of this corps, the 31st, had been sent on October 20th to Flanders.

Chapter VI

south of Ypres. Foch had to engage the 39th Division of the 20th Corps that I had placed at his disposal. By telegram of the same day (at 11:30 a.m.), I authorized him to use the remainder of the 20th Corps that I had placed in reserve at Aubigny, but I ordered that he "use these reserves only in case of absolute necessity and to ensure at all costs the inviolability of the front in the region of Ypres."

On November 10th, although there had been a lull in the previous days, I decided to bring large reinforcements to the north as a matter of urgency, drawing on the special reserves of the various armies, which were left with only what was strictly necessary to ensure the inviolability of their front.

These reinforcements, which represented, in total, two infantry brigades, ten battalions of chasseurs, and a complete infantry division* were no longer intended to fuel the battle. They represented the *last reserves* that I could take from the armies. The purpose of sending them to the north was:

1. To allow the command to put back in order those units for which the very nature of the battle had broken all bonds;

2. To relieve troops who were in urgent need of rest, and, at the same time, to reduce the congestion of this part of the front and to reconstitute reserves for the other armies.

As I had predicted, the German attacks from November 12 onwards became increasingly rare and less violent. Then they stopped, and calm was established for a while on this front. The Germans gave up on going to Calais.

While this final phase of the battle of Flanders was taking place, I had to go to the north once again.

On October 30, the President of the Republic had expressed the desire to go on a tour in this region. If I had been able, I would have gladly postponed this trip; in fact, this presidential trip, in which I had to take part, was going to occupy me for several days,

---

* Six battalions of chasseurs and an infantry brigade soon followed by the rest of the 26th Division (coming from the 2nd Army): four battalions of chasseurs coming from the 1st and 3rd armies; a Moroccan brigade coming from the 5th Army; an active brigade of the 44th Division, taken from the 1st Army.

at a time when hours were precious. However, under the circumstances, I could not put prevent it.*

So I left on Sunday, November 1st, at 7:15 a.m. for Amiens. I arrived there at noon, and found President Poincaré, who kept me for lunch with Messrs Millerand and Ribot, the prefect of the Somme, General Fraysse and the director of the Sûreté. We left at 1 p.m. for Dunkirk, where we found Lord Kitchener, Mr. de Brocqueville, General Foch and Mr. Cambon. We had a short conference with these people during which President Poincaré affirmed the will of the French government to lead the struggle to victory, whatever the cost, but he insisted to Lord Kitchener that England should not delay too long the promised reinforcements.

During the dinner that followed, I remember that I had the opportunity to talk about our soldier, his courage, his good humor and his patience. This last virtue was not exactly the hallmark of our people. And yet our men, after three months of uninterrupted struggle in which they had never shown the slightest trace of moral depression, had just proved that anything could be asked of them. Mr. de Brûcqueville added to what I had just said. He declared that since he had been living among our soldiers, nothing seemed impossible to him from them. I interrupted him sharply to say: "Yes, on the condition that we give them capable leaders who deserve their confidence" and I spoke of the many changes I had been obliged to make in the command, many of which had been cruel to my heart, but which I had executed without hesitation. And I declared that it was my intention to continue this purification of

---

* A few days before, I had sent a certain number of crosses of the Legion of Honor and military medals to King Albert.

The king had answered me by hand on October 28:

My dear general,
    I thank you very much for the distinctions you have kindly placed at my disposal to be given to those who have shown themselves most worthy in the defense of the Yser.
    Your gracious thought so delicately expressed delights me as much as it honors my army.
    Believe my dear general, in the sincere devotion of your affectionate,
                        ALBERT.

our cadres without wavering.

The next day, November 2, the president and I left to greet the King and Queen of the Belgians. The king came to meet us. We arrived at La Panne, where the royal family had settled, to mark its will not to leave the Belgian soil. After having greeted the queen, I solemnly affirmed to her that we would sooner or later put the Germans out of Belgium. From the way in which Her Majesty seemed to listen to the words of hope that I said to her, I felt how much her courageous soul needed to believe in them, and how much she was comforted by them in the hours of unspeakable sadness that she was going through.

We then went to Furnes where the King and the President reviewed two squadrons of the 6th Hussars and two Belgian squadrons. Then at half past nine, accompanied by the king to the border, we left for Cassel where we had lunch with General Foch. In the afternoon, after having visited General d'Urbal, to whom the President gave the necktie of the Legion of Honor, we went to Amiens. There, I took leave of Mr. Poincaré, and returned to my headquarters.

This battle of Flanders was a hard test for the army and for me. If we succeeded in blocking the enemy's route to the sea, I must say that I had hoped for more. In particular, I deeply regretted seeing the front stabilize west of Lille, whose immense resources fell to the enemy for four years. I cannot end this passage of my memories without paying a new tribute to our soldiers who led this hard autumn campaign, and to the leader who commanded them. General Foch, whose difficult conditions I mentioned when I sent him to represent me in this operation, showed rare military virtues and an admirable talent for diplomacy. I have recalled what a beneficial effect he had on our allies, and particularly on the British, by his tact, his enthusiasm, his clear-sighted and communicative will.

It is undoubtedly the place to say here the service that I had the occasion to render to Marshal French, a service of which I would not be proud if it did not aim at confirming that solid bonds of affection and esteem had been established between the English commander-in-chief and me.

General Joffre and General Foch leaving the Hotel du Sauvage in Cassel

Chapter VI

It was no secret that there was frequent friction between Lord Kitchener and Sir John French. At the beginning of November 1914, Kitchener, as I said above, came to France. Among other matters that he proposed to settle, he arrived with the project of replacing Marshal French at the head of the British army by General Sir Ian Hamilton. As soon as I heard of this threat to French, I made an urgent approach to Kitchener during the Dunkirk meeting, which I have described above, to remove him, and I had the satisfaction of succeeding. A few days later, I received a letter from Foch, from which I think it is interesting to quote some passages.

> Cassel, November 9th, 1914
>
> General,
>
> I told General Wilson a few days ago the object of Lord Kitchener's visit to Dunkirk, the plan to replace Marshal French with General Ian Hamilton; I added that it was at your very emphatic request that the plan was stopped. I had this fact from an authorized source.
>
> Wilson notified the Marshal. He connected the news with other clues, and came to thank me wholeheartedly for the communication.
>
> He intends to go without delay to express his gratitude to you. I warn you of this, after advising him to wait until events give us more freedom.
>
> [...]
>
> I write you *currente calamo*[*] a number of questions that come to my mind. Perhaps I will request to go and talk to you in a few days, when things will be settled here. For the moment, the length of the journey holds me back. There is work to be done here, but we must look to the future, which may be near.
>
> We're doing everything we can to consolidate our units, rebuild our resources. This is my constant concern. Today, I had to commit a regiment of the 11th Division. But I believe I will have the equivalent of this division available tomorrow, if necessary.
>
> [...]
>
> Believe, my general, in my deepest respect.
>
> FOCH.

---

[*] "Running the pen."

Chapter VI

At that time I made various changes in my staff.

General Berthelot, whose brilliant services I have recalled several times in the preceding pages, was given the command of a group of reserve divisions.

I replaced him as Assistant General Staff by General Nudant, Chief of Staff of the 4th Army, who was himself replaced in his functions by Lieutenant-Colonel Paquette.

On November 28th, the great headquarters moved to Chantilly. The staff moved to the Hôtel du Grand Condé, where the numerous services that the necessities of the hour obliged me to establish could be accommodated. Personally, I was lodged in a villa belonging to Mr. Poiret.

It was about this time, during a tour in the east, that I made contact for the first time (November 24th) in Thann, with the population of Alsace. "We have been waiting for you for forty-four years!" said one of the delegates.

The welcome I received from these Alsatians, whose loyalty had not been shaken by half a century of captivity, left me with a memory that I have not forgotten.

Looking back at my memories of the end of 1914, I remember the impressions that dominated my mind at that time.

The victory of the Marne and the hard campaign of two months which had followed it, had stopped the most formidable invasion of which France, which had seen so much, had ever suffered until then; it had forced it to retreat, had nailed it to the ground, while leaving in the hands of the enemy, for a time whose duration we could not estimate, a rich portion of our territory: Lille, most of our northern coal basin, the entire metallurgical basin of Briey-Longwy, not to mention the great cities which, on the edge of the front, remained vulnerable to attack, Dunkirk, Arras, Amiens, Reims, Nancy.

It is to the Allies of 1814 and 1815 who disemboweled our northeastern border, and to the German victories of 1870 that we owe this situation in part, especially because nature has placed almost all our mineral wealth – so to speak – on the border.

But the fact remained that at the end of the year 1914, the Germans, whose plan was based on a lightning defeat of the French

General Joffre at his desk at G.Q.G. in Chantilly

armies, had just lost all hope of winning the war. I already had the clear impression of this. The memoirs of the German men of war, Hindenburg, Tirpitz, Falkenhayn, Ludendorff, later made the more or less explicit admission.

But it was not enough to prevent the Germans from winning the war. We had to obtain a complete victory, to reconquer the north of France, Belgium, and our beloved provinces of Alsace and Lorraine.

Here, a frightening problem lay before me.

For lack of anything better, the Germans buried themselves in front of us in a defensive system that was becoming more and more perfect every day. We had to attack this immense fortress, to drive the enemy back into the open country, and to impose our will on him. A terrible war was born to which we had to adapt as soon as possible. The creation of a powerful artillery equipment was necessary, equipped with ammunition stocks the size of which the imagination recoiled before. In this respect, we know where we started from. The modest ammunition program that I had requested from the Minister at a time when I hoped to drive the enemy out of our country by a maneuver executed on his right wing, proved to be overdue. On November 17th, Major Herbillon,[*] arriving from Bordeaux, informed me that the Minister was not able to keep any of the promises concerning the manufacture of munitions and that we would have to wait more than a month before having what I was counting on for the beginning of November. This delay could not be attributed to Mr. Millerand, whose energy was like that of the industrialists he had called upon. But to start a production as difficult as that which the events required, it was necessary to have machines, ore, coal, and workers. The machines were to be made, the ore and coal were now on the other side of the wire, and the workers were mobilized.

The Russians, of whom I have spoken up to now only to recall the immense service they rendered us at the time of the Marne, were beginning to make their weight felt in the operations.

On November 6th I had received a telegram from Grand Duke Nicholas Nicolaievich announcing a great victory over the Austrians who seemed to be in full rout. The generalissimo of the Russian armies thought of sending immediately in the high valley of the Theiss a dozen infantry divisions which would threaten Buda-Pesth. As for the Germans, they also seemed to be in full retreat west of Warsaw. This news gave me hope, for I had reason to think that as Russian pressure increased, the Germans would be forced to send forces to their eastern theater of operations, which would make my own task easier.

---

[*] Major Herbillon was the liaison between the Minister of War and the G.Q.G.

Chapter VI

But on the 17th, the Germans announced by radio a great victory over the Russians. And this contradictory news panicked poor Colonel Ignatief, liaison officer of the Russian G.H.Q. with me. When the information became clearer, this failure seemed to be localized to the region of Thorn; in East Prussia and in the Carpathians our allies continued to advance. From these fluctuations of the battle, it appeared above all that the Russians did not possess, either in terms of staff or in terms of armament, sufficient means to stand up to the Germans, but they had a clear superiority, both material and moral, over the Austro-Hungarians who, in three months, had just added a fairly long sequence to the already long list of defeats suffered in the course of history by the armies of the double monarchy.

As for the Serbs, after a victory in August in the mountainous area of the Tser, which had at once liberated their territory, they had seen a new Austro-Hungarian army penetrate their territory in September. Seeing their position on the verge of being overrun, Royal Prince Alexander and the Voivode Putnick had, at the beginning of November, marked a strategic retreat. The Serbian army suffered from a lack of arms and ammunition. Equipment arrived, sent by us. In the first days of December, the dazzling victory at Rudnik routed the Austrian army again, liberating the territory of our allies for the second time.

At the same time, a new belligerent came into play. At the beginning of November, the Allies had declared war on Turkey, whose cautious policy had been able, for three months, to deceive our diplomacy. This was an important event, although not because the Ottomans had a military state and a financial power that were formidable in themselves. But the Turkish soldier is brave. Armed and directed by Germany, Turkey, the traditional enemy of Russia, was going to strike our allies from behind in the Caucasus. Religious suzerain of Islam, she could create serious embarrassments for England and France, great Muslim powers through their overseas possessions. As the mistress of the Dardanelles, she closed the shortest and safest route that linked us to Russia and threatened the road to India. Moreover, the war, by igniting in the Near East, risked bringing serious complications to the Balkans.

Finally, on November 8th, we learned that the Japanese had taken Kiao-Tchéou from the Germans. I sent my congratulations to the Japanese mission that was with me for this victory that took away from our adversaries the last vestige of their possessions in the Far East.

For the time being, these different theaters of external operations were beyond my control, which was limited to the armies of northeastern France. But it was impossible for me to ignore them, because of the repercussions that they could have on the front that I have never ceased to consider as the main one, the one on which the mass of German armies was joined to French, British and Belgian armies.

With this in mind, on January 8, 1915, I was led to have my 3rd Bureau[*] write a memorandum that aimed to nip in the bud a project, perhaps seductive at first glance, that aimed at nothing less than to create, by means of troops taken from our depots, an army that would be responsible for going to fight Austria.

In this note, I explained that this idea was "unacceptable in its principle as in its methods."

1. The men who are in the depots are not available. They are strictly sufficient in number to fill the holes that the continuation of the campaign until next autumn will produce in our units.[†] An army thus constituted would have neither cadres, nor artillery, nor regimental equipment, nor services;

---

[*] Office of Operations.

[†] In an Appendix to the Note that I summarize here, I gave the following figures:

> In less than five months of war, the final losses for the active and reserve (killed, prisoners, permanently unavailable wounded), were 420,000 men.
> If the war lasts another ten months, the final losses will be 840,000 men. What do the depots have to meet this need?
> They will have on the one hand what they currently contain, on the other hand what they will receive during these ten months.
> They currently contain. . . . . 547,000 men.
> Breakdown: mobilizable 199 000
> untrained 343,000
> They will receive the class of 1916, maximum 270 000
> A total of . . . . 817,000 men.

Chapter VI

2. An army intended to operate against Austria could only be taken from the army corps at the front. Is this withdrawal possible? No, the army corps we have at our disposal are barely sufficient to cover the 600 kilometer front we hold. To reduce the number of them is to forbid us any offensive for the future; it is to expose ourselves, in case of a violent attack on a point, to be breached, and to retreat;

3. Our goal is to reach the enemy in the main theater of operations. It is obvious that the main theater is where Germany has massed the largest and best part of its forces.

It's not Austria that we need to beat, it's Germany.

It is the defeat of Germany that must be planned;

4. Unacceptable in principle, the proposed combination would be difficult to implement.

Salonika is a neutral city where we cannot land our troops.

If we could land in this city, the output of the Salonika-Uskub railroad would be insufficient to supply a large army. The Serbs have the greatest difficulty in supplying the 100,000 men at their disposal. What would it be like if 300,000 Frenchmen were added to these 100,000 Serbs?

These objections apply with greater force to a landing in the Adriatic, from which Admiral de Lapeyrère has just withdrawn his squadrons, which he found unsafe.

Following my observations, the project was discarded. It was to reappear a few weeks later, in the form of the ill-fated Dardanelles expedition.

At the end of December 1914, I suggested to the Minister of War that talks be initiated with Japan with a view to sending Japanese forces to the western theater of the war. This project, transmitted by Mr. Millerand to Mr. Delcassè, received no response at first.

At the beginning of March 1915, I received from the Minister of War a copy of a letter addressed to him by the Minister of Foreign Affairs.[*] In this letter, Mr. Delcassé made it known that talks had been initiated with Tokyo at the beginning of the war.

---

[*] The letter from Mr. Delcassé is dated March 6th, 1915.

Immediately they had come up against Japanese popular sentiment, which was reluctant to see its army, "born of compulsory service, destined to defend its national soil," go off to serve far away as mercenaries, and for foreign interests.

Later the Japanese government objected to this project because of transportation difficulties. Later still, a new fact occurred, which revealed to us the deep cause of Japan's refusal to take military action in Europe. The Tokyo government, which, under cover of the Anglo-Japanese alliance, had proceeded as I have just said to take possession of the German colony of Tsing-Tao, addressed a series of demands to China,* under the pretext of resolving the Chantoung question, to obtain from China a series of regulations and advantages likely to ensure a dominating situation for Japan. In fact, the moment was well chosen for Japan. France, England and Russia were too busy in Europe, and the United States itself was watching the affairs of the old world with too much interest, to remain at liberty to embark on a Chinese adventure. The Foreign Minister concluded by saying that Japan might later accede to our request when public opinion there had sufficiently developed in our favor and when China had given her satisfaction.

We know now that this was not the case, and I have always regretted that the personal interests that Japan was pursuing in the Far East prevented it from sending its brave soldiers to fight in Europe alongside us.

Thus the first phase of the war ended. A new phase was beginning which brought us great hopes, but also serious problems full of dreadful unknowns.

---

* On January 18, 1915, the Japanese minister in Peking, Mr. Hioki, handed over to President Yuan-Chi-K'ai the famous "Twenty-One Demands," which are still relevant today.

Index

Aerschot 281
Africa... 92, 97, 111, 137, 149, 164,
        172, 174, 176, 183
Aix-en-Provence 173
Aix-la-Chapelle 151, 254
Albert, King.... 208, 209, 234, 245,
        247, 248, 259, 428, 434,
        436, 438, 444
Albertville 172
Aldebert, Col. 262, 273
Alexander 451
Alexandre, Lt.-Col............. 22
Algeria.. 13, 23, 111, 113, 136, 163,
        183, 204, 226, 227, 318,
        350
Algiers................ 164, 174
Allenstein 131, 132, 157
Allied Armies .. 126, 248, 285, 365,
        424, 430
Allies.. 31, 103, 116, 118, 124-127,
        130, 184, 204, 209, 234,
        249, 264, 266, 272, 282,
        290, 299, 301, 304-306,
        310, 324, 330, 341, 346,

        366, 379, 399, 411, 428,
        429, 433-435, 440, 445,
        448, 451
Alps..... 23, 28, 96, 104, 111, 113,
        115, 120, 156, 157, 166,
        172, 173, 183, 194, 203,
        256, 262
Alsace 26, 113, 118, 119, 143,
        146, 147, 149, 150, 172,
        185, 188, 204, 206, 208,
        222, 227, 228, 231, 232,
        236, 237, 239, 241, 243,
        246, 248, 259, 260, 266,
        267, 272, 281, 284, 294,
        296, 302, 317, 409, 448,
        449
Altkirch 232, 236, 237
Amagne..................... 30
Amance, Mont d'............ 171
Amel 177
Amiens . 9, 112, 250, 282, 293, 294,
        296-299, 305, 310, 315,
        320, 324, 338, 410, 415,
        421, 436, 444, 445, 448

ammunition . 53, 59, 60, 65, 68, 77-79, 141, 178, 193, 206, 210, 213, 248, 263, 351, 398, 401-403, 407, 442, 450, 451
Ancre..................... 410
André.............. 49, 99, 349
Angers................. 79, 173
Anglo-Boer War 35
Anizy..................... 384
Anthoine, Gen. .. 41, 382, 414, 417, 419-421
Antwerp... 116, 135, 209, 212, 234, 248, 249, 253, 258, 259, 264, 267, 269, 272, 273, 281, 291, 398, 411, 416, 422, 428-436, 438
Aosta..................... 252
Apremont.................. 170
Arches.................... 171
Archinard, Gen.. 195, 197, 243, 294
Arcis-sur-Aube . 325, 327, 337, 356, 357
Ardennes Forest............. 144
Argonne, the 159
Arlon..... 187, 228, 231, 260, 264, 269
Armentières................ 414
armies . 6, 13, 18-20, 23, 25, 26, 29-31, 35, 42-45, 55, 56, 60, 91, 98, 103, 104, 106, 109-111, 113-115, 117, 119, 120, 125-127, 130, 131, 135, 138, 139, 142-155, 158, 161, 164, 168, 170, 171, 178, 180, 183, 184, 189-192, 194, 196, 197, 204, 217, 219, 225, 227, 229, 233, 235, 237, 238, 240-242, 247, 248, 250-252, 255, 259, 261-264, 268, 269, 274-277, 280, 281, 285-291, 293, 294, 296, 297, 299, 300, 302, 308, 311, 312, 314, 316, 317, 322, 323, 325, 327, 329, 331, 332, 334, 335, 337, 340-344, 347, 350-353, 355, 358, 361, 364-366, 368-371, 375-377, 379-386, 389, 391, 392, 394-399, 401-407, 409, 416, 417, 420, 422-426, 430, 431, 435, 442, 443, 449-452
Armistice.............. 235, 244
Arras 285, 294, 410, 414, 419, 422, 448
artillery ... 3, 10-12, 16, 17, 21, 23, 36, 38, 43, 53, 54, 57, 59, 60, 64-79, 81, 82, 86, 92, 94, 130, 133, 139, 144, 157, 161-164, 167, 169, 171, 177, 195, 209, 238, 245, 256, 273, 285, 287, 294, 299, 303, 308, 319, 328, 332, 351, 374, 380, 394, 398, 428, 433, 441, 450, 452
Ath...................... 282
Attigny............ 143, 326, 334
Aube . 323, 325, 327, 335-337, 341, 344, 356, 357, 380
Aubert, Admiral......... 117, 126
Aubreville 406
Audun-le-Roman............ 394
Augagneur, M................ 99
Austria..... 91, 103, 106-109, 125, 202, 206, 208, 212, 220, 252, 276, 452, 453
Austrian Army.......... 131, 451
XIVth Corps 232
Autrécourt................. 307
Aveluy.................... 410
Avesnes.............. 144, 299
Avignon................... 173
Avre River................. 321
Avricourt.......... 112, 177, 215
Avril 177
Azannes................... 284
Baccarat................... 169
Bailleul 438
Bailly..................... 331
Balkans 90, 451

Index

Ballon d'Alsace............. 169
Ballons, the................ 155
Bapaume...... 305, 409, 410, 429
Bapst, M................... 109
Barbot, Gen................ 414
Barcelona.................. 175
Bardonnèche............... 252
Barrère, M................. 104
Barthélemy, Maj............. 138
Barthou, M.................. 99
Bar-le-Duc.. 30, 150, 159, 171, 326, 327, 337, 380, 406
Bar-sur-Aube....... 323, 335, 337
Bastogne.. 153, 187, 231, 245, 262, 264
Baye...................... 389
Bayon 29, 150
Bayonne................... 173
Beaumont 280, 284
Beauraing 260
Beauvais 298, 392, 407, 408
Bel, Maj.... 22, 213, 295, 322, 323, 356, 383
Belfort . 29, 30, 35, 48-50, 109, 143, 149, 150, 154, 167, 169, 176, 180, 194, 243, 247, 251, 296, 330, 335, 382
Belgian Army .. 107, 122, 124, 183, 234, 235, 241, 244, 245, 247-249, 253, 255-258, 261, 264, 265, 267, 268, 272, 273, 300, 411, 415, 416, 422, 426, 428-431, 434-436, 438-440
Belgium... 24-27, 90, 98, 102, 103, 105, 107-110, 113-115, 117-119, 121-123, 134, 135, 138, 141, 143, 144, 146, 149-154, 157-159, 169, 179, 182-187, 190, 192, 194, 209, 212, 219, 222, 223, 226-228, 230, 231, 233, 236, 239, 245, 255, 259, 263, 272, 275, 281, 283, 287, 291, 300, 325, 330, 342, 375, 388, 411, 428, 429, 435-437, 445, 449
Beney..................... 404
Berge, Gen................. 236
Bergères................... 371
Bergheim.................. 245
Berlin... 22, 31, 106, 108, 119, 120, 130, 132, 206, 222, 276, 277, 330
Bernard, Lt.-Col. 191, 252, 321, 349
Berthelot, Gen. . 128, 175, 213, 229, 230, 292, 293, 298, 307, 312, 321, 324, 335, 343, 356-362, 364, 396, 448
Berthier, Louis Alexandre...... 25
Bertie, Sir Francis 120
Bertincourt 305
Bertrix.................... 276
Besançon....... 13, 143, 167, 180
Bessarabia................. 109
Béthune................... 414
Betz.............. 331, 378, 386
Bilsen 254
Blusses 178, 194
Bohain................ 289, 299
Bohemia 208
Boisse, Maj. de la 11
Bonneau .. 232, 236, 237, 243, 246, 251
Bordeaux.. 173, 329, 332, 344, 429, 432, 450
Bosnia.................... 106
Boulogne...... 118, 173, 227, 430
Bourbonnais 180
Bourderiat.................. 37
Bourg-Saint-Maurice......... 172
Braine 396
Bray.. 300, 321, 325, 362, 363, 365
Bray-sur-Seine.......... 325, 362
Bray-sur-Somme 321
Brécard, Lt.-Col..... 213, 226, 230, 231, 233-235, 261, 282, 283, 304-306, 309, 310, 314, 319, 321, 365
Brécart, Col. 409, 435, 437
Breslau 277
Brest 131, 173
Brest-Litowsk 131

Breteuil 415, 421
Brialmont, Gen. 431
Briançon 172, 173
Briand, Aristide 58, 93, 94
bridges 55, 122, 188, 189, 193,
255, 256, 262, 267, 271,
301, 317, 322, 381, 408,
428
Bridoux, Gen. 388, 408, 409
Brienne-le-Château 344
Briey 126, 140, 177, 448
Briey Commission 140
Brissaud-Desmaillet, Maj. 14
British Army ... 119, 144, 145, 154,
183, 220, 257, 258, 261,
264, 269, 274, 281, 290,
291, 294, 298-301, 304,
319-321, 331, 337, 354-
356, 362, 370, 378, 383-
385, 389, 391, 396, 397,
423-425, 427, 428, 447
   1st Army 428
   2nd Corps 426
   3rd Corps 427, 438
   Lahore Division 438
British Cavalry 426
Brittany 173
Brugère, Gen. 141, 408
Bruges 430, 434
Brun, Gen. 9, 13, 66
Brussels ... 116, 122, 193, 219, 222,
227, 230, 233, 234, 245,
258, 261, 264, 267, 268,
273, 274
Buat, Col. 213, 247
Bucquoi 410
Buisson, Gen. 409
Bulgaria 69
Bussy-le-Repos 371
Buzancy 11
Caillaux, Joseph . 14, 21, 22, 31, 57,
104, 106, 298
Calais 69, 70, 74, 173, 430, 438,
440, 443
Cambon, Jules 22, 206, 444
Cambrai 284, 301, 303
Canada 4

Capron, M. 229
Carcassonne 298
Carence, Maj. 11
Carp 109
Cassel 445, 447, 447
Castelnau, Gen. de Curières de . 19-
20, 32, 40, 42, 43,
44, 60, 135, 175-176,
195-196, 226, 241, 247,
251, 266-267, 269-271,
284, 316, 374, 381-383,
391, 404, 407-412, 414-
415, 417-422, 427, 429,
437
Ceccaldi, Corp 298
Celles 282
Cernay 236
Châlons 30, 82, 159, 225, 327,
340, 371, 406, 436
Châlons-sur-Marne 159
Chambéry 173
Chambry 378
Champagne 159, 323, 325, 332,
439
Champaubert 371, 390
Champenoux, Forest of 374
Changis 362, 378
Chantilly 298, 448, 449
Charleroi .. 123, 138, 276, 285, 348
Charmes Forest 170, 194
Chasseurs ... 22, 173, 218, 319, 437,
443
Château-Porcien 326, 334
Château-Salins .. 146-150, 187, 188,
210, 260, 270
Château-Thierry 326, 354, 356,
359, 362, 379, 389, 391
Châtel 154
Châtillon-sur-Seine 360, 368
Chaulnes 305, 324
Chaumont 30
Chauny 322
Chauvoncourt 405
Chavanges 380
Chavonne 428
Chemin des Dames 397
Cherbourg 173, 429

Index

Chéry........................ 393
Chèvreville 387
Chiers, the 251, 279, 283, 292
China....................... 454
Choisy...................... 378
Cholm....................... 131
Chomer, Gen 43, 75, 195
Churchill, Winston .. 431-433, 436
Ciney....................... 283
Cirey....................... 223
Clayeures................... 289
Clemenceau, Georges 62, 231
Clergerie, Gen. 357, 358
Clermont ... 79, 159, 171, 333, 407
Clermont-en-Argonne 159, 171
Clignon 390, 391
Clive, Lt.-Col. 304, 361, 367
Collon, Maj. 234
Colmar............ 188, 189, 227
Cologne....... 186, 191, 210, 245
Commercy..... 169, 171, 326, 381, 391, 404, 406
Compiègne 296, 306, 319, 320, 324, 333, 334, 384, 408, 411, 412, 419, 420, 426, 427, 441
Condé 288, 371, 389, 448
Condé-en-Brie.............. 389
Conflans 169, 295
Conneau, Gen........... 338, 437
Corbie 408, 409
Cornet...................... 367
Cornulier-Lucinière.......... 389
Cotentin.................... 173
Coucy-le-Château 338
Coudren..................... 322
Coulommiers... 362, 370, 378, 387
Courchamps................. 378
Courtacon 370, 378
Courtrai............... 430, 438
Coutanceau, Gen. 392
Craonne.......... 293, 310, 327
Creil............. 167, 180, 438
Creue....................... 404
Crimean War............... 395
Crozat Canal 314, 320
Crusne..................... 279

Dallas, Col. 433
Dammartin..... 340, 346, 356, 387
Dammartin-en-Goële......... 387
Dampvitoux........... 212, 404
Damvillers.. 30, 159, 170, 179, 284
Dannemarie................ 232
Dardanelles 451, 453
Darney..................... 171
Davignon, M. 219
Delarue, Gen................ 128
Delcassé, Théophile... 50, 117, 119, 217, 453
Delle 29
Delme, lake 113, 187, 188, 210, 266
Dender..................... 429
Desaleux, Gen. 128
Dessens, Lt.-Col............. 343
Dieppe..................... 173
Diest 248, 263
Dieulouard............. 150, 177
Dieuze.... 118, 187, 188, 210, 260, 266
Dijon 13, 24, 27, 112, 167, 180, 263
Dinant 144, 153, 235, 249, 256, 260, 275
Directive No. 1 142
Divisions 23-30, 42, 43, 75, 94, 111, 112, 116, 118, 120, 131-133, 143-145, 149, 150, 153, 154, 159-161, 163-173, 177-180, 183-185, 187, 197, 203, 225, 238, 240, 242, 243, 249-251, 253, 255, 259-262, 266, 268, 270, 273, 274, 276, 278, 280, 281, 284, 285, 289, 294-296, 300, 302, 305, 306, 308-310, 313-316, 319, 321, 326, 328, 329, 333, 334, 337, 338, 341, 350, 362, 377, 383, 386, 388, 392, 395, 408, 409, 412, 414, 417-420, 423, 424, 426-430, 436, 437, 439, 441, 442, 448, 450

Dixmude 434
Dôle.................. 167, 180
Donnelay.................. 266
Dormans 327, 371, 391
Douai............. 273, 414, 429
Doubs 143
Doullens 418, 437
Doumer, M.................. 101
Dubail Gen.. 18, 31, 32, 40, 75, 103,
    125, 195, 196, 228, 232,
    236, 237, 243, 251, 266,
    267, 269, 302, 317, 374,
    383, 404, 405, 407
Duchêne, Gen............ 76, 421
Dugny 295
Dun 159, 160
Dunkirk.... 24, 284, 403, 414, 426,
    429, 430, 432, 436, 437,
    444, 447, 448
Duport, Lt.-Col................ 138
Durand, Gen. Léon 11, 302
Durbion.................. 194
Dury 421
Duval, Capt. 14
Dyle...................... 262
East Prussia.... 131, 204, 277, 290,
    330, 451
Ebener, Gen. ... 176, 218, 231, 246,
    248, 314, 315
Eecke..................... 438
Eifel... 26, 114, 151, 152, 154, 158
Enghien................... 282
England.... 91, 103, 105, 107-110,
    118-120, 151, 157, 209,
    222, 226, 227, 231, 249,
    250, 257, 300, 304, 368,
    395, 423, 444, 451, 454
English Channel 118, 173
Entente Cordiale 22
Eparges 178
Epernay................... 356
Ermenonville Forest 377
Esher, Lord 122
Essey.................. 171, 404
Esternay............... 370, 378
Ethe...................... 328
Etienne, M. 44

Eyschen, M............. 219, 223
Falkenhayn, Gen. Erich von ... 449
Fallières, Clement Armand ... 9, 10,
    21, 39, 105, 106, 115,
    116
Faucilles 145
Faulquemont 148
Faulx plateau............... 178
Fayolle, Gen................ 414
Fère-Champenoise... 379, 390, 391,
    394
Ferrières................... 239
Fétizon, Maj..... 22, 213, 270, 415,
    418, 421
Feuillères.................. 409
Fez....................... 13
Filloux, Lt.-Col............... 74
Fismes 396
Flanders... 323, 403, 411, 430, 434,
    435, 442, 443, 445
Flone 256
Foch, Marshal Ferdinand.... 19, 69,
    139, 312, 313, 316, 322,
    328, 329, 332, 343, 349,
    358-360, 362, 364, 371,
    385, 390-394, 396, 416-
    422, 434-437, 441-445,
    447, 447
Fontoy.................... 210
Foreign Office.. 106, 109, 117, 122,
    202
fortifications . 10, 23, 29, 35, 37, 50,
    54, 58-60, 65, 66, 98, 107,
    114, 135, 143, 172, 185,
    193-195, 206, 210, 213,
    236, 334, 340
Foucaucourt................ 409
Fournier, Gen............... 384
Fraize................. 169, 177
France . 6, 13, 14, 21, 22, 25-28, 33,
    52, 54, 57, 58, 65, 68, 69,
    78, 90-92, 102-108, 110,
    120-122, 124-126, 130,
    134, 136, 138, 148, 157,
    174, 175, 182, 193, 207,
    208, 210, 213, 215, 218,
    219, 240, 252, 287, 298,

Index

303, 343, 356, 368, 375, 376, 395, 399, 432, 433, 438, 447-449, 451, 452, 454
Franchet d'Esperey, Gen. . 318, 348, 349, 358-360, 362-365, 371, 378, 384, 387, 389-391, 393, 397, 406
Francheville. 371
Franco-German agreement 31
Fraysse, Gen. 444
French, Sir John 250, 257, 258, 261, 265, 279, 284, 294, 299-301, 304, 305, 309, 312, 314, 320, 324, 327, 331, 339, 341, 345, 353-355, 361, 363, 365-367, 369, 395, 416, 420, 422, 424-427, 430, 434, 437, 445, 447
French Army 3, 27, 42, 74, 77, 119, 123, 124, 136, 151, 231, 232, 235, 245, 248, 273, 299, 304, 306, 312, 314, 324, 366, 367, 425, 438, 473
    Colonial Troops. 13
    1st Army . . . 30, 171, 188, 190, 227, 228, 232, 237, 242, 243, 248, 260, 266, 267, 270, 276, 281, 284, 308, 316-318, 330, 341, 374, 382, 392, 404, 405, 407, 410, 420, 425, 443
    2nd Army. . . 30, 111-112, 171, 177, 228, 241, 260-261, 266-267, 269-271, 275, 281, 284, 289, 341, 374-375, 380, 382, 404, 407-412, 414-415, 417-421, 425, 437, 442-443
    3rd Army . . . 30, 150, 171, 197, 262, 269, 275, 279, 281, 284, 293, 295, 301, 302, 308, 317, 322, 323, 326-329, 332, 334, 337, 341, 359, 360, 374, 380, 381, 383, 390, 393, 397, 404, 405, 425
    4th Army . . . 30, 159, 171, 179, 196, 197, 255, 261, 269, 273, 274, 278, 280, 281, 283, 285, 292, 301, 307, 308, 311, 315-317, 322, 326, 327, 329, 332, 341, 349, 350, 356, 359, 367, 379-381, 390-393, 397, 412, 436, 448
    5th Army . . . 30, 112, 172, 183, 185, 196, 220, 225, 242, 249, 254, 256, 258, 261, 262, 266, 268, 269, 273, 274, 279-284, 289, 292, 293, 299, 301, 303-308, 313-315, 317-319, 321, 322, 324, 326-333, 335, 337, 338, 347-349, 353-363, 378, 384, 386, 387, 389-392, 396-398, 410, 412, 420, 427, 443
    6th Army . 29, 30, 71, 111, 159, 160, 171, 296, 302, 303, 305, 306, 310, 314, 315, 317, 320, 321, 324, 326, 328, 329, 331, 333, 338, 342, 346, 350, 354, 356, 358, 360, 362-364, 370, 378, 379, 383, 384, 386-391, 393, 396, 401, 402, 406-411, 420, 422, 427
    7th Army . . 172, 281, 319, 350
    8th Army 295, 436
    9th Army . . 262, 356, 361, 385, 389-391, 393, 406, 410, 412, 417
    10th Army 412, 418
    Army of Alsace . 243, 246, 248, 266, 267, 284, 294, 296, 302
    Army of Amiens 112
    Army of Paris . . 111, 112, 351
    Army of the Alps. 28, 172, 173, 203
    Army of the North 150

Index

1st Corps .. 255, 256, 274, 276, 282, 348, 427, 438
1st Cavalry Corps 274
2nd Corps . 94, 168, 169, 179, 274, 299, 380, 393, 426, 438
3rd Corps.. 276, 280, 285, 313, 314, 321
4th Corps.. 274, 328, 361, 383, 401, 406, 408, 409, 411, 419
5th Corps.............. 285
6th Corps... 29, 169, 177-179, 295, 322, 323, 390, 405, 441
7th Corps.. 169, 176, 188, 228, 231, 232, 236, 237, 242, 243, 251, 284, 294, 296, 302, 314, 321, 334, 427
8th Corps............ 23, 405
9th Corps . 170, 208, 251, 267, 270, 332, 341, 441
11th Corps. 159, 316, 390, 410, 411
12th Corps. 278, 343, 349, 380
12th Division....... 169, 177
13th Corps.. 13, 284, 396, 401, 407-409
13th Division........... 169
14th Corps.. 91, 169, 251, 285, 407
15th Corps.... 23, 28, 29, 113, 176, 179, 218, 341, 380, 381, 385, 390, 391
16th Corps..... 404, 441, 442
17th Corps. 278, 285, 301, 380
18th Corps. 261, 276, 310, 313, 331, 333, 389
19th Corps... 28, 29, 111, 116, 163, 174
20th Corps.. 23, 168, 169, 171, 177, 178, 218, 270, 271, 276, 290, 407, 408, 421, 443
21st Corps 23, 28, 29, 111, 133, 163, 168, 169, 177, 179, 284, 341, 380, 390, 410, 414, 415, 418, 419
32nd Corps 441
1st Cavalry Division 409
2nd Division 361
2nd Cavalry Division. 177, 247, 270, 381, 391
3rd Division. 91, 169, 170, 177, 309
3rd Algerian Division 298
3rd Cavalry Division . 423, 434
4th Division.... 169, 177, 299, 308, 309
4th Cavalry Division . 177, 410, 412
5th Cavalry Division 388
6th Cavalry Division . 177, 412
7th Cavalry Division . 177, 381, 391, 414
8th Division........ 387, 423
8th Cavalry Division . 172, 176, 228, 232, 243, 247, 410, 426
9th Division........ 170, 177
9th Cavalry Division . 282, 316, 380, 441
10th Cavalry Division 270
31st Division 441
32nd Division 428, 442
37th Division........... 401
38th Division........... 441
39th Division........... 443
40th Division........... 313
41st Division 176
42nd Division .. 322, 328, 378, 390, 437, 440-442
44th Division... 167, 173, 243, 443
45th Division... 318, 334, 350, 411
53rd Division........... 419
56th Division........... 319
63rd Division........... 294
65th Division........... 319
67th Division........... 262
70th Division........... 410
75th Division........... 404
77th Division........... 410

Index

Alpine Division..... 168, 225
French Cavalry............. 412
French Navy............... 126
Fresnes-en-Woëvre........... 30
Fresnières............. 408, 409
Fromentières............... 390
Frouard................... 194
Fumay..................... 112
Furnes............ 435, 437, 445
Galicia............ 126, 131, 346
Gallieni, Gen. 42, 195, 196
Gamelin, Gen.... 22, 229, 293, 307, 312, 361, 363, 364, 367
gap.... 29, 113, 148, 173, 189, 242, 324, 331, 332, 376, 379, 380, 404
Gaucher........... 327, 356, 378
Gembloux............. 259, 264
General Instruction no. 1...... 242
General Instruction no. 4.. 337, 340, 355, 356
General Instruction no. 5...... 359
General Order no. 6.. 364-366, 378, 379
Génie, Col. 234, 249, 262, 264
German Army ... 74, 78, 89, 94, 97, 131-134, 136, 137, 169, 190, 217, 237-239, 241, 245, 249, 253, 261, 267, 277, 290, 305, 306, 324, 325, 330, 333, 335, 338, 342, 346, 354, 357, 360, 378-380, 384, 386, 404, 426
Ist Army........... 342, 346, 354, 357, 360, 378, 379, 384, 386
IInd Army......... 290, 346
IVth Army............. 380
Vth Army............. 404
VIIth Corps........ 233, 234
VIIIth Corps........... 223
IXth Corps......... 386, 387
Xth Corps 262
XVth Corps............ 260
German Cavalry..... 248, 249, 263, 268, 273, 275, 297, 298, 305, 310, 331-333, 338, 379
German Navy............... 107
Germany . 11, 14, 25, 31, 48, 50, 57, 58, 65, 74, 78, 81, 89-93, 96-98, 102, 103, 106, 107, 109, 110, 116, 118-122, 125, 131, 133, 134, 136, 147, 148, 157, 185, 192, 193, 195, 201, 203, 206-208, 213-215, 219, 220, 222, 226, 227, 231, 276, 290, 406, 451, 453
Gerolstein 151, 185, 186
Gette 262
Ghent......... 429, 431, 434, 438
Gilinsky, Gen............... 126
Giromagny.......... 29, 169, 212
Girouville 194
Givet..... 112, 169, 177, 192, 193, 220, 235, 255, 256, 261, 268, 280, 284, 292
Gondrecourt............. 30, 171
Gough, Gen. 420, 427
Gouraud, Gen............... 375
Grandmaison, Lt-Col. de.... 16, 37
Grandvillers................ 408
Gratz 203
Greece.................... 209
Grenoble 172
Grey, Sir Edward.... 122, 431, 432
Grodno 131
Grossetti, Gen... 323, 328, 437, 440
Guerbigny 321
Guignicourt................ 322
Guillaumat................. 202
Guillemin, Maj............... 14
Guiscard 408
Guise..... 299, 303, 319, 321, 347, 348, 372
guns.. 43, 53, 65, 70, 71, 74, 75, 78, 251, 436
Hache, Gen................. 313
Haelen............... 249, 262
Haig, Gen. Sir Douglas 299
Hal................... 273, 274
Haldane, Lord 120

Hallouin, Gen. 135
Ham. 305, 306, 309, 321
Hamilton, Gen. Sir Ian 447
Hannut. 257, 260, 264
Hattonchâtel 30, 155, 159, 187
Haudiomont. . . . 170, 178, 179, 194
Haudiomont-les-Blusses 178
Hautes-Vosges. 154, 169, 176
Hauts-de-Meuse . 11, 155, 159, 170, 178, 179, 194, 284, 295, 325, 337, 397, 404
Havre. 118, 173, 227, 309, 403, 430
Hazebrouck. . . . 414, 428, 430, 438
Heiltz-le-Maurupt 30, 327
Hély d'Oissel, Gen. . . 128, 242, 313
Hem. 320
Hennersdorf. 236
Herbillon, Lt.-Col. 278, 450
Hermalle 256
Hermant, Gen. 273
Herr, Gen. 71
Herzegovina 106
Hindenburg, Field Marshal Paul von
. . . . 449
Hioki, Mr. 454
Hirson 118, 144, 167, 172, 180, 197, 220, 254
Holland 108
Houdremont. 276
Houffalize 144, 186, 253
howitzers . . . 57, 59, 65, 72, 74, 238, 252
Huguet, Col. . . . 249, 250, 265, 279, 301, 304, 305, 308, 314, 345, 354, 359, 360, 365-368
Humbert, Charles 62
Humbert, Gen. 442
Huy . . 187, 234, 256, 260, 262, 264
Infantry . . 14, 16, 17, 22, 38, 45, 51, 53, 66, 78, 82, 86, 92, 94, 100, 116, 118, 123, 137, 158, 161-163, 169, 179, 203, 235, 249, 250, 252-256, 259, 262, 273, 274, 281, 287, 288, 295, 297, 300, 343, 349, 380, 387, 390, 394, 395, 433, 443, 450
Information Service. 135
Isvolsky, M. 208
Italy 22, 28, 91, 103, 105, 108, 109, 120, 125, 157, 179, 209, 212, 220, 227, 252, 256
Jacquand, Maj. 415
Jamoigne 276
Japan 453, 454
Jaurès, Jean Léon. 15, 215
Jeandelize 295
Jemmapes 123, 124, 279
Jeumont. 123
Jodoigne 260, 267
Joffre, Marshal 2-4, 3, 6, 41-44, 83, 121, 128, 205, 210, 247, 248, 288, 336, 345, 351, 353, 375, 417, 424, 432, 433, 447, 449, 473
Joinville. 30, 344
Joppecourt. 276
Jouy. 194, 378
Jungbluth, Gen. 122
Jura Mts. 143, 150, 194
Juvisy. 341
Kessler, Gen. 35
Kiel 212
Killbourg. 151
Kitchener, Lord 140, 250, 298, 300, 339, 384, 430-433, 436, 444, 447
Klein, Gen. 427
Klobukowski, M. 219, 233
Kluck, Gen. von 254, 335, 338, 342, 346, 354, 370, 376, 378, 384, 386-390, 409
Koenigsberg 126, 131, 248
La Bassée. 438
La Fère 16, 293, 308-310, 322
La Ferté 327, 356, 378, 386
La Ferté-sous-Jouarre 356, 386
La Garde 247
La Neuville 212, 321
La Panne 445

Index

Laffont de Ladébat, Gen... 195, 197
Lagny..... 228, 356, 358, 363, 378
Lamothe, Gen............. 67, 70
Landen................ 193, 262
Landrecies............. 144, 284
Langle, Gen. de.. 40, 195-197, 278, 283, 285, 307-308, 312, 315-316, 328, 332, 343, 379, 380, 385, 390-391, 396, 436
Langlois, Gen.... 36, 37, 53, 77, 79
Langres................. 13, 30
Lanrezac, Gen..... 19, 40, 196, 220, 248, 249, 254, 255, 258, 259, 261, 273, 275, 279, 280, 282, 294, 299, 303, 304, 306, 307, 309-313, 315, 318, 319, 322, 324, 331, 332, 338, 347-349, 353
Laon 16, 27, 29, 167, 180, 293, 297, 298, 305, 310, 318, 319, 326, 334, 338
Laroche................... 231
Lartigue, Gen............... 328
Lassigny.................. 408
Le Cateau......... 225, 289, 301
Le Mans.................. 173
Leboucq, Gen....... 323, 328, 393
Legion of Honor 387, 444, 445
Legrand, Gen........... 176, 195
Léman.................... 234
Lens.............. 410, 414, 419
Lesse..................... 283
Leuze..................... 282
Libramont................. 245
Liège..... 123, 135, 192, 209, 212, 233-235, 239, 241, 245, 252, 253, 256, 259-261, 263, 264, 266, 267
Liétard, Gen................ 414
Lieven, Admiral Prince....... 126
Ligny-en-Barrois............. 30
Lihons.............. 324, 409
Lille.. 194, 273, 275, 289, 411, 414, 415, 426, 428, 430, 438, 445, 448

Lizy.............. 362, 377, 386
Lloyd George, David.......... 14
Lombaertzyde.............. 440
Longueville................ 282
Longwy.... 10, 194, 223, 285, 448
Lorient.................... 173
Lorraine.. 24, 25, 98, 113, 114, 118, 119, 143, 146-149, 151-155, 188, 189, 196, 204, 206, 208, 226, 227, 233, 239, 241, 245, 262, 271, 276, 280, 281, 284, 295, 296, 302, 325, 326, 374, 383, 407, 439, 449
Louvain... 193, 234, 247, 255, 261, 267, 273
Louvemont 171
Louvres................... 354
Lublin.................... 131
Ludendorff, Gen.......... 97, 449
Lunéville.......... 177, 271, 276
Lure.................... 29, 30
Luxembourg ... 102, 105, 108-110, 113, 122, 134, 135, 138, 139, 144, 146-153, 158, 159, 185, 186, 190, 219, 220, 222, 223, 228, 240, 253, 254, 256, 264, 268, 269, 275, 280, 281, 292, 376
Luxeuil................... 143
Machault.................. 322
Madagascar........ 195, 225, 275
Mailly .. 60, 66, 70, 71, 79, 82, 166, 167, 172, 380
Maisoncelles............... 378
Maissin................... 276
Maistre, Gen............... 307
Malines................... 262
Malmédy.. 122, 151, 158, 185, 186, 223
maneuvers.... 9, 12, 23, 29, 31, 38, 40-43, 55, 60, 70, 71, 101, 107, 127, 130, 140-142, 162, 172, 175, 182, 184, 195, 209, 232, 334, 359
Mangin................... 356

Manonviller........ 150, 154, 270
Mantes.................... 327
Manteuffel, Gen.............. 13
Marchais-en-Brie............ 384
Marche ... 151, 187, 235, 245, 261
Marcy 321
Marienbourg............... 289
Marines................... 430
Marion, Gen................. 42
Marle............. 307, 311, 312
Marne, Battle of the. . 291, 336, 363, 368, 370, 375-377, 393-395, 398
Marne River 339, 356
Marquion.................. 409
Marsal................ 260, 266
Martin.................... 201
Massevaux................. 236
materiel . . 47, 48, 51, 53, 56, 60, 67, 70, 72, 73, 83, 112, 131, 162, 195, 217
Maubeuge..... 118, 123, 144, 220, 253-256, 282-285, 289, 291, 306, 384, 386, 388
Maud'huy, Gen. de . . 412, 414, 418, 419, 437
Maunoury, Gen.. 262, 263, 295, 302, 305, 314, 315, 319, 321, 333, 341, 351, 354, 356, 357, 363-365, 378, 379, 383-385, 387-389, 392-394, 396, 397, 402, 406, 409, 411, 427
Maurice, Gen........... 172, 212
Maurienne, valley 172, 173
Maurin, Maj.... 213, 247, 267, 269, 315, 357, 361, 362
Mazel, Gen................. 247
Meaux..... 29, 327, 344, 353, 362, 370, 377
Melotte, Maj................ 248
Melun 341, 358, 365, 367
Merzig................. 26, 186
Mesnil.................... 321
Mesple, Maj................. 14
Messimy, M. . 14, 16-19, 21, 31, 56, 63, 67-69, 77, 80, 83, 88, 100, 104, 126, 201-204, 207, 211, 215, 217-219, 222, 225, 228, 246, 254, 263, 277, 286, 287, 289, 298, 302, 303, 307, 311, 314, 332, 395
Messines.................. 442
Metz . 23, 24, 26, 29, 102, 113-115, 117-119, 134, 147-150, 152-155, 159, 170, 187, 189, 190, 196, 206, 208, 233, 239-241, 245, 262, 404, 407
Meurthe River.............. 276
Mézières 29, 30, 144, 151, 154, 160, 169, 170, 172, 177, 197
Michel, Gen. 12, 14, 16, 17, 24, 195, 264
Millerand, Alexandre. . 9, 31, 32, 41, 57, 69, 80, 84, 85, 88, 92, 117, 119, 156, 161, 302, 307, 310, 311, 329, 338, 339, 366, 399, 403, 429, 444, 450, 453
Milon..................... 391
Miraumont................. 410
Mirecourt.................. 171
Mitry, Gen. de 409, 412, 441
Modane............... 172, 173
Molsheim.......... 118, 147, 188
Moltke, Gen. von. . 25, 26, 28, 113, 134, 145, 375, 376
Moltke, Marshal von (elder) ... 375
Mondon Forest 276
Mons............. 275, 280, 282
Montbard................... 10
Montbéliard............ 169, 296
Montdidier..... 319, 321, 333, 384, 410, 420
Montereau............. 357, 359
Montfaucon........ 160, 171, 326
Monthois.................. 328
Monthyon 377
Montmédy... 10, 30, 179, 194, 284
Montreux.................. 215
Morhange 188, 266, 277

Index

Morocco .. 13, 22, 50, 57, 89, 108-111, 136, 163, 164, 204, 227, 275
Mortagne................. 154
Morteau.................. 143
Moscow.................. 232
Mouchin 414
Moutils 378
Mouzon.................. 283
Moy..................... 314
Moyeuvre 210
Mulhouse.. 188, 228, 232, 236, 243, 247, 266
Muller, Capt.... 229, 298, 361, 367
munitions................ 79, 450
Murray, Gen. Sir Archibald.... 257, 299, 300, 320, 359, 367, 395
Mutzig................. 26, 188
Namur 123, 124, 135, 169, 177, 187, 192, 193, 209, 212, 234, 235, 249, 253, 256, 259, 261, 264, 266, 267, 273-276, 280, 282
Nancy ... 11, 41, 69, 102, 114, 133, 150, 151, 153-155, 170, 171, 174, 177, 178, 187, 194, 211, 241, 251, 266, 270, 271, 335, 374, 381-383, 407, 448
Nangis................ 357, 361
Nanteuil-le-Haudouin 331, 340, 388
Neufchâteau.. 24, 35, 143, 153, 171, 187, 220, 231, 245, 260-262, 269, 276
Neufchelles 377
Neuilly................ 327, 391
Neuilly-sur-Marne........... 328
Neuville.......... 212, 321, 419
New York 121
Nice................. 172, 173
Nicholas, Grand Duke..... 41, 127, 128, 276, 450
Nieuport 434
Ninove................ 273, 274
Nivelles 258

Nogent-sur-Seine.... 327, 337, 344
Normée 406
North Africa . 92, 97, 111, 137, 164, 172, 174
North Sea.. 107, 117, 173, 185, 226, 403, 436
Nouart................... 329
Nouvion.............. 144, 318
Nouvion Forest 318
Noyon 301, 304, 305, 308, 401, 408
Nudant................... 448
"O. Dax" 123
Obroutcheff, Gen............ 124
offensives 119, 147, 335
Oise River 333, 338
Ombret................... 262
Oran................. 164, 174
Orchies 414, 429
Ornes................. 177, 179
Ortoncourt................ 171
Ostend 430, 434, 436, 442
Osterode 310
Ourcq River............... 378
Pagny...... 142, 167, 171, 180, 215
Paliseul 144, 276, 394
Panther 14, 21
Paquette, Lt-Col..... 301, 358, 448
Paris.. 4, 23-25, 111, 112, 116, 143, 164-167, 172, 180, 195, 202-204, 206, 210, 216, 223, 225, 231, 246, 257, 263, 277, 285, 286, 289, 292, 296-298, 302, 310, 311, 317, 318, 324-329, 331-334, 337-342, 344, 346, 350-358, 360, 361, 363, 365, 367, 379, 383, 387, 388, 392, 394, 398, 400, 403, 429, 430
Parroy, forest........... 169, 177
Pau, Gen.... 11, 17, 18, 43, 99, 100, 139, 175, 243, 245-247, 251, 317, 431, 434, 435
Payot, Maj. 11
Pellé, Col. 275, 341, 357
Penchard 377

Index

Pénelon, Col. 278, 329
Percin, Gen. 256
Péronne . . . 305, 313-315, 317, 319, 321, 409
Perpignan 116, 173, 298
Pézarches. 378
Philippeville 174, 249
Picardy 294, 407, 411
Pierrefitte. 30
Pilica 126
Plan XVI . . 9, 13, 19, 22, 24, 27, 29, 102, 112, 156, 157, 160, 163, 165, 174
Plan XVII . 73, 102, 138, 156, 160-163, 165, 172, 174, 176, 196, 225
Poincaré, Raymond . . 31, 43, 44, 57, 93, 117, 120-122, 207, 214, 218, 257, 444, 445
Poindron, Col. 181
Poiret, M. 448
Poissy 327
Poix. 262, 408
Poland 27, 131
Pont, Col. . 181, 213, 230, 325, 337, 355, 361, 419
Pontarlier. 194
Pont-Saint-Vincent 171
Pont-sur-Yonne. 344
Port-sur-Seille 177
Posen. 277
Pouydraguin 11
Pradelles 438
Principles of War, The 139
Prinetti, Signor . 104, 105, 108, 217
Prinetti Convention 105, 108
Provence 172, 173
Prussian Guard 391
Przemysl 131
Puisieux. 378
Putnick, Voivode. 451
Railroads . . . 20, 26, 30, 35, 52, 112, 123, 125, 132, 135, 142, 157, 158, 179, 203, 208, 215, 229, 244, 249, 350, 383, 402, 410, 416, 438
Raincy. 354

Rambervillers 171
Ramerupt. 326, 380
Ramillies 264
Ramscapelle 440
Rawlinson, Gen. 434, 438
Recogne. 260
Regiments, . . 17, 162, 163, 173, 433, 440
Regret 304, 328, 374, 428
Regulations for the Conduct of Large Units 44, 45
Reinach, Joseph. 96, 99
Remiremont. 30
Renouard, Maj. 22, 128
Renwez 30
Repington, Lt-Col. A.C. 122
Rethel . . . 11, 23, 29, 172, 255, 343
Rethondes 408
Revigny. 327, 380
Rheims. 320, 397
Ribécourt. 408, 409
Ribot, Alexandre 444
Roberts, Lord. 35
Rochefort. 187, 245
Rochette 178, 212
Rocroi 311, 313, 315, 316
Roget, Gen. 247
Romanche, valley 172
Romilly 406, 438
Roques, Gen. 308, 349
Rosa. 262
Roubaix. 273
Rouen 118, 173, 227, 317, 328, 377
Rougemaison. 428
Rouquerol, Gen. 285
Rouvreux. 256
Roye 409, 419
Ruffey, Gen. . 40, 72, 195, 196, 226, 262, 279, 322, 323, 328
Rupprecht, Crown Prince of Bavaria 335
Russia . . . 25, 26, 31, 70, 91, 96, 97, 101-103, 106-109, 124, 125, 130-132, 134, 175, 184, 191, 202, 204, 208, 214, 215, 220, 227, 232,

Index

239, 240, 252, 276, 330, 342, 398, 451, 454
Russian Army .. 124, 126, 127, 130, 131, 157, 277, 330
Sainte-Menehould.... 30, 159, 172, 356, 405
Saint-Amarin............... 236
Saint-Bernard 252
Saint-Christ................ 314
Saint-Dié.......... 169, 187, 188
Saint-Dizier............. 30, 143
Saint-Front 391
Saint-Georges 378
Saint-Germain.......... 212, 327
Saint-Ghislain 279
Saint-Gond marshes 390
Saint-Hilaire 401
Saint-Hubert 144, 187, 260
Saint-Just.............. 321, 346
Saint-Just-en-Chaussée ... 321, 346
Saint-Laurent............... 321
Saint-Mihiel ... 169, 295, 381, 391, 405, 416, 425
Saint-Nicolas........ 30, 178, 194
Saint-Omer 173, 427, 437
Saint-Pol.............. 418, 437
Saint-Privat................ 210
Saint-Quentin .. 294, 298-300, 303, 305, 307, 309, 312, 314, 317, 319, 321, 322
Saint-Simon............ 309, 314
Saint-Soupplets......... 346, 377
Saint-Waast................ 419
Saint-With..... 152, 153, 185, 186
Saizerais plateau 169
Salonika................... 453
Sanon River................ 276
Sarrail 323, 328, 343, 380, 381, 385, 391, 392, 397, 404, 405, 407, 436
Sarrebourg.. 11, 113, 118, 146-149, 169, 187, 188, 210, 240, 251, 260, 263, 266
Sarreguemines....... 11, 147, 149
Sarry 393
Sartiaux................... 438
Saulx 380, 381, 393, 394, 396

Sazonoff, M................ 208
Scarpe River 412
Schlestadt 169, 188
Schlieffen, Gen. von 26
Schlucht pass............... 169
Schneider............. 69, 71, 74
Schneider, M.......... 209, 210
Schneider, Maj.............. 304
Schoen, Baron von ... 14, 215, 218
Sedan..... 144, 159, 177, 220, 231, 262, 307, 375, 398
Selliers, Lt.-Gen. de...... 234, 273
Selves, M. de. 14, 31, 105, 106, 115
Semoine................... 379
Semoy........... 251, 273, 278
Seneffe.................... 282
Senegalese............ 440, 441
Senlis..................... 354
Sens...................... 367
Seraing 262
Serbia 201-203, 209
Serbian Army 451
Séré de Rivière, Gen... 34, 145, 155
Sermaize 370
Serre 322, 328
Sézanne 348, 349, 362, 378
Silly-le-Long............... 387
Sissonne 9, 82, 397
Soignies............... 269, 282
Soissons..... 24, 27, 167, 180, 319, 324, 326, 331, 333, 346, 384, 427
Solre-le-Château 289
Somain 289, 291
Sommesous 370
Sordet, Gen...... 40, 195, 197, 231, 248, 253, 258, 275, 297, 300, 305, 309, 313, 314, 319, 370, 388
Souain.................... 401
Souilly.................... 327
Soupir 428
South African War............ 36
Southern Group............. 132
Spa....................... 256
Spain 108-110, 173-175
Special Instruction no. 19 305,

Special Instruction no. 20 ..... 385, 390
Special Instruction no. 21 392
Special Instruction no. 32 408
Special Order no. 31 407
Spincourt.................. 150
Stavelot 186, 228
Stenay 111, 159, 160, 283
Strasbourg... 11, 26, 113, 117-119, 147, 169, 188-191, 208, 210, 240, 241
Surmelin 389
Switzerland .. 24, 26, 103, 107, 109, 143, 169, 184, 190, 192, 193, 202, 203, 206, 232, 252
Tamines, bridge.............. 274
Tannenberg 330
Tardieu, André . 205, 277, 302, 349
telegraph .. 203, 210, 352, 377, 406, 409
Temps, Le 303
Tergnier....... 167, 180, 305, 314
Thann 228, 236, 448
Theiss 450
Thiepval................... 411
Thierry, J. . 326, 354, 356, 359, 362, 379, 389, 391
Thillot, le................... 177
Thionville .. 29, 113-115, 117, 118, 147-150, 152-155, 159, 170, 189, 190, 206, 223, 239, 240
Thorn......... 126, 131, 276, 451
Thourout 434, 442
Three-Year Law.. 61, 87, 92-94, 98, 99, 134, 137, 162, 175, 176
Tintigny.................... 276
Tirlemont.............. 262, 267
Tirpitz, Admiral von 449
Tongres 254, 259
Tonnoy 194
Toul.... 11, 24, 30, 35, 48-50, 102, 113, 142, 150, 153, 155, 167-169, 177, 180, 194, 226, 269, 270, 295, 326, 381, 391
Toulon................ 173, 212
Toulouse 180
Tourcoing 273, 275
Tournai 288, 429, 438
Tournoux.............. 172, 173
Tours..................... 393
training camps.... 3, 43, 57, 60, 81, 84, 85, 287
Trémeau, Gen....... 9, 12, 19, 141
Trentinian, Gen. de 328
Triple Alliance.. 107, 108, 124, 125
Triple Entente 27, 31
Troyes 24, 27, 167, 180
Troyon............ 160, 381, 391
Tunisia..... 13, 111, 113, 136, 204
Turkey.......... 28, 90, 108, 451
United States............. 4, 454
Urvillers................... 321
Uskub 453
Vailly..................... 428
Valabrègue, Gen..... 197, 242, 319
Valcourt................... 280
Valenciennes... 282, 284, 289, 291
Vallières, Gen. des 242
Varennes .. 150, 159, 160, 326-329, 405
Varin, Gen. 247
Vautier, Gen................ 251
Vaux 367
Vavincourt................. 171
Verberie.............. 346, 354
Verdun... 11, 23, 24, 29, 35, 48-50, 102, 114, 150, 154, 155, 159, 167, 169, 170, 174, 177-180, 187, 194, 223, 225, 226, 293, 295, 298, 299, 320, 325, 326, 335, 337, 338, 340, 356, 370, 381, 392, 394, 397, 404-406, 436
Verdun, Battle of 406
Verneville 210
Versailles.................. 429
Vertus 327, 371, 393
Verviers... 153, 186, 228, 256, 264
Vervins ... 172, 197, 242, 303, 304

Index

Vesoul . . 13, 30, 143, 150, 154, 172, 197
Vienna. . . . 192, 201, 203, 206, 276
Vienne-la-Ville 401
Vieux. 188, 215
Viffort 389
Vigneulles 170
Villers 205, 327
Ville-en-Tardenois 393
Ville-sur-Tourbe 401
Virton 187, 228, 276
Visé. 254-256, 260
Vitry . 229-231, 242, 298, 308, 313, 320, 322, 323, 325-329, 335, 370, 380, 393
Vitry-le-François. . . . 230, 313, 326, 328, 329, 335, 370, 380
Vittel 171
Viviani, René. . . 207, 208, 214, 215, 218, 277, 278, 287, 339
Vivières. 346
Void. 171, 379
Vosges Mts. . . 23, 84, 111, 113, 114, 118, 134, 148, 150, 153, 154, 169, 176, 185, 188-190, 196, 248, 377, 381, 385
Vouziers 23, 27, 29, 332, 335
War budgets 47, 63
War College. 41
War Ministry. . . . 62, 206, 209, 228, 287
War Office. 157, 209, 250, 431, 433
Waremme 256
Warsaw . . . 126, 131, 232, 248, 252, 450
Wassy 380
weapons. . . . 36, 53, 54, 78, 86, 186, 406
Weygand, Col. 312
William II, Kaiser 132, 208
Wilson, Gen. 22, 108, 122, 306, 310, 320, 362, 365, 367, 368, 395, 426, 434, 447
Woëvre 30, 114, 152, 153, 159, 170, 177, 178, 374, 381, 405, 407
World Crisis, The . . . 432, 433, 436
World War. 3
Xures. 211
Yellow Book. 97
Ypres. 441-443
Ypres, Battle of 441
Yvoir. 260
Zeebrugge 434

About the Author

Joseph Jacques Césaire Joffre (1852-1931) was a French general and the Commander-in-Chief of the French Army from 1911-1916. Born in French Catalonia, he became a career officer in 1870. Originally an engineer, he presided over the modernization of the French Army and the first three years of the Great War. After the war, he became a member of the Académie Français.

www.ingramcontent.com/pod-product-compliance
Lightning Source LLC
Chambersburg PA
CBHW050157240426
43671CB00013B/2163